Russian Research Center Studies, 55

Revolutionary Russia

Richard Pipes, author of numerous books and articles on Russia, including *The Formation of the Soviet Union* (HUP, 1964) and *Social Democracy and the St. Petersburg Labor Movement, 1885-1897* (HUP, 1963) and translator of *Karamzin's Memoir on Ancient and Modern Russia* (HUP, 1959), is Professor of History at Harvard University.

Revolutionary Russia

Oskar Anweiler – Hannah Arendt – Shlomo Avineri – Isaiah Berlin
E. H. Carr – Alexander Dallin – John Erickson – Merle Fainsod
Marc Ferro – Dietrich Geyer – George Katkov – George F. Kennan
John Keep – Jan M. Meijer – Richard Pipes – Henry L. Roberts
Maximilien Rubel – Leonard Schapiro – Hugh Seton-Watson – John M.
Thompson – Adam B. Ulam – Bertram D. Wolfe

Edited by Richard Pipes

Harvard University Press   Cambridge, Massachusetts   1968

Library of Congress Catalog Card Number 68–15641
Printed in the United States of America

Editor's Foreword

In April 1967, on the fiftieth anniversary year of the Russian Revolution, a group of scholars assembled in Cambridge, Massachusetts, to discuss its events and their significance. The present collection of papers, comments, and discussion reports represents the proceedings of that conference.*

In planning the meeting, no effort was made to achieve either comprehensiveness of treatment or a consensus of opinion. The invited participants were left virtually free to choose their subjects and, of course, were allowed to treat them as they saw fit. This feature represents a certain disadvantage from the point of view of the lay reader, who, in return for the effort he puts into a large volume, likes to be rewarded with the sense of having to some extent mastered a subject. Comprehensiveness and consensus, however, are largely illusory. In scholarship, as in natural science, knowledge involves not so much authoritative opinion on the totality of a given subject as the drawing of limits within which serious discussion of its varied aspects can take place. Its purpose is to ascertain the boundaries of the probable, the plausible, the likely.

Although more than half a century has passed since the Russian Revolution, the historical literature devoted to it is still in many respects in a rudimentary stage of development. The questions that have been asked of it are less sophisticated than those historians have for some

* The conference was cosponsored by the Joint Committee for Slavic Studies of the American Council of Learned Societies and the Russian Research Center of Harvard University. Particular thanks are due to Mr. Gordon Turner, the Vice-President of the ACLS, for his assistance and to Professor Abram Bergson of the Russian Research Center for agreeing to the Center's acting as host. Professor Alex Rabinowitch has given generously of his time to summarizing the general discussions that followed each presentation. Mrs. Barbara Hunt deserves gratitude for her varied contributions to the organization of the conference and the preparation of the manuscript for publication.

time been in the habit of addressing to such comparable events as the French Revolution of 1789, the European revolutions of 1848, or the totalitarian revolution in Nazi Germany. There are good reasons why this should be the case—after all, the Russian Revolution is still not completed, insofar as the present rulers of Russia are the heirs of the men who in October 1917 made the revolution. Even so, it should be possible now to look at this event with some detachment and perspective and to pose about it questions of the kind that have yielded better understanding when applied to other revolutionary phenomena.

The papers fall into three categories. One group is narrative, seeking to reconstruct and give some meaningful pattern to extremely complicated events, such as the activities of German intelligence in Russia on the eve of the revolution, the spread of Bolshevik power in the provinces, and the creation of the Red Army. Another set is essentially reflective and speculative: it inquires about the reasons for the revolution and the extent to which it has succeeded or failed to succeed in fulfilling its aims. There is also a third category of papers, lying between the two, and constituting the bulk of the volume. It raises analytic questions of a specific kind: By what precise steps did Lenin arrive at his political philosophy? What was the political outlook of the men who took power in February 1917? What were the demands of Russian workers and peasants in the first weeks of the revolution? What theoretical and practical considerations influenced the Bolshevik power seizure in October? What effect on the course of the revolution can be ascribed to the predominantly urban outlook of the Bolsheviks?

We hope that in their totality the three kinds of papers and the comments and discussions that follow them will give the reader a sense of the Russian Revolution: not so much of what happened (this he can obtain from general histories), but how it was and what it meant.

Cambridge, Massachusetts   Richard Pipes
July 1967

Contents

Participants in the Conference on the Russian Revolution

Oskar Anweiler – Professor, Ruhr University, Bochum

Hannah Arendt – University Professor, Graduate Faculty, New School for Social Research, New York

Shlomo Avineri – Lecturer in Political Theory, Hebrew University, Jerusalem

Sir Isaiah Berlin – President of Wolfson College, Oxford; Professor in Humanities, The City University of New York

Edward Hallett Carr – Fellow, Trinity College, Cambridge University

Alexander Dallin – Professor of International Relations, Columbia University

Fritz T. Epstein – Professor of History and Curator of Slavic Collections, Indiana University

John Erickson – Reader in Defense Studies, University of Edinburgh

Merle Fainsod – Carl H. Pforzheimer University Professor, Harvard University

Marc Ferro – Sous-Directeur d'Etudes, Ecole Pratique des Hautes Etudes, Paris; Editor of *Annales*

Dietrich Geyer – Professor of East European History, University of Tübingen

George Katkov – Fellow, St. Antony's College, Oxford University

John L. H. Keep – Reader in Russian Studies, School of Slavonic and East European Studies, University of London

Paul Kecskemeti – Consultant to the RAND Corporation, Santa Monica, California

George F. Kennan – Permanent Professor, The Institute for Advanced Study, Princeton University

Leon Lipson – Professor of Law, Yale University

Jan M. Meijer – Professor of Russian, University of Utrecht

Richard Pipes – Professor of History, Harvard University

Henry L. Roberts – Professor of History, Dartmouth College

Hans Rogger – Professor of History, University of California at Los Angeles

Maximilien Rubel – Director of Research, Centre National de la Recherche Scientifique, Paris

Leonard Schapiro – Professor of Political Science, The London School of Economics and Political Science, University of London

Hugh Seton-Watson – Professor of History, School of Slavonic and East European Studies, University of London

John M. Thompson – Associate Professor of History, Indiana University

Donald W. Treadgold – Professor of History, University of Wash-
ington
Adam B. Ulam   – Professor of Government, Harvard University
Bertram D. Wolfe – Senior Research Fellow, The Hoover Institution,
Stanford, California

Revolutionary Russia

The Breakdown of the Tsarist Autocracy —

George F. Kennan

The discussion that follows proceeds from the premise that what occurred in Russia in February–March 1917 was, precisely, a *breakdown* of the autocracy under a fortuitous combination of momentary strains—not the overthrow of the existing order by revolutionary forces. In essence, the regime may be said to have collapsed because it was not able to muster sufficient support to enable it to withstand this sudden combination of strains. In quarters whose support would have been essential to enable it to do this, there was either distrust, indifference, outright hostility, or, in the particular case of the bureaucracy and the army, a mixture of disorientation, demoralization, and ineptness. The central question involved is therefore the question as to which of the regime's policies—that is, what elements of its behavior, what errors of commission or omission, or possibly what circumstances outside its control—were decisive or outstandingly important in bringing it to the helpless and fatal predicament in which it found itself at the beginning of 1917.

Such an inquiry presents special difficulty in view of the bewildering interaction of long-term and short-term causes. One is compelled to ask not just what were the long-term weaknesses that rendered the regime susceptible to the danger of collapse under relatively trivial pressures in the first place, but also what it was that caused the collapse to come at this particular moment.

I should like to begin with an examination of some of the long-term weaknesses and failures of the regime and then conclude with some brief reflections about the developments of the final wartime period just preceding its fall.

Long-term Weaknesses and Failures of the Regime

When one looks for those more basic mistakes and failings that undermined the tsarist autocracy and caused it to lose what the Chinese would call the "mandate of Heaven," one is obliged first to deal with certain broadly held misimpressions on this score—misimpressions that Soviet historians, in particular, have been at no pains to dispel. One of these is that the autocracy lost the confidence and respect of the people because it failed to bring a proper degree of modernization to Russian society in the economic, technological, and educational fields—that it made no adequate effort to overcome Russia's backwardness. Another is that the regime was intolerably cruel and despotic in its treatment of the populace generally; and that a revolution was required to correct this situation. In each of these impressions there are, of course, elements of truth; but both represent dangerous, and in general misleading, over-simplifications. That this is true is so well known to experts in the field that it needs, I think, no great elaboration here. But I shall just mention briefly, to avoid unclarity, my own impressions of the situation.

Let us take first the subject of industrialization. Here, it seems to me, we have one of those fields in which the tsar's regime had least to be apologetic about from the standpoint of responsibility for the moderniz-ing of the country. The rates of industrial growth achieved in Russia in the final decades of tsardom would appear to compare not at all unfavorably with those achieved in Western countries at comparable stages of development. The 8 percent growth rate that I understand to have been achieved in the 1890's, and the comparable 6 percent figure for the period from 1906 to 1914, are respectable figures, to say the least. One must doubt that the pace of industrialization could have been pushed much further without producing adverse social consequences out of all proportion in seriousness to the gains involved. Nor does there seem to be any reason to suppose that if revolution had not intervened, and if the dynamics of growth observable in the final decades of tsardom had been projected into mid-century, the results achieved would have been significantly inferior to those that have actually been achieved under Soviet power. This is, of course, only another way of saying that if industrialization was the main concern then no revolution was needed at all: there were easier and no less promising ways of doing it.

It has often been pointed out by way of reproach to the tsar's regime —both at the time and since—that this growth was achieved only by an excessive acceptance of investment and equity participation by foreigners in Russian industry, as well as by excessive state borrowing from other governments. Certainly, the proportion of foreign equity participation in Russian industrial concerns was very high, particularly in mining and metallurgy; and it is perfectly true that the Russian government was the most heavily indebted, externally, of any government in the world at the time. But I am not sure how well these charges stand up as reproaches to the policies of the tsar's government. Whether the high rate of foreign industrial investment was a bad thing depends on whether one accepts the Marxist thesis that any important degree of such external financing represented a form of enslavement to the foreign investors. The experience of the United States, where foreign capital also played a prominent part in nineteenth century industrial development, would not suggest that this is the case. And as for the government borrowing: much of this, of course, found its way, directly or indirectly, into the process of industrialization, and particularly into the building of railways. But the main stimulus to such borrowing was not the need for industrial capital but rather the effort by the government to maintain a military posture, and to engage in military ventures, that were far beyond its means. These practices, and the heavy indebtedness to which they led, were indeed among the significant weaknesses of the regime; but they do not constitute a proper source of reproach to the regime in connection with its program of industrialization. Had the foreign borrowings of the government been restricted to what it required in order to do its share in the stimulation of the growth of industry, the resulting burden of debt would surely have been well within its means.

Another reproach often leveled at the tsar's government in this connection was that industrialization was given precedence over agriculture and that it was partially financed by the exploitation of the peasantry through such devices as high indirect taxation, rigged prices for agricultural products, forced exportation of grain, and so on. Certainly there is much substance in these charges. The program of rapid industrialization was indeed put in hand long before any attack of comparable vigor was made on the problems of the peasantry, and the peasant was made to contribute heavily to its costs. But these circumstances seem to me to be illustrative less of any error or unfeeling quality on the part of tsarist statesmen than of the cruelty of the dilemmas with which they were faced. Without at least a certain prior development of industry, and particularly without the construction of railway network, no modernization of Russian agriculture would have been conceivable at all. And while somewhat more might perhaps have been extracted from the upper classes through ruthless taxation, there is no reason to suppose that this could have changed basically the logic of the situation, which was that the cost of industrialization, to the extent it was not covered by foreign borrowing, had to be covered by limitations on consumption by the great mass of the Russian people—which meant, in fact, the peasantry. To have tried, through the device of heavy taxation, to switch this entire burden to the relatively well-to-do or property-owning classes would merely have tended to destroy existing possibilities for the accumulation of private industrial capital; but such private accumulation was precisely what the government was concerned, and for very respectable reason, to stimulate and promote.

The truth is that the tsar's government, if it wished to get on in a serious way with the industrial development of the country, had no alternatives other than foreign borrowing and an extensive taxation of the peasantry. The claim that it should have avoided one or the other of these devices is thus equivalent to the allegation that it moved not too slowly but much too fast in the whole field of industrialization. For this there might be much to be said. But this is not the way the reproach is usually heard.

In the case of agriculture, the pattern is obviously more complex. Certainly, the reform of the 1860's left much to be desired: it was not properly followed through; the burdens resting on the peasantry down to 1905 were inordinate; the economic situation of large portions of the peasant population remained miserable. In all this there were just grounds for reproach to the regime; and I have no desire to minimize its significance. It seems reasonable to suppose that the additional burden of bitterness that accumulated in peasant minds in the final decades of the nineteenth century contributed importantly both to the peasant disorders of the first years of the new century, and to that spirit of sullen contempt for the dynasty, and indifference to its fate, that manifested itself at the time of the revolution.

Against these reflections must be set, however, two compensatory considerations. One has, first, the fact that the most important single factor involved in producing the land hunger and economic misery of the central-Russian village in these decades was nothing having to do with governmental policy but simply the enormous increase in the rural population that occurred at that time—a doubling, and more, just in the years between the emancipation and the outbreak of the world war. Second, there is the fact that after 1906 the government did finally address itself vigorously, intelligently, and in general quite effectively to the problems of the Russian countryside. The fact that this effort came late —too late to be successful in the political and psychological sense— should not blind us to its imposing dimensions. What was achieved in those final years from 1907 to 1914 in a whole series of fields affecting the peasant's situation—in the purchase of land by small peasant holders; in the break-up of the peasant commune and the facilitating of the transition from communal to hereditary tenure; in the consolidation of strip holdings, with all the enormous labor of surveying and adjudication this involved; in resettlement and in colonization of outlying regions of the empire; in the development of the cooperative movement in the countryside—strikes me as impressive in the extreme.

One can truthfully say that the tsar's government deserved reproach for its failures in relation to the peasant throughout most of the nineteenth century. And there can be no doubt that the price of these failures figured prominently in the reckoning the autocracy had to face in 1917. No one would deny, in particular, the importance of the impact that the spectacle of all this rural misery and degradation had on the growth of the Russian revolutionary movement in the nineteenth century. And one can well say that such efforts as were made to improve the situation of the peasantry came much too late in the game. What one cannot say is that they did not come at all or that revolution was necessary because the tsar's government, as of 1917, had still done nothing effective about agriculture. The fact is that the revolution came precisely at the moment when the prospects for the development of Russian agriculture, the war aside, had never looked more hopeful.

Similar conclusions could be drawn, I should think, with relation to education. That Russia was slow in coming to popular education no one would deny. But that the progress made in this field in the final years of tsardom was rapid and impressive seems to me equally undeniable. If, as I understand to be the case, enrollments in primary schools throughout the empire more than doubled in the final two decades before 1914; if in this same period enrollments in institutions of higher learning more than tripled and those in secondary schools nearly quadrupled; or if, for example, the incidence of literacy among military recruits increased from 38 percent in 1894 to 73 percent in 1913—then it may be argued, I think, that all this might have been done earlier; but it cannot be said that nothing consequential was being done at all. The official goal, as adopted five or six years before the outbreak of the world war, was the achievement of universal, compulsory primary school education. The tsarist authorities hoped to achieve this goal by 1922. The rate of progress made prior to the war suggests that it would probably have been achieved at the latest by the mid-1920's had not war and revolution intervened. This is certainly no later than the date at which it was finally achieved by the Soviet regime. Again, one simply cannot accept the thesis that the old regime kept the Russian people in darkness to the end and that a revolution was necessary in 1917 to correct this situation.

In all these fields of modernization, the pattern is in fact much the same: initial backwardness, long sluggishness and delay, then a veritable burst of activity in the final years. If it was in these fields that one was to look for the decisive failures of the autocracy and the reasons for revolution, then it would have to be said that there was much less reason for an overthrow of the regime in 1917 than there was in 1905. Had the 1905 Revolution succeeded, one might well have concluded that the tsar's regime had been overthrown because it failed to bring the Russian people into the modern age. To account for an overthrow coming in 1917, one has to look for other and deeper causes.

The first and most decisive of these causes seems to me to have been, unquestionably, the failure of the autocracy to supplement the political system in good time with some sort of a parliamentary institution—the failure, in other words, to meet the needs of the land-owning nobility and then, increasingly, of the new intelligentsia from all classes for some sort of institutional framework that would associate them with the undertakings of the regime, give them a sense of participation in the governmental process, and provide a forum through which they, or their representatives, could air their views and make their suggestions with regard to governmental policy. In the absence of any such institution, literally hundreds of thousands of people—student youth, commoners (*raznochintsy*), sons of priests, members of the national minorities, members of the gentry, even members of the land-owning nobility itself —people bursting with energies and of the love of life in all its forms; people vibrating with intellectual excitement under the flood of impressions that swept over Russian society as its contacts with the West developed during the nineteenth and early twentieth centuries; people passionately concerned with public affairs, intensely aware of Russia's backwardness, and possessed by no more consuming passion than the desire to contribute to its correction—all these people found themselves, insofar as they did not become associated with the armed forces or the administrative bureaucracy, repelled by the regime, held at a distance from its doings and responsibilities, condemned either to a passive submissiveness in public affairs that did violence to their consciences as well as their energies or to the development of forms of association and political activity that could not, in the circumstances, appear to the regime as other than subversive. What was required, initially, was not a widely popular assembly. There was much to be said for the view that the Russian people at large were not yet ready for this. At any time in the nineteenth century, even a central assembly of the local government boards (*zemstva*) would have constituted an important safety valve, and in fact a very suitable one, insofar as it would have enlisted as collaborators in the tasks of government at the central level not mere theorists devoid of practical experience but people who had had the best sort of preparation: namely, experience at the local, provincial level in the fields of administration intimately connected with the lives and interests of common people. To attempt, with relation to so great and complex a process as that of the loss of public confidence by the Russian autocracy, to identify any single error as a crucial one is, of course, always to commit an act of oversimplification; but if one were to inquire what, by way of example, might appear as outstanding historical errors of the regime, I should think one would have to name such things as the flat repulsion by Alexander II in 1862 of the initiative taken by the gentry of Tver, under the leadership of Unkovskii, in favor of a central *zemstvo* organ; or the rebuff administered by Nicholas II to the representatives of the *zemstva* and the nobility who called on him in 1895 to urge—if only in the mildest of language—the recognition of the need for a more representative system of government. In the entire record of the last decades of tsarist power, I can think of no mistakes more calamitous than these.

There was, of course, eventually, the Duma; and it was, as an institution, not really so bad as it has often been portrayed. Its initial members could, as Vasilii Maklakov pointed out, have made much better use of it than they actually did. The franchise was indeed a limited one, but it was not so severely limited as to prevent both First and Second Dumas from being violently oppositional, and even extensively revolutionary, in spirit. Nor can I develop any lively sympathy for the great unhappiness manifested by the Kadets over the fact that the Duma was not given the right to appoint and control the government. For an American, in particular, it is hard to regard a fusing of the legislative and executive powers as absolutely essential to a sound political system. But leaving aside the adequacy of the arrangements governing the constitution and functioning of the Duma, it is obvious that the granting of it by Nicholas II came far too late and in precisely the wrong way—under pressure, that is, and with obvious reluctance and suspicion on his part. Given the situation that existed at that particular moment, it was natural enough for him to do so. There could have been no more than a minority of the members of the First Duma whose political aspirations, if satisfied, would not have ended in the violent destruction of the autocracy; and the tsar understood this very well. And yet it was Nicholas himself, his father, and his grandfather who were responsible for the fact that this was the way things were. Had they acted earlier—and the 1860's would not have been too soon—they might have had a different, more respectful, and less menacing sort of a parliamentary body before them. And the difference would, I think, have been decisive. The conservative and liberal intelligentsia, from which the dynasty really had something to hope, might have rallied to its side and the radical revolutionary movement, from which it could expect nothing good, would have been split. The effect of waiting forty years and establishing the Duma in 1906 instead of in the 1860's was just the opposite: it unified the radical-revolutionary movement against the regime and split the conservative and liberal intelligentsia, whose united support was essential if the dynasty was to survive.

It was true, of course, that to grant a parliamentary institution would have involved at any time on the tsar's part a readiness to share the power which the dynasty had previously exercised absolutely. But in the mid-nineteenth century, there were still people on the other side who would have been willing to content themselves with this sharing of supreme power. By 1906 there was practically no one left, not only in the revolutionary movement but among the liberals as well, who did not insist, by implication at least, on destroying the tsar's powers entirely rather than just sharing in them. It was the destruction of the autocracy as such, not really its limitation, that was implicit in the demands of the First Duma for a responsible government, for control in effect of the police, and above all for a general amnesty.

In the 1860's the dynasty might still have had before it, in a parliamentary institution, people who were anxious to see it succeed in its tasks and willing to help it do so. By 1906 it was confronted, in every political party to the left of the Octobrists and even partly in the ranks of that grouping, not by people who constituted a loyal opposition, not by people who really wanted the dynasty to succeed with the tasks of modernization to which I referred earlier on, not by people who wished to have a share in the dynasty's power, but by rivals for the exercise of that power, by people whose chief grievance against the regime was not that it was dilatory or incompetent but that it stood in their own path, whose complaint was not really that the autocracy misruled Russia, but that it prevented *them* from ruling—or misruling, as history would probably have revealed—in its place.

With Unkovskii and his associates in 1862, Alexander II might, it seems to me, have come to some sort of political terms. With Miliukov and his associates, decorous and mild-mannered as they outwardly were, this same possibility no longer existed. It had become by that time a case of *kto kogo* (who whom)—either the tsar or they. Yet without their help, as February 1917 revealed, the dynasty itself could not be defended.

In the mid-nineteenth century, in other words, the autocracy could still have opted for the status of a limited monarchy. In 1906 this option no longer remained open to it. And the failure to accept it when it *had been* open left only one possibility, which was its final and total destruction.

This great deficiency—namely the denial of political expression—must be clearly distinguished from the question of physical cruelty and oppression in the treatment of the population. It was suggested, at the outset of this discussion, that it was a misimpression that the regime was intolerably cruel and despotic in this respect. This is, of course, a controversial statement; and I do not wish to make it unnecessarily so. I am well aware of the fact that the tsarist police and prison authorities, as well as the military courts, were guilty of many acts of stupidity, injustice, and cruelty. I am not unmindful of the observations of my distinguished namesake, the elder George Kennan, on the exile system in Siberia. But the standards of the present age are different from those of the latter—unfortunately so. The tsarist autocracy did not engage in the sort of prophylactic terror—the punishment of great numbers of the innocent as a means of frightening the potentially guilty—of which we have seen so much in our age. Its treatment of many individual revolutionaries, including incidentally Chernyshevskii, seems to have been, if anything, on the lenient side. The censorship was irritating and often silly, but it was not sufficiently severe to prevent the appearance in Russia of a great critical literature. Most important of all, one has to distinguish, when one speaks of police terrorism, between that element of it that is spontaneous and the element that is provoked. That the Russian revolutionaries behaved provocatively, and deliberately so, on countless occasions is something that few, I think, would deny. Now, it is a habit of political regimes to resist their own violent overthrow; it is something to be expected of them. Stolypin used harsh measures—yes—in suppressing the disorders of the period following the war with Japan, but measures no more harsh than the situation required from the standpoint of the regime. Had there been a time in the history of the United States when political assassinations—assassinations of public officials—were running at the rate of more than one and a half thousand per annum, as was the case in Russia in 1906, I rather shudder to think what would have been the reaction of the official establishment here. In situations of this nature, where there is a constant interaction between the strivings of revolutionaries and the defensive efforts of a political regime, the question of responsibility for violence becomes a matter of the chicken and the egg. If one abstracts from the behavior of the regime in the administration of justice and in the imposition of political discipline that element that was provided by provocation from the revolutionary side, then the use of police terror cannot be regarded as more than a minor determinant of the alienation of great sectors of society that underlay the breakdown of 1917.

So much for the denial of parliamentary government and political liberty. A second crucial deficiency of the autocracy was one that it shared with a large part of upper-class Russian society, and with a portion of the lower classes as well, and that was for this reason not only much more difficult to recognize at the time but has been more difficult of recognition even in the light of history. This was extreme nationalism—that romantic, linguistic nationalism that was the disease of the age.

The spirit of modern nationalism was pernicious for the Russian autocracy for two reasons: first, because it reflected itself unfortunately on the treatment by the tsar's government of the national minorities; but second, because it led to an adventurous foreign policy, far beyond what the capacities of the Russian state at that time could support.

In an empire of which nearly half, or something more than one half (depending on where the Ukrainians were ranked) of the population was made up of national minorities, an absolute monarchy was confronted, in the age of nationalism, with a basic choice. It could make political concessions to the Great-Russian plurality and thus at least keep the strongest single national element firmly associated with it in an effort to hold down the minorities; or, if it did not wish to do this, it could employ a light touch with the minorities, do everything possible to reconcile them to the Russian state, and play them off against the potentially rebellious central Great-Russian group. The tsar's government did neither. Operating against the background of a sullen Russian peasantry, a frustrated Russian upper class, and a lower-class Russian intelligentsia veritably seething with sedition, it set about to treat the national minorities in the name of Russian nationalism with an utterly senseless provocation of their national cultures and feelings and a rigid repression of all their efforts to establish a separate national political identity. This was a policy calculated to make sure that if there were anyone among the minority elements who was not already alienated from the autocracy by virtue of its general social and political policies, he would sooner or later be brought into the opposition by the offense to his national feelings. Among the manifestations of this stupidity none was more serious than the anti-Semitism that set in after the murder of Alexander II—an aberration of policy that was at first simply clumsy and reactionary in an old-fashioned religious sense but then assumed, under Nicholas II, forms that were truly disgraceful and bespoke a profound perversion of political and philosophic understanding. This tendency was particularly unfortunate because it came at a period when, for the first time, a great many young Jews would have been prepared, given half a chance, to forget the specific circumstances of their religious and cultural origin and to become essentially russified. And this anti-

Semitism was of course only a part of nationalistic policies that affected in some way and at some time practically every one of the minorities that lined the periphery of the empire. The revenge for this extraordinary blindness became apparent, quite naturally, in the form of the high percentage of members of the national minorities to be found in the revolutionary movement. It is impossible to say what 1917 would have been like without the Chkheidzes and Martovs, the Trotskys, Dzerzhinskiis, Radeks, Sverdlovs, Stalins, and Ordzhonikidzes; but certainly the non-Great-Russian component in the revolutionary opposition to tsardom was a great one, particularly after 1881, and it must be assumed to have added greatly to the difficulty of the predicament of the autocracy at that final moment.

The second manner in which the disease of extreme nationalism manifested itself in tsarist policy was, as already noted, in the field of foreign affairs. Particularly was this true under Nicholas II. The origins of the war with Japan were, from the Russian side, disreputable and inexcusable. There was no need for this involvement; it could easily have been avoided; the attendant military effort was clearly beyond the physical resources of the country at that moment of rapid economic and social transition; and the folly of the venture from the domestic-political standpoint was at once apparent in the events of the Revolution of 1905. And as though this war were not folly enough in itself, it had the further effect of making it more difficult than ever for Russia to resist involvement in the much greater and even more dangerous European war that was shortly to come. The financial distress in which the tsar's government finished the war with Japan left it more dependent than ever on the financial bounty of the French government and the French bankers and more helpless than ever before the French demands that Russia become in effect an instrument of French policy against Germany.

Whether this added element of financial dependence was decisive in bringing Russia into World War I may well be doubted. The same result would very possibly have been achieved by the nationalistic tendencies now raging unchecked among the Russian bureaucracy, the military caste, and the upper classes generally, coupled with the tsar's strange weakness for military adventurism. To people still imbued with a strong conviction of the iniquity of the kaiser's Germany or Franz Josef's Austria, it may seem strange to hear it suggested that the Russian monarchy might have done better, in the interests of its own preservation, to remain aloof from involvement in a war against Germany. In the light of the prevailing nationalistic emotionalism of the time, it would no doubt have seemed preposterous to suggest that Serbia should have been left to Austria's mercy and that Russian prestige, just recently so painfully injured in the crisis over the annexation of Bosnia and Herzegovina, should suffer another and perhaps even greater reverse of this nature. The fact remains that in 1914 Russia was in no condition to participate in a major war—the experience of the war with Japan had demonstrated this; and neither the fate of Serbia nor the question of control over the Dardanelles really represented for her a vital interest, comparable to what she stood to suffer by courting another domestic upheaval on the heels of the one she had just experienced in 1904–05.

The Franco-Russian alliance served, in Russia's case, a financial interest but not really a political one. The kaiser's Germany may have been a threat to Britain; it was not in great measure a threat to Russia. Some of the more sober statesmen, Witte and even the otherwise nationalistic Stolypin, saw this, and would have tried betimes to avoid the catastrophe to which this alliance, which took no proper account of Russia's internal condition, was leading. But it was the pervasive nationalism of the age that defeated them; and I am inclined, for this reason, to attribute to that nationalism a major role in the causes of the final collapse of the regime. A tsarist autocracy that saw things clearly and wished to exert itself effectively in the interest of its own preservation would have practiced a rigid abstention from involvement in world political problems generally, and from exhausting foreign wars in particular, at that crucial juncture in its domestic-political development.

The third of the weaknesses of the autocracy that I should like to mention was the personality of the last Russian tsar himself. Poorly educated, narrow in intellectual horizon, a wretchedly bad judge of people, isolated from Russian society at large, in contact only with the most narrow military and bureaucratic circles, intimidated by the ghost of his imposing father and the glowering proximity of his numerous gigantic uncles, helpless under the destructive influence of his endlessly unfortunate wife: Nicholas II was obviously inadequate to the demands of his exalted position; and this was an inadequacy for which no degree of charm, of courtesy, of delicacy of manner, could compensate. It is ironic that this man, who fought so tenaciously against the granting of a constitution, had many of the qualities that would have fitted him excellently for the position of a constitutional monarch and practically none of those that were needed for the exercise of that absolute power to which he stubbornly clung. Time and time again, in the record of his reign, one finds the evidences of his short-sightedness and his lack of grasp of the realities of the life of the country interfering with the political process in ways that were for him veritably suicidal. True, he was the product of the vagaries of genetics; another tsar might not have been so bad. But the experience of his reign only illustrates the fact that these accidents of royal birth, tolerable in earlier centuries where the feudal nobility bore a good portion of the load, and tolerable again in the modern age wherever the main burden is borne or shared by parliamentary institutions, were not tolerable in the age of economic development and mass education and in a political system where the monarch claimed the rights of personal absolutism.

So much for the leading and crucial weaknesses of the autocracy itself in the final decades of its power. Mention must be made, in conclusion, of the Russian revolutionary movement. It was, of course, not the revolutionary parties that overthrew the autocracy in 1917. Nevertheless, there were indirect ways in which their existence and activity affected the situation of the regime; and these must be briefly noted.

First of all, by providing a somewhat romantic alternative to any association with the governing establishment, the revolutionary movement drew many talented youths into an attitude of defiance and revolutionary disobedience to it, thereby impoverishing it in talent, energy, and intelligence. Every time that a young person of ability was drawn into the ranks of its revolutionary opponents, the bureaucracy, deprived of these sources of recruitment, became just that more stupid, unimaginative, and inept.

Second, there was the effect the revolutionary elements had on the development of governmental policy. They obviously had no interest in seeing the modernization of the country proceed successfully under tsarist tutelage, and they did as little as they could to support it. I find it significant that more useful social legislation appears to have been passed by the two final and supposedly reactionary Dumas than by the first two relatively liberal, and partially revolutionary, ones. But more important still was the influence of the revolutionaries in frightening the regime out of possible initiatives in the field of political reform. These revolutionary parties and groupings had, as a rule, no interest in seeing genuine progress made in the creation of liberal institutions. Their aim was generally not to reform the system but to cause it to fall and to replace it. For this reason, the more the regime could be provoked into stupid, self-defeating behavior, the better from their standpoint. They often found themselves, in this respect, sharing the same aspirations and purposes as the extreme right wing of the political spectrum, which also—though for other reasons—did not wish to see any liberalization of the autocracy. And in this respect one has to concede to the revolutionary movement a series of important successes. In one instance after another where there appeared to be a possibility of political liberalization or where the pressures in this direction were intense the timely intervention of revolutionary activity of one sort or another sufficed to assure that no progress should be made. One has only to recall, as examples, the effect of the Polish uprising of 1863 on the policies of Alexander II or the effect of his assassination in 1881 on the projects then being entertained by Loris-Melikov.

The War and the Final Crisis

So much, then, for the major weaknesses, failures, and strains that entered into the undermining of the tsarist system of power. It remains only to note the manner in which the effect of all of them was magnified by the world war that began in 1914: magnified to a point where the system could no longer stand the strain. Wartime patriotic fervor, engulfing the liberal-parliamentary circles even more hopelessly than the government itself, brought them in at this point as critics of the government on new grounds: on the grounds that it was not *sufficiently* nationalistic, not *sufficiently* inspired and determined in its conduct of the war effort. And to this there was now added the quite erroneous but heady and dangerous charge that it was pro-German and even treasonable in its relations to the enemy. These charges were utilized by the liberal-parliamentary circles as the excuse for setting up new organizational entities, such as the various war industry councils, which were able to function as rival authorities to the governmental bureaucracy, to provide channels for political activity hostile to the regime, and eventually to contribute significantly to the circumstances surrounding its collapse. Meanwhile, the strictly military aspects of the war effort had a whole series of effects—such as the weakening by losses in battle of the loyal portion of the officers' corps, the stationing of undisciplined garrisons in the vicinity of the capital city, the removal of the tsar himself to field headquarters, and so on—that were to have important connotations, unfavorable to the security of the regime, at the moment of supreme trial. In a number of ways, furthermore, the war effort exacerbated relations between the government and members of the national minorities, who for obvious reasons did not always share the Russian emotional commitment to the war. Finally, not perhaps as a consequence of the war (this is hard to judge), but certainly simultaneously with it, there were the grotesque developments in the tsar's own personal situation, particularly the ripening and the denouement of the Rasputin affair—developments that finally succeeded in alienating from his cause not only large elements of the immediate bureaucratic and military entourage that had constituted his last comfort and protection, but even a portion of the imperial family itself, thus completing his isolation and removing, or disqualifying, his last potential defenders.

Conclusions

Prior to the undertaking of this review, I was inclined to feel that had the war not intervened, the chances for survival of the autocracy and for its gradual evolution into a constitutional monarchy would not have been bad. On reviewing once more the events of these last decades, I find myself obliged to question that opinion. Neither the tardiness in the granting of political reform, nor the excesses of an extravagant and foolish nationalism, nor the personal limitations of the imperial couple began with the war or were primarily responses to the existence of the war. None of the consequences of these deficiencies were in process of any significant correction as the war approached. The spectacle of the final years of tsardom prior to 1914 is that of an impressive program of social, economic, and cultural modernization of a great country being conducted, somewhat incongruously, under the general authority of a governmental system that was itself in the advanced stages of political disintegration. The successes in the field of modernization might indeed, if allowed to continue, have brought Russia rapidly and safely into the modern age. It is doubtful that they could for long have overbalanced the serious deficiencies of the political system or averted the consequences to which they were—even as war broke out—inexorably leading.

Comment by Hugh Seton-Watson on — "The Breakdown of the Tsarist Autocracy" by George F. Kennan

To speak in reply to Mr. Kennan is a great privilege. The paper we have heard combines all the clarity and eloquence that over many years we have learned to expect from him. It seems to me that the issues he raised are the important ones and that the ones he did not raise are less important. I also found myself agreeing very largely with his opinions. I shall, however, concentrate on those points on which I would differ from him in interpretation or in emphasis.

First, as regards modernization, I concur with what I take to be Mr. Kennan's main thesis: the strains and stresses of nineteenth-century Russian society were largely due to the attempt by the state machine to modernize Russia from above. The process was in some ways mishandled, but the direction was on the whole the right one, and in the last ten years particularly impressive progress was made. In fact, it was not inability to confront the tasks of economic and cultural modernization that brought about the collapse. My general view would be the same, but I would like to comment on two important aspects of modernization —agriculture and education.

Mr. Kennan observes that the cost of industrialization, to the extent it was not covered by foreign borrowing, had to be covered by limitations on consumption by the great mass of the Russian people, which meant, in fact, the peasantry. This is certainly true, not only of Russia, but of virtually all countries that have undergone industrialization, whether in modern times or, for example in eighteenth-century England. But the Russian government's treatment of the peasants, if not absolutely unique, at least contrasted strikingly with the policy of many of the "modernizing" countries. The essence of the Russian policy was that virtually none of the wealth that was taken from the Russian peasants was put back into agriculture. To compare Russia with Japan in the same period: the Japanese peasants, like the Russians, were squeezed by taxation, but part at least, even a rather large part, of the proceeds reverted to agriculture. Thus, the output per unit of arable land in Japan rose quite strikingly, whereas in Russia there was practically no improvement at all between the emancipation of the serfs and 1905, or at best the improvement was very slight. This lack was the real cause of the Russian peasants' misery. The rising population pressed on the same resources, whereas with a more intelligent policy the resources could have been greatly increased. The population pressure was not the fault of the government, but the government did nothing to cope with it. This population pressure was not absolute, but was caused by excessive population in relation to land incompetently cultivated. Land efficiently cultivated could have supported a much larger population. The government's failure to act was far more important as a cause of misery than the survival of large landed estates. One should remember that in 1914 the noble landowners' share of the arable land of Russia was between 15 and 20 percent. That is a substantial share, of course, but it can hardly be said that Russian agriculture was dominated by noble landowners.

Second, education. As a general proposition, it seems to me that historical experience shows us that at the beginning of every process of modernization from above, willed by the ruler—of which Russia is an outstanding example and of which we have had many others in other parts of Eastern Europe, Asia, and the rest of the world in recent decades—there is bound to be a tremendous gap between the elite and the masses. This gap is bound to be a source of frustration to the new, modern, intellectual elite and a source of painful strain in the society as a whole. The gap can only be narrowed by raising the cultural level of the masses toward that of the intelligentsia—in other words, by the creation of a modern system of primary education. It was here that nineteenth-century Russia failed most abysmally. In education, nineteenth-century Russia had proud achievements to show, but they were at the higher levels of the educational pyramid and in the upper social classes. In the first half of the nineteenth century, this situation was, I think, inevitable. Neither funds nor personnel were available to create a system of primary education. I do not think Uvarov, the Minister of Education of Nicholas I, should be judged too harshly. His achievements affected only the nobility and the children of medium-level officials or merchants. But to have educated even these classes was a real achievement. The regime of Nicholas I deserves more credit than it is usually given. By the 1880's, however, the situation was entirely different: then the funds and the personnel could have been found much more easily, but they were withheld. You will remember Delianov's circular of 1887, which recommended that secondary education should not be extended to the children of coachmen, servants, cooks, washerwomen, small shopkeepers and people of that sort (*takogo roda liudei*).

The picture of Russian primary education at the turn of the century is not only a shocking one, but one which could have been avoided with good will and intelligence. The truth is that the Russian government of the end of the century believed that the people were better off without education. This was retrogression from the time of Alexander I, or even of Peter the Great.

Again, compare the situation with that of Japan: within forty years of the Meiji restoration the Japanese had a system of effective primary education, embracing over 90 percent of the boys and girls. Japanese reformers were not liberal humanitarians. They believed that educated peasants would provide better soldiers and workers and would make Japan a more powerful empire, and that was why they developed schools. The Russian government, whose political motivation was almost exactly the same, acted on the opposite premise.

After 1906 all this changed, as Mr. Kennan has rightly stressed. Stolypin's peasant policy may or may not have been effective (opinions vary on this), but undoubtedly its aim was greater agricultural efficiency, and undoubtedly it put back into agriculture some of what was taken out in taxes. This was a new policy. Again, in education great progress was made. In 1913 the Ministry of Education received four times as much from the state budget as in 1900: it was still far too little, but it was real progress. It is true that the Council of State turned down the elementary education law of the Third Duma, but it was largely put into practice by government financial assistance to the *zemstva* and city councils, this of course being the exact reverse of the trend of the 1880's and 1890's, when the *zemstva* were actually impeded and obstructed. Education even during the war went ahead. Count Ignatiev, the penultimate minister of education, was an energetic, progressive man, who was able to achieve something, even in war conditions.

If then we look at the regime's policy from the point of view of economic and cultural modernization, we must conclude, I think, that progress had been made and that the orientation toward the end of the regime was rather intelligent.

It was not here that the failure lay. It was in the persistence of feelings of massive social and political discontent, which had their origins in the past century. These feelings resulted largely from the two great failures of the nineteenth century that I have mentioned—in agriculture and education. But the essence, I think, was not a feeling that Russia should be, and was not being, modernized but rather rage against the whole social and political system. Resentment grew not so much from a desire for modernization as from a passion for justice. This was true particularly of the intelligentsia, but to some extent it was true also of the people as a whole. The non-Russian peoples, as Mr. Kennan has well pointed out, were more and more resentful of Russian domination and more and more inclined to follow leaders who thought in terms of autonomy or even of independent states. The peasants were becoming politically conscious. It is a curious irony that, as the proportion of arable land held by the nobility diminished, so the resentment of the peasants against noble landowners, if anything, increased. The working class had the same reasons for discontent that working classes in the early stages of industrial development have had or have in all countries. And here, too, material improvements probably made for more discontent and more political radicalization. The emergence of a minority of skilled urban workers—quite a large minority by 1914—who were materially much better off than the exploited, unskilled laborers of the 1880's provided cadres for political action by the workers.

But we should not, I think, exaggerate the importance of mass discontent. I think there is a point worth making here about the peasants. The peasants did not bring about the revolution. At the most, one can say that the peasants in uniform played their part in February 1917, but they did not operate as peasants, but as soldiers. Their motivation was military, not social, except in the most indirect way. The peasantry played an enormous part after February, but that is another story. Indeed, it is an interesting point, which goes beyond the experience of Russia, that in all those great mass revolutions of our time in which peasants have played a major part, their actions followed, rather than preceded, the collapse of the old regime and its state machine. Peasant participation in revolutionary action has been a consequence of political collapse, not its cause. This is true of China, Mexico, Yugoslavia, as well as of Russia. As for the workers, no one can deny their part in February. But workers' discontent, strikes and street demonstrations are things that any reasonably efficient government can normally handle. It is not enough to say that the workers made the February Revolution. The point is that the government was no longer reasonably efficient.

Here, two factors have to be considered: the impact of war and the alienation of the political class. Let us take the second factor first. The social and cultural conditions that had produced the original alienation of the intelligentsia from the regime were beginning to disappear in the last decade of the imperial regime, but the state of mind they had created for generations on end had not disappeared—it had hardly even begun to disappear. On the contrary, it had extended into wider sections of the upper and middle classes, into the business class, the bureaucracy, and probably into the officer class of the regular armed forces. (Incidentally, this subject, it seems to me, deserves much more research—the study of the officer cadres of the Imperial Russian army.)

Exasperation against the regime became more, rather than less, bitter in the last years of peace and in the war. There is already a large polemical literature on this subject. The faults and naiveté of the political class of Russia are much more easily discerned now in 1967 than they were then, and the few contemporary criticisms, such as Struve's famous essay in *Vekhi*, appear rather impressive. But I must admit that I am rather less impressed by Maklakov's arguments. Also, although the point is perhaps marginal, I differ from Mr. Kennan about the issue of responsible government. It seems to me the matter was more important than he has allowed. The opposition of the Kadets was surely not due only to their insistence in 1906 on a doctrinaire imitation of some West European parliamentary system, with its responsibility of the executive branch to the legislative. They were not being offered, and dogmatically rejecting, an American-type presidential government with the executive and legislative branches separate but both subject to popular control. What they were being offered was the perpetuation of Nicholas II's autocracy, with the departments of the executive under the control of men chosen arbitrarily by him, with the representative assembly reduced to the status of a talking shop, quite unable to affect policy. Admittedly, for a time things worked out a little better than that. Stolypin at least was a real prime minister. Under him the Council of Ministers had a sort of embryonic unity, and the restricted-franchise Third and Fourth Dumas acted as some sort of a forum for political discussion. But I do not see how, in 1906, the Kadets could have anticipated this, or, if they had, could have accepted the prospect with equanimity, or indeed, how they could have acted otherwise than they did. With Mr. Kennan's argument that the decisive chance was missed in the 1860's and that in 1906 it was too late, I am in absolute agreement, but I have rather more sympathy for such men as Miliukov than has become fashionable in recent times in the West.

And now the last point—the war. The actual impact of the war on the army and on the civil population, the changes in the composition of the officer corps after the tremendous blood-letting of September 1914 and the summer of 1915, the state of morale in the higher reaches of the civil ministry and in the governor's offices: these are things of which I know far too little but of which I am inclined to suspect that too little is known still by anyone at all. They are, of course, decisive for the revolution. Without failure in war, even the regime of Nicholas II and Goremykin might have carried on. There have been many examples in recent decades, in other countries besides Russia, of fantastically incompetent, tyrannical, and grotesque governments being able to carry on in peacetime if they are not subjected to external pressure. It is by no means impossible that even Nicholas II and Goremykin could have stayed in power if there had not been a war. It is meaningless to make the observation that if there had not been a war when there was, there would still have been some sort of revolution some time: the revolution we know, with the consequences we know, would not have taken place.

However, the war was not just something which happened to Russia; it was brought on in large part by Russia's own policies. I am extremely glad that Mr. Kennan stressed the importance of Russian official nationalism and anti-Semitism and their connections with the revolutionary movement in the sense that a disproportionately large number of Jews and non-Russians were recruited into the revolutionary groups. This consequence is not usually sufficiently stressed. I think, too, that he is right in suggesting a connection between these russifying policies and the Russian imperialism in foreign policy that contributed to the outbreak of the war. However, it must be admitted that Russia was not the only country whose government pursued policies of "official nationalism"—that is, an attempt to use the state machine to force one nationality upon all the subjects of a multinational state. Official nationalism was to be found also in contemporary Prussia and Hungary. Anti-Semitism, too, was widespread (though not, it is true, officially sponsored as in Russia) in Austria and in the eastern provinces of Prussia and Hungary. Mr. Kennan is surely right in linking Russian nationalism with a foreign policy that brought Russia to war, but I think he overrates Russia's responsibility for its outbreak. I would agree that the kaiser's Germany was not really a threat to Russia. But the war did not happen because Russia needlessly joined the conflict between Germany and Britain, the eventuality that you will remember, was foreseen in Durnovo's famous memorandum of early 1914. The war happened because Austria was determined to take over the whole Balkan peninsula, and Germany backed her. Russia had the alternatives of letting this happen or going to war. If she had let it happen, then, leaving out any sentimental considerations about obligations of honor towards Serbia, whom she had twice already urged to give way—in 1909 and 1913—she would have been serving notice to all that she was abdicating from great power status, that she was no longer *bündnisfähig*, that she was willing to be a junior partner, not only to Germany, but to Austria too, to adopt something like the status of Austria after Wagram. No Russian government could have been expected to do so.

The counter-arguments are obvious enough. Russia's basic strength in manpower and economic resources was bound to assure her great power status in the end. Political defeat in 1914 would at most have held her back for a decade or two. What did Serbia matter, or the Straits either, in comparison with the earth-shaking events of 1917? How pitiable the conflicts of the European powers in 1914 seem in the ages of Hitler and Stalin and Mao! How much more convenient it would be for all of us if the war of 1914 had not come! We can all, from time to time, feel the force of such arguments, but it seems to me that they are unhistorical. In 1914 no one could think in these terms. In fact, Russia's decision to go to war in 1914 proved disastrous for the Russian imperial regime. But according to the conventional wisdom of 1914, there was no other choice. And if we must apportion blame, surely we cannot forget Austria. The Hapsburg monarchy gave its subjects better government, and perhaps a finer civilization, than the Russian autocracy, but it suffered from many of the same faults. Official nationalism in Budapest, *Schlamperei* in Vienna, an intellectual elite consumed with brilliant destructive criticism, rising national and social groups contemptuously excluded from a share in their own government, and occasional outbursts of futile rage from a ruling class that was on the way out, all these factors helped to turn Central Europe into a powder barrel. One may or may not prefer Vienna to St. Petersburg, but one must note the similarity. Perhaps, in the late 1960's, one may have more sympathy with the predicament of declining rulers, elites, empires, and nations than an earlier generation of any English-speaking nation would have felt. But one must also realize that these phenomena are likely to give rise to dangerous and explosive situations.

Discussion

Mr. Kennan found Mr. Seton-Watson's remarks penetrating and helpful. With regard to the question of Russia and the outbreak of World War I, he said that it had not been his intention to suggest that remaining aloof from complications in the Balkans was a feasible choice for the tsarist government in 1914. His comments in that regard were meant to indicate the fully tragic situation that had been produced in Russia by the effects of modern nationalism. The tragedy had already occurred by 1914; it could not have been stopped in its final act.

Mr. Rogger asked whether the irregular supply of enlightened despots in general and the personality of the last tsar in particular did not call into question the right of the autocracy to exist. In other words, the fundamental problem was not so much with the personality of the despot as with the system. He also wondered whether there actually was much connection between domestic nationalism and foreign policy. He pointed out that those rightists who were most imbued with Great Russian chauvinism were also the most peaceful in foreign policy.

Mr. Wolfe commented that, as a congenital exceptionalist when examining the history of any country, he had reservations about Mr. Seton-Watson's statement that all countries undergoing industrialization did so largely at the expense of the peasantry. Mr. Seton-Watson had himself spoken of developments in Japan where so much capital had been plowed back into education and into the development of the Japanese as a unified people. With the benefit of huge areas of free land and an enormous reserve of imported labor, the United States had industrialized without grinding the peasant into the ground. In view of all this, Mr. Wolfe wondered whether it was not best to avoid hazarding generalizations about industrialization and peasant hardship and to put the Russian problem back into Russian perspective. As Mr. Kennan had suggested, the peasant had been a beneficiary of Russian economic expansion after 1906. Mr. Wolfe expressed confidence that this trend would have continued.

Mr. Wolfe also took issue with Mr. Rogger's thoughts on the right of the autocracy to exist. He believed that nothing in the way of wholesome new institutions could have been expected of Nicholas II and his family. A change was inevitable. However, this did not mean that the right of the autocracy to exist was in question. Right or no right, the fact remained that the tsarist political system had been replaced by a new and far worse form of autocracy.

Finally, Mr. Wolfe expressed the hope that during the conference attention would be paid to the ideological side of the revolution. Among problems he suggested for consideration were the historical background of Russia's ardent ideology of autocracy, the ideology of the tsarist bureaucracy, the deeply rooted anarchism of the Russian peasantry, and the anarchical extremism of the intelligentsia.

Mr. Pipes wondered whether it were not in fact true that the root of *both* the ideology of the autocracy and the social revolutionary movement was a tremendous dread of the Western pattern and the hope that Russia might be able to avoid it. The desire of the radical left to avoid capitalism with all its consequences was paralleled by the desire of the right to escape industrialization, urbanization, social revolution, mass culture, and everything else that followed.

Mr. Kennan thought that behind these fears of the Western path lay a deeply ingrained aversion to all compromise as a pollution of truth. The Russian political mind found it very difficult to deal with a complexity of truth or to admit that truth could be complex and contain contradictory elements. Thus the autocracy and revolutionaries alike rejected Western European civilization in the social sense that involved some sort of accommodation between capital and labor, as well as in the political sense that involved the whole messy, imperfect, Western parliamentary system. Speculating on the roots of this attitude, Mr. Kennan wondered if it did not stem from Byzantium and the original concept of the integrity of the religion as something absolutely essential to the success of the system.

Mr. Seton-Watson noted that there was one form into which the Russian autocratic political system might have developed that had not yet been considered. The autocracy might have tried to marshal the peasantry and working class behind a right-wing dictatorship, owing allegiance to the tsar. The Union of the Russian People (*Soiuz russkogo naroda*), pegged to extreme Russian nationalism and anti-Semitism, had been a step in this direction. It had not got very far before the war, but in the following thirty years similar proto-fascist political systems had been successful in Eastern European countries that in many ways resembled Russia. He was not saying that such a development would have been a good thing; however, it was an alternative which historians had to bear in mind.

To Mr. Treadgold it seemed that along with the critical moments mentioned by Mr. Kennan, the decade of the 1880's deserved a bit more attention as decisive for Russia's development. From the very beginning of the 1880's, as Mr. Seton-Watson had noted, tsarist educational policies had failed to take advantage of existing opportunities. It was at this time that the oppression of national minorities was intensified and that Russian nationalism came to the fore. Moreover, precisely such a representative consultative body as Mr. Kennan had spoken of had actually been authorized hours before the assassination of Alexander II. That these hopes for popular representation had faded away after Ignatiev's term as Minister of the Interior was only partly a consequence of the tsar's murder. Mr. Treadgold felt that all this threw light on what could have been reasonably expected of the tsarist regime in terms of transforming itself.

Mr. Epstein observed that the thesis which Mr. Kennan seemed to be expounding, namely that Russia was modernizing effectively before World War I and that without war the Russian political system might have evolved peacefully into a parliamentary monarchy, had been presented by the conservative German historian Otto Hoetzsch in 1913. Hoetzsch had also stressed the importance of the *zemstva* as the nucleus for the parliamentarization of Russia. Mr. Kennan had referred to the time when the *zemstva* were introduced as a moment when some kind of national parliament might have been established. Mr. Epstein did not think this argument persuasive. To him the possibility of such a development seemed precluded by the example which the Prussian constitutional struggle offered to Russian statesmen.

In regard to the Russian nationality problem, Mr. Epstein thought it necessary to indicate precisely when national consciousness on the part of minority peoples became a problem for Russia. Only Polish nationalism and to a certain extent that of the Baltic Germans constituted a problem for the Russian government in the nineteenth century.

Mr. Kennan replied that, at precisely the time when the spirit of nationalism stimulated russification efforts by the tsarist regime, it also enormously heightened both the ambitions and the sensitivities of certain of the national minorities themselves, so that, for example, what the Poles had been prepared to accept in 1815 was no longer acceptable to them in 1863. Mr. Kennan felt that this was something that should have been clarified in his paper. He also remarked that having been a student of Hoetzsch, he had perhaps been influenced by his views. However, he was now inclined to doubt the thesis that prospects for the survival of the tsarist regime were good had war not intervened.

A statement by Miss Arendt to the effect that Russian nationalism was fundamentally different from nationalism in Western Europe and that from the middle of the nineteenth century Russian nationalism was actually Pan-Slavism prompted several comments. Mr. Kennan pointed out that Russian nationalism was only in part Pan-Slav. Sir Isaiah Berlin recalled Mr. Karpovich's view that Pan-Slavism lasted in Russia for a mere fifteen years—from about 1865 to at most the late 1870's. There was really no Pan-Slavism in existence by 1900, or at least no political Pan-Slavism in the sense that there were persons interested in Slavic areas outside Russia. Mr. Rogger added that at that time the tsarist government was in fact deathly afraid of Pan-Slavism.

Mr. Seton-Watson remarked that while Pan-Slavism probably lasted only fifteen years as a government policy, a certain amount of Pan-Slav sympathy among Russians survived later. However, to him this was not the point. In referring to Russian nationalism he had in mind official nationalism, the imposition through the Russian state machine of Russian nationality on everyone else in the empire. This seemed to be the sense in which Mr. Kennan had discussed nationalism in his paper and here an important change had taken place between the middle and end of the nineteenth century. Sometime in the 1890's the Russian government had begun directing russification policies not only at the Poles, but against such loyal friends as the Finns, the Baltic Germans, and the Armenians. Although these peoples asked for nothing better than to serve the Russian empire, they had been persecuted merely because they were not Russian. For reasons that could only be speculated about, this policy had been deliberately adopted by the Russian government; its results were fatal for the empire.

Mr. Seton-Watson agreed with Mr. Treadgold's emphasis on the importance of the 1880's for Russia. However, to Mr. Treadgold's list of crucial developments he would add the change in official attitudes toward the commune that had also occurred at this time. The future of the commune had, after all, been left open by the Emancipation Statute; thus provision had been made for the individual peasant to leave the commune and set himself up as a private landowner. However, for reasons of administration, in the 1880's this door was almost completely closed.

Mr. Seton-Watson traced the adoption of this economically repressive policy to changes in the composition of the Ministry of the Interior. At the time of the emancipation, the Ministry of Interior had contained the most progressive figures in the Russian bureaucracy, and by the 1880's it had become a center of reaction. Mr. Seton-Watson compared the effects of the Meiji restoration upon the Japanese bureaucracy with what had occurred in Russia during the reform period. The Meiji restoration had come about as the result of a bloody struggle and had brought with it a complete transformation in the composition of the ruling elites. However, no such fundamental change had occurred in Russia; this had made it possible for the old Russian bureaucracy to bring reform to a halt merely by pushing aside a few outstanding people.

To Mr. Seton-Watson this lack of any kind of purge or revolution at the beginning of Alexander II's reign was as important a gap as the failure to come to terms with people like Unkovskii. Indeed, the two were related in that the failure of the tsarist regime to deal with the liberals at the time when limited liberalism could have got somewhere was connected with the failure to purge the machine. Bearing this in mind, Mr. Seton-Watson wondered if the great tragedy of Russia was not that its defeat in the Crimean War had not been severe enough.

The Origins of Bolshevism: The Intellectual Evolution of Young Lenin — *Richard Pipes*

The formulation in 1900–1902 by Lenin of Bolshevik theory is an event that in importance far exceeds the obvious influence it has had on the history of Russia and other countries with Communist governments or movements. Bolshevism originated that characteristic institution of the twentieth century, the one-party state. By dissociating socialism from democracy, and institutionalizing this cleavage in the dictatorial elite that goes by the name of "party" but bears little relationship to what is ordinarily meant by this word, Lenin has turned out to be the most influential political theorist of modern times.

The origins of Lenin's political theory have to be sought at least as much in psychology as in ideas. But Lenin's psyche is a separate subject, and we shall not occupy ourselves with it, except in passing. Our concern shall be with political theory. We shall trace Lenin's thirteen-year-old search for a revolutionary strategy, which began upon his expulsion from the university in 1887 and ended in the closing days of the century when he formulated the basic principles of bolshevism. As we shall indicate, the central question confronting Lenin was the relation between socialism and democracy or, more concretely, the relationship of revolutionary socialists to three social classes: the peasantry, the industrial working class, and the bourgeoisie. His intellectual evolution went through four phases, each distinguished by a specific answer to this question. During the first phase, extending from 1887–1892, Lenin sympathized with the Jacobin wing of the People's Will. He believed that the revolution would derive its force from the peasant masses and its leadership from a conspiratorial group employing terror and aiming at a power seizure. The second transitional phase began in 1892–93 when Lenin lost faith in the revolutionary capacity of the peasantry. He now turned his attention to the industrial proletariat but continued to cling to the techniques of terror and power seizure. In the summer of 1895, Lenin entered the third phase, at which time he became a full-fledged

Social Democrat of the Western type. He concluded that socialism could triumph only as a result of a broad oppositional movement of all the social classes, including the liberal bourgeoisie, and that socialism presupposed democracy. In mid-1899, under the shock of various disappointments, he experienced a personal crisis. He now lost faith in both the working class and the liberal bourgeoisie and evolved an undemocratic philosophy of socialism, which fused Jacobin and Marxist elements to produce that peculiar amalgam known as bolshevism.

The difficulties one confronts in attempting to trace Lenin's intellectual evolution are formidable. Lenin left us virtually no autobiographical information, and we possess almost nothing from his pen during the first twenty-three years of his life.[1] The difficulty is compounded by the fact that the Moscow Institute of Marxism-Leninism and other Russian archival repositories have not seen it fit to publish, except in brief excerpts, many documents from the 1880's and 1890's bearing on Lenin, including the correspondence of his sisters and the memoirs of his brother.[2] Nearly all the secondary accounts of Lenin are of post-1917 vintage. By then friend and foe alike sought to link Lenin, the leader of the October Revolution, with Vladimir Ulianov, the young radical intellectual. As a result, Lenin emerges in most Western and nearly all Communist biographies as a person fashioned of one piece: a man unchanging and unhesitating, who from his earliest years (at any rate from the age of 16, when his brother was executed) knew and followed his path. This picture may well be true in the psychological sense, but it certainly does not hold of Lenin's political ideas. He was a politician long before he had an opportunity of practicing politics. He was forever adapting his ideas to realities, and he changed his strategy and tactics more frequently and more abruptly than any other prominent Russian revolutionary. Unlike typical radical intellectuals of his time, he had no commitment to any set of ideas; and

1. The most complete bibliography of Lenin's writings is that published by the Institute of Marxism-Leninism under the title *Khronologicheskii ukazatel' proizvedenii V. I. Lenina*, 2 vols. (Moscow, 1959–1962). Prior to the spring of 1893 it lists a total of 25 items (nos. 1–23, 10375 and 10376) of which 17 are official petitions or certificates, 3 marginalia, 2 telegrams, 2 legal defense briefs, and one an advertisement.

2. The Institute of Marxism-Leninism has, among other pertinent documents, the letters of Maria, Anna, and Olga Ulianovas from the late 1880's. Excerpts from them have appeared in B. Volin's *V. I. Lenin v Povolzh'e* (Moscow, 1955), pp. 53, 57–58, 92. References to unpublished memoirs of brother Dimitrii deposited at the Kokushkino Lenin Museum are made in *Uchenye Zapiski Kazanskogo Universiteta*, vol. 114 (1954), no. 9, pp. 24–25. Other pertinent memoirs, such as those of M. L. Mandelshtam (see below, note 19), remain unpublished as well.

it is ironic that he, the most flexible of revolutionaries, should have acquired the reputation as the most constant.

Virtually all Lenin's biographers mention his early contacts with the People's Will (*Narodnaia volia*), the terrorist organization that, beginning in 1879, engaged in systematic attacks on tsarist officials and in 1881 succeeded in assassinating Alexander II. Lenin is said in his early years to have sought out veterans of the terrorist underground, and questioned them closely on their conspiratorial techniques, in this manner acquiring knowledge which he later put to use in organizing the Bolshevik Party. Soviet historians, although vehemently denying any connection between bolshevism and the People's Will, do not, as a rule, gainsay Lenin's admiration for the old terrorists. Nor can they, since Lenin himself, as well as his widow and sister, left unequivocal testimony to this effect.[3]

Lenin's involvement with terrorism and terrorist organizations, however, can be shown to have been much deeper and longer than it is usually depicted. His concern for terrorism was not merely that of an interested outsider: between 1887 and 1893, he was affiliated with three organizations composed almost exclusively of adherents of the People's Will. Even the sparse documentary evidence available to the foreign scholar leaves no doubt that Lenin spent the first five or six years of his revolutionary career in the very midst of the most extreme Jacobin elements of the People's Will.

Lenin's initiation into politics occurred rather accidentally during his first term at the University of Kazan. He had arrived at the university in the autumn of 1887 surprisingly innocent of any political ideas or connections. In the gymnasium at Simbirsk he had been a model student with a nearly perfect record in all subjects, behavior included, and had

---

3. "Many [Social Democrats] began to think in a revolutionary manner as *Narodovol'tsy*. From their early youth onwards, almost all bowed in exultation before the heroes of terror. The rejection of the adored image of this terroristic tradition required a struggle accompanied by a break with those who, regardless of the consequences wished to remain loyal to the People's Will, and whom the young Social Democrats regarded so highly." *Chto delat'?* in V. I. Lenin, *Sochineniia*, 2nd ed., IV, p. 499. (All further references to Lenin's Works, unless otherwise noted, are to this second edition.) Krupskaya, citing this passage in her Memoirs, calls it "a piece of Vladimir Il'ich's biography." (N. K. Krupskaia, *Vospominaniia o Lenine*, 2nd ed., Moscow, 1933, p. 37.) Lenin's sister, Anna, also states that "[Lenin] always felt a deep regard for the old *Narodovol'tsy*" (Entsiklopedicheskii Slovar' *Granat*, vol. XLI, pt. 1, p. 309). So does Zinoviev in his early biography (N. *Lenin*, Moscow, 1920, p. 8).

graduated at the top of his class. It is only because of this impeccable record that he was allowed to enroll at Kazan. The previous spring his elder brother, Alexander, had been executed with four other members of a People's Will organization for participating in a plot to assassinate Alexander III. Normally this family record would have barred Lenin from the university. But he was admitted on the strength of an enthusiastic endorsement supplied by the principal of the Simbirsk gymnasium, Fedor Kerensky, the father of the future head of the Provisional Government whom Lenin was to overthrow. Vladimir Ilich, he wrote, although "reticent" and "unsociable" was in every respect an excellent young man, who "neither in school nor out of it gave his superiors or teachers by a single word or deed any cause to form of him an unfavorable opinion."[4] There is no reason to doubt the accuracy of this characterization. The only contrary evidence comes from his sister, who denies that Lenin was quite so perfect because he was known to have ridiculed his French teacher. Even she concedes, however, that on completing the gymnasium Lenin held no "definite" political views.[5]

Despite this background, within a few weeks after his arrival at the university, Lenin associated himself with a highly subversive organization. What happened is that he was recognized by fellow students as the brother of a recently executed terrorist and was approached by members of a revolutionary circle headed by one Lazar Bogoraz. Early in the academic year, Lenin joined this group.[6] Insofar as we can judge from the available documentation, the Bogoraz circle intended to reconstitute the People's Will and possibly to complete the mission which Alexander Ulianov and his associates had failed to carry out, namely

4. *Molodaia gvardiia*, no. 1 (1924), p. 89.

5. A. I. Ulianova-Elizarova in *Aleksandr Il'ich Ul'ianov i delo 1 marta 1887 g.*, (Moscow-Leningrad, 1927), p. 97. Lenin's lack of political concerns during his gymnasium years is confirmed by V. Alekseev and A. Shver in *Sem'ia Ul'ianovykh v Simbirske, 1896–1897* (Leningrad, 1925), pp. 48–51.

6. Documents bearing on the Bogoraz circle are deposited at the Central State Historical Archive in Moscow (TsGIAM), Delo Departamenta Politsii. They have been partly reproduced by M. K. Korbut in "Kazanskoe revoliutsionnoe podpol'e kontsa 80–kh godov i Lenin," *Katorga i ssylka*, no. 8/9 (81/82), (1931), pp. 7–27 and in *Krasnyi arkhiv*, no. 62 (1934), pp. 65–66. The background of this circle is sketched in G. E. Khait, "V kazanskom kruzhke," *Novyi mir*, no. 4 (1958), pp. 189–193. On Bogoraz, see V. I. Nevskii, ed., *Deiateli revoliutsionnogo dvizheniia v Rossii—Bio-bibliograficheskii slovar'*, vol. V, vyp. 1 (Moscow, 1931), p. 398. B. Volin's *V. I. Lenin v Povol'zhe* concedes that Lenin belonged to Bogoraz's circle (p. 52) but misleadingly describes the latter as a circle for "political self-education." See also, *Novyi mir*, no. 4 (1957), p. 147.

the assassination of the tsar. To this end, Bogoraz established contact with terrorists in St. Petersburg.[7]

The designs of Bogoraz's circle were abruptly terminated on December 4, 1887, when many of its members, Lenin among them, became involved in a student demonstration against the new university regulations. As the demonstrators were dispersed, their student cards were taken away. Having returned home that evening, Lenin wrote a formal letter to the university announcing his withdrawal.[8] This desperate effort to prevent expulsion failed. Later that night he was arrested, and a few days later expelled, together with 39 fellow students.[9]

We have at our disposal two interesting glimpses of Lenin at the time of this, his first police detention. In 1924, a Bolshevik writer recalled what he had heard from Lenin in 1905 about his arrest in Kazan. A guard who escorted Lenin is said to have asked him: "Young man, what are you doing? You are up against a wall!" To which Lenin is said to have replied: "Yes, a wall—but a rotten one—touch it, and it will fall apart."[10] The belief that the imperial regime was on the verge of collapse, was, of course, typical of the adherents of the People's Will. And in 1926, a fellow prisoner of Lenin's in Kazan wrote down the story of their detention. He said that the majority of the arrested students were gay and bantered about their future. At one point, someone turned to Lenin, who was sitting apart, lost in thought, and asked what he intended to do after his release. Lenin, we are told, replied: "What is there for me to think about? . . . My road has been paved by my elder brother."[11]

At the time of Lenin's arrest, the Kazan police had not been aware of his association with the Bogoraz circle. This they discovered only subsequently, in the course of investigations of his background carried out on instructions of the governor.[12] Once Lenin's connections with

7. The St. Petersburg contact was one Vassilii Zelenenko, whom the police arrested in 1888. Documents found on him told of the organization's desire to "display activity and thereby demonstrate the revival of the revolutionary party" [that is, the *Narodnaia Volia*]. Khait, "V kazanskom kruzhke," pp. 190–192; Korbut, "Kazanskoe revoliutsionnoe podpol'e," p. 16; *Krasnyi arkhiv*, no. 62 (1934), p. 65.

8. This letter is reproduced in A. I. Ivanskii, *Molodye gody V. I. Lenina* [(Moscow), 1958], p. 278.

9. The names of the students expelled with Lenin are listed in M. K. Korbut, *Kazanskii Gosudarstvennyi Universitet imeni V. I. Ul'ianova-Lenina za 125 let*, II (Kazan, 1930), pp. 199–201.

10. V. Adoratskii, "Za 18 let (Vstrechi s Vladimirom Il'ichem)," *Proletarskaia Revoliutsiia*, no. 3 (26), (1924), p. 94.

11. E. Foss, "Pervaia tiurma V. I. Lenina," *Ogonek*, no. 11 (1926), p. 5.

12. "Spisok lits nakhodivshikhsia v blizkom znakomstve i snosheniiakh s . . . Vl. Il. Ul'ianovym," *Delo Departamenta Politsii, 1886 g.*, no. 151, 3 deloproiz-

the terrorists became known, he was placed under permanent police surveillance. Because of his brother's and sister's compromising record, and his own association with "undesirables," petitions for pardon, which he and his mother regularly submitted, were equally regularly rejected. Lenin therefore spent the next four years in forced idleness. He engaged during this period in no gainful employment and lived entirely off his mother's widow's pension. It is during these four years that he probably developed that consuming hatred of the "bourgeois" and "cultured" society that remained with him all his life. (How deeply embedded this estrangement became may be illustrated by the fact that years later, when escorting Trotsky around London, Lenin habitually described the sights as "theirs," by which he meant not the English, but the "enemy." "This meaning was always present when [Lenin] spoke of any kind of cultural values or new conquests . . . ," Trotsky adds, "*they* understand or *they* have, *they* have accomplished or succeeded—but always as enemies.")[13] A brilliant, hard-working student, a recent gold-medallist, he found himself condemned because of a minor breach of discipline to a parasitic existence without any hope of reprieve. How desperate his psychic condition must have been at this time may be gathered from one of his mother's petitions for her son, in which she voiced fears that he may be driven to suicide.[14] Accounts dealing with this period depict Lenin as a singularly disagreeable young man: aggressive, sarcastic, uncommunicative, and friendless.[15]

So far Lenin's involvement in the revolution had been spontaneous and almost accidental; now it became conscious and deliberate. Immediately after his expulsion, during the winter of 1887–88, which he spent with his family in virtual isolation at a country dacha, Lenin interested himself for the first time in social questions. As he later recalled, he never again in his life read as much as during the year that followed.[16] He went over old copies of "fat journals" and the works of "progressive" writers of the preceding quarter century. It was now that he became acquainted with Chernyshevskii, the leading radical publicist of the 1860's. Lenin read and reread Chernyshevskii's essays in the

---

vodstvo, 1. 108 i sl., dated February 4, 1888, and cited in Korbut, "Kazanskoe revoliutsionnoe podpol'e," pp. 19–20.

13. L. Trotsky, *Lenin* (New York, 1925), pp. 7–8.

14. Petition of May 17, 1890, *Krasnaia Letopis'*, no. 2/11 (1924), p. 35.

15. Ivanskii, *Molodye gody*, pp. 210, 249, 264. A. I. Ulianova in Institut MELS, *Vospominaniia rodnykh o V. I. Lenine* (Moscow, 1955), pp. 22–26.

16. N. Valentinov, *Vstrechi s Leninym* (New York, 1953), p. 106. Valentinov cites an account written down by V. V. Vorovskii in 1919 on the basis of talks which he and Valentinov had had with Lenin fifteen years earlier.

Contemporary and his novel, *What Is to Be Done?*, with such thoroughness and involvement that years later he spoke of having been "deeply plowed over" by Chernyshevskii.[17] Precisely what he assimilated from him we cannot tell; later he claimed to have been introduced by Chernyshevskii to Hegel and to philosophical materialism. But there can be little doubt that he came under the spell of Chernyshevskii's style of discourse: his biting sarcasm, utter self-assurance, impatience with ideas unrelated to action, and unwillingness to see anything but stupidity or depravity in any opponent on any issue.

In the autumn of 1888, the Ulianovs resettled in Kazan. At this time there appeared in Kazan a few radicals claiming to profess "Marxism" or "Social Democracy." The most influential among them was N. Fedoseev, who in December 1888 formed his "Marxist" circle. What kind of Marxism Fedoseev and his friends espoused we shall discuss below. Here, suffice it to say that they were moving toward Social Democracy of a Western kind but were still some distance from their goal. Lenin is sometimes mentioned as a member of Fedoseev's circle,[18] but this is clearly wrong. Not only is there no archival information linking Lenin with Fedoseev, but we are told by Lenin himself that he did not know him: "I heard about Fedoseev during my stay in Kazan," Lenin wrote shortly before his death, "but I never met him personally. In the spring of 1889 I left [Kazan] for the Samara province, where at the end of the summer I learned of the arrest of Fedoseev and other members of the Kazan circles, including the one of which I was a member."[19]

17. Valentinov, *Vstrechi s Leninym*, p. 103. See also the accurate and illuminating essay by the same author, "Chernyshevskii i Lenin," *Novyi Zhurnal*, no. XXVI (1951), pp. 193–216, and no. XXVII (1951), pp. 225–249. Valentinov considers Chernyshevskii to have been the single most important influence in the formation of Lenin's political views. Without denying the influence of Chernyshevskii, we would attach even greater importance to the whole People's Will-Jacobin tradition which Lenin absorbed during his formative years.

18. For example, Volin in *Lenin v Povolzh'e*, pp. 60–67.

19. "Neskol'ko slov o N. E. Fedoseeve," *Sochineniia*, XXVII, p. 376. Lenin's sister Anna confirms that Lenin did not belong to Fedoseev's circle (A. I. Ul'ianova in *Vospominaniia rodnykh*, p. 26). There was in Kazan at this time another circle in which Marx was seriously studied, headed by M. L. Mandelshtam. Lenin is sometimes listed as belonging to Mandelshtam's group by Soviet historians desperate to find a Marxist alibi for him during the Kazan days (for example, Korbut, "Kazanskoe revoliutsionnoe podpol'e," p. 24). But since Mandelshtam himself "learned" of Lenin's alleged membership in his circle only in 1928, we may safely disregard this claim. (See the excerpt from Mandelshtam's unpublished memoirs in *Moskva*, no. 4 (1958), p. 57.) On the other hand it is entirely possible that Lenin first became acquainted with Marx at a lecture delivered by Mandelshtam, as stated in an article in *Rabochaia Moskva*, no. 92, April 22, 1924, "Iz rasskazov tov. Lenina o ego vstuplenii v revoliutsionnoe dvizhenie," cited in *Moskva*, no. 4 (1958), p. 55.

Lenin was always parsimonious with autobiographical statements, and with good reason, for he did not want to divulge his early Jacobin associations. It is significant that in this remark he did not see fit to mention what "Kazan circle" he did belong to. It now can be established, however, that in the autumn of 1888 he had joined a circle organized by Maria Chetvergova, a prominent adherent of the People's Will. This circle formed part of a nationwide network established by an escaped Siberian convict, M. V. Sabunaev, with the intention of reviving the People's Will. Chetvergova participated in September 1889 in a secret convocation of these circles held in Kazan, for which she and other of its participants were shortly afterwards arrested.[20] Lenin escaped the same fate only because a few months earlier his mother, alarmed by his contact with revolutionaries in Kazan, decided to move the family to Samara.[21]

There, Lenin continued his association with the People's Will. In Samara he found himself in the heartland of socialist revolutionary sentiment. Samara and its environs were inhabited by many released political prisoners, veterans of both the "Going to the People" and the terrorist movements, who, forbidden to take up residence in the capital cities chose to settle in this agrarian region. Shortly after his arrival, Lenin contacted N. S. Dolgov, who had once been a close associate of Nechaev, the most Jacobin radical of the 1860's.[22] Dolgov in turn

20. We know that Lenin attended Chetvergova's circle from information provided in *Rabochaia Moskva*, no. 92, April 22, 1924, cited in *Moskva*, no. 4 (1958), p. 55, and in *Novyi mir*, no. 4 (1957), p. 147. Lenin visited Chetvergova in Ufa in 1900, as he was returning from his Siberian exile. Krupskaya notes that Lenin "displayed [toward her] a special gentleness in his voice and expression" (*Vospominaniia*, p. 37). Krupskaya's statement about Lenin and the *Narodovol'tsy*, cited above in note 3, refers to Chetvergova. See also N. Valentinov, *Vstrechi s Leninym* (New York, 1953), pp. 38–39. According to S. Livshits ("Ocherki istorii Kazanskoi sotsial-demokratii, 1888–1916 gg.," pt. 1, *Puti Revoliutsii*, no. 1, Kazan, 1922, pp. 98–99), Chetvergova's circle was originally formed by Aleksei Trofimov, but he must be mistaken in dating its formation summer 1889. Chetvergova, born about 1845 and educated in Zürich and Vienna, was first arrested in 1875 for "propaganda," that is, for participating in the "Going to the People" movement. The 1889 conference of *Narodovol'tsy* organized by Sabunaev is described in *Obzor vazhneishikh doznanii, proizvodivshikhsia v zhandarmskikh upravleniiakh imperii po delam o gosudarstvennykh prestupleniiakh* for 1890, pp. 39–40, 125. See also *Moskva*, no. 4 (1958), p. 56.

21. The fears of Lenin's mother are recalled by Lenin's sister in *Puti revoliutsii*, no. 2 (Kazan, 1922), p. 9. A recent historian of the People's Will, S. S. Volk states that in December 1889 Lenin himself participated in discussions with Sabunaev but provides no further details. (*Narodnaia Volia*, 1879–1882, Moscow-Leningrad, 1966, p. 448.)

22. On Dolgov, see F. Venturi, *Roots of Revolution* (New York, 1960), p. 374. In 1869 he had belonged to Nechaev's main circle, *Narodnaia rasprava* (People's

introduced Lenin to other local revolutionaries, including two women belonging to the Jacobin organization headed by Zaichnevskii.[23] Lenin thus surrounded himself with Jacobins and terrorists, including persons associated with the leading figures of Russian Jacobinism. In addition, he joined in Samara an illegal circle, headed by A. P. Skliarenko. This circle professed typical "populist" ideas of the time and maintained connections with People's Will adherents in other cities.[24]

Many years after the events here described, when he headed the Soviet government, Lenin, in reply to a party questionnaire inquiring when and where he had begun his revolutionary career, replied "In 1892–1893, in Samara."[25] This unelaborated statement carries striking implications. As we have seen, by 1892–93 Lenin had been arrested and expelled from the university, spent nearly a year under administrative exile, and participated in three illegal circles—those of Bogoraz, Chetvergova, and Skliarenko. Only thanks to good luck he had managed to escape imprisonment when each of these circles in turn was broken up by the police.[26] Why then should he have begun his revolutionary

Summary Justice) and later participated in the so-called Dolgushin conspiracy organized by Nechaev's followers. Another friend of Lenin's in Samara, A. I. Livanov, had also belonged to the Dolgushin group. (See Ivanskii, *Molodye gody*, p. 328, and V. I. Lenin v Samare, 1889–1893—Sbornik vospominanii (Moscow, 1933), p. 6.

23. They were Mariia Petrovna Golubeva-Iasneva and Adelaida Ivanovna Romanova, both recently returned from Siberian exile. See M. Golubeva, "Poslednii karaul," *Molodaia gvardiia* no. 2/3 (1924), pp. 29–31, and "Iunosha Ul'ianov (V. I. Lenin)," *Staryi Bol'shevik*, no. 5/8 (1933), pp. 160–164. Golubeva was a close associate of Zaichnevskii's and left recollections of him [*Proletarskaia revoliutsiia*, no. 6/7 (18/19), (1923), pp. 27–31]. Both women later joined the Bolshevik party.

24. Our principal information on the Skliarenko circle comes from one of its members, M. I. Semenov (M. Blan): "Pamiati druga" in *Staryi tovarishch Aleksei Pavlovich Skliarenko* (Moscow, 1922), pp. 7–19 and *Lenin v Samare 1889–1893* (Moscow, 1933; a second, revised edition came out in Kuibyshev in 1940 under the title *Revoliutsionnaia Samara 80–90-kh godov*). There are also memoirs of A. Beliakov, *Iunost' Vozhdia*, 2nd ed. (Moscow, 1960), originally written in 1926; the printed version, however, according to a publisher's note, has been "slightly abbreviated" and given a "literary working-over," for which reason it must be regarded a suspect source. According to Semenov, in 1889 when Lenin joined his circle, Skliarenko was a follower of Mikhailovskii and V. V. (Vorontsov), that is, of the two leading agrarian socialists (*K Samarskomu periodu*, p. 37). Semenov also tells us that before turning "Marxist," Skliarenko and his group were adherents of the People's Will ("Staryi tovarishch," pp. 7 and 10; *K Samarskomu periodu*, p. 44).

25. *Leninskii Sbornik*, XX, p. 51. Written in 1921.

26. The Bogoraz circle was arrested in the winter of 1887–88; Chetvergova was jailed in 1890, and Skliarenko and his group in late 1893.

reckoning five years late? To this question the answer is twofold: partly to conceal his past involvement with the People's Will, and partly to mark the beginning of his conversion to Marxism.

Anyone who tries to ascertain precisely when Lenin became a Marxist runs into wide differences of opinion. The earliest date suggested is 1887, that is, when Lenin was sixteen. The source of this dating is Lenin's sister, Maria. According to her, Lenin, upon hearing of his brother's execution, proclaimed, "No, we shall not take this road"— presumably in this manner announcing his conversion to Marxism.[27] Apart from the fact that Maria was not quite ten when this alleged statement had been made, this anecdote (given currency in 1924) deserves no attention because, as we have seen, by immediately joining the terrorist group of Bogoraz, Lenin followed precisely his brother's road. But even serious studies differ on the dating of Lenin's Marxism, some going back as far as 1888–89, others placing it as late as 1892.[28] The differences of opinion on this matter are due less to lack of evidence than to disagreement over the meaning of the word "Marxism."

In the Russian context of the 1880's and early 1890's, Marxism could have one of four meanings. It could refer to Marx's economic analysis as presented in the *Capital*, a work legally circulating in imperial Russia. In this guise it was accepted by many Russian professional economists, even including one with monarchist convictions.[29] On another level, "Marxism" referred to the theory that social relations, political institutions, as well as ideas and all culture constitute a superstructure determined by the economic base. In this sense, Marxism was, of course, hardly compatible with monarchism, but it could be adapted to a variety of oppositional philosophies. Certain of the People's Will adherents, for example, embraced Marx's social doctrine and grafted onto it ideas of terror and power seizure. This held true of the organization with which Lenin's brother had been associated. Its program asserted that every country moved toward socialism by virtue of its economic development, and that under modern conditions the

27. Institut MELS, *Vospominaniia rodnykh o V. I. Lenine* (Moscow, 1955), p. 85.

28. The question of Lenin's exposure to Marx (see below, note 35) must be kept distinct from his "conversion" to Marxism. The sources date the "conversion" of Skliarenko's circle either in 1891 (Semenov, *Revoliutsionnaia Samara*, p. 44) or 1892 (V. Chuev, *V. I. Lenin v Samare, 1889–1893gg.*, Moscow, 1960, p. 75). But as we shall see (note 48), a Marxist visitor to Samara in early 1893 passes in silence over Lenin's "Marxism."

29. For example, A. I. Skvortsov, the author of a book on the influence of steam transport on the Russian economy, published in Warsaw in 1890. For a while he was considered by young Russian radicals a fellow Marxist, but when they discovered he was a monarchist and an anti-Semite, they dropped him.

urban proletariat constituted the main socialist force.[30] A liberal like Peter Struve, on the other hand, could accept Marx's social doctrine without subscribing to its revolutionary implications. In the third sense, Marxism meant Social Democracy: a comprehensive theory based on the writings of Marx and Engels as systematized by the theorists of the German Social Democratic Party, and formalized in 1891 in that party's Erfurt Program. The distinguishing feature of the Erfurt Program was its view that liberalism and democracy constituted essential ingredients of socialism. Therefore, it exhorted the working class to strive for full political liberty: that is, civil rights, the universal suffrage, and a genuine parliamentary system of government. Finally, in the fourth sense, Marxism referred to a theory of revolutionary action as presented in the publicistic writings of Marx and Engels. In Russia around 1890 it was by no means clear to which of these four meanings the word "Marxism" referred; hence much of the ensuing confusion over the date of Lenin's "conversion" to it.

Plekhanov and his fellow émigrés who in 1883 had founded in Geneva the first Russian Marxist party espoused from the beginning the Social Democratic brand of Marxism, declaring political liberty to be the immediate and indispensable goal of Russian socialism.[31] Inside Russia, however, it took a long time for self-proclaimed Marxists and Social Democrats to reach this position. The heritage of anarchism here was very strong. The majority of radical intellectuals continued to reject political freedom and representative institutions, because in their eyes these would only serve to ensconce the exploiting classes in power. Fedoseev, whose interesting letters from the early 1890's have been recently published, agonized over this question for some time after he had become a "Marxist."[32] There must have been in Russia many revolutionaries like him: men who accepted Marx's economic and social theory, but who rejected as unsuitable to Russia the political program of Social Democracy and adhered, as before, to terror and power seizure.

The available evidence strongly suggests that from 1892, or at the latest 1893, until mid-1895 Lenin was precisely this kind of a transi-

30. *Aleksandr Il'ich Ul'ianov i delo 1 marta 1887g.* It is a great mistake to contrast "populism" with "Marxism." In fact, the so-called "populists" absorbed a great deal of Marxist theory. This holds particularly true of the People's Will, which both Marx and Engels greatly admired, as stated below by Mr. Rubel. See also my essay "Russian Marxism and Its Populist Background," *The Russian Review*, October 1960, pp. 316–337.

31. See for example, "Sovremennye zadachi russkikh rabochikh" (1885), in G. V. Plekhanov, *Sochineniia*, II (Moscow-Petrograd, n.d.), p. 371 and "Vtoroi proekt programmy russkikh sotsial-demokratov (1887–88)," *ibid*, pp. 400–404.

32. N. Fedoseev, *Stat'i i pis'ma* (Moscow, 1958), p. 77.

tional Marxist. At bottom, he was still an adherent of the People's Will of the kind his brother had been, combining with terror, conspiracy, and power seizure the Marxist beliefs in the inexorable force of economic progress and in the revolutionary hegemony of the proletariat. He exemplified that very type which Fedoseev had in mind in 1893 when he wrote of Russian Marxists as "striving to become Social Democrats"[33]—words Lenin was to repeat almost verbatim many years later in recalling his own Samara days.[34]

Lenin seems to have read Marx as early as 1888,[35] but he became seriously interested in him only in 1892. The previous year, the agrarian regions where Lenin lived were struck by a famine. The famine engendered a lively debate among Russian radical intellectuals concerning its causes and long-term implications. One group blamed the hunger on capitalism, claiming that it destroyed cottage industries and impoverished the peasantry to the point where it could no longer support itself. They saw in the hunger conclusive proof that capitalism undercut its own market and therefore had no future in Russia.[36] Their opponents, Marxist publicists led by Peter Struve, interpreted the famine as a by-product of nascent capitalism and saw in it, on the contrary, incontrovertible evidence that the money economy was conquering the country. In this debate, Struve gave currency to the word "populism" as a generic term embracing all those who thought capitalism in Russia either unlikely or undesirable.[37]

Lenin did not at first participate in these discussions. In June 1890 he had at last received authorization to take the bar examinations in St. Petersburg, and the next year and a half he was busy studying. But in November 1891, when he had passed the tests and returned to Samara, he tackled the polemical literature in earnest. He now read

33. *Ibid.*, p. 98.

34. Lenin, *Sochineniia*, XXVII, p. 376.

35. There is general agreement that Lenin first read Marx in the fall or winter of 1888–89. Cf. A. I. Ulianova in *Vospominaniia rodnykh*, p. 25; *Rabochaia Moskva*, no. 92, April 22, 1924; and V. Valentinov, "Vstrecha Lenina s Marksizmom," *Novyi zhurnal*, LIII (1958), pp. 189–208. Valentinov recalls having heard from Lenin that he became acquainted with Marx's work in January 1889. I. I. Bliumental, in *V. I. Lenin v Samare* (Samara, 1925), says Lenin began to read *Das Kapital* in the fall of 1888 (p. 6).

36. The leading exponent of this view was Nikolai-on (N. F. Danielson), whose principal book is *Ocherki nashego poreformennogo obshchestvennogo khoziaistva* (St. Petersburg, 1893).

37. Struve's review of Nikolai-on's book, "Zur Beurtheilung der Kapitalistischen Entwickelung Russlands," *Sozialpolitisches Centralblatt*, vol. III, no. 1, October 2, 1893, pp. 1–3, and his subsequent works of the mid-1890's. On the history of the term "populism," see my article "*Narodnichestvo*: A Semantic Inquiry," *Slavic Review*, XXIII, no. 3 (1964), pp. 441–458.

the main publicistic works, as well as numerous statistical surveys issued by local government boards in order to ascertain what was in fact happening to the Russian peasant economy. Among these writings were three manuscripts by Fedoseev on agrarian history and conditions. Lenin was much impressed by Fedoseev's arguments, although there is some dispute whether he did or did not agree with them.[38] These researches he continued throughout 1892 and 1893. His purpose, in his sister's words, was to determine the "feasibility of Social Democracy in Russia."[39]

It was some time at the end of these two years that Lenin reached an important conclusion, one at odds with the leading proponents as well as opponents of the theory of Russia's inevitable capitalization. While they argued about the future, Lenin decided that Russia *already was in the capitalist phase*: capitalism was not a problem; it was a fact. This conclusion is astonishing considering that at the time 87 percent of the population of the Russian empire was rural. But Lenin reached this verdict on the basis of agrarian, not of industrial data. He seems to have been particularly impressed by a study of rural conditions in southern Russia brought out in the winter of 1891–92 by V. E. Postnikov. Postnikov demonstrated to Lenin's satisfaction that the Russian village was in the throes of "class differentiation" in the course of which the landowning peasant turned into a "petty bourgeois" who exploited hired labor, while the rest of the rural population became proletariarized.[40] According to one of Lenin's calculations at that time, 20 percent of the peasantry of certain provinces could be fully classified as "bourgeois."[41] With such a "middle class" Russia was indeed "capitalist." In 1893, in his earliest writings, Lenin declared: "Capitalism already at the present time is the basic background of Russian economic life;"[42] and

38. Fedoseev's manuscripts have not been published and may be lost. They are summarized in Semenov, *Revoliutsionnaia Samara*, pp. 56–57.

39. A. I. Ulianova-Elizarova in *Vospominaniia rodnykh*, p. 29.

40. V. E. Postnikov, *Iuzhno-russkoe krest'ianskoe khoziaistvo* [Moscow, 1891 (but probably beginning of 1892)]. Lenin's first extant writings of substance are his marginalia on Postnikov's book, reprinted in his *Polnoe Sobranie Sochinenii*, 5th ed., I, pp. 537–546, which the editors date not later than March 1893, and a review of this book, under the title "New Economic Movements in Peasant Life," written in the spring of 1893 and first published in 1923 (*Sochineniia*, I, pp. 1–49). In the autumn of 1892, Lenin delivered in Samara an oral report on Postnikov's book (Semenov, *Revoliutsionnaia Samara*, p. 65) and in 1893–1894 he entered into correspondence with P. Maslov on this subject (*Leninskii Sbornik*, XXXIII, pp. 15–19). Clearly, the book had an enormous impact on him.

41. "Po povodu tak nazyvaemogo voprosa o rynkakh," *Polnoe sobranie sochinenii*, I, p. 110.

42. *Ibid.*, p. 105 (written in the autumn of 1893).

"Essentially, our order does not differ from the Western European [that is, capitalist] one."[43]

This remarkable appraisal of Russia's economy had three corollaries.

First, the peasantry could no longer be relied upon to serve revolutionary purposes. The land-owning peasant was bourgeois and as such committed to the *status quo*. Intellectuals who defended his interests—those whom Lenin, adopting Struve's usage, now addressed as "populists"—became reactionaries. This attitude explains why almost alone among Samara intellectuals Lenin in 1892 refused to join relief committees formed by the local intelligentsia to help feed the starving peasants.[44] To him such philanthropy merely strengthened capitalism.

Second, Russia had no need for political liberty in the form of civil freedoms, constitution, and parliament. In a capitalistic country, political liberalization fortified the position of the bourgeoisie. In none of his works written before mid-1895 did Lenin advocate liberalism or democracy. Indeed, in *Who Are the Friends of the People*, written in 1894, he described demands for liberalization as "reactionary" and stated that the time had come to separate democracy from socialism.[45]

Third, as a capitalistic country, Russia was ripe for a socialist revolution of the kind envisaged in the *Communist Manifesto*. "The Russian economic order is a bourgeois system," Lenin wrote in 1894, "from which there is only one way out . . . namely the struggle of the proletariat against the bourgeoisie."[46] This revolutionary struggle had to be directed simultaneously against both the autocracy and the bourgeoisie. In other words, Russia was ready for communism.[47]

43. *Leninskii Sbornik*, XXXIII, p. 16. Letter to Maslov, dated May 30, 1894.

44. Golubeva, "Iunosha Ul'ianov," p. 162; Semenov, *K Samarskomu periodu*, p. 62. V. Vodovozov, "Moe znakomstvo s Leninym," *Na chuzhoi storone*, XII (1925), pp. 174–80. See below, note 55.

45. "The era in the social development of Russia when democratism and socialism fused into one indissoluble, inseparable whole (as it had been, for example, in the era of Chernyshevskii), is gone forever. Now there is absolutely no longer any basis for this idea . . . that allegedly in Russia there is no deep, qualitative difference between the ideas of democrats and socialists. Quite on the contrary: between these two ideas lies a whole gulf, and Russian socialists should have long realized this, the *inevitability* and *necessity of a full and final break with the ideas of the democrats*." *Sochineniia*, I, pp. 170–71 (written in the summer of 1894; emphasis in the original).

46. *Ibid.*, p. 77.

47. *Ibid.*, p. 194. "The Russian *worker*, leading all democratic elements, will bring down absolutism and will lead the *Russian proletariat* (together with the proletariat of *all countries*) *by the direct road of open political struggle to the triumphant Communist Revolution*." These words were written in the summer of 1894 (emphasis in the original).

Lenin thus retained his earlier Jacobin beliefs but in a modernized, Marxist guise. By proclaiming Russia capitalist, he could still call for an immediate socialist revolution, without having to wait patiently for capitalism to mature. We are not surprised, therefore, to learn from persons acquainted with Lenin in 1892–93 that at this time, while ostensibly a "Marxist" and even a "Social Democrat," he continued to advocate terror and power seizure and in discussions with admirers of German Social Democracy to challenge their "constitutional illusions."[48] After six years of quest, Lenin had reached the same position that his brother, unknown to him, had formulated in 1887, on the eve of his execution.

This second phase of Lenin's intellectual development came to an abrupt end in the summer of 1895, when he converted to Social Democracy in the ordinary, Western meaning of the word then current. This particular conversion was so smooth and sudden, so devoid of the crisis atmosphere attending Lenin's other intellectual shifts, that it is natural to wonder whether it represented, at least initially, a genuine intellectual commitment rather than merely a tactical maneuver.

In the autumn of 1893, Lenin had established himself in St. Petersburg. Outwardly, he made a living as a practicing lawyer, but since no evidence has been found connecting him in the capital with any legal proceedings, we may assume that he continued as before to live off his mother. Shortly after his arrival, he contacted a small group of radicals who conducted tutorial sessions with skilled workers—activity known as "propaganda." Its purpose was to lead the workers through a

48. Golubeva ("Poslednii karaul," *Molodaia gvardiia*, no. 2/3, 1924, pp. 30–31) held conversations with Lenin sometime between November 1891 when Lenin returned to Samara from St. Petersburg and the autumn of 1892 when she, herself, left Samara. She reports that "Lenin questioned neither the possibility nor the desirability of a power seizure, but he simply could not understand on what 'people' (*narod*) we intended to base ourselves. He began elaborately to explain that the people is not something unified and homogeneous, that it consists of classes with different interests, and so on." See also her remarks in *V. I. Lenin v Samare* (Moscow, 1933), p. 65n where she emphatically denies Lenin was anti-Jacobin. I. Lalaiants, an associate of Fedoseev, who arrived in Samara in March 1893 detected in Lenin "certain sympathies for *Narodnaia volia* terror" and notes that this propensity caused conflicts between the two of them. [I. Lalaiants, "O moikh vstrechakh s V. I. Leninym za vremia 1893–1900gg.," *Proletarskaia Revoliutsiia*, no. 1 (84), 1929, p. 49]. Lalaiants, it may be noted, describes Skliarenko as a full-blown Marxist (p. 44); since he does not make the same assertion about Lenin, it is likely that he did not regard him as such. As late as the autumn of 1893, when Lenin sought entrance into a circle of St. Petersburg "propagandists," he was examined thoroughly on terror and found temperamentally "too red," that is, too favorably disposed to it. (G. M. Krzhizhanovskii, *O Vladimire Il'iche*, Moscow, 1924, pp. 13–14). On Lenin's attacks on German Social Democrats parliamentary tactics, see M. Golubeva in *Staryi Bol'shevik*, 5 (1933), pp. 162–163.

broad educational program to an acceptance of socialism and in this manner to build up cadres of socialist labor leaders—"Russian Bebels." Lenin himself had little confidence in this activity that at best produced a labor intelligentsia with all of the intelligentsia's shortcomings and at worst promised speedy arrest and jail for the propagandists as well as their pupils. As far as can be determined, he conducted no regular worker propaganda in St. Petersburg for a year and a half after his arrival, although on a few occasions he did contribute leaflets urging workers to strike.[49] During this time Lenin concentrated on literary activity, drafting reviews and essays in which he expounded his strange views on the advanced level of Russia's capitalist development and the need for an imminent anti-bourgeois, Communist revolution. None of these writings, including those intended for the legal press, found a publisher.

In September 1894 there appeared on the bookstalls a Marxist analysis of Russia's current economic situation, Struve's *Critical Remarks on the Question of Russia's Economic Development*,[50] in which he depicted the advent of capitalism in Russia as both inevitable and beneficial. The book created a sensation not only because it was one of the first Marxist studies legally published in Russia, but because Struve took the position, unfamiliar in that country, of defending the progressive function of capitalism from a socialist standpoint.

As soon as Lenin had read Struve's book, he subjected it to a scathing critique in a lengthy essay called "The Reflection of Marxism in Russian Bourgeois Literature." Unfortunately, the original version of this essay is lost, and our knowledge of it derives mainly from the recollections of Struve told to a third person a quarter of a century later and reconstructed by that person from memory after another third of a century had lapsed.[51] Lenin seems to have objected prin-

49. See my *Social Democracy and the St. Petersburg Labor Movement, 1885–1897*, (Cambridge, Mass., 1963), p. 53 and *passim*.

50. *Kriticheskie zametki k voprosu ob ekonomicheskom razvitii Rossii* (St. Petersburg, 1894).

51. N. Valentinov, "Iz proshlogo: P. B. Struve o Lenine," *Sotsialisticheskii vestnik*, no. 8/9 (673–674), (1954), pp. 169–172. Valentinov heard Struve on this subject in 1918. A. Potresov, who knew Lenin well at this time, also recalled that in Lenin's critiques of Struve "behind the Marxist manner of expression one could discern that traditional view of developing capitalist society as a reactionary mass, an attitude characteristically underlying all revolutionary-utopian movements" ("Lenin-Versuch einer Charakterisierung," *Die Gesellschaft*, no. 11, 1927, p. 407). Struve in his recollections ("My Contacts and Conflicts with Lenin," *Slavonic Review*, July, 1934, p. 71) says that "until his very advent to power Lenin held a jump from 'Capitalism' to 'Socialism' to be utterly impossible." But this opinion is based not so much on personal impressions as on retrospective reading of Lenin's writings and is therefore unreliable.

cipally to Struve's timetable of capitalist development. "Lenin showed," Struve recalled, "that capitalism had completely taken over the country, and that I did not sufficiently appreciate this fact, depicting capitalism not so much as a factor already present in all its vigor, but as something lying in the future."[52] In the winter of 1894–95 the two men met, and engaged in long discussions. According to Struve, although Lenin denied in these conversations the possibility of a "leap into the future," that is, of an immediate transition to socialism, "all the same one felt that the thought of such a leap was stuck somewhere in his head."[53]

Despite these differences, Struve and Lenin agreed in their hostility to the so-called "populists," and this permitted them to form a working alliance. Its immediate purpose was to arrange for the publication of another Marxist volume, a collective undertaking directed against the "populists": but beyond this, the agreement represented the first stage in the projected formation of a Social Democratic party. Long negotiations ensued, for Lenin insisted on printing in the symposium his critique of Struve in its original form. Being pressed by Struve and his associates to revise it, he sought the advice of another reader, namely Fedoseev.[54] Fedoseev by this time had become a full-fledged Social Democrat, and as such had little patience with Lenin's basic assumption. Two years earlier he had characterized as "fools" or "corrupt Pharisees" those who considered Russia already in the midst of capitalism because they ignored the difference between "primary capitalist accumulation" and capitalism proper.[55] On his advice, Lenin agreed to alter the manuscript. In the form in which it finally appeared it mainly criticized Struve for his failure to point out that the "populists" represented the interests of the "petty bourgeoisie" and for its "objective," "professorial" approach.[56]

During their long discussions Struve once told Lenin that he would

52. Valentinov, *ibid.*, p. 171.

53. *Ibid.*, p. 171.

54. *Ibid.*, p. 172. We know from other sources that Lenin was in correspondence with Fedoseev since 1893: I. S. Zilbershtein, "Nekotorye voprosy biografii molodogo Lenina," *Katorga i ssylka*, no. 1, (62), (1930), pp. 7–23.

55. Fedoseev, *Stat'i i pisma*, p. 126: "Personally, I attach serious importance to separating from the ranks of Marxists those fools or corrupt Pharisees who, confusing capitalism with primary capitalistic accumulation, protest against all help to the village." These strictures were aimed at those who, like Lenin, refused in 1891–92 to help the starving peasants on the grounds that to do so would mean strengthening capitalism (cf. *Ibid.*, p. 176).

56. K. Tulin [V. I. Lenin], "Ekonomicheskoe soderzhanie narodnichestva i kritika ego v knige g. Struve, "*Materialy dlia kharakteristiki nashego ekonomicheskogo razvitiia* (St. Petersburg, 1895), pt. II, pp. 1–144; reprinted in Lenin, *Sochineniia*, I, pp. 223–362.

understand true capitalism only after he had been abroad, especially to Germany.[57] In the summer of 1895 Lenin undertook his first foreign journey, in the course of which he visited Germany, Switzerland, and France. There he read a great deal of current Social Democratic literature and attended meetings organized by the German Social Democratic Party. He also met with Plekhanov, Akselrod, and the other veterans of Russian Social Democracy residing in Geneva. He made a good impression on Plekhanov and Akselrod but disconcerted them with his views on the liberals. "We turn our faces toward the liberals," Plekhanov told Lenin, "whereas you turn on them your back."[58] Behind these differences, as behind Lenin's disagreements with Struve, lay, of course, divergent estimates of the level of Russia's capitalist development.

Whatever he had thought upon leaving Russia, upon his return there in the autumn of 1895 Lenin presented himself as a regular Social Democrat, determined to work with others for the creation of a Russian Social Democratic party on the German model. This object required several efforts: one of them being to secure a political following among the industrial workers and another to constitute a common front against the autocracy with all oppositional groups, notably the "bourgeois" liberals.

How did one obtain leadership over the working class? The workers were very suspicious of intellectuals, connections with whom were certain to attract the attention of the police. At this time, the bulk of the working population was as conservative and unapproachable as the peasantry had been during the "going to the people" crusades twenty years previous. Even the labor elite, the well paid workers organized in study circles with whom the intellectuals maintained tenuous connections, showed no interest in socialism or politics, being exclusively concerned with intellectual and economic self-improvement.

To overcome this indifference and to involve workers in politics, Polish and Jewish socialists active in the Western provinces of the empire, had devised in the late 1880's and early 1890's a technique known as "agitation." Rather than preach politics as the propagandists had done, the proponents of "agitation" hoped to make the worker

57. Valentinov, "Struve o Lenine," p. 171. Struve recorded the impression that German "capitalism" had made on him on his trip there in 1890, in an essay reprinted in his book *Na raznye temy* (St. Petersburg, 1902), p. 279.

58. *Perepiska G. V. Plekhanova i P. B. Aksel'roda*, I (Moscow, 1925), p. 271. Valentinov ("Chernyshevskii i Lenin," *Novyi Zhurnal*, no. XXVII, 1951, p. 225) attaches great importance to Akselrod's arguments in favor of collaboration with the liberals in causing Lenin to change his mind.

aware of the need for political action by encouraging him to pursue his immediate economic aims. The plan was to enlighten the workers about their legal rights, to show how employers violated them, and in this manner to incite industrial strikes. Once the workers struck, they were bound to discover that behind the employers stood the whole apparatus of the state and from this discovery, it was hoped, realize that they could not improve their economic situation without gaining political influence, that is, without supporting the cause of Social Democracy. In brief, labor would become politicized and open to socialist influence through essentially trade-unionist activities.[59]

In the autumn of 1895 Iulii Martov, a Jewish socialist from Lithuania, persuaded Lenin and his associates to abandon "propaganda" in favor of "agitation." For three months the group gathered facts on violations of labor laws in various St. Petersburg factories and from them drafted leaflets inciting the workers to strike. Then in December 1895 to January 1896 the police rounded up the leading "agitators," including Lenin and Martov, and put them in prison. Despite this fiasco, the "agitators" did not lose heart, for others continued their work. In May, 1896, 30,000 St. Petersburg textile workers went on strike. This was the greatest work stoppage experienced in Russia until then; and although the intellectuals had next to nothing to do with either its outbreak or management, they interpreted the strike as a brilliant vindication of the "agitational" method. Lenin was so much carried away that in a second of two drafts of a Social Democratic party program that he composed in prison, he stated that Social Democrats should henceforth concentrate their *main attention* on helping workers improve their condition. "The struggle of workers with the factory owners for their daily needs," he wrote, "confronts them *of itself and inevitably* with problems of state and politics."[60]

If we now turn to Lenin's political ideas after mid-1895, we find a striking change. As late as the summer of 1894 he had written that socialism and democracy had to part ways;[61] now he asserted with equal conviction that socialism and democracy were inseparable.[62]

Lenin first made approving mention of constitution and parliament in an obituary of Engels, which he wrote in the autumn of 1895.[63] He

59. The "agitational" method was formulated by two Jewish socialists, Iu. Martov and Al. Kremer in *Ob agitatsii* (first printed in Geneva, 1896). See my *Social Democracy and the St. Petersburg Labor Movement*, chap. IV.

60. *Sochineniia*, I, 440, 441 (emphasis added).

61. See above, note 45.

62. See below, note 66.

63. *Sochineniia*, I, pp. 415–416.

developed the argument more fully in the first draft of the party program, which he composed in prison shortly after his arrest. He now no longer viewed Russia as a country in the throes of capitalism, but rather as one with a semi-feudal complexion; the main enemy of the working class was not, as it had been previously for him, the bourgeoisie, but the autocracy. "The struggle of the Russian working class for its liberation is a political struggle, and its goal is the attainment of political liberty."[64] In accord with this thought, Lenin called for the convocation of a Land Assembly (*Zemskii Sobor*) to draft a constitution and for the introduction of universal suffrage and of full civil liberties. "The Social Democratic Party declares," Lenin says in this draft, "that it will support all strata of the bourgeoisie engaged in a struggle against the autocratic government."[65] In another programmatic statement, drafted in 1897, Lenin insisted on the connection between socialism and democracy even more forcefully: "The democratic struggle is inseparable from the socialist one; [it is] impossible to wage a successful fight for the cause of labor without the attainment of full liberty and the democratization of Russia's political and social order."[66] At the same time, he condemned as outdated conspiracy and power seizure.

There is no need to go into Lenin's ideas during this phase, because they are those familiar from the history of Western Social Democracy. This was a happy time for Lenin. Even though he spent two years in prison and three in Siberia, he was confident of the future, entertaining no doubts about the ultimate triumph of the revolutionary cause. He felt himself a member of an irresistible movement and experienced none of the crises or fits of destructive rage so characteristic of him at other periods. His self-assured mood is evidenced by the unusual tolerance he now displayed toward diverse opinions voiced by fellow Social Democrats. He even expressed admiration for Sidney and Beatrice Webb, whose *Industrial Democracy* he translated into Russian at this time.[67]

This happy period came to an abrupt end in the summer of 1899, when Lenin experienced a new crisis, the most prolonged and important

64. *Ibid.*, p. 426.

65. *Ibid.*, p. 444.

66. *Zadachi russkikh sotsial'demokratov* (Geneva, 1898), pp. 11–12 (reprinted in *Sochineniia*, II, p. 167–190). In the introduction to the original (1898) edition of this pamphlet, Akselrod enthusiastically endorsed Lenin's stress on the bond between socialism and democracy.

67. *Teoriia i praktika angliiskogo tred-unionizma*, 2 vols. (St. Petersburg, 1900–01). In April 1899 Lenin described the Webbs as representatives of one of the "most advanced currents of English social thought" (*Sochineniia*, II, p. 389).

of his life. This crisis came to a head in December 1900—the last flicker of the nineteenth century—when Lenin found a way out of his perplexity by devising a new political doctrine.

The original cause of this crisis was Lenin's disillusionment with the industrial proletariat. While Lenin, Martov, and the other members of the initial group of St. Petersburg "agitators" were under confinement, the relations between labor and the radical intelligentsia in Russia underwent subtle change. In the late 1890's the working class grew so rapidly both in numbers and in strength that the handful of radical intellectuals who had managed to stay out of jail could no longer pretend to lead it. Russian labor had become an independent force. Under the direction of its own intelligentsia, many of them graduates of propaganda circles, it was moving toward mature trade unionism. In these circumstances, socialist "agitators," if they wished to retain any contacts with labor, had to acquiesce to a status of auxiliaries or functionaries of an essentially trade-union machinery. In late 1897 voices began to be heard among radical intellectuals favoring a frank acknowledgment of the changed situation: that is, an indefinite postponement of the political struggle in favor of helping labor in its struggle for economic improvement. This heresy, later known as "economism," proposed to divest agitation—at least temporarily—of that political function for the sake of which it had been originally devised.[68] The labor newspaper, *Worker's Thought*, founded in October 1897, served as the organ of the "economist" school, which in 1898 and 1899 gained ascendancy within the Russian Social Democrat movement both at home and abroad.[69]

Lenin was not entirely oblivious of this development. In 1897, during a few days freedom granted them before their departure for Siberia, he and Martov met with a group of "agitators" in St. Petersburg and found to their dismay that the latter were wholly absorbed in setting up mutual assistance funds for labor.[70] Nor could Lenin have been unaware of the skepticism of some of the older Social Democrats, like Akselrod, who as early as 1896 had expressed their misgivings about the whole

68. Some historians consider "economism" to have been a polemical device invented by Plekhanov, Lenin, and other Social Democrats to neutralize their opponents within the Social Democratic movement. (See for example, Leonard Schapiro, *The Communist Party of the Soviet Union*, London, 1960, pp. 33–35). Whatever the merits of the case, there can be little doubt, however, that Lenin himself was genuinely alarmed over what he considered "economist" tendencies.

69. The first editorial of this newspaper is translated in my *Social Democracy and the St. Petersburg Labor Movement*, pp. 129–131.

70. *Ibid.*, pp. 114–115. See also Martov's recollections of Lenin's cautious initial reaction to *Rabochaia mysl'* and "economism" in Lenin, *Sochineniia*, II, pp. 585–586.

"agitational" method.[71] But neither then, nor in 1898 and the first half of 1899, did Lenin attach significance to these warnings.

Then, in the summer of 1899, when his term of exile was drawing to a close, Lenin received from his sister a document drafted by one of the exponents of the "economist" tendency, a document which subsequently became known as the "Credo." Its author urged the socialists to abandon the political struggle to the bourgeoisie and to concentrate their own efforts on promoting the economic well-being of the working class.[72] Why it was this casually drafted document that should suddenly have so alarmed Lenin, it is difficult to tell. But it is certain that it immediately alerted him to the threat to the revolutionary cause implicit in "agitation" and before long caused him to reconsider his entire attitude toward industrial labor.

Lenin's unhappiness with the "economists" was exacerbated by the emergence in Russia of revisionism. In early 1899, several leading Russian socialists, led by Struve, called publicly for a reappraisal of some of Marx's theories and, like Bernstein and his German followers, began to question the feasibility of social revolution.[73] Lenin at first attached much less importance to revisionism than to economism. He disliked it all along, considering it a "scholastic" exercise and therefore a waste of time, but he did not think it prudent to weaken the Social Democratic movement by exposing its internal theoretical differences to the common enemy, the "populists." Indeed, he at first urged his colleagues to keep on good terms with Struve even after Struve had enraged Plekhanov with his calls for a massive "reappraisal" of Marx.[74] Still, revisionism was a bad portent, the more so that it came to Lenin's attention concurrently with economism and before long became confounded with it in his mind.

Krupskaya, Lenin's wife, reports that in the summer of 1899 Lenin underwent a visible change: he lost weight and began to suffer from sleeplessness.[75] He now spent all his time pondering the causes of the

71. For example, in his introduction to *Ob agitatsii* (Geneva, 1896).

72. The text of the "Credo" (the name had been given it by Lenin's sister) can be found in "Protest rossiiskikh sotsial-demokratov," *Sochineniia*, II, pp. 477–480. Its author, E. Kuskova, describing later how this document came to be written, denied it had any programmatic significance; *Byloe*, no. 10 (1906), pp. 320–330.

73. The "revisionist" controversy made itself first felt in Russia early in 1899 when S. Bulgakov took to task K. Kautsky, Lenin defended Kautsky, and Struve came out in favor of "criticism." See R. Kindersley, *The First Russian Revisionists* (Oxford, 1962).

74. Lenin's letters to Potresov, *Sochineniia*, XXVIII, p. 31 (4th ed., XXXIV, p. 22). See also L. Martov, *Zapiski Sotsial Demokrata*, I, (Berlin, 1922), p. 401.

75. Krupskaia, *Vospominaniia*, p. 35.

malaise in the Social Democratic movement and devising remedies capable of curing it.

He concluded initially that economism was a result of the dispersion and isolation of socialist and labor groups operating in various parts of Russia. Separated from each other, the local circles inevitably lost sight of the movement as a whole and lapsed into apolitical trade unionism. To extricate them from this rut, it was necessary to found an all-Russian socialist newspaper.[76] This newspaper Lenin and Martov conceived on the model of the *Sozialdmokrat*, the central organ of the German Social Democratic party during the years of Bismarck's Anti-Socialist Law. It was to be an organ of Social Democrats uniting all politically minded oppositional groups and specifically directed against economism. Such was the origin of what later became *Iskra*.

But a newspaper was not enough, and Lenin now began seriously to rethink the function and structure of the socialist party. In late 1899 he observed ominously that the Social Democrats lagged behind the "old revolutionaries," that is, the People's Will, in matters of party organization.[77] These were the first indications that Lenin was beginning to question current Social Democratic practices.

Lenin spent the year 1900 in Germany and Switzerland on exhausting negotiations leading to the founding of *Iskra*. Now everything went wrong. Plekhanov sneered at the concessions Lenin had made to Struve in order to secure Struve's financial and editorial help for *Iskra* and altogether treated him disdainfully.[78] Struve, in turn, objected to being publicly labeled a turncoat to the movement by Plekhanov and others with whom he had undertaken to collaborate. Money was short. To make matters worse, the Socialist-Revolutionaries, successors to the old People's Will, gave indications of launching a rival party. In August 1900 Martov and Lenin, driven to desperation, considered giving up *Iskra* and returning to Russia.[79]

76. One of the earliest references to the need for a party newspaper is to be found in "Nasha blizhaishaia zadacha," *Sochineniia*, II, p. 499, written not later than October 1899.

77. "The improvement of revolutionary organizations and discipline, the perfecting of conspiratorial technique are urgently needed. One must openly admit that in this respect we lag behind the old Russian revolutionary parties and that we must apply all efforts to catch up and overtake them. Without an improvement of the organization, our labor movement can make no progress at all." "Nasushchii vopros," *Sochineniia*, II, p. 500. Written about October 1899.

78. See Lenin's revealing "Kak chut' ne potukhla Iskra," *Sochineniia*, IV, pp. 15–31.

79. D. Geyer, *Lenin in der Russischen Sozialdemokratie* (Köln-Graz, 1962), p. 204. This monograph is an excellent study of Russian Social Democratic politics of the period with which we are concerned.

The whole Social Democratic movement, in which Lenin had placed so much confidence, suddenly seemed on the verge of disintegration. "Russian Social Democracy is living through a period of wavering, a period of doubts which approach self-denial," Lenin wrote in November–December 1900 in a seminal paper called "Urgent Questions of Our Movement." "On the one hand, the labor movement separates itself from socialism . . . , on the other, socialism separates itself from the labor movement."[80] This process presents enormous dangers because—and here Lenin first utters the fateful words—"the labor movement, separated from Social Democracy . . . inevitably becomes bourgeois."[81]

We have reached a critical moment in Lenin's intellectual evolution. Seven or eight years earlier he had rejected the peasantry as a petty bourgeois, reactionary class; now he comes to doubt the revolutionary potential of labor. The working class, as he henceforth sees it, is revolutionary *only* insofar as it fuses with, that is, is led by Social Democrats. Therefore, Social Democrats must aspire not to assist labor but to direct it: "to inculcate socialist ideas and political self-consciousness into the mass of the proletariat and to organize a revolutionary party, indissolubly bound with the spontaneous labor movement."[82] "No single class in history," Lenin writes in "Urgent Questions," "has ever attained mastery unless it has produced political leaders, its leading representatives, capable of organizing the movement and leading it . . . It is necessary to prepare men who devote to the revolution not only their free evenings, but their whole lives."[83]

Here Lenin formulates the basic tenets of bolshevism and outlines a practical policy in the shape of a professional body of full-time revolutionaries, to direct the labor movement and to keep it from straying into the bourgeois morass where its own inclinations push it. His unspoken assumption is that the majority of the population is actually or potentially reactionary; his unspoken conclusion, that democracy leads to reaction. Democracy is incompatible with revolution and therefore must be disassociated from socialism. Indeed, Lenin now begins to talk of the "dictatorship of the proletariat" not in the usual Marxist sense of the hegemony of the once exploited multitude over their previous exploiters, but of the rule by a "revolutionary" segment over the "petty bourgeois" segment.[84] The principles of *Führertum* and the one-

80. "Nasushchnie zadachi nashego dvizheniia," *Sochineniia*, IV, p. 55.
81. *Ibid.*, p. 56.
82. *Ibid.*, p. 57.
83. *Ibid.*, p. 58.
84. For example, "If we really *positively* knew that the petty bourgeoisie would support the proletariat when the latter achieved its proletarian revolution, then we

party totalitarian state in all its numerous guises are fully inherent in these sentiments.

Having lost faith in the working class, Lenin did not take long to break away from the liberal bourgeoisie, with whom he had never felt comfortable anyway. Throughout 1900 he had engaged in protracted negotiations with Struve, who in that year left the Social Democrats and became a spokesman of liberal groups. By December 1900 Lenin concluded that Struve and the liberals wanted to exploit the Social Democratic movement in order to wring from autocracy concessions for the bourgeoisie. After one of the stormy meetings Lenin noted that these negotiations had marked for him "the close of a period in his life,"[85] by which he meant, the end of that era when he had believed it possible to collaborate with the liberal bourgeoisie—in other words, his Social Democratic phase.

Lenin finally severed ties with the liberals in the spring of 1901. At that time Struve published Sergei Witte's *Autocracy and zemstvo*, with a substantial introduction of his own. Witte, in what was intended as a memorandum to the tsar, urged the curtailment of the organs of local self-rule, the so-called *zemstva*, as a threat to autocratic authority. In his introduction, Struve took the opposition position. He argued that it was in the interest of the monarchy to preserve and strengthen *zemstva* as protection against revolutionary movements. The curtailment of the *zemstva*, he wrote, would hand the revolutionaries their "trump card."[86]

In arguing this point, Struve used language calculated to persuade the government that it lay in its own interest to preserve the *zemstva*: language the government could understand and possibly find convincing. But Lenin interpreted Struve's argument quite differently. He concluded that Struve was betraying the revolutionaries: he was deliberately conducting a double policy, helping the revolutionaries only as a means of exerting pressure on the monarchy on behalf of the bourgeoisie. From now on, in correspondence, he often referred to Struve as "Judas." Later that spring Lenin wrote an essay in which he

---

would have no need to speak about a 'dictatorship,' because then we would be assured of so overwhelming a majority that we could manage beautifully without the dictatorship." "Zamechaniia na proekt programmy," *Leninskii sbornik*, II, p. 80. Written in March 1902.

85. *Sochineniia*, IV, p. 67.

86. S. Iu. Witte, *Samoderzhavie i zemstvo*, 2nd ed. (Stuttgart, 1903), pp. vii–xlvii. This work was brought out by *Iskra* in accord with an arrangement made with Struve the previous year by Lenin himself. Struve had used the same approach in 1895 in his "Open Letter to Nicholas II," V. Burtsev, ed., *Za sto let, 1800–1896*, pt. I (London, 1897), pp. 264–267.

took to task not only Struve but the liberals in general. A striking feature of this essay was the description of the *zemstva* as "tools" of autocracy.[87] Lenin was now reverting to the position he had held before 1895, when he had regarded the entire bourgeoisie as a reactionary class allied with the autocracy against socialism. As a concession to Plekhanov and Akselrod he somewhat softened the language of this essay, but he kept his convictions. "Zemstvo liberalism," Lenin wrote Plekhanov in 1901, "is in respect to its influence on society a counterpart of what economism is in respect to labor. We must persecute both one and the other."[88]

Lenin now burnt his bridges. He disassociated himself from all those forces, the alliance with which in the preceding five years he had regarded as essential for the triumph of socialism: the labor movement; the liberals; even Plekhanov and the other patriarchs of the movement. He saw himself as the only genuine revolutionary—a leader with followers but no longer any allies. Around him were nothing but reactionaries, opportunists, traitors. "We are moving in a tight band along a precipitous and difficult path, clutching each other's hands," Lenin wrote that winter, "We are surrounded on all sides by enemies, and we must always advance under their fire."[89]

Lenin had tried all possible allies and found them wanting: the peasantry, he had decided long before was "petty bourgeois"; the proletariat, potentially the most revolutionary class, left to its own devices, turned "bourgeois"; and the bourgeoisie proper was at one with the autocracy. A socialist revolution could be achieved, therefore, only in the teeth of the majority: Social Democracy was unrealizable. Although in 1905 and again in 1917 Lenin was to attach great importance to mass movements in the cities and the countryside, he did so for tactical reasons only. He never again reverted to that faith in democratic socialism that he had briefly entertained in the late 1890's.

In 1903 Lenin had a chance to find confirmation of his political views in the early writings of Marx and Engels brought out by Franz Mehring the preceding year.[90] Henceforth, he proudly adopted the name "Ja-

87. "Goniteli zemstva i annibaly liberalizma," *Sochineniia*, IV, pp. 119–157.
88. *Sochineniia*, IV, p. 577.
89. "Chto delat'?" *Sochineniia*, IV, p. 368.
90. Franz Mehring, *Aus dem literarischen Nachlass von Karl Marx, Friedrich Engels, und Ferdinand Lassalle*, I–IV (Stuttgart, 1902). (Vols. I–III contain writings from 1841–1850). That Lenin first learned the favorable opinions of Marx and Engels of the Jacobins from Mehring's edition is attested to by V. G. Revunenkov in *Marksizm i problema iakobinskoi diktatury* (Leningrad, 1966), pp. 84–85. According to Revunenkov, the anti-Jacobin views which Marx and Engels had formulated later were not known to Lenin, being first published after his death (pp. 83–84).

cobin" which the Mensheviks had taunted him with after he had made known his unorthodox views, and proudly identified the Bolsheviks as the "Jacobins of contemporary Social Democracy."[91]

Bertolt Brecht, reflecting on the Berlin uprising of 1953, asked himself: since the government has lost confidence in the people, why not dissolve the people? This thought was not far from Lenin's mind in the closing days of the nineteenth century when, realistically surveying the forces available for a socialist revolution, he formulated his political strategy.

Comment by Sir Isaiah Berlin on — "The Origins of Bolshevism: The Intellectual Evolution of Young Lenin" by Richard Pipes

I should like to begin by saying that I am not a "Leninologist." I do not know a great many facts about him, and therefore what I say is not likely to be of very great importance. I would like to begin by thanking Mr. Pipes for his extremely lucid and interesting chronological exposition, in particular for his discoveries about Lenin's populist phase before 1892, namely the fact that Lenin belonged to various circles.

To begin with, I accept Mr. Pipes' periodization of Lenin's evolution to the beginning of the twentieth century. It seems to me extremely clear and convincing. Also I am grateful to him—I think we all should be— for the discrimination of the four types of Marxism about which he speaks. It sheds a great deal of light on that rather vague term. It could be made to recrystalize a little.

I think it is perfectly true to say that the Marxism that came to Russia earlier than to almost any other non-German reading country did, at the beginning, simply mean some kind of economic doctrine that did not necessarily affect political opinions. Mr. Pipes quoted the case

---

91. *Sochineniia*, VIII, p. 64 (written in 1905). " 'Terrible words' like Jacobinism and so forth, express exactly nothing *but opportunism*," he wrote in the spring of 1904. "A Jacobin who is indissolubly bound with the *organization* of the proletariat *which has become aware* of its class interests—this is *a revolutionary Social Democrat*. A Girondist, one who longs for professors, gymnasium students, who fears the dictatorship of the proletariat, who sighs about the absolute value of democratic demands—this is an *opportunist*." *Ibid.*, VI, p. 303.

of a monarchist economist. Even Ziber who, I suppose, was as devoted to spreading Marx's economic doctrines as anybody else, by translating, by lecturing, and by writing on them, was a fanatical liberal during the whole of his life and never showed the slightest inclination to accept Marxist class theories or theory of revolution. Marxism entered into all kinds of amalgams in the thought of people like Chernyshevskii, Mikhailovskii, Lavrov, and others, without necessarily converting them to Marxism. Marx was regarded by some Russians simply as an able economic analyst, by others as a proponent of an interesting theory of historical materialism, which some students of his work accepted in part, some people rejected in part, but which did not immediately produce converts. The real penetration of Marxism into Russia begins with the conversion to Marxism of *narodniks* like Akselrod, Plekhanov, and others.

Why did Lenin say nothing about belonging to these early circles? Mr. Pipes says that possibly he did not want it known that he had ever been a *narodnik*. I do not know. It seems to me there would have been nothing shaming in admitting this, even for Lenin. After all, all the prominent Russian Marxists had gone through this corridor. Plekhanov did not conceal his past. Akselrod did not conceal it. Nobody else concealed it. Why should Lenin be so particularly reticent? I think—and I am going to make this purely as a tentative suggestion—that perhaps while the others who belonged to these circles (which was no doubt dangerous) got into a certain amount of trouble, he did not. He may have anticipated trouble at the university, but he was not expelled for this and did not regard what he did in these circles as of sufficient weight or importance. He was not a full participant in the kind of systematic revolutionary activity that made him think about himself retrospectively as an active and prominent member of an organized movement. But when he became a Marxist, Lenin did become precisely this and early saw himself as a leader. He was in no sense a leader at the age of seventeen, eighteen, or nineteen. I think this is a possible explanation. At any rate he was, as Mr. Pipes says, in general rather reticent about his past and perhaps not very anxious to reveal it.

Now the next point I want to come to is Lenin's view that Russia was already in a capitalist phase. I mean his extraordinary view in the early 1890's that Russia was not merely facing the probability of capitalism, as the Marxists in Geneva were saying, but were already plunged into a capitalist phase. His position is extraordinary and extravagant. Where does it come from? I think it comes from two sources; one factual, the other psychological. The psychological source is obviously a certain reluctance, during his entire life, to accept any kind of mechanical gradualism: the view that although you can help a process on and encourage it, stimulate it, men, even revolutionaries, are nevertheless rigidly confined to some kind of unalterable timetable, and what must inevitably happen may happen at a very distant date—at best, the movement can be helped, can be brought nearer, but its course cannot be dramatically altered. Lenin was an activist. Everyone knows that. I think what have been called the voluntarist aspects of his character derive from his early *narodnik* days, and from his own character. I think that this volitional—*volevoi*—desire to mold events is probably characteristic of him at all times.

As to ideological tactics, Mr. Pipes describes the impression that Postnikov's survey made on Lenin in the early 1890's. I expect it did. At the same time, I think Lenin could have derived these ideas earlier from the reading of the early works of Plekhanov. If one looks at Plekhanov's works written in exile in the 1880's—essays like *Socialism and the Political Struggle* and *Our Differences*—one finds that in these works Plekhanov emphasizes, though not in the highly dramatized, exaggerated form in which Lenin later states it, the doom of the peasant commune, declares that it is disintegrating, and even gives a specific analysis of the disintegration into the three familiar elements—the rich, the middling, and the poor peasants. He then attributes this process to the entrance of the money economy into the villages, leading to the emergence of rich peasants as in some sense exploiting capitalists, the corresponding classification of the poor peasants as a landless proletariat or something very like it. Only people who might want to hold on to the communes, to whom they may still promise something economically and socially, are the third element—the middle peasants. I cannot remember whether or not Plekhanov talks about *kulaks, seredniaks, bedniaks,* as such, but the distinction is already there. And since Plekhanov was presumably read by persons like Lenin in the late 1880's and early 1890's, he could have certainly obtained that original impulse from him. No doubt it was much strengthened and invigorated by Postnikov's actual figures about the Russian village organization in southern Russia.

As a result of this, Lenin certainly began to reflect on the possibilities of an early revolution in Russia on Marxist lines. Mr. Pipes very plausibly says that his Marxism was still, at this period, at any rate, mixed with some kind of Jacobinism. Lenin's Marxism is closer to the views and temper of the activist Jacobin wing of what is called the populist movement, than to, say, the legal populists: there is the Blanquist strain that is always recognizable in Lenin. I wonder whether his Marxism need be called Jacobin? I think it is clear that sometime during this period he became a Marxist. But we must not confound various Marxist doctrines with each other. Not only are there inconsistencies, but there are "periods" in Marx's views too: all Lenin needed to do in order to hold the views that he did in fact hold, was to go to the earlier writings of Marx. It seems fairly clear that Marx's writings from 1847 to about 1852 are genuinely different in tone and the content from some of his later works. In this earlier period Marx supposes that what is necessary is an organization, some kind of organization of determined persons needed for the purpose of pushing, harrying, the bourgeoisie into the particular historical phase which it has to play. Certainly in the famous address to the Communist League, the references to the dictatorship of the proletariat are clear indications that his thought was, at that time directed toward the formation of a small, coherent party of revolutionary intellectuals that had to play the part of a "ginger group." If the party was to be mentor, it was not exactly to use the methods of kindness— but rather whips and scorpions. In any event, these persons were to prod, to force, the development of the bourgeoisie in a direction not likely to be agreeable to the bourgeoisie in the end. That is to say, this has to be the beginning of the period of dual control by which there were to be two persons riding the horse of society, the bourgeois democrats who would have to make their bourgeois revolution, and, seated behind them, a small group of revolutionaries quietly sabotaging them from behind in order ultimately to throw them out. To change the metaphor, it is a theory of the cuckoo in the nest, which, I think, marks this particular phase in Marx's thought in 1847–1852.

Now, if one looked at the Russian political, economic, and social scene in the 1880's or 1890's and if one were convinced of the validity of Marx's general schema, what could one possibly do? After all, Marx himself changed his tactics and his tone simply because after 1851 the possibility of revolution in Germany appeared to recede; the economic and social picture changed sufficiently to convince him that the party of the proletariat must wait; it must educate, must build up majorities, must not engage in putsches, must not be Blanquist. Nothing is worse, as Engels afterwards said, than to have a premature revolution, that is, for a socialist party to come into power before the time is ripe, before industrialism is developed properly. Revolution requires a preliminary phase of development in which the bourgeoisie is performing its historic task. As Marx said to Engels, "The old boy [Bismarck] is doing our work for us." Bismarck was uniting, centralizing, concentralizing, organizing, accelerating the pace of all the various economic and social forces that in the end would bring about a situation in which the revolutionary transformation of society was bound to occur. But it was very clear that the same thing was not happening in Russia. Supposing one wanted to have a Social Democratic Party, founded upon the admired model of the German Social Democratic Party, even the kind and degree of political liberty in which Lassalle could function in Germany in the mid-nineteenth century was obviously excluded in Russia in the 1890's by the nature of the political regime. One could not begin to do what Lassalle did. One could not even do what the socialists did under Bismarck's Anti-Socialist Laws.

The only way in which one could prepare, agitate, organize in Russia, and presumably indoctrinate the proletariat or any other revolutionary forces at hand was not possible under legal conditions. Therefore, the formation of some kind of revolutionary elite would inevitably be required, presumably working from outside, or working wherever it could, and would inject its ideas and its organizational methods by illegal methods into this very difficult, political and economically "backward" situation. This may not have been the orthodox Marxism of the 1870's and 1880's—it certainly was not—but it seems to be perfectly orthodox Marxism of, say, 1847–1852.

As for Lenin and Social Democracy: let us consider his original espousal of German Social Democratic policies and his later rejection of them. The reasons are a matter of conjecture. But I should be inclined to agree with something I think is suggested in Professor Pipes' thesis—that it was not simply a question of his agreement with Struve or with anybody else about the precise timetable, about the scientific evidence concerning the exact pace at which capitalism was developing in Russia, but an overwhelming desire to believe that Russia was already in the full bloom of capitalism, so that all that was needed now was the "classical" anti-capitalist revolution according to the orthodox Marxist prescription. Lenin's thesis that Russia already possessed millions of capitalists—namely, the peasants—is, as I said, an extraordinary, view (I mean his bold denial of the equation of developed capitalism— in Marx's sense—with industrialization) and it is, to say the least, open to question. His discovery of many million capitalists in Russia surely springs from an extreme anxiety to see the Russian situation of his day as one that would make revolutionary action legitimate according to Marxist rules. And because Lenin always was very anxious to act, the advocacy of an alliance of socialism and democracy was, I think, simply a more or less mechanical adoption of German Social Democratic doctrine in its orthodox form, in the belief that this could lead to action. Perhaps he hoped, perhaps he believed, that it was possible to collaborate with the liberal bourgeoisie at this period or possible to collaborate with the semi-legal organizations of the workers and to drive them on to drastic action of some sort. This hope was doomed to disappointment.

Hence 1899 was probably a relief to him, in the sense that his temperament asserted itself much more genuinely when he was able to find reasons for shedding his allies and, as Mr. Pipes suggests, go forward on his own, without one leg being tied to someone else's.

Why did he rebel in 1899? I think Mr. Pipes is probably quite right in the reasons he gives. I think that if Lenin feared anything, it was a lowering of tension, a lowering of the revolutionary initiative. Kuskova's "Credo" was perhaps a symptom of the fact that the workers might easily be lured into some kind of Bernsteinian path, easily lured into pure trade-unionist, economic activity: this he condemned. The one thesis that I think Lenin held to all his life was that any kind of diversion of the energies of the workers into daily bread and butter, trade-unionist activities would necessarily delay the revolution and lower the possibility of the change which he desired and anticipated. I am sure this is so.

Lenin's treatment of the question of democracy and anti-democracy seems to me largely tactical. I do not know that Lenin did much more than Marx did with the Commune, for example. It is well known that the Paris Commune was made largely by non-Marxists, indeed that it was made against Marx's advice and took a form which was certainly not compatible with what could be regarded as Marxist orthodoxy or even that of the International—the orthodoxy of the Workingmen's International of 1871. Nevertheless, Marx saw quite correctly that it was necessary to bless this workers' movement as the first rising of workers as workers, and that it therefore had to be assimilated, integrated into what might be called revolutionary hagiography. In the same sort of way, Lenin adopted the democratic standpoint simply from a need for a framework, for historical solidarity—because it was then the standpoint of the admired German Social Democratic Party, which was the universal model for organizing, for creating a sensible party with firm intellectual foundations and some kind of clear organizational program. However, as soon as this program began to flow into what might be called peace-loving channels in Russia and began, as he thought, to divert the energies of the workers from the revolutionary task before them, or from political struggle, or from anything dynamic at all into some kind of self-help, into some kind of trade-unionist activity of which he accused the economists and revisionists, he rebelled against it and took the path with which we are all familiar.

Now about Chernyshevskii. I think that Valentinov was perfectly right in supposing that Chernyshevskii had a dominant influence on Lenin, not simply in acquainting him with Hegel (if he did), or with revolutionary theories, or the materialist conception of history, but in having a dominant influence on him by the very tone and the very nature of his work. Chernyshevskii was a very rigid, serious, industrious, erudite man, dedicated to dry facts and statistics. He detested every form of liberalism, every form of the attitude that Herzen at that time represented, particularly the gradualism Herzen developed toward the end of the 1860's, including his regret for the kind of older humane civilization that the new life was likely to overthrow. Chernyshevskii's enormous emphasis on the "new men," on the fact that the new world could be created only by grimly dedicated revolutionaries, Jacobin in temper if not in ideas, detached from the world in which they lived, with all their energies directed to its overthrow, with no moral bonds uniting them to the mass of philistines by whom they were surrounded, which was Chernyshevskii's fundamental doctrine, and what he captured young men with—this was, I think, extremely consonant with Lenin's temperament; and so was the loss of all possible hope of reform from above and the denunciation of it as a fatal delusion, ideas that became Chernyshevskii's passionate refrain. Hatred of liberals, hatred of compromises, hatred of alliances of any kind, especially with the bourgeoisie, the harsh tone not only of the polemic, but of his whole attitude, the emphasis on the need for unswerving heroic figures probably made a greater impression on Lenin than anything else written in Russian. That is what he meant when, according to Valentinov, he said about Chernyshevskii: *"On menia vsego perepakhal,"* "He plowed me over," "He wholly transformed me." Every turn from gradualism and a united front with liberals or other moderates throughout Lenin's life stems from this stern puritan.

There is one further point what I would like to make. I do not believe that even Lenin supposed at any period before 1905 that the Russian Revolution would be the first revolution to set off the world conflagration. Of course, he believed with Marx, that is, according to Marx's letters to the *narodniks*, that the Russian timetable was not to be adjusted to the general European timetable. He held this view and believed in the proposition—almost to the end of his life—that the Russian Revolution would not be a success unless there also broke out a world, or at least a European, revolution to carry it on its shoulders. But I do not believe that Lenin supposed that the Russian Revolution would be the first event in this particular series—the first spark to ignite the world fire. The "weakest link" doctrine seems to me to have been supplied by Parvus and Trotsky and never to have been fully adopted by Lenin; at any rate, I think that this is where he obtained it. Nor is there any touch of *ouvrierisme* in Lenin at any stage: no wish to follow the workers' movement, to learn from workers, to identify himself with their actual aspirations. At all periods—and this is a consistent strain—he was convinced that there must exist a small group of leaders who formulate the program and push the others on. In this respect he is very consistent, and probably from the earliest beginnings.

The only real point of issue between myself and Mr. Pipes is whether one needs to assume a Jacobin (or populist) strain in the Lenin of the early years, in order to account for his anti-democratic, elitist behavior and beliefs after 1901. What I should like to suggest is simply that there were at least two Marxes if not more, and that Lenin was appealing to the earlier Marx because conditions in Russia in the early twentieth century were far more familiar to conditions in Germany in Marx's youth than they were to conditions in Western Europe in later years of the century. I believe there was in him a psychological strain of a kind that took him originally toward *narodnik* groups, a desire for activism, militancy, an elite of men of action, a craving for revolution, soon not late. But one should remember that the Jacobins, whether the French Jacobins of the eighteenth century or the Russian Jacobins of the nineteenth, had no sense of timetables, of inexorable historical stages. The whole notion of a cosmic timetable, which leads men to ask themselves whether conditions are ripe or not ripe, whether the Mensheviks are correct about the stage reached or not, what constitutes ripeness, what kind of capitalism is needed, how far advanced it should be in order to certify the revolution as both probable and of the correct kind—this whole historicist notion of stages of looking at the calendar of history and considering a particular date for the revolution, when the times are fulfilled—this is absent from the thought of Russian Jacobins as much as it is from those of the French Jacobins. In this respect I think Lenin is truly Marxist and dissimilar from the Jacobins. I do not think Mr. Pipes will disagree. He only speaks of a combination of Marxism and Jacobinism. But I should like to repeat again that Lenin's faithful and, I think, orthodox, adoption of Marx's earlier views, whether conscious or not, stemmed from his perception that conditions in Russia resembled the condition of early capitalism in Germany much more than they resembled conditions of developed capitalism in Europe in his, Lenin's lifetime. There is no need to look for other sources.

Discussion

Replying to Mr. Berlin, Mr. Pipes expressed doubts that Lenin's unwillingness to reveal his early associations stemmed from his failure to consider them sufficiently serious. The deliberate effort to cover up these connections indicates that more was involved. After Lenin seized power in 1917 he was charged with being unMarxist, an anarchist and a Jacobin. To admit his earlier anarchist-Jacobin associations would have fed the anti-Bolshevik accusations and given ammunition to the Mensheviks who had been making this charge all along.

Mr. Kennan inquired how the Bund's views on party organization affected Lenin.

Mr. Pipes replied that he had encountered no evidence of any interest of Lenin in the Bund at this time.

Mr. Schapiro commented that a recently published document, Lenin's marginal comments on Chernyshevskii, bore out Mr. Berlin's statements about the influence of Chernyshevskii on Lenin. In regard to what is sometimes referred to as Lenin's "Menshevik phase" after 1895, Mr. Schapiro disagreed with Mr. Pipes' suggestions that it might have been a tactical maneuver. He also thought that the impact of Bernsteinianism on Lenin's crisis of 1899 was greater than Mr. Pipes allowed, because it meant the end of revolutionary hopes.

Mr. Pipes answered that although he did not deny totally the genuineness of Lenin's psychological conversion to Social Democracy in the summer of 1895, he found it inexplicable. The sudden conversion is so unlike Lenin at any other phase that the possibility of its being a tactical maneuver must be considered. In regard to the importance of Bernstein, Mr. Pipes maintained that in the late 1890's Lenin worried less about revisionism than about the threat of economism or the defection of the working class from Social Democracy. After all, Struve said many of the same things in 1894–96, and yet Lenin cooperated with him; in fact, as late as 1900 Lenin worked hard and against Plekhanov's wishes to secure Struve's cooperation on *Iskra*. Revisionism became significant only in the light of the possibility of the detachment of labor from the Social Democrats—that is, after the publication of Kuskova's "Credo."

Mr. Keep suggested that if the "Credo" was this important in the formation of Lenin's thought, one would expect Lenin to have checked whether the information it contained was accurate. He does not seem to have done that. According to Mr. Keep, revisionism was probably at least as dangerous as economism in Lenin's view, and the change in his attitude toward it depended on his personal relations with Struve and the acute psychological shock of their sudden change. Personal relations were more important than the other influences.

Mr. Katkov said that Mr. Pipes' presentation did not answer clearly the question of whether Lenin was made revolutionary by Marx, or Marxism made revolutionary by Lenin. Why should Lenin deny being a revolutionary before becoming a Marxist? The answer must be that he felt it necessary to show a scientific basis for the conversion to a revolutionary attitude in order to create an atmosphere of charisma.

Mr. Wolfe suggested that Paul Avrich's new book on anarchism casts some light on Lenin's detestation of the trade union leaders by pointing out the degree of anti-intellectualism that was felt by anarchists and syndicalists in the 1890's. The same attitude on the part of the workers' leaders no doubt contributed to Lenin's view of them as tools to be exploited. Mr. Wolfe also suggested that Lenin's total rejection of the world into which he was born and of all his teachers along the way makes this side of his character important for his historians. Last, Mr. Wolfe pointed out Lenin's extreme sense of mission.

Mr. Thompson inquired at what point and how Lenin came to change his views about the nature of Russia's economic and social structure.

Mr. Pipes answered that the party program prepared by Lenin in 1896 no longer referred to Russia as a fully capitalistic country. This interpretation was probably given not because Lenin had changed his mind but in order to gain the broadest acceptance as the Social Democratic Party platform. It is particularly in the programmatic statements that he is found to abandon his earlier—and later—stand that Russia was already fully capitalistic and speaks of it as rapidly "becoming" capitalistic.

Mr. Avineri suggested, qualifying Mr. Berlin's statement that Lenin's last phase of development was a rejection of German Social-Democratic Marxism, that Lenin's attempts to organize the party in the 1890's were markedly different from Marx's views of an elite pushing the bourgeoisie. This distinction makes the populist or Jacobin elements in Lenin's background more important.

Mr. Berlin agreed that Lenin's conception of the party owed a great debt to the populists. The need for a dedicated nucleus, however, was due to the repressive regime in Russia, not to a conscious adoption of the ideas of 1793. It was his Marxist conviction that made him turn to *narodnik* tactics as the only way to achieve revolution in Russia. In regard to the change of Lenin in 1899 and his great fear of economism, Mr. Berlin suggested that perhaps the death of Engels was a factor in Lenin's total rejection of gradualism.

Mr. Seton-Watson maintained that, although logical, Mr. Katkov's argument that the desire for a charisma founded on scientific study caused Lenin to deny his populist past would apply equally to Plekhanov. Since Plekhanov did not feel it necessary to deny his past and Lenin admired him, some other explanation must be sought. Mr. Seton-Watson inquired into the extent of Tkachev's influence, particularly in regard to imparting the sense of urgency of action.

Mr. Pipes called attention to the fact that Lenin's *narodnik* period was in the late 1880's and early 1890's, when there was a Russian Social Democratic movement, whereas Plekhanov's populist phase had occurred earlier, in the 1870's, and therefore involved no rejection of Social Democracy. Their populist episodes, therefore, could not be regarded or treated similarly. This difference might explain why Plekhanov acknowledged it and Lenin did not. Mr. Pipes said that he had found no direct evidence of Lenin's having been

influenced by Tkachev in the 1890's. At the time, however, he was surrounded by social revolutionary Jacobins: he absorbed their ideas and thus
no doubt was indirectly influenced by Tkachev.

Miss Arendt suggested that in tracing the intellectual biography of Lenin,
the important consideration was not what men or movements his changes
echoed, but that everything he did reflected the moves of one determined
for action, who would dictate or reject something on the basis of whether
or not it permitted him to do something. In this sense he was not a Marxist.
For Marx, circumstances determined whether he would be a revolutionary,
but Lenin would be nothing if not an activist. Lenin used the scientific
aspect of Marxism for charisma, but Marx took it more seriously.

Mr. Berlin remarked in reply to Miss Arendt that most of the activists
did not become Marxists but Social Revolutionaries or terrorists.

Mr. Epstein commented that we still know very little about the intellectual climate in which Lenin lived in the years he attended populist cicrles.
We do not know what was discussed in those circles.

Mr. Pipes agreed that this subject deserves intensive study. One of the
main occupations of the circles such as those to which Lenin belonged was
drawing up reading lists. These lists provide a clue to a given group's political
complexion. Indeed, the Skliarenko group originally split into its two wings
over the issue of a reading list, Lenin and a few incipient Social Democrats
demanding that the list be based on Marxist literature.

German Political Intervention in Russia during World War I — George Katkov (with the assistance of Michael Futrell)

Es gibt also in Wirklichkeit zwei Geistesverfassungen, die einander nicht nur bekämpfen, sondern die gewöhnlich, was schlimmer ist, nebeneinander bestehen, ohne ein Wort zu wechseln, ausser dass sie sich gegenseitig versichern, sie seien beide wünschenswert, jede auf ihrem Platz. Die eine begnügt sich damit, genau zu sein, und hält sich an die Tatsachen; die andere begnügt sich nicht damit, sondern schaut immer auf das Ganze und leitet ihre Erkentnisse von sogenannten ewigen und grossen Wahrheiten her. Die eine gewinnt dabei an Erfolg, und die andere an Umfang und Würde. Es ist klar, dass ein Pessimist auch sagen könnte, die Ergebnisse der einen seien nichts wert und die der anderen nicht wahr.*

We shall consider in this paper the part played by Germany in revolutionizing Russia during World War I.** We shall try to answer three separate questions—or if this is not possible, to find out the reasons that prevent us finding a satisfactory answer to them. (1) When the German leaders envisaged war with Russia, did they expect a revolution there and did they take this expectation into consideration in

---

* There are thus in reality two attitudes, which not only fight each other but, what is even worse, usually exist side by side without exchanging a single word except insofar as they assure each other they are both desirable, both in their proper place. The one is content to be precise and sticks to the facts; the other is not content with this, but always looks at the whole and derives its knowledge from the so-called eternal and great truths. The one gains success, the other comprehensiveness and dignity. Clearly, a pessimist could also say of the findings of one that they are without value, and of the other, that they are without truth. (Robert Musil, *Der Mann ohne Eigenschaften* (Book I, Chapter 62).

** I very much regret that the articles by Nicolaus Fritz Platten, published in a series in the Swiss paper *Volksrecht* (March–April 1967) were unknown to me when I wrote this article. Although most of the evidence was known to me, there are important points made by Mr. Platten that illuminate circumstances on which I did not want to be too definite and that require careful consideration.

their decision making? (2) If so, what were the means at their disposal, and what use did they make of them to support, organize, and control a revolutionary movement in Russia? (3) Were they successful? In other words, in what measure can the revolutionary events in Russia be explained by German intervention?

Unfortunately, we cannot claim to have found much support in archivists' publications or in other research on World War I in our efforts to solve these questions. The historiography of the Russian Revolution in the Soviet Union is dominated by conceptions that preclude any discussion of this problem. Even a reference to German intentions of fostering a Russian Revolution would amount there to something like blasphemy. No help, except involuntary and inadvertent, can be expected to come from those quarters. We meet with the same dearth of information on the German side, but for different reasons. Memoirs of German statesmen and officials of that epoch, often voluble and sometimes informative, are extremely reticent on the matters with which we are concerned here. This is understandable. The German efforts to revolutionize Russia would have been defeated if total secrecy had not been observed. The opening of the German Foreign Office files and other archives after the end of World War II altered this situation only partially. Political warfare in Russia was only a side branch of the activities of the Foreign Office (*Auswärtiges Amt*—AA in the following pages). The archives of the agencies concerned—the political department (*Abteilung*) of the High Command and the Sektion Politik of the General Staff in Berlin—were presumably destroyed in the last weeks of World War II. A perusal of the AA archives provides, however, limited and often indirect information, and some of these documents are of the greatest importance.

Let us take, for instance, the report of Count Pourtalès, the German ambassador to Petersburg, of March 13, 1913, on an amazing interview that the elder Russian statesman, Count S. Iu. Witte, gave to a certain Joseph Melnik, whom Pourtalès described as a contributor on Russian affairs to the Berlin paper *Börsenkurier*.[1] In fact, Joseph Melnik had been for years a man of confidence of Count Witte, had published and prefaced some of his writings, and after Witte had retired from his official position, continued to look after his considerable financial interests in Germany.[2] In 1913 he worked for a German shipping company owned by Ballin. Pourtalès reports that Melnik put Witte's remarks at

1. AA archives, Russland 61, vol. 121. All dates in this paper, unless marked (OS) are in New Style.
2. Letter of Ballin to Bethmann-Hollweg, December 28, 1914, in A. Scherer and J. Grunewald, *L'Allemagne et les problèmes de la paix* (Paris, 1962), p. 40.

his disposal. One may wonder for whom else these remarks could have been intended! It seems that Witte was speaking to Melnik for Pourtalès and the German government and for nobody else. This is the full text in English translation:

It is utterly impossible for Russia to go to war at present; even if the whole of the Balkans were to be divided up, Russia would not strike [nicht losschlagen], provided her frontiers were not directly threatened. The army shows but little improvement, and out of the 50 million non-Russian subjects which Russia possesses, 30 million would render espionage service to the attacker, and would start a civil war inside the country. Besides, revolution would break out immediately in Poland and Finland. A Slav movement that could drive the government into war simply does not exist. The Slav gatherings that have taken place here in Petersburg and in other places have no significance whatever and are a plaything of rich gentlemen like Monsieur Brianchaninov. Austria pursues the right policy, when she protects herself against her enemies who have already penetrated inside her house.

I cannot understand however why Austria does not strike [nicht losschlägt]!

As far as Germany is concerned, I admire its economic progress, its army, administration, and so on. But Germany does not have outstanding diplomats. Nor indeed has Russia, with perhaps only one exception: Hartwig, who has the mettle of a statesman. He would have been minister of foreign affairs long ago, but for his German name. Izvolsky is not stupid, but too vain. Sazonov is insignificant, but intelligent enough to take the advice of sensible people—he is not thickheaded. The tsar, who cannot stand me, would call me back only in the extreme case of a revolution. On no account does he want a war. France would not shirk a war with Germany at present, even wishes one perhaps, but would strike only if she were quite sure of Russia's support, and as I have already said at the beginning, Russia cannot. In Germany one is not at all aware of the internal conditions in Russia. Yesterday I was visited by one of the members of the "Union of the True Russian People," who told me "My estate is situated close to the Austrian frontier: I would be quite satisfied if there were a war and my land possessions became Austrian by annexation. This would double the estate's value." This is how all these scoundrels think.

The importance of this document by far transcends the theme of the present paper. It would deserve cautious analysis sentence by sentence. What we can do here is only try to understand why Witte did such a thing, bordering on treason, as to invite German pressure on Austria to attack Serbia. Possibly the answer lies in his personal relations with Nicholas II. "The tsar cannot stand me," he said. And these feelings were fully reciprocated, for Witte hated and despised Nicholas II. We might well think that the revolution in Russia may not have been the only situation in which Witte hoped to be reinstated in power. Had Russia not stood by the Serbs in the eventuality of an Austrian invasion, it would have meant the end of the Entente Cordiale. Then, the question of a new system of alliances would have arisen, with Germany as the prospective ally. Russian diplomats like Sazonov and Izvolsky would hardly have qualified to deal with the Germans after their involvement with France and England. Witte on the other hand would have had every chance, once again in his life, of becoming a brilliant mediator; he was highly regarded in Germany, where he possessed a large fortune deposited in the Mendelssohn-Bartholdy Bank. His financial and economic connections would in such circumstances have helped him to become one of the greatest manipulators of wealth and diplomacy of this century. He may well have considered that this possibility made it worth while taking the risk of making this approach to Germany. The German government can hardly have understood all this and may not have known at that time of Witte's financial interests in Germany.[3] What must have struck them was Witte's emphatic assurance that Nicholas II would hardly go to war over an awkward development in the Balkans and that, should he do so, the regime in Russia would be on the verge of collapse right from the beginning, with Poland and Finland in open insurrection, the national minorities ready to assist the enemy in every way, and the rest of the country seething with revolution. Coming from a man of Witte's stature and importance, such assurances cannot have failed to impress Bethmann-Hollweg. The latter's position in the July 1914 crisis, only sixteen months after Witte's statement, might well have been influenced by these unsolicited and disturbing confidential revelations. The disappointments that the attitude of the tsar and the upsurge of patriotic feeling in the Russian empire at the beginning of the war brought the Germans explain why the AA tried so frantically to get in touch with Witte in the first months of the war. They were, however, once more disappointed, because Witte had little useful advice to give them and was merely concerned with getting his money out of Germany as soon as possible.

Witte's estimate of the situation was not isolated. News of a recrudescence of revolutionary activity in Russia reached the AA from various sides. For example, a certain Leo Winz, who at that time and up to 1917 kept the AA informed on such matters, reported on October 13,

3. *Ibid.*, p. 64; and George Katkov, *Russia 1917: The February Revolution* (New York, 1967), pp. 65 ff.

1913, that revolutionary pressure in Russia was once more gaining strength. One of the officials of the AA minuted Winz's report: "Schiemann says exactly the same" (*Russland*, 61, vol. 121). This comment gave Leo Winz's report an importance it otherwise might not have had. For Theodor Schiemann was no ordinary informant on Russian affairs. Schiemann, born in 1847 in the Baltic provinces of Russia, was educated in a German gymnasium and the University of Dorpat before its russification; he considered himself originally a German subject of Tsar Alexander II for whom, he once said, he would have gladly sacrificed his life. The policy of russification of the Baltic provinces made him a passionate hater of Russia and the Russians.

In 1887 he left an honorable and safe job as the archivist of the city of Reval (Tallinn) in order to go to Germany, from where he hoped to serve the cause of the *"neue Heimat"* (that is, the Baltic provinces) even better. He became the first professor of East European history at the University of Berlin, wrote a history of the reign of Tsar Nicholas I, and lectured on Russian affairs to the officers of the German General Staff. From 1904, he began a rather intimate friendship with the kaiser, whom he profoundly influenced in his attitude to Russia. Of course, this relationship enhanced his position in German society and politics immeasurably. He was invited to dinners at the kaiser's almost weekly; he became an unofficial adviser of the AA, to whom he communicated the private letters he received from a fellow historian, the Grand Duke Nikolai Mikhailovich, from Russia. The Grand Duke was by no means a paragon of discretion, and the information he gave must have been of some value to the AA, even if in their bureaucratic rigidity they may have resented the intrusion of a professor into their sacred bureaucratic domain. He not only gave information to the AA, but was also allowed to take cognizance of extremely secret reports, including those received from an official of the Russian embassy in London, von Siebert, who had been bribed by the German government.

Schiemann was neither a diplomat nor a courtier in the proper sense, and yet his political influence was probably greater than that of any of the people belonging to these categories. He maintained close personal contacts with Chancellors Bülow and Bethmann-Hollweg. Schiemann was no more a revolutionary than Witte himself. But he believed that if no greater effort was made in Russia to strengthen legality, revolution would become inevitable, and the realm would disintegrate. He did not believe that this development could be averted by the introduction of a constitution or other liberal reforms. Schiemann's interest in revolution stemmed less from general historical considerations than from his extreme Baltic German chauvinism; should the Russian emperor prove unable to curb the revolutionary wave that, according to Schiemann, would gain in amplitude every time it swept over Russia, the duty of the German government would be to protect German interests and "Kultur" in the Baltic by extending the borders of the Reich to include both Livland and Courland. All these ideas were poured out with a great amount of flattery and adulation to the kaiser, who was far more receptive to the intellectual ravings of a Schiemann, a Harnack, a Houston Stewart Chamberlain, than was his government.

It is through Schiemann that the idea of a possible revolution in Russia was spread in the circles where the aspirations of the German ruling cliques found their expression. After the outbreak of the war he became the main German adviser on Russian affairs. In 1915 he forecast in his brochure *Russland auf dem Wege zur Revolution* the regime's imminent collapse, which would end in anarchy and the advent of "a new tyranny." He was a definite opponent of all attempts at winning over the tsar and the Russians to the idea of a separate peace, to which the kaiser was inclined in 1916. Only a *hard* solution, resulting in a weakening of Russia and a reduction of its territory, could secure a lasting peace for Europe. In his public utterances Schiemann went as far as he could in supporting the idea of *Aufwiegelung* (subversion) and *Revolutionierung* (revolutionizing). He expressed regret that Germany had not used the 1905 Revolution to improve its frontiers with Russia. With all that, his practical demands did not go further than raising a claim on the whole of the Baltic coast, including Courland, and in proclaiming support for national minorities' separatist movements elsewhere.[4] Thus, he was brought into conflict both with Bethmann-Hollweg and with General Falkenhayn, and closer to the extremist attitude of Ludendorff. There are definite indications that during the war Schiemann did not remain aloof from the work directed by the General Staff toward a rapid disintegration of Russia. In the brochure mentioned above he admitted that the hopes for an early outbreak of revolution in Russia had not been fulfilled, but that did not, according to him, mean that Russia could hold out for a long time because there would come a moment "when the disintegration of the army, with the worsening defeats and under the influence of propaganda, will go so far that a military mutiny will break out. This will mean general anarchy." Of course, the "worsening defeats of the Russians" mentioned by Schiemann materialized only after the revolution. All the more important must have been, from the Schiemann point of view, the

4. See Klaus Meyer, *Theodor Schiemann als politischer Publizist* (Frankfurt am Main, 1965), pp. 213 ff.

role of propaganda. There are indications that in 1915 or 1916 he had been given to study the papers seized on Stolypin's estate near Kovno; they contained much information about the organization of anti-revolutionary propaganda.[5] There is also evidence that one of the most active German agents working in Stockholm among the Bolsheviks and the Ukrainian separatists, a certain Altdorffer, was in contact with Schiemann.[6]

The relative importance of Schiemann or any other German specialist on Russian affairs who was dominated by the idea of "the Russian danger" may be assessed differently by various writers. We have picked on him here merely as an exponent of the hopes and visions of a future that permeated German nationalist journalism and got a ready audience in high places, not least with the kaiser. If Russia was to be thrown into anarchy, it served her and her rulers right, as a punishment for her aggression against the Baltic Germans and for having entered the war. Certainly, it was disappointing that the revolution, contrary to expectations, did not occur immediately after the outbreak of war. The Germans had difficulty in understanding that Finnish or Polish dislike of Russian rule did not necessarily lead to a desire for liberation by the Germans and for the status of buffer satellites in a system of German spheres of influence. This lack of understanding explains the efforts made by the AA and the General Staff in the months immediately following September 1914 to substitute for the expected spontaneous risings that had failed to materialize less spontaneous and far more expensive *Aufwiegelung*-operations for which they created and supported all kinds of "liberation committees," recruited by German embassies mainly in Constantinople, Bern, and the Scandinavian countries.

The history of the outbreak of World War I is now again an open question. Until clear and conclusive new evidence is adduced, I must stick to the old conception that Germany had drifted into a world war on two fronts without actually having planned it and after considerable diplomatic efforts to avoid it.

In the first weeks of the war the internal situation in Russia was not the main concern of the Germans; while Russia mobilized and deployed her armies there was plenty of time to implement the Schlieffen Plan of a *Blitzkrieg*, which would have created an entirely new basis for diplomatic negotiations.

The Schlieffen Plan came to grief on the banks of the Marne early in

5. See *Padeniie tsarskogo rezhima*, ed. Shchegolev, V (Moscow–Leningrad, 1926), p. 413.

6. Altdorffer to Wesendonk 9/7/17. AA archives, Russland 61, vol. 131.

September 1914. From then on, it was clear to rationally thinking military leaders like Falkenhayn that Germany could not win a war on two fronts by military action alone. Secret diplomatic action was launched to bring about a separate peace with any one of the members of the Entente in order to make it easier to crush the others by force. As far as Russia was concerned, approaches through the relatives of both empresses, the dowager and the reigning one, were clumsy and tactless and brought absolutely no result.

On the other hand, the policy of subversion of the Russian, British, and French empires to knock one of them out of the war had been an integral part of the German war plans. As far as Russia was concerned, the first risings were expected to come spontaneously. On August 5, General Moltke reported to the AA that risings in Poland had been actively prepared and that the Polish population was already meeting the Germans with bread and salt. In fact, there had been very little sedition in those first weeks of the war, and the Germans were surprised by the success of Russian counteraction in political warfare among the Ukrainian population during the first Russian advance in Galicia.[7]

The agencies directly concerned with the organization of subversion—the so-called *Aufwiegelung*—were mainly two. The general direction seems to have been in the hands of the AA, which decided what seditious movements inside Russia should be encouraged and supported. The operational side of this work was concentrated in a special agency, the *Sektion Politik* of the General Staff in Berlin, subordinated to the Political Department of the High Command. The AA dealt with this department almost exclusively through the Berlin Office (the *Sektion Politik*), except when questions of the highest importance had to be solved directly and urgently, such as the transport of Lenin and other revolutionaries through Germany or the beginning of armistice negotiations in December 1917.

This structure showed a certain untidiness, typical of wartime relations between military and civil authorities. The various German embassies and legations were approached by numerous representatives of Russia's national minorities, who were looking to Germany for support of their liberation committees, the maintenance of contacts with their fellow countrymen inside Russia, and even for the opportunity of fighting Russians and carrying out sabotage in Russia. Among them were a few Russian revolutionaries who were ready to work for Germany as

7. An excellent survey of political warfare in the first months of the war will be found in Professor Egmont Zechlin's "Friedensbestrebungen und Revolutionierungsversuche," in *Aus Politik und Zeitgeschichte* (appendix to the weekly *Das Parlament*), for May 17, June 14 and 21, 1961, and May 15 and 29, 1963.

paid agents. The German embassies and the AA kept some of these people under their control, whereas others were directed through the intermediary of the military attachés into purely military channels and became attached to the various establishments set up by the *Sektion Politik* of the General Staff. There was no complete interchange of information between the AA and the *Sektion Politik*. Their relations were ruled more by personal contacts than by rigid protocol. The first head of the *Sektion Politik* was actually a career diplomat, R. Nadolny. The AA also delegated for a time one of its officials, Kurt Riezler, to the *Sektion Politik*; he became one of the main organizers of the *Revolutionierungspolitik* and in 1918 served as a counselor in the German embassy in Moscow under Count Mirbach.

It is difficult to say which of the two main branches of control of subversive activities blundered more in the initial stages of the war. The diplomats were all promoting their own particular favorites, whereas the *Sektion Politik* seems to have fallen prey to the deceptive methods of their protégés and trainees in the various camps they organized. The *Sektion Politik* of the General Staff embarked on a number of small-scale political actions, using adventurers of all sorts and supporting conflicting tendencies among the enemies of the Russian empire, so that these efforts were largely neutralized. The Germans did not seem to realize that it was not possible to foster a holy Muslim war in the Caucasus and at the same time to give effective support to Georgian separatist tendencies. They had no understanding of the conflicting social and political trends among Ukrainian separatists. They blundered criminally in supporting the so-called "Committee for the Liberation of Russian Jews" headed by a crackpot called Bodenheimer, which only led to cruel deportations of Jews in Russia. But above all, having become themselves the victims of the golems which they had created, they started believing that some of these organizations of national minorities abroad really represented substantial groups inside Russia and heaped on them financial, moral, and military support. Only in one case, that of the Finnish activists, was a serious attempt made at establishing a military training camp and something like regular fighting units.[8] Disillusionment came very late, after the February Revolution. Thus, in the summer of 1917, one of the best qualified German agents in Scandinavia, Altdorffer, found that many of the "old friends"—that is, representatives in Germany of Russia's national minorities—had by then become useless. They could be reactivated only by obtaining fresh

8. See a detailed account of the Finnish operation by the then head of the *Sektion Politik* himself, Ernst von Hülsen, in the Swedish-language history of the Finnish Civil War, *Finlands Frihetskrig*, I (Helsingfors, 1921), pp. 198–273.

mandates from inside Russia. "I have no hope of duping anybody with the League [the German-sponsored League of Oppressed Nations of Russia] as I did in Lausanne," Altdorffer wrote. "Should, however, the Ukrainians and, following them, the other national minorities from Russia send their representatives here [that is, to Stockholm from Russia], all these friends of ours could become of great use for us if they would serve under or at the side of the newly arrived delegates [from Russia], say in a similar capacity as the Galician-born Radek serves under Lenin's man, Fuerstenberg."[9]

The various enterprises of the *Sektion Politik* were partially financed by the AA, for which Ludendorff duly thanked the AA.[10] Although both institutions had their own staff and their own agents, the AA could convey its desires to the *Sektion* for inclusion in the instructions given to such agents. On the other hand, when the *Sektion* needed passports or diplomatic cover for its employees and agents, it approached the AA. In fact, it is such communications from Hülsen (Nadolny's successor as head of the *Sektion Politik*) to the AA that provide evidence of the contacts of such agents with the *Sektion*. However, the AA did not always comply with the demands of the *Sektion*. An interesting case is that of Robert Grimm, the editor of the *Berner Tagwacht*.

When in 1916 Grimm planned to go to Holland to attend a socialist conference, Hülsen, as head of the *Sektion*, recalled a hitch on a previous occasion and insisted that the AA grant a visa to Grimm without delay. Hülsen wanted Grimm to be treated as *persona grata*. The AA refused because Romberg, the German minister in Bern, had complained about some articles by Grimm betraying a pro-Entente attitude. Later, however, when Romberg was organizing Lenin's return to Russia in the "sealed train," he was originally instructed to entrust the operation to Grimm, who was replaced by Platten only on Lenin's insistence. Even so, Grimm applied for a visa through Germany in order to go to Russia and work "for peace," and this time not only was the visa given him, but he was charged with the extremely delicate mission of transmitting German peace conditions to the socialists of the Petrograd Soviet. All this shows that Grimm's connection with the *Sektion Politik* was highly conspiratorial and was kept secret even from the AA. Grimm's ostensible pro-Entente attitude was only a cover to make his entry into Russia more easy. We know that this action ended in his complete discomfiture, but that is another story. The Grimm case of 1916 shows us what

9. Altdorffer to Wesendonk 9/7/17. AA archives, Russland 61, vol. 131.

10. Z. Zeman, *Germany and the Revolution in Russia* (1915–1918) (London, 1958), p. 71n.

we can learn of the activities of the *Sektion Politik* from the documents of the AA.

Sometimes the AA learned about certain machinations of the *Sektion* only because they had misfired. Thus when the ensign Ermolenko was reported in the press as being under arrest in Russia, as having made revelations naming the German officers who had trained him, and as denouncing Lenin as a German agent, the AA became alarmed and asked for an explanation. The *Sektion Politik* forwarded a report on July 17, 1917, by an officer, a Lieutenant Schoening, who in the absence of von Luebbers, whom Ermolenko had mentioned to the Russian authorities, was in charge of the camp where Ermolenko had been trained. Schoening's explanations are most revealing about the technique of the *Sektion's* work. According to Schoening there was no reason for losing confidence in Ermolenko:

I believe that after his exposure he is using his old trick, providing the Russian government with ostensibly important information, only in the best of our interests. As far as I can see up to now, he has carried out to a large extent his political assignment: of the program which was set up by the AA, he has carried out (1) the organization of a Ukrainian administration in the provinces, towns, and communes, the formation of a Ukrainian army (convening a military congress in spite of Kerensky's ban), the formation of a General Staff and of Ukrainian army units, and the establishment of contact with the Black Sea fleet and (2) a Ukrainian government on its own, with eight ministers (General Secretariat).

The German officer then reported that it was not clear how far the preparations for a Ukrainian rising in case of a German offensive had progressed but that information had been received according to which Ermolenko's son-in-law and daughter had gone to Odessa and Sevastopol. Schoening closed with the words: "As Ermolenko has not yet managed to establish the direct contact for reporting on which we had agreed, our press service must closely follow the news of the Ukrainian and Russian press. On further details I believe that oral reports are necessary."[11]

It is clear from Schoening's report that Ermolenko was a trained agent, with whom the task of organizing a rising in the Ukraine, coordinated with a German offensive, "had been discussed . . . very frequently." There can hardly be any doubt either that he was leading the Germans up the garden path. In these circumstances there is no particular reason to disbelieve that these German officers mentioned

11. AA archives, WkIIa, vol. 14.

Lenin and the Bolsheviks as part of the forces on which they relied for the disruption of Russia. The complicated explanation that Trotsky gave[12] when he tried to construe Ermolenko's revelations about Lenin as an invention of the Russian military intelligence intended to compromise Lenin is both improbable in itself and based on the assumption that Ermolenko had never been a trusted (although unfaithful) German agent.[13]

If Ermolenko was a child of the *Sektion Politik*, Stepankowski, whom the Germans considered another prominent Ukrainian politician, was preeminently a creature of German diplomacy. He enjoyed every form of support from the German government, including generous financing. He was running a Ukrainian bureau of information in Lausanne with the assistance of the Polish Count Tyszkewicz, a Swiss resident, who occasionally met Entente diplomats as well. Much of the gossip from Entente circles passed to the AA via Stepankowski. In May 1917, Stepankowski decided to return to Russia in order to launch a "legal campaign" for a wide autonomy for the Ukraine. The AA gave him half a million marks, of which he took with him to Russia only some 140,000, the rest to be transferred to Petrograd by Director Steinwachs of the *Sektion Politik*. The case is interesting because of the ease with which a sum of half a million marks was spent on an agent whom nobody should really have taken very seriously. One wonders how much more the Germans were prepared to put at the disposal of really worth-while people. Stepankowski crossed the Russian frontier, was arrested in the process and talked profusely, and on the whole not utterly untruthfully, about his dealings with the Germans.[14] Stepankowski's revelations are largely borne out by the documents found after World War II in the AA archives.

For representatives of national minorities such as Stepankowski, or such Georgians as Prince Matchabeli and Michael Tseretelli, some Muslims, Poles, and Finns (for example, Zilliacus), it was politically possible to enter openly into contact with the Germans in their fight against Russia. Any such approach by Russian revolutionary parties

12. L. Trotsky, *History of the Russian Revolution*, II (London, 1932), p. 98.

13. Ermolenko's later career is not clear. The Provisional Government which, to begin with, made so much of his revelations, never published the result of the investigation, only increasing the entirely unfounded suspicion that Ermolenko was a man of straw set up by the Russian High Command in order to compromise the Bolsheviks. Later on, in the late summer of 1918, we find him in prison in the Kremlin, where he bitterly complained of physical ill treatment and indignities inflicted on him by that prominent lawyer of the early Lenin regime, M. Iu. Kozlovsky. See *Kreml za reshetkoi* (Berlin, 1922), p. 10.

14. P. Miliukov, *Istoriia vtoroi russkoi revoliutsii*, I (Sofia, 1921), pp. 153–154.

or their representatives would have been self-defeating. In relation to them the initiative was taken by the Germans and was based on propaganda among prisoners of war. The idea may have come from the Japanese who had applied it in 1905, or it may have been inspired by the agent provocateur, Roman Malinovskii, whom the Germans employed as a propagandist in POW camps already in the early weeks of the war. The Germans were keen to enlist the collaboration of Russian émigré revolutionaries of every creed to spread revolutionary ideas among POWs, both national minorities and Great Russians. Some émigrés, including the SR leader V. Chernov (writing under the name of Gardenin) and even the bibliographer Rubakin who lived in Switzerland, did actually contribute to the German magazine for prisoners of war, *Na chuzhbine* (On Foreign Soil). Compared with the national minorities' representatives, the Russians proved difficult partners, especially Rubakin, who in the German documents was referred to as "Dr. Martel." He insisted that any propaganda he might address to the Russian POWs should also be distributed to German soldiers! However ludicrous this demand might have appeared, the German authorities negotiated with Rubakin, hoping that, once thoroughly compromised, he would become less difficult. Lenin, as far as we know, was not approached in this connection, although there is strong evidence that he did not object to such activities among his closest collaborators. Zinoviev's wife Lilina was engaged in transmitting propaganda to Russian prisoners of war in camps in Germany and Austria.[15] The Germans, however, were most concerned not to compromise Lenin personally by openly supporting him. So, for instance, when Romberg, the German minister in Bern, planned to spread Lenin's "program" by means of "various French confidential agents for distribution among the ranks of the French opposition," he was prevented from doing so by Jagow, under the pretext that this might lead to a stepping up of action against revolutionaries in Russia.[16] Actually, Jagow had no reason to fear any such outcome, since it might well have provoked the revolutionary situation for which he hoped. But the risk of losing Lenin as a "burnt-out case" before the great fireworks started was from the point of view of the Germans highly undesirable. So Romberg was told to keep quiet and the matter was dropped.

The scruples in connection with Lenin did not apply in the case of

15. M. Futrell points out that this fact was mentioned in Lilina's obituary published in *Proletarskaia Revoliutsiia*, 1929, 6 (89), p. 208. More evidence to this effect can be found in a note to A. L. Sidorov *Revoliutsionnoe dvizheniie v armii i na flote v gody pervoi mirovoi voiny* (Moscow, 1966), p. 423.

16. Zeman, *Germany and the Revolution*, pp. 7 ff.

agents employed to foster a revolutionary movement. Such agents received considerable funds for smuggling revolutionary literature and even arms into Russia. Occasionally they would undertake sabotage work. In fact, many of them were probably swindlers, preying on the credulity of the Germans. In only one case, to my knowledge, did the activities of such an agent have a considerable (though unforeseen) political importance. In 1916 the Austrian military attaché in Bern handed over to the Germans a certain agent Zivin, who became one of the major informers on the Russian revolutionary movement to Romberg and the AA. Zivin was a Russian Jew of independent means, who had been undergoing treatment for consumption in Switzerland for years and was well known in revolutionary circles. He belonged to the SR party and claimed to be a close friend of Chernov. He was assisted in his activities by a friend called Levinstein (Löwenstein), and they were known in the AA correspondence as *Weiss* and *Blau*. Zivin received funds from Romberg, made one abortive journey to Scandinavia to contact SRs there, and was about to be dropped by his employers when the February Revolution occurred. From then on his importance for the Germans grew. In June 1917 he decided to return to Russia via France and England in the company of Madame Chernov.[17] He promised to work on his return to Russia against the tsarist warmongers and for peace but doubted whether it would be possible for him to maintain contact with the Germans when in Russia. However, Zivin-Weiss had left behind in Switzerland his partner Levinstein-Blau, with whom he kept in contact and who continued to inform the Germans about the military situation in Russia. Zivin's story, a rather banal one, would not have been worth relating but for one peculiar circumstance: the information that Zivin conveyed to the Germans was picked up directly or indirectly from Chernov, both in Switzerland and after Zivin's return to Russia when Chernov became a member of the Provisional Government. This information must have been of exceptional interest to the Germans. Some leak through Chernov must have become known to the rudimentary counterespionage service established by the Provisional Government under Savinkov. During a meeting of the cabinet on August 3, 1917 (OS), at which the commander-in-chief, Kornilov, made a report on the situation at the front, Savinkov warned Kornilov not to reveal operational details. After the meeting he let Kornilov understand that Chernov was a possible security risk. Kornilov attributed this risk to Chernov's contacts with members of the Petrograd Soviet. The consequences of Savinkov's remark to Kornilov are incommensurate with the minuteness of the incident, for

17. See Romberg to AA, 18/6/17 in AA archives, Wk, No. 2, geh. vol. 4.

Kornilov concluded that the government had among its members potential spies. His confidence in the reliability and patriotism of the government was shaken, and this was an important factor in the dismal episode now known as the "Kornilov mutiny" or the "Kornilov Affair."

Zivin was, of course, not the only one of his type. But on the whole the efforts of the various German paid agents, as far as they can be detected from the documents of the AA, were not on anything like the scale necessary to bring about a popular uprising that would develop into a social revolution. This task was undertaken by persons who can hardly be called agents in the proper sense of the word, but who were rather political allies of the Germans in destroying Russia as an empire. The key man in this campaign was certainly Alexander Helphand (Parvus). His amazing life has been studied in detail in the work of Scharlau and Zeman.[18] He saw the aim of his life in the destruction of the Russian empire and its dismemberment into a number of independent democratic states. He did not believe in the possibility of a spontaneous Russian Revolution, and indeed was sceptical of the revolutionaries' ability to achieve their aims. Therefore, he created an underground organization of his own, which, operating in the south from Bucharest and Sofia, and in the north from Copenhagen and Stockholm, sought directly to foment unrest among Russian industrial workers, at first on the basis of economic demands, but with the gradual introduction of a political element. The progress of liberal ideas in Russia appeared to him neither probable nor desirable. He laid down his ideas in a pamphlet published in Constantinople in October 1914, and at the beginning of 1915 he managed to win the support of important German diplomats in various embassies as well as in the AA. At that time his southern base for operations became active. On January 20, 1915, the German ambassador in Sofia reported: "As is known here, there exists in Sofia and Bucharest an organization of Russian revolutionaries, and these elements seem now to have gone to work."[19] With what success, we shall see. It is unnecessary here to repeat what has been unearthed by Zeman, Scharlau, Futrell, and myself on the manifold activities of Parvus, but the available material has by no means been exhausted, and new evidence can still be found, as for example the above-quoted message from Sofia, apparently unknown to previous researchers.

The important thing is that the Germans could in a sense farm out

18. W. B. Scharlau and Z. A. B. Zeman, *Freibeuter der Revolution* (Cologne, 1964): English version, *Merchant of Revolution: A Life of Alexander Helphand* (Oxford University Press, 1965).

19. AA archives, Russland 61, vol. 121.

the task of revolutionizing Russia, mainly to Parvus, but also to a very few other persons, like Alexander Kesküla, an Estonian political adventurer and former member of the Bolshevik party. There is ample evidence to show how closely Parvus worked not only with the AA but also with the *Sektion Politik*. Some people connected with his trade enterprises also were working with the *Sektion Politik*. On the other hand, the sums put at Parvus' disposal, and in particular the one million marks he received for starting a large-scale strike movement in Petrograd in January 1916, came from the AA. Later, of course, with the rapid increase of Parvus' trading operations, part of the money he had, and especially the profits of blockade-breaking commercial operations with Russia, could be used to further his political plans inside Russia. We have no reason to believe that Parvus was in any way discouraged by the partial failure of his "revolutionizing" offensive in January 1916. He was never sure of its immediate success and always considered it only as the initial push that could set off the avalanche in Russia. As Brockdorff-Rantzau said later, no one had done more to bring about the revolution in Russia. But in official circles and especially in the AA, the idea of removing Russia from the war by means of a revolution seems to have been competing with a conflicting tendency in favor of concluding a separate peace with a Russian right-wing party, which was allegedly prepared to make a deal with the Germans behind the back of Russia's allies. This idea had a particular attraction for the kaiser, who on July 26, 1916, wrote in a long memorandum: "If the Right (in Russia) really wants, as has been suggested, a separate peace, whatever their reasons may be, we must, from a military point of view, get the best out of it and sign on the line."[20] The kaiser believed that if a separate peace with Russia were signed, France would withdraw from the war and England could be punished for her treachery toward Germany by a humiliating defeat. We know now that these somewhat delirious hopes and expectations of the kaiser and some of his ministers were inspired in large part by the activities of a notorious crook, a certain Kolyshko, who posed in Stockholm as an intermediary between some mysterious pro-German circles in Russia and the German chargé d'affaires, Lucius. Later on, early in 1917, the same Kolyshko, who had claimed to be on close terms with Stuermer, had the effrontery to pose as an intimate of the members of the Provisional Government and of Kerensky himself. Such was the desire of the Germans for a separate peace that even then Kolyshko was put in touch with the Reichstag deputy Erzberger, with whom he worked out the terms of a possible

20. *Ibid.*, vol. 124.

armistice. When Kolyshko returned with this amazing document to Petrograd, he was arrested by the Provisional Government, and Erzberger was reprimanded by the kaiser himself.

While all this was going on in a world of fantasy, the *Sektion Politik* of the General Staff and the Parvus organization were not inactive. In any case they seem to have been the only people to whom the February Revolution did not come as a complete surprise. Even the AA did not seem to expect it at that time. But the German military authorities apparently did. In the absence of German sources, there is important Russian evidence. In his testimony before the investigation committee in Irkutsk shortly before he was shot, Kolchak recalls in great detail his movements during the revolutionary days. Kolchak first learned of the revolution from the Minister of the Navy, Grigorovich, while in conference in Batum with the Commander-in-Chief of the Caucasian front, the Grand Duke Nikolai Nikolaevich. That must have been on Monday, February 27/March 12. Kolchak left the same day in a destroyer for Sevastopol. "On the way I picked up a German radio broadcast in clear from Constantinople, which had a powerful radio station. The broadcast gave a shattering picture of the events in Petrograd, saying that a revolution was taking place and there was fierce fighting and bloodshed. In short, all this information was highly colored and exaggerated, as came out later. But the essence, of course, was correct. The form and the tone in which it was all described did not correspond to reality. The broadcast was of German origin, in broken Russian, with Bulgarian turns of speech, and was obviously delivered by some Bulgarian speaking in Russian so that all stations could pick it up." On his arrival in Sevastopol, Kolchak found that his chief of staff had only the vaguest information about a mutiny in Petrograd; but after having received Rodzianko's announcement of the fall of the tsarist government and the formation of the Duma Committee, "a whole series of broadcasts from Constantinople were received, which reported that mutinies were taking place at the front and in the army, that the Germans were victoriously advancing, and that in the Baltic Fleet there was a total mutiny and a massacre of officers. I personally," Kolchak adds, "immediately took these Constantinople broadcasts as a definite act of provocation, which it was quite impossible to stop spreading as all radio messages were picked up by the telegraphists on duty on all the ships."[21]

It is clear that the German High Command was not only quick in transmitting the information but that it had prepared beforehand a

---

21. *Arkhiv russkoi revoliutsii*, vol. X (Berlin, 1923), pp. 214–215.

version of the events which would cause the maximum disarray in the Russian camp.

In my book on the February Revolution, I have tried to show how closely the events in February 1917 resemble what happened in 1916, approximately a year earlier. In 1916 we have definite proof that the effervescence in the capital had been intended and supported by Parvus and his organization. At that time Parvus' activities can be traced in the documents of the AA, which financed them rather freely. For 1917 I have no such direct indication. But we know for certain that Parvus' organization was in close contact with the *Sektion Politik*, and we can assume that the latter was as active in support of Parvus' policy as it had been before, and as well informed about it as was necessary for producing the lurid reports broadcast from Constantinople.

So much for the German *Revolutionierungspolitik* before the fall of the tsarist regime.

Basically, the change of regime in Russia did not resolve the dilemma of German policy toward the enemy in the East. On the same day, April 2, 1917, on which he had asked Zimmermann to receive Parvus, Brockdorff-Rantzau reported that there were two ways open to Germany in her Eastern policy: either to come to an understanding with the Provisional Government and conclude a separate peace straight away, or else continue supporting the extremist movement in Russia, bringing about a collapse of the state without any further military pressure. It is obvious that Parvus favored the second solution. The dilemma was complicated by the fact that, perhaps for the first time, a separate peace was not entirely phantasmagoric. After the appeal of the Petrograd Soviet to all belligerents for a "peace without annexations or indemnities," the Germans probably could have obtained such a peace, had they conceded these principles at least in their dealings with Russia. Neither the German government nor the High Command was prepared to go so far. The talk about peace was merely an instrument for undermining Russian morale. It was skillfully used at the front in a large-scale action of fraternization launched immediately after Lenin's arrival in Russia and enjoying full support of Lenin and the Bolshevik party. The co-ordination of Lenin's efforts with the German efforts in organizing fraternization is indeed subtle and far-going. Right from the beginning, immediately after his arrival in Petrograd, Lenin demanded a large-scale spontaneous fraternization between the soldiers at the front.[22]

22. For example, V. I. Lenin, *Sochineniia*, 3rd ed., XX, pp. 76 ff., speech of April 4/17, 1917.

When, in order to counter this Bolshevik appeal supported by an organized effort across the trenches with the use of bottles of vodka, packets of cigarettes and chocolate, and appropriate printed material, the Russian High Command denounced fraternization as an organized German campaign, *Pravda* published on May 16, 1917 (OS), an article maintaining that the German General Staff had forbidden fraternization. The aim was, of course, to increase the confidence of the Russian soldiers in the honest efforts to those Germans "who," in Lenin's words, "do not want to make a trap out of fraternization." In fact, on the German side the fraternization campaign was a well thought-out military operation by the German High Command, reports on which were regularly communicated from every district of the front to the AA by the General Staff.

The other important operation carried out in these months was the supplying of the Bolshevik party with sufficient funds to carry out their various publications and propaganda campaigns. This was a major operation, not because there would have been any difficulty in transferring funds from a neutral country such as Sweden to Petrograd, but because the subsidizing of the Bolshevik party would be self-defeating if it were exposed, and yet it had to be done quickly and on a massive scale. Some of the methods used to this end may never be disclosed; one channel, however, has been sufficiently exposed to show how the operation worked. I have summarized the results of much research by myself and others in my book.[23] I have little to add or modify here. It is important to stress, however, how futile it would be to attempt to add up the funds that at various times had been allocated by the German government in order to help the Bolshevik regime to seize power and to maintain it. The funds expended by the AA were obviously only a part of the allocations for that purpose; more must have gone from the budget of the General Staff, more possibly under some cover directly from the Ministry of Finance. One of the key operating figures in these deals was Moritz von Saemisch, an official of the German Treasury, who dealt personally with the agents concerned working in Stockholm, behind the back of the AA as such.

The extremely touchy, almost hysterical, reactions of Soviet historians to this problem make futile any discussion of Lenin's personal knowledge of these subsidies. None of his henchmen involved in these operations would either then or later admit any knowledge of them.

Another important point is the switch to different channels of political pressure in Russia after the revolution. Although Parvus' biogra-

23. Katkov, *Russia 1917*, pp. 105–115.

phers are right in pointing out that his reputation with the AA had been enhanced by the February Revolution, his task was completed and his influence on the revolutionary unrest in Russia was at an end. Parvus had never worked through Bolshevik committees in plotting the February Revolution. He had never been on good terms with Lenin, and in early summer 1915 when he put definite proposals to Lenin, the latter snubbed him. Moreover Parvus as well as his German protectors knew very well of the infiltration of the Bolshevik party by the Okhrana, and they were too security-minded to get involved with organizations compromised in that way. But there were plenty of other channels open to them for using funds to organize strikes and demonstrations.[24]

Dr. Gustav Mayer, who served as an academic letter-box in communications between Saemisch and the one-time German assistant military attaché in Bern, Walter Nasse on the one hand and the Bolsheviks on the other, as well as Altdorffer, a confidential agent of Legation Counsellor Wesendonk, was in close contact with Radek. (See above, page 72.) Lenin himself in the article we have just mentioned attacking the Kadet paper *Rech* which inquired how *Pravda* got special information from Germany, wrote: "Where from, Messrs. slanderers? From the telegrams and letters of our correspondent, comrade Radek, a Polish Social Democrat who for a number of years has been in tsarist prisons and who has been working for over ten years in the ranks of German Social Democracy, who was banned from Germany for revolutionary agitation against Wilhelm and against the war, and who has specially gone to Stockholm in order to inform us."[25]

In view of what both the Germans and Lenin himself said, we can assume that Radek was at that time the main pivot of German-Bolshevik relations.

The AA did not concentrate exclusively on contacts with the Bolsheviks in order to bring about an early separate peace with Russia. The Danish socialist Borgbjerg (a friend of Parvus) and later Robert Grimm went to Russia in the spring of 1917 with peace proposals, which they communicated to the socialists of the Petrograd Soviet. Both missions failed, and Grimm's ended in a memorable international scandal. Lenin was most scathing about these efforts to bypass him in peace-making negotiations. His concern is understandable. For him, peace propaganda was but a means to destroy the Russian army, which was the only serious force standing in the way of his bid for power. A separate peace concluded before the complete disintegration of the Russian armed

24. *Ibid.*, pp. 252–261, particularly p. 258.
25. Lenin, *Sochineniia*, XX, pp. 374–375.

forces might well have led to a consolidation of the Provisional Government and of the socialist parties whom Lenin denounced as social chauvinists—hence his emphatic rejection of a separate peace, combined with intensive propaganda against offensive military operations and in favor of fraternization in the trenches. After Grimm's failure and Kerensky's June offensive, the only way for the Germans to work for early peace with Russia was to give every possible support to Bolshevik policy, both legal and subversive.

The AA tended to underestimate in the summer of 1917 the extent and speed of Russian disintegration. It is possible that the failure of the Bolshevik July coup discouraged them and made them think that the money they had spent on building up the Bolshevik party had been wasted. However, by the end of August the situation had changed again. In an extremely well informed report of a "reliable confidential agent" it is stated:

"*Forces are again at work in Russia in an enterprising and energetic attempt at overthrowing the existing government, which in its system and methods is hardly different from the tsarist one. The Bolsheviks have greatly increased in numbers and authority, and their time will come earlier than it would appear at present. The failure of the Bolshevik uprising has not discouraged them. It was only a prelude preceding the great action. What this formidable party requires most is money, and this in large quantities. The Finnish Social Democratic Party has just transferred to the Bolsheviks 50,000 Swedish kronor.*"[26]

The German authorities involved seem to have taken the hint seriously, for it is about that time that their agent, the Swiss Karl Moor, discovered that he had received a large inheritance, which he was ready to put at the disposal of the Bolshevik central committee. When finally the Provisional Government collapsed and the Council of People's Commissars proclaimed themselves the provisional government of Russia, the AA welcomed this development as the crowning of many years of effort towards this aim. Kühlmann, the German Minister of Foreign Affairs, admitted that the seizure of power by the Bolsheviks had been substantially helped by financial means made available to them by the German government "through various channels and under different labels."[27] There was an element of self-glorification in this attitude. The state to which Russia as a great power was reduced by the autumn of

26. AA archives, Wk 2c, vol. 9, report from Stockholm dated August 31, 1917.
27. See the text of this important document of December 3, 1917, in *International Affairs* (London), April 1956, pp. 181–189. Also cf. Zeman, *Germany and the Revolution*, pp. 94–95, and Katkov, *Russia 1917*, pp. 108 and 229.

1917 had many other causes besides the systematic efforts directed by the German government and High Command at what they called "Aufwiegelung." But the conviction that it was they who had put Lenin in the saddle was sustained by the knowledge that the German army could at any moment intervene and overthrow the initially weak and unstable Bolshevik regime. The Germans were right in thinking that Lenin remained in power by their good graces. This feeling was general, both in Berlin and in the various missions in Russia up to the beginning of July 1918.

It became even stronger after the conclusion of the Brest-Litovsk treaty. On March 8, 1918, Riezler, the counselor of the Mirbach embassy in Moscow, wrote that a treaty like Brest-Litovsk could have been imposed only on the Bolshevik government; if at any time the Germans felt like replacing the Bolshevik puppet administration by another government pursuing national aims, they would have to alter considerably the harshest elements of the Brest-Litovsk treaty.[28] But unexpectedly for him, at the very moment when the puppet show operator was about to change his cast, he had to leave, and the puppets remained to grow into an independent and awesome Grand Guignol company.

The Russian authorities were certainly aware of the extent of the German *Revolutionierungspolitik* and of the agencies involved, in particular of Parvus' activities, but probably underestimated their effectiveness. The methods employed to counteract the German action were typical for the Russian bureaucracy and secret police. While relying on secret informers and agents inside Russia to control the various revolutionary parties and groups, the Russian counterespionage service concentrated on curbing the entirely legitimate activities of people of German extraction living in Russia by launching national discriminatory campaigns against Baltic Germans and by interning German and Austrian aliens residing in Russia. The long-established bureau of the Russian security police in Paris made a determined attempt to penetrate German agencies spreading subversive revolutionary propaganda in Russia. The task was entrusted to one of their most reliable agents, Dolin, who worked under the aliases of Lenin or Sharl. The man managed to interest Bismarck, the German military attaché in Bern, under the pretense of having carried out large-scale sabotage action in Russia. In 1916 he claimed that the German authorities were willing to entrust him with the spreading of revolutionary propaganda in Russia. Before accepting the German proposal, he demanded from the Germans that they stop the work of all other groups involved in this task and tried to

28. AA archives, Russland 61, vol. 148.

persuade them that he had every means of checking whether this condition had been complied with.

Negotiations about propaganda were, according to an unpublished Okhrana report to be found in Paris Okhrana files at the Hoover Institution, carried out directly with Romberg, the German minister in Bern. One of these reports presents a certain interest because it gives the general lines on which, according to the views of the AA, such propaganda should be conducted. Dated April 28/May 11, 1916, no. 111, it states:

The proposers [that is, the German representatives in Bern] pointed out the desirability of exploiting in the first instance the alleged discontent of large masses of the population in order to provoke a large-scale strike movement in works engaged on war production, and of a general strike similar to the one of 1905. Even if no such results could be achieved immediately, one should persist in efforts in this direction bearing in mind as the main purpose the slowing down of work in such factories. Secondly, one should carry out large-scale propaganda among peasants, inciting them against large landowners and provoking enmity toward landowners. For this purpose it is recommended that, as far as possible, economic and agrarian terrorism be applied. The proposers consider it particularly important at the present moment to carry on agitation among soldiers, and in view of the fact that this is technically impossible at the front, the proposers indicated that such agitation should be carried out in places where the troops are being trained and reserves are concentrated. It is recommended that it be pointed out in leaflets and in private conversation with soldiers that it is futile to carry on with the war because it is already irredeemably lost, to remind the soldiers that life as prisoners of war is not all that bad, and that the end of the war can be speeded up by their refusal to carry out the task entrusted to them by their superiors.

All this is, of course, fairly commonplace, but certain elements of these instructions remind us of Parvus' original plan and give us a foretaste of the propaganda methods employed in 1917 during the intensive fraternization campaign.

I have found no trace of reports by Bismarck on his negotiations with Sharl, but of course such matters were reported not to the AA but to the military authorities directly. On the other hand, the Okhrana documents kept in the Hoover Institution throw no light on the further development of this rather adventuresome enterprise which anyway came at the last hour before the revolution.[29]

29. See the pamphlet by V. K. Agafonov, *Zagranichnaia Okhranka* (Petrograd, 1918), pp. 177–182 and 335–340.

We have seen how Germany, on entering World War I, had been given assurances from authoritative quarters that Russia could not embark on the war without facing immediate unrest and revolution at home. It must be assumed that these assurances encouraged the Germans to risk a war on two fronts. In the second part of this paper, I have shown how the Germans, when the predicted revolution did not appear to be materializing, set up machinery to encourage revolution (in case it should prove impossible to induce the tsar to conclude a separate peace). The question remains: did these elaborate efforts have any influence on what happened, or did events unfold by themselves, totally unaffected by the complicated, secret, and extremely costly arrangements made by the AA and the political branches of the German war machine?

From an epistemological point of view, this is very much like asking whether the fact that Oswald's wife refused to sleep with him affected his decision to assassinate the President of the United States. This is not the place to discuss the semantics of such statements. What we can do is recall a few events of the prerevolutionary and revolutionary situation in Russia that, although trivial and unremarkable by themselves, sometimes acquire a fascination and glimmer of significance if related to our knowledge of German efforts to weaken Russia's military power. May I recall, first of all, the report Michahelles sent from Sofia in January 1915, announcing that revolutionary organizations set up there and in Romania had just gone to work; and next, the memorandum compiled by Parvus in March 1915, in which he stressed to the Germans the importance of organizing local strikes in Nikolaev and Odessa as early as possible because they would have "a symptomatic significance by disturbing the peace which descended on internal strife within the tsarist empire at the beginning of the war."[30] Does not the enigmatic strike during the spring of 1916 in the shipbuilding yard of Naval in Nikolaev, concerning which the investigating admiral said he could not decide whether it was provoked by revolutionaries or by the Germans, appear as a fulfillment of Parvus' plans? Would we be justified in sneering at the same admiral's findings, when he points out that the demands put forward in the Naval works were the same as those of Petrograd strikers, whose conditions of work were quite different; or when he states that the Naval strike was actually political, although camouflaged as an economic one, exactly as was proposed by Parvus?[31]

30. Zeman, *Germany and the Revolution*, p. 141.
31. See my *Russia 1917*, p. 92 ff.

And if we look at the internal struggle in the Russian Social Democratic movement, can we help being struck at finding in 1916 a legally published paper in Samara coming out with a long apologia for Parvus and his enterprises and denouncing as an unjustifiable and malicious slander the entirely truthful exposure of Parvus as a collaborator of the German and Turkish governments?[32] Is not the appearance in Russia in 1915–16 of Bukharin's antiwar pamphlets, printed in Germany under the auspices of Kesküla, and their dissemination in Russia, a further sign of the effectiveness of German penetration? Is the outbreak of political unrest in Petrograd in January and February 1916 merely coincidental with the transfer of one million marks by Parvus to his agents in Petrograd for the promotion of exactly this kind of unrest? And is the figure of one hundred thousand demonstrators, which Parvus claimed to be able to bring into the street and which is also reported by Fleer, a Social Democrat observer, nothing but another such coincidence?

With the return of Lenin and his retinue to Russia through Germany in April 1917, we can abandon the interrogative and go over to the indicative. Gustav Mayer reports in his memoirs:

My absolutely inconspicuous address was the thing that interested him [Nasse] most. Letters, manuscripts, on occasion money transfers also, were to come from time to time by post or through messengers, mostly women, and were to be kept unopened until either Nasse himself or a messenger authorized by him would take them.[33]

When we remember that Nasse was the man who was entrusted in Bern with finding a way to convey funds to the Bolsheviks in a manner

32. *Nash golos*, January 17, 1916. This letter to the editor dated December 28, 1915 (OS), in defense of Parvus-Helphand and the "Society for the Study of the Social Consequences of the War," which he had founded, is signed E. Groman, S. Dalin, A. Zurabov, G. Osipov and V. Perazich. The contents of the paper are very indicative of the penetration of German propaganda through Social Democratic channels. In the same issue the paper brings a correspondent's report on the satisfactory development of Social Democratic enterprises in German-occupied Warsaw and in Belgium. Probably the most drastic example of the impudence of such propaganda penetration during the war is a report signed G. O. [G. Osipov, that is, G. D. Bienstock] on March 29, 1916 (OS), advertising the *Russkii Vestnik* printed in Berlin by the German General Staff for prisoners of war. G. O. claims that this paper is "in private ownership" and is hardly distinguishable from any other "Russian liberal provincial newspaper." No wonder Lord Milner found, in spite of general complaints about lack of freedom of speech, that Russian censorship was slack and the liberty taken by the press astonishing in wartime.

33. *Erinnerungen* (Zurich, 1949), p. 260.

that would not compromise them; when we recall Gustav Mayer's rather intimate friendship with the inhabitants of a luxurious villa in a fashionable suburb of Stockholm, Hanecki and Radek; the innocent letter of Lenin to Hanecki and Radek of April 12, 1917 (OS), beginning: "Dear friends, until now we have received nothing, neither letters nor parcels nor money from you," begins to glow with a particular significance.[34] (Incidentally, the letters, parcels, and money were delayed because Gustav Mayer had to nurse a flu and was late in arriving in Stockholm.) Does not the cautious and suspicious remark of Lenin from his hiding-place in Finland, asking who Karl Moor was anyway, come alive when one recalls the dealings between Lenin and Moor in 1916?[35] One is no more astounded to hear that Karl Moor, who must have been born under a particularly lucky star, inherited in the summer of 1917 a lot of money which he immediately offered to the Bolshevik Central Committee. The latter recorded in a formal minute its refusal to accept it but then noted that the suspicions against Moor were unfounded. It makes Kühlmann's claim, of having helped the growth of bolshevism by conveying financial aid through various channels and changing labels, appear less of a boast than an account of calculated and at least partially successful political action. The discovery of such links and threads, which should not necessarily be interpreted as cause-and-effect relations, brings sense and significance into the tangled, porous, and shimmering texture of historical reality.

Comment by Alexander Dallin on — "German Political Intervention in Russia During World War I" by George Katkov

To venture into the maze of problems that is Mr. Katkov's topic is to court disaster. To challenge the conclusions of one who has spent many years exploring this difficult terrain is to rush in where better scholars have feared to tread. Yet the one thing worse than challenging his views would be not challenging them.

The three questions Mr. Katkov raises in his paper are legitimate ones. It is the answers, not the questions, that give me trouble.

Let us turn to the first question. Did Germany expect a revolution

34. V. I. Lenin, *Polnoe sobranie sochinenii*, XLIX (Moscow, 1964), p. 437.
35. *Leninskii Sbornik*, XI (1929), pp. 214 and 226.

when considering war with Russia? I do not believe the paper answers this question. We are told of a conversation with, or communication from, Count Witte to Ambassador Pourtalès in 1913, but I fail to see its relevance. I do not believe it tells us very much about the decisions taken in Berlin. Moreover, one could show, I believe, that Witte made similar statements on Russia's gloom and doom to other people, on other occasions—say, to the British and French ambassadors. It was no secret that Witte had become something of a crank who candidly berated "this insane regime, this tangle of cowardice, blindness, craftiness, and stupidity."

And, secondly, we are told of the view of people like Theodor Schiemann, who looked forward to the disintegration of the Russian empire. Mr. Katkov quite correctly identifies his views as those of a Baltic German nationalist, but he fails to show the impact of these views, or of others like his, on the decision makers in Berlin. More generally, we fail to learn what the assumptions of the German cabinet or the military leadership were about Russia and what they expected, in August 1914 or before, to take place in Russia once war began. For instance, how did the Schlieffen Plan fit this vision of inevitable disintegration? We are told, it is true, in the conclusions of Mr. Katkov's paper that "Germany, on entering World War I, had been given assurances from authoritative quarters that Russia could not embark on the war without facing immediate unrest and revolution at home. It must be assumed [Mr. Katkov continues] that these assurances encouraged the Germans to risk a war on two fronts." Mr. Katkov's statement, "It must be assumed," can also be taken to mean "We have no proof." At any rate, German expectations were geared, I believe, to hopes for splintering Russia primarily along national rather than social lines.

Most of the paper deals with German wartime support of the Russian revolutionaries. What do the various individual sketches, fascinating as they are, add up to? In the period from 1914 to February 1917, the Germans were interested in promoting separate peace sentiments in Russia or in stirring up trouble and revolt behind the enemy lines or in both. This is what every warring power does to its enemies (except when it calls for "unconditional surrender"). Indeed, Mr. Katkov recognizes that the Germans sought to do the same to the British and French empires, too. They did wish to encourage divisive elements in Russia, and they therefore supported certain émigré politicians—some directly, some not. All this had very little effect inside Russia. The Germans' main hope and "contact," Parvus, obviously deceived them about what he could accomplish inside Russia. With some skepticism, the Germans finally did finance his effort to promote a strike movement in January 1916. It failed to develop into the massive disruptive affair that the Germans thought they had "bought." And for the following year—until February 1917—as Mr. Katkov agrees, there is no evidence of German-supported activity inside Russia.

In regard to the period from February to October 1917, I have even greater difficulty following Mr. Katkov. His evidence for the "German hand" in the February Revolution is essentially this: the German military were the only ones *not* to have been surprised by the events; hence presumably, they knew in advance what was coming. How do we know they were not surprised? Not from documents or memoirs or diaries of the German military, but from a statement made from memory, three years later, by Admiral Kolchak in Irkutsk, before he was shot. And that statement refers merely to a radio broadcast from Constantinople, which, Kolchak recalled, seemed to have been premature or excessive.

As for Parvus' (or anybody else's) role, the evidence is also indirect. Let me quote from Mr. Katkov's paper (p. 80 above):

In 1916 *we have definite proof that the effervescence in the* [Russian] *capital had been intended and supported by Parvus and his organization. At that time, Parvus' activities can be traced in the documents of the* Auswärtiges Amt, *which financed them rather freely. For 1917 I have no such direct indication. But we know for certain that Parvus' organization was in close contact with the* Sektion Politik, *and we can assume that the latter was as active in support of Parvus' policy as it had been before, and as well informed about it as was necessary for producing the lurid reports broadcast from Constantinople.*

My own translation of this paragraph is: "There is no evidence whatsoever." Yet a few pages later this vagueness has already turned into firmer fact, for here Mr. Katkov says that "Parvus had never worked through *Bolshevik* organizations in preparing the February Revolution." And next we are told with regard to appeals to fraternization that there was "subtle and far-going" coordination between Lenin's and the Germans' efforts. I do not know of any evidence to support this claim. In his recent book Mr. Katkov sums up this problem, more sharply perhaps than in his article, by suggesting that the fall of the tsarist regime was "the reward of [the German authorities'] own relentless efforts."

I shall not dwell on the inevitable issue of German money transferred to Lenin, which is also discussed with great skill in Mr. Katkov's book. I do not question the fact that money was somehow passed to the Bolsheviks. But what we are told is that German money had "built up" the Bolshevik party, and the Germans soon had the "conviction of having put Lenin in the saddle." How they accomplished this remarkable feat we are not told; nor is it revealed how, after October, Lenin remained in power "by the Germans' tolerance." The former allegation is implausible to me, I must admit; and the latter flies in the face of what we know about the German efforts, at the end of 1917, to work with forces opposing the new Russian regime—such as Ukrainian nationalists, and some of the Kadets—and also of Lenin's willingness in early 1918, so long as the Germans were "enemy number one," to accept ammunition and food "from the Anglo-French imperialist robbers."

What then are Mr. Katkov's conclusions regarding the impact of German efforts on the Russian Revolution? I regret to say that I do not see such things as the republication of a pamphlet that had first been published in Germany, in Russia in time of war as evidence of the effectiveness of German manipulation or penetration. As for Lenin himself, all we find is a letter in which he complains that he is *not* getting money. We are asked to accept this as proof, I presume, that on other occasions he did receive money from the Germans.

Mr. Katkov refers twice to the famous Kühlmann document, in which Kühlmann boasted, in December 1917, of having conveyed financial aid to the Bolsheviks and took credit for what had occurred. What I miss is any attempt to analyze this document further. Just as Parvus and Kesküla were prone to exaggerate *their* contacts and accomplishments, so German agencies and individuals were apt to exaggerate their own contribution to history. What independent proof is there, and what is Kühlmann's record in general? For, unless we know more, we might just as well credit the evidence left by Kühlmann's successor, State Secretary Admiral von Hintze, who wrote in 1918: "What do we want in the East? The military paralysis of Russia. The Bolsheviks are taking care of this better than any other Russian party, *without our contributing a single man or a single penny* . . . We are not cooperating with the Bolsheviks; we are exploiting them."[1]

Mr. Katkov concludes that there were "links and threads" between Germans and Bolsheviks (incontestably there were); that they were "not necessarily cause and effect" (true, indeed); but that they had "sense and significance." Now I am not sure; what sense, what significance? Is it not the impact, *as a cause*, that we had set out to survey? Was it not implied in the arguments that this is what the documents meant? Mr. Katkov is far too good a historian to allege flatly that the Germans caused both the February and the October Revolutions. But then I am not sure just what weight we are to attach to these things.

1. Cited in Fritz Fischer, *Griff nach der Weltmacht* (Düsseldorf, 1964), pp. 770–771; English in Z. A. B. Zeman and W. B. Scharlau, *Merchant of Revolution* (London, 1965), p. 254 (italics mine).

Disarmingly, Mr. Katkov starts out by telling us that there is a lack of documentary evidence, but he seeks to turn this circumstance to his advantage: he argues that the Soviet authorities would wish to suppress the facts; hence, the lack of evidence supports his thesis; and the Germans likewise have found this too ticklish a matter to elaborate or confirm. Thus, he is obliged to provide various "non-proofs" of the German role. The argument seems to rest on the premise that if you find supporting evidence, it strengthens your case; if you do not find any evidence, it also proves your case. Moreover, vigorous denial by the protagonists is also taken to strengthen the case against them.

How important was German aid to Lenin? Helphand-Parvus claimed to have a total of ten agents, some or most of whom were fictitious. Of the German agents, Mr. Katkov says, many were crooks and swindlers, and only one (Zivin) was important. In substance, the Germans fell for Parvus' fraud, and it is important that we should not.

How much money did they get to him? Mr. Katkov implies that it is absurd to count the money on which we have information because there is so much more on which we do *not* have any information. But this becomes a circular argument: because we do not know how much money there was, we cannot tell how relevant it is to the discussion. On the face of it, what the Germans spent was only one tenth of what they spent in other countries.[2]

Regardless of the amounts of money, was Lenin a German agent of any sort? (I shall not bother to differentiate here among the various categories of agent status one should distinguish.) By nature and disposition Lenin was nobody's agent. He used the Germans as he used the French, his friends as well as his enemies. He would take funds or guns from any quarter any time, just as his successors would.[3] Lenin would never accept any sense of dependence or obligation, let alone to the Germany of Wilhelm II. The parallelism of momentary goals is something that Bolshevik strategy and tactics have, of course, elaborately acknowledged, but it by no means implies any causal relationship.

2. *Times Literary Supplement* (London), June 30, 1966.
3. Insofar as the German documents are concerned, their leading analyst on our subject writes: "There is no evidence among the documents of the Foreign Ministry that Lenin, a circumspect man, was in direct contact with any of the official German agencies. How much he knew about the activities of the men around him is difficult to tell . . . But it cannot be said even about Radek and Fürstenberg [Hanecki], who had more contacts with the Germans than anyone else among the Bolsheviks, that the interests of the Imperial German government lay close to their hearts. A socialist revolution was their aim. To achieve and further it they were prepared to use every means." (Z. A. B. Zeman, ed., *Germany and the Revolution in Russia 1915–1918* [London, 1958], p. x.)

In our search for analogies we are helped by the recent disclosures of the role of the CIA. To say or imply that Lenin was a tool of the Germans is to argue with the same kind of evidence and in the same fashion that any one of the prominent figures who have recently been revealed to have, directly or indirectly, received support originating with the Central Intelligence Agency was its agent.

Students of Soviet history need not be reminded that the question of "German gold" is as old as the revolution itself. From April 1917 on, rumors and forgeries circulated. In the July Days, the charges against Lenin were central to the crisis. The allegations of German support for the Czech Legion; the Sisson Documents, whose falsity Mr. Kennan so brilliantly exposed; and all the other fabrications should make us doubly cautious about now reversing course without having the most indisputable evidence for it. Mr. Leonard Schapiro has spoken, very aptly, of the thesis of "treason in high circles" during World War I as a gesture of Russian patriots in search of alibis for failure. "German gold" provides a similar kind of alibi. If ever in Russia there were created an "un-Russian activities committee," these would be the kind of findings which, a priori, they would want to have. One need not go to the extreme of Vladimir Nabokov's characterization of the revolution as a "trite *deus ex machina*" to see the political and psychological comfort which such a view can provide.

As for its plausibility, this is another matter; and this is not the place to argue the case for the *organic* nature of developments in Russia in 1917—of both *stikhiia* and organization—a case, incidentally, that Mr. Katkov's admirable book greatly strengthens.

As for the charges—or what I assume to be the charges that Mr. Katkov levels—the verdict I believe remains, "not proven."

Discussion

In reply to Mr. Dallin's comments, Mr. Katkov acknowledged that considerable disagreement had emerged between them on matters of historical proof. He said that the evidence he had compiled against Lenin would not have been conclusive enough to justify hanging him. At the same time he emphasized that he was not acting in the capacity of a judge. He could only weigh one probability against another, and in this regard evidence that had come to light in the past ten or fifteen years was certainly weighted in favor of a greater German role in the Russian Revolution than had been believed earlier. Mr. Katkov stressed that the evidence he had come across quite unexpectedly in the German archives had greatly surprised and distressed him, and he expressed dismay that it appeared to make so little impression upon Mr. Dallin.

Mr. Rogger voiced skepticism regarding the importance of Pourtalès' report for the formation of German policy toward Russia during the war. Noting that considerably more optimistic appraisals of the Russian situation could be found in British and French documents, he asked what role selective perception played in all this. Mr. Rogger added that reports of this kind did not alter the alliance system or the attitudes or expectations of political leaders toward what was going to happen.

Mr. Katkov responded with the thought that such reports were of importance simply as indicators of the probability of success of a given policy and hence the amount of money that should be invested in it.

Speaking as a lawyer, Mr. Schapiro took issue with the remarks made by Mr. Dallin. He pointed out that in his mind there was a fundamental difference between the legal evidence admissible in a court of law and the kind of information with which the historian is forced to deal. In attempting to reconstruct a whole picture, and particularly in handling the difficult problem of causation, the historian has to consider such factors as myth, atmosphere, and the most diverse fragments of information.

Mr. Schapiro stressed that he would not have much to say if Mr. Katkov had actually stated that Lenin was a German agent, as Mr. Dallin had suggested. To him it was quite obvious that such an accusation was impossible. There was also no evidence that Parvus had used the money given him by the Germans before April 1917 to foment unrest in Russia. However, it was indisputable that German money on a vast scale had helped to finance Bolshevik propaganda after April, and no one could say that the money did not affect the course of the revolution. Mr. Schapiro thought this kind of approach to history necessary and valuable even though Germany's role in causing the revolution obviously could never be proved with a lawyer's certainty.

Mr. Anweiler agreed that it was necessary to make a distinction between the positions of the lawyer and the historian. However, it seemed to him that when it came to dealing with facts a position might be found somewhere between the legal and historical definitions of evidence offered by Mr. Schapiro. Mr. Anweiler referred to passages in Mr. Katkov's book (*Russia 1917*, pp. 258–260) which asserted that in February 1917 there existed an anonymous strike committee organized by Helphand's agents, and which strongly suggested that the strike movement in February 1917 had been started by people who received their instructions from Berlin via Copenhagen and Stockholm. Commenting that all this was important in that it cast doubts on the spontaneity of the February Revolution, Mr. Anweiler asked for more evidence to support such a view.

Mr. Katkov replied that he would also like to have more evidence. He had based his suggestions in regard to the activities of a German-sponsored anonymous strike committee in the February strike movement on references by Shliapnikov to small Social Democratic groups that were not under

Bolshevik control. These groups were attached to the *bolnichnye kassy* (workers' aid committees) which paid the strikers. It was unclear where the *bolnichnye kassy* got their money; according to the tsarist government the money had come from Germany. The February strikes had occurred in the same places that Parvus had mentioned in his plans. Mr. Katkov explained that he had drawn the connections between these facts and interpolated the missing evidence.

Mr. Kennan returned to the theme of the differences in the points of view of the lawyer and the historian toward facts. He remarked that there was another point of view that had struck him in listening to the discussion— the point of view of one like himself who had been in government for twenty-five years and had dealt with these matters. From this perspective, said Mr. Kennan, the picture appeared reasonably clear. In wartime, intelligence services customarily finance a great many things on the chance that one or another of them would turn out to be a good bet. Mr. Kennan expressed confidence that this was precisely what the Germans had done during World War I. After the February Revolution the Germans would naturally have been interested in pouring money into the Russian political faction that seemed to hold the greatest potential for provoking divisiveness and trouble, if not a separate peace. That the Germans did support the Bolsheviks financially seemed clear to Mr. Kennan from Kühlmann's statement. Hintze probably was not aware of these dealings. After Brest-Litovsk the Germans would certainly have recognized that the success of the pact depended on keeping the Bolsheviks in power. Mr. Kennan emphasized that this was quite a different thing from using the Bolsheviks as conscious agents and giving them orders. For this he saw no evidence at all. From the materials collected by Mr. Katkov and Mr. Zeman, Mr. Kennan concluded that there was somewhat more substance to claims of German-Bolshevik collaboration than he had previously believed.

Mr. Kennan went on to say that he had not seen Mr. Zeman's book nor Mr. Katkov's when he wrote his paper on the Sisson documents. He noted that they did not change his estimate of the falsity of these documents, though they did show that there was a bit more substance than he had previously thought to support the theory that the Germans had aided the Bolsheviks in 1917.

Mr. Keep thought it worth noting that Soviet historians were now much more forthcoming than they had been heretofore about such questions as German support for the Bolsheviks in 1917. In view of this he suggested approaching the problem from another angle. According to Soviet sources, the Bolsheviks were publishing some eighty newspapers and journals in October 1917. How these publications were financed is unclear, but it seems apparent that neither local nor Central Committee resources were sufficient to support so vast an enterprise. Mr. Keep proposed pursuing this line of approach in the hope that it might perhaps encourage Soviet historians to deal with the problem.

Mr. Epstein returned to the question raised by Mr. Rogger in regard to the importance of the Pourtalès document. Mr. Katkov had not shown that it influenced Bethmann-Holweg or any other leading German statesman; on the contrary, the information contained in the document did not fit into the picture of Russia then commonly held by the Germans. Many leading Germans, Bethmann-Holweg included, were already at this time apprehensive about Russia's growing power and contemplating the possibility of a preventive war.

Referring to the Musil epigraph, Mr. Dallin noted that its point was that there were two kinds of truths—the great eternal verities and great insights, on the one hand, and the petty little facts on the other. He assumed that in this contest between the possessors of the great verities and the footnote-mongers Mr. Katkov ranged himself on the side of those who had the insight even if it could not be supported by the factual evidence. Mr. Katkov was calling on his listeners to accept his interpretation on the basis of intuition, faith, or partisan politics and Mr. Dallin remarked that for him none of these was adequate.

The Political Thought of the First Provisional Government — *Leonard Schapiro*

The First Provisional Government was formed on March 2, 1917, on the day of the tsar's abdication. It lasted until May 5, 1917, when it gave way to the first coalition Provisional Government. The coalition was inspired by a crisis which provoked the government to issue on April 26 a declaration explaining its own record and views and urging the broadening of its composition to include Socialists. This declaration[1] forms a convenient starting point from which to approach the political thought of the first Provisional Government.

The crisis that led to the formation of the coalition government was the result of demonstrations on April 21 in Petrograd against the Provisional Government. These were ostensibly provoked by a note of April 18 by the Foreign Minister, P. N. Miliukov, prepared for transmission to the Allied Powers, setting out the principles of the foreign policy of the Provisional Government.[2] The roots of the crisis, however, lay deeper. They derived from the growing rift between the Provisional Government and the "masses"—in other words, the anarchical Petrograd garrison, the Red Guards, and the mob—elements the Petrograd Soviet itself at this stage was only barely able to control.[3]

Note: All dates in this article are given in Old Style.

1. Reprinted as doc. 1075 in *The Russian Provisional Government, 1917—Documents,* selected and edited by Robert Paul Browder and Alexander F. Kerensky, 3 vols. (Stanford, Calif., 1961), Hereinafter cited as Browder and Kerensky, III, pp. 1249–1251.

2. *Ibid.,* II, doc. 964, p. 1098.

3. The report of the examining magistrate on the demonstrations of April 21 leaves no doubt at all that this was carefully organized as a move against the Provisional Government with the aid of the armed, Bolshevik-controlled Red Guards. The role of the Bolsheviks in planning the disturbance was evident, but the magistrate either could not or thought it more politic not to pin responsibility on any individuals. *Ibid.,* III, doc. 1071, pp. 1242–1244. Lenin on April 21 called for the overthrow of the Provisional Government by demanding that the "handful of

The main points of the declaration were as follows:

(1) That the Provisional Government had assumed power with the "unanimous support of the people" and with a policy "unanimously" endorsed by the country.

(2) This policy comprised the following: convocation of a Constituent Assembly at the earliest moment; civil liberties and equality for all; democratic local self-government; extension of civil rights to the army with the preservation of military order and discipline; and continuation of the war "in close union with our allies."

(3) An enumeration of the extent to which these aims had already been achieved or embarked on.

(4) An expression of the anxieties of the Provisional Government over the difficulties that "threaten to become insurmountable." The Provisional Government "believes that the power of the state should be based not on violence and coercion, but on the consent of free citizens to submit to the power they themselves created." But "the repudiation of past coercive methods" has led to the result that "the less conscious and less organized strata of the population threaten to destroy the [country's] internal civil cohesion and discipline" and to produce internal disintegration and defeat at the front, raising the spectre of civil war and of anarchy, with consequent "reaction and the return of despotism."

(5) An appeal for order, coupled with a promise "of expanding its [own] composition by drawing into responsible government work representatives of those active creative forces of the country who have not previously taken direct . . . part in the government of the state." The declaration was accompanied by personal appeals to the socialists from Prince G. E. Lvov and A. F. Kerensky.

Although the first Provisional Government included a predominant number of leading Kadets (Miliukov, Shingarev, Manuilov, Nekrasov, Tereshchenko), it was for a variety of reasons in no way predominantly Kadet in its outlook or policy, and indeed it often departed from the official Kadet platform. There were a number of reasons for this phenomenon.

In the first place, there had been for some years past a considerable lack of agreement on policy among the Kadets themselves. In the course of the war a strong left wing had grown up inside the Kadet party with

capitalists" be made to yield to the soviets. However, two days later, on April 23, he had recognized the authority that the Soviet still exercised over the crowds, and he now called for strict observance by all Bolsheviks of the prohibitions against armed demonstrations that the Soviet had issued. See V. I. Lenin, *Sochineniia*, 3rd ed., XX, pp. 208 and 224–225.

a leaning toward a mass movement, as distinct from the parliamentary opposition within the Duma constantly advocated by Miliukov.[4]

Second, this mass-oriented trend, insofar as it involved cutting across parties and institutions, had been traditional to the *zemstvo* constitutionalist movement that had grown up early in the century under the aegis of the Union of Liberation movement—Prince Lvov was perhaps most representative of it. So, in a sense, was the Progressive Bloc in the Duma. For the Progressive Bloc (like the Liberation Movement) was a union of like-minded men, not a coalition of political parties. The Progressive Bloc cut across the program of the parties, whose members had agreed to form the Bloc. The Liberation Movement had sought the widest possible agreement on the simplest formula: "Down with the Autocracy." The Progressive Bloc sought and found the same wide basis of appeal in two single policy demands: first, a government enjoying the confidence of the country; and second, a full legislative program to bring into being civil freedom and the rule of law.[5]

As the war wore on there was a growing sense both among the Progressive Bloc leaders and among the *zemstvo* leaders like Prince G. E. Lvov that it was essential for the liberal leaders to try to assume leadership over the masses for fear that otherwise the latter would spill over into anarchy and disorder. At the time of the formation of the Progressive Bloc (August 1915), a Central Committee had been formed in Moscow for the promotion of the aims of the Bloc by mass means which were very reminiscent of those of 1905—that is, by pressure on the emperor by *zemstvo* congresses and deputations. This Central Committee included among its leaders Prince G. E. Lvov and another future member of the Provisional Government, Konovalov.[6] A Moscow *okhrana* report on the mood of society at the end of February 1916 stressed first that in general all were agreed on the need to do nothing about the tsar until the end of the war and then "to settle the score"; and second, that there was strong feeling in *zemgor* (union of *zemstva* and municipalities) circles on the need to link up with the working class movement and to assert influence and leadership over it.[7] This was also essentially the view at this time of the left wing of the Kadets, of whom Nekrasov

---

4. See B. B. Grave, ed., *Burzhuaziia nakanune fevral'skoi revoliutsii* (Moscow-Leningrad 1927), doc. 62, pp. 145–148, reproducing a Moscow *okhrana* report on the October 1916 Kadet conference. See also docs. 77 and 78, *ibid.*, pp. 175–178, for similar left-wing trends on the eve of the revolution, in January 1917.

5. See Grave, *Burzhuaziia*, doc. 12, pp. 26–29, for their agreed policy program published on August 25, 1915.

6. *Ibid.*, doc. 14, pp. 33–38.

7. *Ibid.*, doc. 32, pp. 75–81.

was typical.[8] The tactics to be adopted were outlined by Nekrasov in a *zemstvo* banquet speech on March 13, 1916: what he had in mind was in fact nothing less than the recreation of the *Soiuz Soiuzov* of 1905— a super-union of all kinds and shapes of unions, forming one national front united on the slogan "Down with the autocracy."

Although very little can be confidently asserted about it, some evidence has come to light suggesting that the members of the First Provisional Government were further divided by the fact that, with the exception of Miliukov, its leading members were bound by some form of Free Masonry, which revived in Russia after 1905. In her guarded letter on the subject to N. V. Volsky (Valentinov) of November 15, 1955, E. D. Kuskova significantly said the aim of this movement was "to restore in this form the Union of Liberation and to work in the underground for the liberation of Russia." Miliukov, she states, had refused to have anything to do with this organization. However A. I. Guchkov (the Minister of War in the First Provisional Government), although a member of this Masonic organization, "was repeatedly threatened with exclusion" from it, according to Kuskova. This was because Guchkov had been involved in conspiratorial activity aimed at a "palace revolution"—of which, it would appear, his fellow masons disapproved.[9] Certainly, this account by Kuskova is borne out by the evident manner in which Miliukov and Guchkov (the only two monarchists in the First Provisional Government) fell more and more out of step with their colleagues and were forced to resign within two months. It may also help explain why the bond of common membership of the Kadet party was of so little importance in maintaining any solidarity of political outlook between Miliukov, on the one hand, and Nekrasov and Tereshchenko (who were Masons), on the other.

Finally the predominant traditions of the Liberation Movement had little to do with liberalism or constitutionalism in any normal sense of the terms. They were in fact much closer to a form of populism: faith in the perfectability of the people, regarded as being corrupted only by its institutions; and the lack of any sense of a danger from the left— a danger many Kadets understood. The Union of Liberation, on the

8. *Ibid.*, doc. 33, pp. 81–83. See also doc. 64, pp. 152–154, dated November 1, 1916, that shows that Protopopov was aware of this policy and was trying to counteract it by the methods which had once been used by Plehve, the prohibition of *zemstvo* gatherings.

9. Kuskova's letter to Volsky was published, together with some other relevant letters, in Grigorii Aronson, *Rossiia nakanune revoliutsii—Istoricheskiie etiudy* (New York, 1962), pp. 138–143. The evidence on the whole question has now been examined by G. Katkov in *Russia 1917—The February Revolution* (London, 1967), pp. 163–173. For A. F. Kerensky's account of the matter, see Alexander Kerensky, *Russia and History's Turning Point* (New York, 1965), pp. 88–91.

contrary, believed that all opposition in Russia necessarily had to be extreme and violent and that the most extreme and violent elements would become milder once the autocracy had fallen. Similarly, the sense of the importance of order and institutions, not only on paper but of a kind that could in Russian conditions work in practice, formed no part of the tradition of Liberation. In short, here was a tradition typical of the Russian intelligentsia, which Lenin was the first to challenge from the left.

It is therefore easy to see why the declaration of April 26 found it necessary to stress repeatedly the unanimous support of the people at the moment when the authorities were trying to deal with the anarchy that was eventually to engulf the whole Provisional Government. This attitude to "the masses" was quite consistent with the views of a Lvov, Nekrasov, or Kerensky—though not of Miliukov. The weakness of the situation of the Provisional Government was already evident in the nature of this Declaration of April 26. Such legitimacy as the government could claim was in reality based on the precarious support and goodwill of the Petrograd "masses": in theory and formally the position was very different.

The Provisional Government that emerged from the Temporary Committee of the State Duma on March 2 received formal legitimacy from the Grand Duke Michael in his act of abdication of March 3 where it was described as having "come into existence at the initiative of the State Duma and being endowed with full power until such time as the Constituent Assembly . . . gave expression to the will of the people."[10] This act of abdication was drawn up by two eminent lawyers, Baron B. E. Nolde and V. D. Nabokov. It was a valiant attempt to endow the new government with legitimacy, and therefore with authority, by stressing its continuity both with the Duma and the emperor. Legitimacy, however, requires more than an ingenious formula if it is to exercise its function of bolstering authority. In plain fact, the new government had not come into existence at the initiative of the Duma. It was brought about by an agreement concluded, on the one hand, between certain individual members of the Duma who called themselves a "Temporary Committee of the Duma" but who had never been approved, let alone elected, by the Duma and, on the other, by the Executive Committee of the Petrograd Soviet. Moreover, neither the Duma nor the Grand Duke disposed of full powers in Russian constitutional law. The Duma merely enjoyed certain legislative powers in conjunction with the State Council and the emperor. The Grand Duke—even if one assumes that he inherited the powers of Nicholas II

10. Browder and Kerensky, I, doc. 101, p. 116.

by the abdication of the latter, which is open to doubt—could not have inherited "full power," but only the limited powers the emperor enjoyed after 1906. The formation of the Provisional Government was therefore a revolutionary act from the start.[11]

The Provisional Government would have been in a more solid and independent position had it really been appointed by and had it owed responsibility to the Duma. The problem of continuity would to some extent have been resolved. At this time the Duma still retained considerable popular support. Had the Duma survived it would have provided the basis of a legislative assembly that any government claiming to be democratic has to have. Without such a link to the Duma, the natural tendency was for the Provisional Government to become in the eyes of the public an executive government responsible to the Petrograd Soviet.[12] There were several factors that made it improbable that the Duma could in any circumstances assume the leadership at the critical moment, however theoretically desirable this course might have been.

First, although there had been some attempts both before the collapse of the tsar's ministry in February and immediately after it to turn the Duma into the leader of the revolution, in general the Duma leaders were at no time fired with any determination to do this.

Second, even Miliukov, for whom the Duma was theoretically the natural institution to lead and guide popular discontent, had doubts

11. For a full discussion of this question see S. P. Melgunov, *Martovskie dni 1917 goda* (Paris, 1961), pp. 356–367; and Katkov, *Russia 1917*, pp. 409–415.

12. The popular attitude toward the Duma before and just after the revolution is far from clear. There is no doubt that, perhaps for lack of an alternative, many sectors of discontent at different times looked to it with hope and confidence. Even if confidence in the Duma was fairly low among the masses, according to the police reports for October 1916 quoted in Grave, *Burzhuaziia* in docs. 58 and 75 (pp. 136–139, 168–169), the vigorous attacks by the Duma on the government at the end of the year certainly raised its stock by January 1917. In the early period of the Petrograd Soviet there was apparently a tendency among the Mensheviks to look upon the Duma as a kind of brake that would "prevent the revolution from serving as a foundation for a bourgeois dictatorship." (See Marc Ferro, "Les Débuts du soviet de Petrograd (27/28 février 1917 ancien style)" *Revue Historique*, CCXXIII, April/June 1960, pp. 353–380.) Above all, among the troops of the army in the field, as contrasted with the garrison troops of the capital, during the first weeks after the abdication confidence in the Duma was high—see N. E. Kakurin, ed., *Razlozhenie armii v 1917 godu* (Moscow-Leningrad, 1925), pp. 25–27. In this context it is worth recalling the argument of a right-wing defensist Social Democratic delegate to the First Conference of Soviets held in April that in effect an unwritten constitution had come into being under which the Provisional Government represented the ministry and the Soviet corresponded to the legislature or the legislative chamber, to which the ministry is responsible. This was not an unreasonable picture of the situation as it must have appeared to many at the time. See Melgunov, *Martovskie dni*, p. 401.

about the moral right of the "June 1907" Duma—a product of Stolypin's coup d'état—to claim leadership of the revolution. At any rate, writing later in exile he tended to treat the Progressive Bloc as having in some way expiated the "original sin" of the June 1907 Duma and of having thereby acquired (after transforming itself into the Provisional Government) a moral right to lead the revolution that the Duma had lacked.[13]

And, lastly, the Duma was overtaken to some extent even before the revolution by the mass organizations that had been forming within and outside it and that exercised the real political influence—the Progressive Bloc, zemgor, and the like—in a word: Liberation redivivum. The Duma died, therefore, with the revolution, for which it was not prepared and which it did not really, as an institution, desire.

In plain fact—as distinct from myth—the Provisional Government from the start owed its existence not to the Duma, but to an agreement made between certain individual members of the Duma who had long overthrown the Duma and who became the Provisional Government; and to the Petrograd Soviet, which even if it did not represent the "people," certainly acted under the pressure, and in the interests, of the mutinous garrison. This becomes quite evident from the comparison of two documents: first, the list of demands made by the Executive Committee of the Soviet on March 2 to the Temporary Committee of the Duma as a condition for its support of the new government; and second, the "guiding principles" of policy enunciated by the Temporary Committee of the Duma at the time when the Provisional Government was formed. The two documents are virtually identical.[14]

The "guiding principles" were much more than principles: they were concrete policies, laying down the course of action the future government would follow. It was these policies that predetermined the impotence of the government and laid the foundations for future anarchy. The two documents contained the same eight points, which can be summarized as follows:

(1) Amnesty in all cases of a political and religious nature, including terrorist acts and military revolts.

(2) The basic civil freedoms and the extension of political freedoms to persons serving in the armed forces.

(3) The abolition of all restrictions based on class, religion, and nationality.

(4) The immediate preparation for the convocation of the Constituent Assembly on the basis of universal equal direct suffrage and

13. P. N. Miliukov. Vospominaniia (1859–1917), II (New York, 1955), pp. 207, 215, 275, 303.
14. Browder and Kerensky, I, docs. 104 and 112, pp. 125–126, 135–136.

secret ballot, which would determine the form of government and the constitution of the country.

(5) Substitution of the people's militia for the police.

(6) Elections to the organs of self-government to be held on the basis of universal equal and direct suffrage and secret ballot.

(7) Military units that took part in the revolutionary movement to be neither disarmed nor withdrawn from Petrograd.

(8) Soldiers to be freed from all restrictions in the exercise of civil rights to which other citizens are entitled, while preserving military discipline on duty.

There is nothing to suggest any serious disagreement between the future ministers of the Provisional Government and the Soviet representatives—indeed, the basic attitude to authority that is implied in the "guiding principles" closely follows the main lines of the populist philosophy of Prince Lvov, Kerensky, and Nekrasov. It was an outlook more remote than that of Miliukov and Guchkov—though, according to Sukhanov, our main source for the meeting of March 1 at which this agreement took place, Guchkov was not present. Miliukov's efforts were mainly directed to settling the issue of the legitimacy of the new government, a point to which all other persons present seem to have been completely blind. His vain efforts were aimed at the hopeless task (in which no one else supported him) of preserving the Romanov dynasty. There had as yet been no abdication, and it was still conceivable that the Grand Duke Michael would consent to act as regent for the heir. Miliukov's chance of success on this issue was of course negligible. It was for the same reason—the desire to preserve continuity and therefore to invest the new regime with legitimacy—that he insisted that the Soviet should issue a strong appeal for the support of the Provisional Government and the maintenance of order.[15] On the main question, that of yielding to the mutinous and anarchical garrison, Miliukov apparently contented himself with pointing out the dangers and with inserting into the guiding principles some phrases on discipline.[16]

V. A. Maklakov maintains that the only hope of survival of the Provisional Government would have been to use the old machinery to

15. In the end the appeal was very lukewarm indeed and in qualified terms. See Browder and Kerensky, I, doc. 113, p. 136.

16. The extracts from Sukhanov are reprinted in Browder and Kerensky as doc. 102, I, pp. 117–124. Miliukov's account in his memoirs (*Vospominaniia*, II, pp. 306–309) differs in some respects from Sukhanov's. In particular he states that Prince Lvov was absent, while Sukhanov says he kept quiet. Miliukov also refers to a late appearance on the second day of Guchkov and says that Guchkov insisted on some expression of continuity between the Duma and the Provisional Government.

keep order and to replace the garrison with loyal troops.[17] Although this evaluation is no doubt correct hypothetically, it was in practice inconceivable that any member of this particular government would for a moment have thought of it. It was indeed contrary to the very being of the Russian *intelligent* to take action of this kind.

The term "dyarchy," referring to the dual role by the Provisional Government and its rival, the Soviet, launched by Guchkov (whose relations with the Soviet were strained from the very first) and then taken up by Lenin, scarcely fits the facts. There was indeed little dyarchy in the sense of rule by two opposed and conflicting institutions. The real dyarchy was more in the hearts of men than in rival institutions. The Provisional Government and the Soviet were at one in many respects, at any rate during the first Provisional Government— a fact correctly symbolized by the presence of Kerensky in the government. They started out on their path that was to lead to anarchy and mob rule jointly, not because one forced the other onto this course, but because they both ultimately believed in some of the same things. There were, of course, deep latent divisions between the two bodies—on the issue of the war above all. But the effect of these divisions was to become apparent only at a later stage.

The amnesty, the civil freedoms, the removal of discriminatory legislation, and the like were certainly fully carried out—too fully, perhaps, for a time of war and incipient anarchy. No one could doubt the intoxication of the first Provisional Government with liberty or deny it the right to its proud boast that no blood had been spilt. It deserves some credit for rescuing the ex-emperor in the early stages from the bloodthirsty clamor raised against him by the mob. On the other hand, the failure to remove the royal family to safety in Britain has been blamed equally on the hesitations of the Provisional Government and on those of Lloyd George: the former is alleged to have been restrained in its efforts through fear of popular feelings against the ex-emperor and empress, whereas the English premier is accused of pandering to radical opinion in England. This debatable question cannot be resolved here.[18]

17. *La chute du régime tsariste. Interrogatoires des ministres etc. du Gouvernement provisoire de 1917 (Comptes rendus sténographiques)*, préface de B. Maklakoff (Paris, 1927).

18. All the available evidence on the question was examined by S. P. Melgunov. See his *Sud'ba Imperatora Nikolaia II posle otrecheniia.* (Paris, n.d. [1944]), pp. 51–58 and 162–190. Melgunov was inclined to blame the Provisional Government rather more than the British. This much debated question should now be capable of final solution since the British cabinet papers for 1917 are open to public inspection.

There was, however, one respect in which the Provisional Government showed lack of understanding of the elementary principles of justice, and that was the case of the Commission of Inquiry into the collapse of the monarchy. True, the Commission was not a trial. But persons brought before it were in effect forced to incriminate themselves; and though possibly secure so long as the Provisional Government lasted, the accumulated evidence assured their execution once the Bolsheviks took over. The legal foundation of the commission is strange: insofar as the Provisional Government was a revolutionary government (which most of its members claimed it to be, even Miliukov, the one minister always most anxious to stress the need for continuity of legitimacy), it was entitled to exact vengeance on the officials of the fallen regime. But vengeance was expressly contrary to the very first point of the Government's "guiding principles": amnesty in respect of *all* political matters. Surely this could not have been intended to apply to revolutionary acts only? If, as indeed the Provisional Government claimed, this was a judicial inquiry in respect of breaches of the law and practice ("malfeasance in office")[19] as they were before the revolution, there can be no doubt that the inquiry went much further—to the extent of investigating and bringing into the open actions by ministers that had been perfectly legal and within their duties at the time. Among such actions were abuse of Article 87 of the Fundamental Laws, the use of police agents and provocateurs among revolutionaries, and the like. Much of the time spent by the Commission of Inquiry related precisely to such issues.

The Constituent Assembly was the keystone of the political arch. Insofar as there was to be any legitimation of the Provisional Government the Constituent Assembly alone could provide it. Everyone realized the urgency for summoning the Constituent Assembly. But those concerned, impressed by the solemnity of the whole matter, insisted on the most detailed preparations in order to assure the most equitable franchise possible. In hindsight such scruples may appear a terrible mistake, but at the time they accorded with the cardinal principle of the sanctity of the people's will. In this respect the Soviet was perhaps more realistic than the Provisional Government, in perceiving the need for speed in convoking a Constituent Assembly: indeed, it was as a concession to the Soviet that the government agreed that the Constituent Assembly should be convoked "no later than the middle of summer."[20] A council was set up on March 25, 1917, the expert members of which were to elect a drafting commission from among their

19. The act of March 11, 1917, setting up the Extraordinary Commission of Inquiry is doc. 165 in Browder and Kerensky, I, p. 194.
20. Browder and Kerensky, I, doc. 401, p. 434.

own number "for the preliminary technical study" of the complicated questions involved.[21] At the time the task seemed to require a few weeks: but two months elapsed before the second Provisional Government fixed the first meeting of the council for May 25.[22] The idealism and perfectionism of the Provisional Government were its own undoing: it never saw the Constituent Assembly as a device to secure its own legitimacy—indeed, there is nothing to indicate that, with the exception of Miliukov, any member of the Provisional Government from the outset entertained any doubts on the subject of the Government's legitimacy. As Prince Lvov told the first meeting of the council called to draft measures for the convocation of the Constituent Assembly, they would lay the foundation of the future order: "the Constituent Assembly must be the essence of all the spiritual and mental forces of the people, it must be the spokesman of their mind and heart." No effort was considered too great for the achievement of this ideal; but the practical results of this attitude, as is now so obvious, were catastrophic. The council could have done the work faster, the chairman (Kokoshkin) told its members, by appointing a small commission of experts to draft the electoral law. But the Provisional Government would not allow this procedure: it took the view that "it was not merely a matter of technical or theoretical perfection of the electoral law." The law should conform to the wishes and interests of all sections of the population, and these had to be ascertained.[23] The rest of the story is outside the scope of this paper: the date for the elections was fixed on June 14 for September 17, in the teeth of objections from the council members that November was the earliest possible date, since the compilation of the electoral rolls depended upon the completion of the *zemstvo* and municipal reforms which were then still in their early stages. On August 9 the date of the elections was postponed until November 12. The course of history might have been different if the members of the Provisional Government had been swayed less by populist idealism and more by a sense of practical urgency.

Enough has been said to show that the cardinal axis around which the faith of the Provisional Government revolved was the belief that the new order must be based on cooperation and trust in the people, and not on force. So far as its members were concerned this was the purpose of the revolution (which they had, after all, not wanted to happen when it did). This outlook was reflected in the government's actions; and its political philosophy may be said to have directly influenced the three major acts that sealed the fate of the Provisional Gov-

21. *Ibid.*, doc. 403, pp. 435–436.
22. *Ibid.*, doc. 405, p. 437.
23. *Ibid.*, doc. 407, pp. 438–441.

ernment: its policy towards the Petrograd garrison, the reform of the militia, and the reform of the administration. The course of action of the Provisional Government in these matters can only be sketched in outline here, in order to illustrate its basic political outlook, resting on confidence in the people as its central concept of the government of men, and the initial rejection of force, which was soon to lead to the fatal sequence of anarchy followed by force—reluctance, inadequacy, and the fact of being too late.

The decision to leave the Petrograd garrison its arms and to guarantee it from being sent to the front was already sealed in the first days by the promise contained in the "guiding principles." There is nothing to suggest that this promise had been wrung from reluctant ministers by the Soviet. Indeed, the whole mood of euphoria which characterized the first chaotic days, when realization dawned that the revolution had actually happened, was not conducive to sober thinking. Anarchical, idle, and demoralized, the Petrograd mutineers were to become an important element in Lenin's strategy. It may be that in theory the replacement of the garrison by the better disciplined and more loyal groups from the area of the front could have saved the Provisional Government: the question is academic, since the Government rejected any such move in the first days of its existence. Subsequently, even if it had desired to take such action, it was too late.

Consequences equally grave flowed from the decision of the first Provisional Government on the nature of the new instruments of coercion that the Government considered it right to create: the militia and the administrative machine. The legislation on these matters was put into effect under the direct control of the Prime Minister, Prince G. E. Lvov, who also held the post of Minister of the Interior. Lvov's somewhat sentimental populism was perhaps greater than that of his colleagues, but again the "guiding principles," as agreed on from the start, do not lead one to infer that Lvov met with any serious dissent from his colleagues. The details cannot be dealt with here: the main outline illustrates the political principles behind the actions. The immediate abolition of the death penalty (a sign of "genuine magnanimity" reflecting "the impulse of the popular soul," as Vladimir Nabokov wrote at the time) was a foregone conclusion, as were also a series of enactments designed to mitigate the severe and brutal Russian penal regime. The Department of Police was abolished on March 10, and the gendarmerie on March 19.[24] After a short period in which policing was entrusted to a temporary militia, a new militia was estab-

24. *Ibid.*, docs. 196 and 198, pp. 216, 217–218.

lished on April 17. It was placed under the *zemstvo* and municipal authorities, in contrast to the former police, which had been highly centralized; and its powers and responsibilities were carefully circumscribed in what on paper was a very liberal and fair police statute.[25]

But, unhappily, good intentions were not sufficient. The truth seems to be that the Provisional Government in the critical first days was more anxious to assert its good intentions than to give proof of any awareness of the danger of anarchy. Two documents, of March 4 and 6 respectively, illustrate this frame of mind most clearly. The first contains the decision of the Provisional Government to "remove temporarily from their duties governors and vice-governors"—the backbone of the existing administrative machine. Their powers were "temporarily" vested in chairmen of *zemstvo* boards; the question of their position in the provinces where *zemstvo* institutions did not exist was to be "left open for the time being." The second document, of March 6, is an appeal by the Provisional Government to the population. After reciting how the failure of the constitution granted in 1905 forced the people to take power in its own hands in 1917, it records that "the unanimous revolutionary upsurge of the people" led to the setting up of the Provisional Government thanks to the resolution of the Duma. There then followed two new promises, as well as others that were in part already contained in the "guiding principles": to carry the war to a victorious conclusion and to observe all agreements entered into with the Allies (neither of these provisions had been included on March 2 in the "guiding principles"), civil liberties, amnesty, democracy, the Constituent Assembly, and the like. The appeal ends: "In carrying out these tasks the Provisional Government is inspired by the faith that in so doing it will be carrying out the people's will, and that the whole people will support it in an honest endeavor to ensure the happiness of Russia. From this faith it draws its courage. Only in the friendly cooperation of all in its efforts does it see the guarantee for the triumph of a new order."[26] There is not a word in the whole document about the need for discipline, order, and obedience to the new authorities.

The reform of the administration envisaged not only the abolition of the gubernatorial system, but also the extension and democratization of the whole system of municipal government. It was an ambitious and idealistic scheme doomed to failure in face of the anarchy that the Provisional Government had done so much itself to encourage. For in

25. *Ibid.*, doc. 200, pp. 218–221.
26. *Velikaia oktiabr'skaia sotsialisticheskaia revoliutsiia. Dokumenty i materialy. Revoliutsionnoe dvizhenie v Rossii posle sverzheniia samoderzhaviia* (Moscow, 1957), I, docs. 323 and 326, pp. 422, 424–426.

truth it placed its faith in a greater response from a free people than that people, after centuries of despotic government, was capable of giving.[27]

There were two topics on which the "guiding principles" agreed upon with the Soviet had remained silent: land and war. Their omission provoked criticism in the Soviet from the left-wing minority.[28] Because these were the topics on which most controversy was likely to arise, their omission from the original agreement was perhaps inevitable. In the case of the land question the Provisional Government could quite properly take refuge in the view that this issue was so momentous in its consequences for the future of Russia that only the Constituent Assembly could decide it. It was not until after the end of the term of office of the First Provisional Government that any broad principles of future agrarian policy were enunciated. The Central Land Committee, at its first session, on May 20, stated its views on the "general direction" of the future land reform: these included nationalization of land for the benefit of the toiling peasants as a basic principle.[29] Since the villagers remained relatively quiet for the first few weeks of the new regime, this shelving of the question did not immediately raise serious difficulties. Such peasant disturbances as did arise, for example in the Kazan Province, were dealt with by the Provisional Government not by force, which was rejected, but by persuasion and exhortation.[30] It was only after April, with the tide of agrarian disorders mounting, that the Provisional Government felt compelled to take more concrete steps toward the solution of the land problem. On April 21 a series of Land Committees (first promised on March 19) were set up and charged with the task of collecting the information upon which the ultimate future of the land would be decided.[31] At that date it was still believed to be possible to hold off the assaults of the peasants.

The question of war and peace was to prove the key to the whole situation—though this was not yet apparent at the start of the first Provisional Government's term of office. Both the government and the

27. See Browder and Kerensky, docs. 219–272, I, pp. 243–316 for details of the municipal and *zemstvo* reforms and for details of the mounting chaos in the provinces.

28. A. Shliapnikov, *Semnadtsatyi god*, I, 2nd ed. (Moscow, n.d.), p. 197.

29. See Browder and Kerensky, II, doc. 476, pp. 538–544 and p. 543.

30. See *Revoliutsionnoe dvizhenie* (cited in note 26), I, doc. 35, p. 46, for a minute of a meeting of the Provisional Government of March 9.

31. Browder and Kerensky, II, docs. 467 and 471, pp. 524–525, 528–532. See also *ibid.*, doc. 474, pp. 534–536, which shows that at that date the Soviet was in complete agreement with the Provisional Government on the question of leaving all the ultimate decisions until the Constituent Assembly met.

Soviet majority were agreed at the outset on a broad policy of "war to victory," supported by a "democratized" army, liberated from the indignities which the old regime had inflicted upon it. But as time went on and the effects of Bolshevik propaganda and of impatience over the land problem grew in the army, the question of the war began to assume gigantic proportions. The whole issue as to whether the policy of democratization of the army also helped to bring about this aggravation is perhaps debatable; but there is no doubt that the policy had the effect of creating favorable conditions for the conduct of the antiwar propaganda to which the Bolsheviks were soon devoting their main effort and financial resources. The question of war aims is outside the scope of this paper. But the incident over Miliukov's note of April 18, which caused the reshuffling of the First Provisional Government, illustrates the explosive nature of the whole problem. The note, by its omission of phrases renouncing the intention to annex foreign territory after victory, could be interpreted by the radical minded as an affirmation of Russian enthusiasm to exact after victory the territorial compensations agreed on with the Allies. Miliukov's views on war aims and on Russia's national interests were certainly closer to Kadet policy than to the views of his more radical colleagues, who were much more inclined to accept as their own the Soviet view of "peace without annexations." Of course, Miliukov could argue that the reference to the strict observance of the treaties made with the Allies included in the Appeal of the Provisional Government published on March 6 (which was discussed above) also included by implication Russia's claim to the Straits after victory. But such an argument (though no doubt correct) would have been really impossible to maintain in the atmosphere prevailing at the time in the capital. And so, although the text of Miliukov's note had been approved by the whole government, the same government considered it expedient to jettison Miliukov.[32] Miliukov's note was now "explained" in an explanatory note of April 22, which embodied the hallowed renunciation of annexation, and the principle of a just peace based upon the self-determination of all peoples. Such was the success of the Provisional Government's political diplomacy that the explanation was accepted by the Soviet without qualification or dissent.[33] And yet, the harmony between the majority of the first Provisional Government and the Petrograd Soviet at this date probably reflected more accurately the realities of the situation than the incongruous presence

32. For the note of April 18 see Browder and Kerensky, II, doc. 964, p. 1098. The note of April 22 is reprinted as doc. 966, *ibid.*, p. 1100. For the reference to the Appeal of March 6, see note 26 above.

33. *Ibid.*, doc. 967, pp. 1100–1101.

in the Government of Guchkov and Miliukov. When these two ministers resigned, a coalition cabinet including Socialists was formed, and this change represented a recognition of what had been a fact from the start—that the first Provisional Government had never been a liberal government based (as it claimed) on the Duma, but a radical revolutionary government based on "the people."

What bound the members of the first Provisional Government together was not so much a political philosophy as an intellectual tradition. This was true of all, except for Guchkov and possibly Miliukov. They were the heirs of the Russian intelligentsia, alienated from all institutions of the old regime, leaning on "the people" with an almost religious faith, passionate for liberty without any strong sense that liberty can only exist within the framework of order. They had hated the old order, but they had also feared revolution. When it came they could not lead it because they were the slaves of their own vision of the people—a people only too easy a prey to extremism and anarchy. Because they rejected coercion, their only hope and indeed policy was to woo the people with concessions, exhortations, trust, and love—and they failed.

Writing in August or September 1915, Zinaida Gippius recorded this penetrating judgment in her diary:

The right—they understand nothing, they are going nowhere, and they refuse to let anyone else go anywhere.
The center—they understand, but they are going nowhere, they stand and wait (for what?).
The left—they understand nothing but are going like the blind without knowing whither or to what ultimate aim.[34]

So it came about that in March 1917 it was the blind who led the halt along to the final drama of October. This is not to condemn the Provisional Government, so much as to record that, being what they were, they could not have acted otherwise. The causes lie farther back than in the period between March and May 1917, or March and October 1917. There are many stages in the story: the failure of the moderate zemstvo movement around the turn of the century to achieve that degree of cooperation between society and the monarchy that it sought and that the monarchy repeatedly rejected; the success of the more extreme Union of Liberation movement that, in the shape of the October Manifesto of 1905, won a constitution which was, in Russian

34. Z. Gippius, Siniaia kniga. Peterburgskii dnevnik, 1914–1918 (Belgrade, 1929), p. 32.

conditions, unworkable; Stolypin's coup d'état of June 1907, which certainly made the Duma more workable, but which also alienated the more impatient and idealistic liberals from the Duma for which they had labored; and then, finally, the turning away during the war of the liberals to the wider mass organizations as instruments of influence that had the effect of undermining the one institution that rightfully should have become the center of authority when the monarchy fell—the Duma. These wider organizations—the Progressive Bloc, the *zemgor*, even perhaps the mysterious Masonic organization—provided a basis for unity that the more tightly knit institutions like the political parties could not provide. But it was a unity based on visions and on myths, rather than on concrete policies—"the people," "democracy," "government of confidence." There was danger in these visions, as events were to show. Pasternak most perceptively records the sense of "the people" in 1917. "The revolution burst forth against our will like a sigh that has been too long repressed. Everyone breathed again, was born again; all suffered transformation and complete change. One could almost say that there were two revolutions for each of us: one, the personal one, and the other the common one."[35] It would be quite untrue to say that the members of the first Provisional Government did not perceive the dangers inherent in this situation. But they obstinately believed, or persuaded themselves, or hoped, that the virtue and wisdom of the Russian people must triumph in the end.

As heirs of the intelligentsia the members of the first Provisional Government shared both its virtue and its main vice: the idealism; the innocent faith in the perfectibility of man; the detestation of violence and coercion; the love of freedom; the compassion for and the sense of debt to the people—but also the lack of practical sense in discerning Russian reality. "What right have we, the brains of the country, to insult with our rotten bourgeois distrust the wise, calm, and knowing revolutionary people?"—so wrote Alexander Blok in his diary on June 19, 1917.[36]

Two weeks later the Bolshevik dress rehearsal for October was in progress in the streets of Petrograd. It was Lenin, himself sprung from the intelligentsia (but who rejected, or who reinterpreted, the traditional virtues of the *intelligent*) who was soon to provide that discernment of Russian reality that his opponents lacked and to restore in a new form the overthrown autocracy.

35. Boris Pasternak, *Doktor Zhivago* (Ann Arbor, 1958), p. 148.

36. *Dnevnik A. A. Bloka, 1917–1921*, ed. P. M. Medvedev (Leningrad, 1928), II, p. 26.

The Political Ideology of the Leaders of the Petrograd Soviet in the Spring of 1917

— Oskar Anweiler

The Russian Revolution of 1917 has its victors, whose heirs still rule the country. It has its victims too, but fifty years after the event, their names survive mostly in archives. The historiography of the Russian Revolution is devoted, in the main, to the leading figures of the victorious party and to their actions, while the defeated have been swept away into the "dustbin of history" as Trotsky had prophesied on the night of the victorious October insurrection.[1] The power of these political dreamers, it has been often said, ran through their fingers like water. They have been called prisoners of their own fictitious ideology, men who did not understand the signs of the times. The representatives of "Socialist Democracy"—Tseretelli, Martov, Chernov, or Avksentiev, appear at best as champions of high ideals, as honest and sincere socialists, but also as men unwilling to strive for power and to use it unscrupulously. They stood in direct contrast to the two stars of October, Lenin and Trotsky, who subjected the social dynamics of the revolution to their political calculations. The usual judgment of historians is that the inevitability of the Bolshevik victory resulted from the failure of the democratic forces, and that this failure in turn derived from their political ideas, which, applied to Russia of 1917, proved illusory.

The critical attention of historians has been mainly directed at the politics of the socialist parties who from the February Revolution until autumn enjoyed a majority in the different public organizations and institutions; that is, the Socialist Revolutionaries and the Mensheviks who claimed to embody the "revolutionary democracy" as opposed to the "bourgeois democracy" of the liberals. This socialist center, which viewed itself as the left, has been put on trial by two different historical

Note: All dates in this article are given in Old Style.

1. I. L. Trotsky, *History of the Russian Revolution*, III (New York, 1932), p. 311.

persecutors. It has been blamed for lack of revolutionary energy and radical decisiveness, for example by O. H. Radkey, who demonstrates with grim pleasure and in precise detail all the mistakes and errors of the Socialist Revolutionary Party.[2] Or, on the contrary, it has been accused by Miliukov and the liberal-conservative Russian émigré writers of clinging to a particular class interest instead of showing readiness to assume all-Russian responsibility. The difference in expectations—already evidenced in 1917—toward the policies of the Soviet majority on the part of the Bolsheviks and the Liberals then revealed that "dilemma of ideas within the struggle for power" which afterwards resounds time and again in the memoirs of a Chernov or a Tseretelli.

It is the purpose of this paper to analyze the political ideas of the leaders of the "revolutionary democracy," that is, the leaders of the Soviet majority, in the first months of the revolution, insofar as they concern the vital question of state power and the establishment of a new political order in Russia.

The ideological dilemma of the majority parties in the spring of 1917 originated in the tension between former political goals, as laid down in doctrines at the beginning of the century and during the Revolution of 1905, and the new revolutionary situation. The crisis that resulted from this confrontation was resolved with the entrance of the socialist representatives into the Provisional Government—a process accompanied as well as impeded by a simultaneous confrontation with a new state model, the Soviet Republic, proclaimed by Lenin. Because in the spring and summer of 1917 the moderate Socialist parties had their political basis in the Soviets of Workers', Soldiers', and Peasants' Deputies, they suddenly found themselves closely bound to the existence and destiny of the soviets, although the soviets had previously assumed no importance either in their political programs or their concepts of the future state and society. Until October 1917, the non-Bolshevik socialists had not clarified their position toward the soviets; their factional splits revealed trends leading in divergent directions.

In general, the origin and the political structure of the Soviets of Workers' and Soldiers' Deputies of 1917 and, to a lesser degree, of the Soviets of the Peasants' Deputies are known, although some aspects still require research.[3] Among the soviets, the Petrograd Soviet was virtually alone to function as a political organ of countrywide importance, at least up to the time of the First All-Russian Conference (March 29 to April 3) and the First All-Russian Congress of Workers' and Soldiers'

2. O. H. Radkey, *The Agrarian Foes of Bolshevism* (New York, 1958).
3. Oskar Anweiler, *Die Rätebewegung in Russland, 1905–1921* (Leiden, 1958).

Soviets (June 3–24). But even after the formation of all-Russian central soviet organs, the Petrograd Soviet maintained in effect the political predominance established in the first days of the revolution. This fact proved later to be decisive for the victory of the Bolsheviks in execution of the October insurrection.

The initial stage in the development of the Petrograd Soviet extends from the period of the first meeting of the "Provisional Executive Committee" in the afternoon of February 27 to the formation of the first coalition cabinet on May 5. During these two months the Petrograd Soviet not only developed and consolidated its structure, but acquired new political self-confidence as an organ of political control that the "revolutionary democracy" exercised over the government.

Before proceeding to analyze the political ideology of the Petrograd Soviet in March–April 1917, we must sketch its political and social profile. Unfortunately, the sources at our disposal are not as abundant as they should be for a precise sociological analysis (a statement that might also be applied to the history of the soviet movement as a whole).

The representation ratio for the election of the deputies until the electoral readjustment of mid-April, gave a certain preference to the soldiers, who therefore enjoyed a majority in the plenary meetings. Among the workers, deputies of the big factories were at a numerical disadvantage compared to those of the smaller ones. Thus, the social physiognomy of the Petrograd Soviet in the first period was not predominantly proletarian in the Marxist sense, but rather peasant and petty bourgeois (because a relatively high proportion of the soldiers' deputies came from the middle ranks and had a higher education). Trotsky saw in this fact the main reason for the initial preponderance of the Socialist Revolutionaries in the Petrograd Soviet.

More important for the political function of the Soviet, however, was the fact that from the very beginning the control was mainly in the hands of socialist intellectuals who, as Trotsky again rightly maintained, created a sort of "reserve and shadow government."[4] Toward the end of March, only seven of the 42 members of the Executive Committee were workers. Besides such journalists as Sukhanov and Steklov, the Committee was dominated by socialist Duma deputies, as, for example, Chkheidze, Skobelev, and (after March 19) Tseretelli.

The predominance of intellectuals differentiated the 1917 Petrograd Soviet from its predecessor of 1905. The latter had originated as a strike committee and therefore never lost its character as an organ of worker "self-government." In 1917, by contrast, the structure of political parties,

4. Trotsky, *History of the Russian Revolution*, I (New York, 1932), p. 216.

emerging from illegal or semi-legal status, with their theoretical, tactical, and personal contradictions, overlapped with the fundamentally different structure of the soviets. The "pure" soviet principle, which Hannah Arendt has recently depicted as the antithesis of the party system,[5] existed only in the first elections to the Petrograd Soviet; the factions in the soviet constituted themselves along party lines. Political party leaders like Lenin, Trotsky, Chernov, and others managed immediately on their arrival from the emigration to secure a seat in the soviet. Before 1917, the conflict among the socialists in Russia had taken place less in the Duma than in the underground. Now it was brought into the open, into the arena of the Soviet.

This crystallization of the Soviet along party lines occurred already in March 1917. The process is interesting because it is symptomatic of the transformation of the soviets from a supra-party, revolutionary organ into a semi-parliamentary deputation of workers and the garrison, a body that embraced the entire spectrum of Russian socialism and its parties. By the end of March, all Russian and non-Russian socialist parties and groups of any importance were represented in the Executive Committee of the soviet, alongside trade union representatives, whether with a voting or merely a consultative vote. For the participants as well as for the non-socialist public at large, the whole embodied "revolutionary democracy." In the provincial soviets this process of crystallization along party lines took longer than in the capital cities of Petrograd and Moscow. In some localities, the political physiognomy of the soviets remained unclear even in the summer and autumn of 1917, not the least because at the beginning the contrasts between the local Bolshevik organizations and the other socialist parties were less pronounced.

All the socialist parties (in contrast to the anarchists) regarded the soviets as an organizing machinery for the activation and articulation of the political consciousness of the toiling masses in accord with their revolutionary party programs. This attitude led to fundamental difficulties: the tendency to organize and lead from "above" ran into the opposite pressure from "below." In the eyes of the soldiers and workers who were about to be organized by the parties assisted by the soviets, these improvised institutions of direct democracy were in most cases not substitutes for parliaments but rather revolutionary clubs and permanent assemblies of the revolutionary masses. The revolutionary *stikhiia* in the soviets and soviet-like committees was always on the alert. Already, during the April demonstrations in Petrograd one could observe an estrangement between the leadership of the Petrograd Soviet

5. Hannah Arendt, *On Revolution* (New York, 1963).

and parts of the working class and the garrison, both of which followed more radical slogans and sought to exert pressure on the Executive Committee of the Soviet. The quick settlement of the dispute, however, demonstrated that the authority of the soviet leadership was as yet unshaken.

In the early summer of 1917, the spread of Factory Councils (*fabrichno-zavodskie komitety*) produced in the form of the Central Council of the Petrograd Factory Committees, a political organ competing with the Petrograd Soviet. The Bolsheviks held in it a preponderance from the very outset. There was no fixed delimitation of functions between the Soviet and the Central Council of the Factory Committees, even though the former concerned itself mainly with political problems and the latter with questions of economics and internal factory issues.[6] Because they served the worker directly at his working place, their revolutionary influence increased in proportion as the Soviet became a permanent institution and lost close contact with the masses. In the eyes of the non-Bolshevik majority of the Soviet, the instability of the Factory Councils—their membership was undergoing constant change—demonstrated the lack of maturity of the Russian working class, its unpreparedness for "a dictatorship of the proletariat." For the Bolsheviks, on the contrary, it served as the basis of agitation. It was Lenin's and Trotsky's masterly tactic to connect their political program, aimed at taming and leading the revolutionary masses, with the *stikhiia* latent in the soviets and incited by the Bolsheviks since the spring of 1917, and in this manner to seize power. One might say that on the eve of October, the Bolsheviks retransformed the soviets from semi-parliamentary institutions into fighting organs.

The political situation that made this possible is generally referred to in the historiography of the Russian Revolution as "dyarchy" (*dvoevlastie*). This expression was no mere invention of Lenin in his "Letters from Abroad." It was used already in the first days of the revolution by adherents of bourgeois Duma parties and their affiliated newspapers as a means of combatting the ambitions of the Petrograd Soviet. The Soviet majority, however, rejected this expression. The division of power between the Provisional Government and the Petrograd Soviet is quite correctly regarded as a decisive and central fact, at least in the first months of the revolution. The issue of the future revolutionary authority in Russia also produced from the very outset divergent views within the Petrograd Soviet itself. These differences continued and were exacerbated until October.

6. See Paul H. Avrich, "Russian Factory Committees in 1917," *Jahrbücher für Geschichte Osteuropas*, NF, XI (1963), pp. 161–182.

Trotsky spoke of "the paradox of the February Revolution," referring to the voluntary renunciation by the Petrograd Soviet of the seizure
of power by the revolutionary democracy, possible at the time of the
fall of the monarchy.[7] On closer examination, however, this thesis proves
fictitious. Neither its real power potenial nor the spiritual prepared-
ness of the revolutionaries were such as to enable the Petrograd Soviet
in February 1917 to take over the government of the country alone.
Even the Bolsheviks in Petrograd were split on that question. On
March 1, only a minority in the Executive Committee of the Soviet
came out in favor of a Provisional Revolutionary Government by the
socialist parties, incidentally in a characteristic combination foreshadow-
ing that of October: three Bolsheviks, one Left SR, one Mezhdu-
raionnyi, two unaffiliated soldiers. The opposition—at that time standing
for a coalition government with the bourgeois groups—was nearly of the
same strength. As is known, the majority decided on March 2 for that
conditional support of the Provisional Government combined with a
simultaneous control of it by the "revolutionary soviet democracy,"
based on the formula *postolku-poskolku* (insofar as), which has entered the historical vocabulary as "dyarchy."

Since that time there has been no lack of explanations, justifications,
and naturally also accusations. In fact, these differences of opinion
began already in the first hours of the agreement which Chkheidze,
Sokolov, Steklov, and Sukhanov had worked out with the Duma Committee. Within the first three weeks of March—until the arrival of
Tseretelli from Irkutsk—the Soviet majority could not decide whether
to stress assistance to the Provisional Government or distrustful, vigi-
lant control. The *Izvestiia* of the Soviet, edited by Steklov, urged the
"hard" course, but this was more a hysterical reaction to alleged counterrevolutionary plots than a carefully established program. The Siberian
group of Mensheviks and Socialist Revolutionaries (the "Siberian Zim-
merwaldists") then on its way to the capital, looked in vain for clear
lines in the announcements of the Soviet organ. Considering, on the one
hand, the revolutionary atmosphere, the external circumstances, and
the capability of the Soviet leaders and, on the other, the urgent problems of the day, no such clear lines could have been expected.

Posterior historical analysis, however, may find some reason for the
decision of the Soviet majority to assume the stance of "the controlling
organ of revolutionary democracy," at some distance from the Provisional Government. The seemingly most obvious explanation is the
weightiest. That handful of socialist intellectuals, whose very names
were hardly familiar to the public, grew frightened of the burden of

7. Trotsky, *History of the Russian Revolution*, I, p. 171.

power, feeling that exercise of government demands more than a few revolutionary ideas and skillful tactics. The hour of the collapse of the monarchy and situation in the streets of the capital were anything but conducive to the seizure of power. The experiences of the Revolution of 1905 were not sufficient to produce a concrete plan of power seizure. The form of the organization itself, namely the soviet, as Trotsky correctly remarked, was "beyond discussion,"[8] but the revolutionary tradition as handed down from the Petersburg Soviet of Workers' Deputies of 1905 did not contain the political program of a government based on soviets. The almost simultaneous formation of the Duma Committee, which in spite of its own insecurity and casual composition could better claim to act as the representative of the whole state, relieved the Soviet leaders in the early stages from the responsibility of making an unequivocal decision on the question of power seizure.

In his speech at the All-Russian Conference of the Soviets of Workers' and Soldiers' Deputies on March 30, Steklov gave a precise description of the situation:

Why is it that at that moment we did not consider the question of taking power into our hands? I will attempt to answer this . . . At the time when this agreement [with the Temporary Committee of the Duma] was contemplated, it was not at all clear as to whether the revolution would emerge victorious, either in a revolutionary-democratic form or even in a moderate-bourgeois form. Those of you, comrades, who were not here in Petrograd and did not experience this revolutionary fever cannot imagine how we lived: The Duma was surrounded by soldiers' platoons that did not even have any noncommissioned officers; we did not have time even to formulate any political program for the movement and at the same time we learned that the ministers were at large and were convening somewhere, either in the Admiralty, or in the Mariinskii Palace. We were not informed on the general attitude of the troops or the attitude of the Tsarskoe Selo garrison, and it was reported that they were marching on us. There were rumors that five regiments were marching from the north, that General Ivanov was leading 26 echelons: shooting resounded through the streets, and we had grounds to assume that this weak group that was surrounding the palace would be routed. We expected from minute to minute that they would arrive, and, if they did not shoot us, they would take us away. However, we sat proudly, like ancient Romans, and conferred, but there was no complete conviction whatsoever in the success of the revolution.[9]

8. *Ibid.*, p. 158.
9. *Izvestiia,* no. 32, April 4, 1917, in R. P. Browder and A. F. Kerensky, eds., *The Russian Provisional Government, 1917,* III (Stanford, Calif., 1961), pp. 1223 ff.

The ideological justification for a decision taken in response to a concrete situation was soon elaborated. But the theoretical explanation for abstaining from government and assuming the position of a controlling organ was not merely a kind of posterior rationalization of spontaneous decisions. It was actually rooted in the world of political ideas of the socialist parties before 1917. The discussions in the newspapers of the Soviet majority or in the Petrograd Soviet itself to justify the attitudes of the "revolutionary democracy" and simultaneously to counter charges of inactivity, rested, above all, on the ideological thesis of the "bourgeois" character of the Russian Revolution, which forbade the participation of socialists in the bourgeois government in the interests of the forthcoming socialist revolution. Steklov called this in his speech of March 30 the "basic aspect" of the decision of the Executive Committee not to attempt to take power:

> *You understand that the attempt on the part of the extreme revolutionary democratic forces to take power into their own hands can have a historical basis and can rely on the support of the broad national masses only in the event that moderate liberalism becomes bankrupt while carrying its program into effect. And it stands to reason that when this moment arrives, when the liberal bourgeoisie turns out to be politically incapable of carrying out its own political program and not simply satisfying the demands of the national masses, and if it meets with decisive opposition in carrying out its own program and proves to be incapable of realizing the aspirations and demands of the working masses, then at this moment we may be confronted with the question of the revolutionary democratic forces seizing power against the desires and the will of broad sections of the bourgeoisie. Such a situation did not exist at the moment, and it does not exist even now. On the contrary, we have seen that the privileged [tsensovaia] bourgeoisie, whose representatives constitute the majority in the Provisional Government, had come to the realization that the time was such and the forces of the revolution were such that it was necessary for them to make broad, democratic concessions.*[10]

The situation after the overthrow of the tsarist regime seemed to match exactly the prognosis Martov had made in March 1905. At that time he had spoken of a possible situation in Russia "where the struggle of the proletariat to secure and develop the revolution might coincide with the struggle to take power." For this eventuality the socialists should be prepared by

10. *Ibid.*, p. 1224.

*organizing the proletariat in a party standing in opposition to the bour-
geois democratic state. And the best way to create such an organization
is to influence the bourgeois revolution from below by the pressure of
the proletariat against the democracy in power. The class which is prepared for the role of an oppositional motor force* (dvigatel') *of the revolution will also play the role of its political master should the historical
events, against its ambitions, bring it close to governmental power.*[11]

The revolutionary tactics formulated by Martov, Dan, and Martynov
in 1905 preshaped the relation between the soviets and the Provisional
Government during the February Revolution. The spontaneous spread
of "revolutionary self-government" (*revoliutsionnoe samoupravlenie*),
operating everywhere in the open, was thought of as a means of liquidating autocracy, but also as an instrument of the "pressure" against the
bourgeois democracy that hastened the revolution toward socialism.[12]
Even the historical reminiscences of the French Revolution of 1789 and
of the Commune of Paris of 1871 played their part in forming "revolutionary communes" to disorganize the governmental apparatus and to
prepare the soil for a broad proletarian mass party.

If one looks for an ideological basis for the attitudes of the Soviet
leaders during the first hours it might be found in the above-mentioned
revolutionary strategy of the Mensheviks of the spring and summer of
1905. Sukhanov, who had decisively shaped the Soviet program until
the middle of March, was in the same boat with the Menshevik Internationalists led by Martov. Martov himself, although criticizing the
policy of the Soviet majority from May to October, had arrived by
July—in accord with his basic attitudes—to the demand that "revolutionary democracy" in the form of soviets, embodying the "political
self-government of the people" and the "new revolutionary statehood,"
take over full political power. The "oppositional motor force" of the
revolution was to become its political master.[13]

This radical Menshevik tendency is not usually given sufficient consideration by historians of the Russian Revolution. As an organized
power it remained always in the minority in the Petrograd Soviet. But
its ideological influence was in the first three weeks of the February
Revolution stronger than at any time later: an influence favored by the
feverish revolutionary excitement of the early days, by the fear of
counterrevolutionary attacks, and by the political vacuum within the

11. *Iskra*, no. 93, March 17, 1905, p. 4.
12. *Wiener Arbeiter-Zeitung*, August 24, 1905, cited in Lenin, *Collected Works*,
IX (London, 1962), pp. 224 ff.
13. See Martov's speech of July 17 and at the Democratic Conference in September, in *Revolutsiia 1917 goda; khronika sobytii* (Moscow-Leningrad, 1923–1924),
III, p. 192, IV, pp. 385 ff.

socialist camp, whose recognized leaders were still absent from the capital.

As the socialist party groupings in the Soviet consolidated into parliamentary factions and the ideological positions gained ground, the moderate majority tried to systematize the unsettled relations between the Soviet and the Provisional Government. This occurred particularly after the return of the Siberian group whose main representatives—Tseretelli, Dan, and Gots—together with Chkheidze and Skobelev henceforth took over the Soviet Executive Committee.

The basic ideological conviction that the revolution was "bourgeois" also prevailed among the new leaders of the Soviet majority—less among the Socialist Revolutionaries, more among the Mensheviks. But this was only a general framework and a form of ideological insurance. Among Soviet leaders, practical calculations, emerging from the concrete situation in which revolutionary Russia found itself, were more influential than abstract considerations. In the case of Tseretelli particularly, the all-Russian national tasks of "revolutionary democracy" emerged early, especially as concerned the fact of war. Among the leaders of the Menshevik-Socialist-Revolutionary Soviet bloc it was Tseretelli who recognized best the necessity for "revolutionary democracy" not to confine itself to one-sided class interests but to assume responsibility for the whole nation confronted with the question of war and peace. In his "Memoirs" he speaks of the "psychological break" that he and his friends experienced in the first days of March when deciding on the question whether or not to permit passage of a train with reservists moving westward from Vladivostok to the front. "Of all practical questions which the revolution had posed us, we were least prepared for this. But we felt that the old, accustomed formulas must be supplemented with new ones, in accord with the exigencies of the revolution."[14] The train was allowed to proceed. Thus was laid the foundation of the "revolutionary defense of the country." On March 22 this line was accepted also by the Soviet Executive Committee and ten days later by an overwhelming majority at the All-Russian Conference of Soviets. The resolution drafted by Tseretelli and adopted by a majority of 325 votes against 57 with 20 abstentions, stated:

The revolutionary people of Russia will persist in their efforts to bring about an early conclusion of peace on the basis of the brotherhood and equality of free peoples. An official renunciation of all programs of conquest on the part of all governments is a powerful means of terminating the war on such conditions.

14. I. G. Tseretelli, *Vospominaniia o Fevral'skoi revoliutsii,* I (Paris-The Hague, 1963), p. 24.

As long as these conditions have not been met, as long as the war continues, the Russian democracy recognizes that the downfall of the army, the weakening of its resistance, its strength, and its combat potential, would be the heaviest blow to the cause of freedom and to the vital interests of the country. For the purpose of [achieving] the most energetic defense against all external attacks on revolutionary Russia, and against attempts at interference in the further successes of the revolution, the Conference of the Soviets of Workers' and Soldiers' deputies calls on the democratic forces in Russia to mobilize all the vital forces of the country in all the spheres of its national life to reinforce the front and the rear. This is an imperative demand, dictated by the present moment in the life of Russia; it is essential to the success of the great revolution.[15]

The attitude of the soviets toward the Provisional Government also received at about this time a clearer theoretical formulation. The new stress in Tseretelli's speech at the conference of April 3 lay on "the unity of national will." "The national masses," he said, "understood the nature of the immediate task and when they advanced the democratic republic as the platform on which all the people of Russia agreed, they understood that this republic would be a bourgeois republic, but that, on the other hand, it would also be democratic, and one which, at that given moment, could unite around itself the proletariat, the peasantry, and all the groups of the bourgeoisie which understood the immediate task before the whole nation."[16]

This policy could also be interpreted in the way Trotsky did when he wrote that at the moment of revolutionary ascendancy the moderate Soviet leaders did not feel themselves called upon "to assume leadership of the people—they preferred to form the left wing of the bourgeois order."[17] He omitted, however, to add that this bourgeois order represented in the eyes of the leaders of the Soviet and even in those of the Bolsheviks in Russia led by Kamenev, an enormous revolutionary achievement against the tsarist regime, a decisive step forward on the way to a socialist democracy. The discussions at the All-Russian Conference of the Soviets showed surprising unanimity on the relationship between Soviets and Provisional Government. The final resolution was unanimously adopted, being supported even by the Bolsheviks. It stated, among other things:

The Conference recognizes the necessity of gradually gaining political control and influence over the Provisional Government and its local

15. *The Russian Provisional Government*, II, p. 1084.
16. *Izvestiia*, no. 35, April 8, 1917, cited in *The Russian Provisional Government*, III, pp. 1226 ff.
17. Trotsky, *History of the Russian Revolution*, I, p. 171.

organs in order to induce it to pursue the most energetic struggle against counterrevolutionary forces, to take the most resolute steps in the direction of a complete democratization of all walks of Russian life, and to make preparations for universal peace without annexations and indemnities based on the self-determination of nations.

The Conference appeals to the democracy to lend its support to the Provisional Government without assuming responsibility for all the work of the government, in so far as the Government is working steadfastly in the direction of regulating and expanding revolutionary gains and in so far as the formulation of its foreign policy is based on the renunciation of ambitions of territorial expansion.[18]

Only Lenin's unconditional fight against the Provisional Government put an end to this attempt at a common policy by the "revolutionary democracy."

The urgent problem was, however, how to shape a long-range relation between the local soviets—at the end of March there were 140 of them, not counting the army committees and some isolated peasant soviets—and the local state organs, as well as between the Petrograd Executive Committee and the Provisional Government. This question could be answered only in a partial manner by the ideological principles. During the first weeks of the revolution a bearable coexistence between the soviets and the local institutions of the Provisional Government had been worked out, whereby instructions from Petrograd warned the local soviets not to assume governmental functions. The leadership of the Petrograd Soviet, however, could not be absolved of the charge of "anarchy" and keeping a constant threat over the Provisional Government, for the claim to a permanent control over the activities of the Government caused continuous political tensions and conflicts.

The responsible leaders of the Soviet majority were not oblivious of the dilemma resulting therefrom. They hoped, as the resolutions of the April Conference and the contact with the Government through the Liaison Commission proved, to harmonize the policy of the Provisional Government with the aims and demands of the Soviet majority. By and large, this led toward a common platform of the socialist center and the left liberal democratic circles, in which case the Provisional Government would not have to fear mistrustful control organs in the Soviet but, on the contrary, could regard them as a benevolent auxiliary.

This new constellation seemed to appear with the formation of the first coalition government at the beginning of May. Its establishment demonstrated within a few days the weakening of the old ideological formulas but also how half-heartedly the socialist majority parties strove

18. *The Russian Provisional Government*, III, p. 1229.

for political power. Participation in a bourgeois government required most of all that the Mensheviks revise their previous theory. They justified their decision in the first place with the exigencies of war and the defense of the revolution. "The Executive Committee realized that Russian revolutionary democracy, bearing on its shoulders the burden of the revolution, could not suffer to see its work ruined. It had to assume responsibility for the salvation of the country."[19] It is typical that Tseretelli, who soon after the revolution approved privately of a national democratic front of socialists and left liberals, now shrank from direct participation in the Government and agreed to the inevitable only when there was no alternative.

The fact that on the question of a participation of the Soviet majority parties in the government opinions partly contradicted former political attitudes—Sukhanov, for example, advocated a coalition—reveals once again the ideological transitory stage at which the Mensheviks had arrived since the February Revolution. Tseretelli feared that the socialist ministers would disappoint the hopes of the masses supporting the soviets and thereby weaken the influence of the Soviet majority to the advantage of the "maximalistic" tendencies of the left. The Petrograd Soviet leaders were aware of the fragile foundation on which they were standing but they had nothing else. This explains why the socialist ministers in the coalition government were linked to the Executive Committee, first of the Petrograd Soviet, and then of the All-Russian Soviet Congress. "The pressure from below" on the bourgeois Provisional Government originally intended by the soviets, transformed itself henceforth into conditional cooperation, but even that was half-heartedly exercised. The parties of the Soviet majority were not prepared to assume the leading role in the coalition government and fully to exploit the semi-parliamentary basis which at this time they still retained in the soviets.

Such a policy would have required two conditions: a clear line of separation from the Bolsheviks and a simultaneous readiness to put into power a pure socialist government composed of the majority Soviet parties if the moderate circles of the bourgeois liberals should have refused further cooperation. The majority of the Menshevik-Socialist Revolutionary leadership was at that time not prepared to accept either of these conditions. The Leninist left was not excluded from the ranks of "revolutionary democracy," in spite of the break it had made with "revolutionary democracy" following Lenin's "April theses," and in spite of the evident signs that it intended to pursue tactics leading to civil

19. *Izvestiia*, no. 56, May 3, 1917.

war. It was not excluded even after the insurrection in July. The common revolutionary tradition of Russian socialism proved stronger than the danger of a dictatorship from the left, which was increasingly felt but until October not really recognized in all its dimensions.

On the other hand, the socialist center, especially its Menshevik nucleus opposed until autumn a homogeneous government of the Soviet majority and the withdrawal of cooperation with the bourgeois left. The First All-Russian Congress of Soviets held in June adopted with a majority of 543 votes against 126 with 52 abstentions a resolution rejecting the seizure of power by the soviets at that stage of the revolution as detrimental because "it would repel all the elements of the population which might still serve the cause of revolution."[20] The burden of undivided responsibility for war and revolution seemed to be too heavy for the socialists. Because of the growing economic disorder and the need for social reforms—especially in rural Russia—the active assistance of the *zemstvo* intelligentsia, of the technical and administrative middle class, and of the bourgeois entrepreneurs as well, could not be dispensed with. These forces, however, were mainly concentrated in the organs of urban and rural self-government, not in the soviets. Lenin's slogan "All power to the soviets" ran into the resistance of the socialists striving for a broad democratic basis as leading to the virtual exclusion of certain classes, among them the peasants, since the soviet organization in the villages was still but poorly developed.

Here a final dilemma arose, which the democratic socialists of the center were unprepared to solve if only because they were guided by the political model of the parliamentary republic, which, even in 1917, appeared to them as the unique form of statehood of a socialist society. In this, Russian socialists, with the exception of unimportant left maximalistic groups, followed the example set by the European socialist parties, for whom the parliamentary system, with all its faults, had become increasingly an axiomatic ingredient of political ideology. Until Lenin's "April theses," the Soviets of 1905 had left virtually no traces on the governmental and social thought of the Russian Marxists and socialists. What, therefore, was to be done with the soviets once the revolution had consolidated itself and a stable political order had been established?

The parties of the old soviet majority were spared the necessity of formulating an answer to this question because the Bolshevik October Revolution had made it irrelevant. But there can be no doubt that,

20. *Pervyi Vserossiiskii s"ezd sovetov rabochikh i soldatskikh deputatov 1917 g.,* I (Moscow, 1930), p. 286.

from the summer of 1917, the moderate socialists—in contrast to the Menshevik Internationalists around Martov and the Left Socialist Revolutionaries—not only were disinclined to assign to the soviets any functions in the future organization of the state, in the sense in which Lenin did, but that they envisioned their role as revolutionary organs of "toiling democracy" in purely provisional terms. With the convocation of the Constituent Assembly and the consolidation of organs of local self-government, the tasks of the soviets would be fulfilled. A parallel with the fate of the soviets in the German November 1918 Revolution comes to mind.

The difference lay in the fact that in Russia the fate of the socialist center was indissolubly connected with that of the soviets. The revolution had not yet produced a national parliament by the time the basis of the moderate socialists within the soviets had become so narrow that the Bolsheviks in the October Revolution could pretend to act on the ground of "soviet legality" and claim pseudo-democratic legitimacy. The break in the "revolutionary democracy" proved irreparable. Looking back, the Soviet leaders of 1917 acknowledged that their worst political mistake and the main reason for Lenin's victory was their failure not to have recognized this break until it was too late.

Comment by Bertram D. Wolfe on — "The Political Thought of the First Provisional Government" by Leonard B. Schapiro and "The Political Ideology of the Leaders of the Petrograd Soviet" by Oskar Anweiler

The choice of reporters and subjects for this session springs from the notion of *dvoevlastie* or "dyarchy," Mr. Schapiro representing the Provisional Government and Mr. Anweiler the Soviet. It must be said that whatever their difference of temperament, background, natural audience, and language, they have cooperated with each other at least as closely as Kerensky and Tseretelli, and have refrained from using on each other the cautious formula of "support insofar as . . ."

Actually, as both reporters have implied, there were not two powers, since only one of them commanded great mass prestige but was reluctant to take power, while the other greatly desired power but commanded little support from the barracks and the street. Hence the two together, in mutual if uneasy collaboration, made up the "Provisional Government" in the broader sense of that term.

I should like to examine the ideology and source of power that under-lay both institutional forms of the so-called dyarchy, and for this pur-pose shall address myself principally to two points: (1) the ideology, or rather the moods, of the barracks and the street, where I think the real power lay; and (2) the problem of "the continuity of power," as Mr. Schapiro called it, or, as I should prefer to call it, the problem of legitimacy.

In short, to the two forces represented by our two reporters, the official Provisional Government and the Soviet, I am adding a third to which both they, and the Bolsheviks as well, appealed, which for brevity we can call the *stikhiia*—the elemental force.

Nowhere in Europe was there greater hostility toward the educated classes, from which the leadership of both government and soviet were drawn, than there was in the villages of Russia. When the peasants came from the villages to the city to work in the factories, or to loaf in the barracks of Petrograd, they brought this suspicion and hostility with them.

The two leading bodies, the Duma Committee and the Soviet Execu-tive, negotiated with each other and came to agreements on a number of matters. But we must note that the ministers of the Provisional Government continued to act pretty much as their own judgment dic-tated, or as they were moved to act by pressures coming from the street. On the other hand, Soviet decisions, majorities, and attitudes remained fluid, too, changing from day to day in response to the changing moods and day-to-day accidental makeup of that vast mass meeting called the Soviet and the scarcely less fluid and unwieldy Executive Committee. They too felt the pressure and influence of that underlying third power, the *stikhiia*. Now they made attempts to enlist its support, again to placate it, and yet again to restrain and direct its reactions. But always the *stikhiia* made itself felt.

The downfall of Foreign Minister Miliukov is a typical example of how the street asserted itself. To be sure, Lenin and his partisans did their best to stir up and utilize this reaction of the street, but the street acted on impulses of its own, particularly the soldiers from the bar-racks acted out of an obscure feeling that the repudiation of the Foreign Minister and his pledge to carry out prior agreements with Russia's allies would somehow make the continuation of the war by Russia impossible. Most of the major actions of the barracks and the street in 1917 flowed from this same deeply rooted desire to get out of the war, now that the apparatus of compulsion and consent, of command, obedience, and discipline had broken down.

This brings us to the problem of the unexpected and sudden rupture of legitimacy in the midst of total war. Total war is a stern and jealous god that demands of a people automatic, traditional, unquestioning, total obedience. Total war demands, too, an unparalleled effort on the part of society to find or create charismatic leaders and to organize with unprecedented strain and imagination the total mobilization of men, money, materials, and emotions. The last tsar was no charismatic leader, nor was he capable of finding anyone equal to the tasks of total war or willing to entrust power to such a leader had one offered himself. After Nicholas fell, neither a Guchkov nor a Kerensky nor a Tseretelli nor a Martov nor any other of the individuals who made up the complex of Provisional Government and Soviet, was comparable to a Lloyd George in England or a Clemenceau in France. Thus the continuation of total effort in the war was complicated alike by the rupture of legitimacy, by the lack of charismatic or even adequately dynamic leaders, and by the lack of the will of the people to continue the all-out effort, the strain, the sacrifices, the unquestioning loyalty and obedience that total war requires.

Even in time of peace, it is hard enough to organize a new order after the legitimacy of the old has been ruptured. But during a time of total war, one involving prolonged stalemate and serious reverses, the task required superhuman wisdom, a large measure of consensus, and a grant of more than ordinary trust and credit by masses of men who were bewildered and confused by the breakdown of their traditional institutions, traditional leadership, and traditional habits of obedience.

The tsar fell because some soldiers impulsively and unexpectedly to themselves, disobeyed the command of their officers to fire on a demonstrating crowd. It was fear of punishment for their violation of discipline that frightened the demoralized soldiery, causing them to appeal to other regiments, give up their rifles and seek to lose themselves in the crowds. And the same fear caused the mutineers to look eagerly for larger justifications and meanings for their first impulsive act.

If order were restored they would be doomed. One of the reasons for the well-aimed, "accidental, stray bullets" that killed young officers and even the high officer on an inspection tour in an automobile with War Minister Guchkov, was that the soldiers were frightened but with weapons in their hands. They had violated discipline unexpectedly even to themselves. Fearing punishment, they asked the Duma Committee, the Soviet, and the unknown spokesmen of unfamiliar parties to give their mutinous action sanction, legitimation, and guarantees that punishment would not follow. All these things they got in full measure.

After a moment of hesitation and fear, society gave them celebration and glorification. Men who had disobeyed orders learned that they were conquering heroes who had freed the nation from unbearable chains. With adulation came self-confidence, whereupon the problem arose of discipline and control by their frightened and inexperienced officers (most of the officers in these inactive reserves were like the men scratched together from the bottom of the barrel). Discipline became an insoluble problem from that moment. Moreover, their desire to avoid transfer to the front was now proclaimed a revolutionary duty, for they were the guardians of the glorious revolution they had wrought.

Their deeds were welcomed by the men who had been conspiring at Court and in the Duma circles, and in the *zemgor* or War Industries councils, to replace Nicholas II by a more active and able tsar with advisers—themselves—deemed better fitted to the demands of total war.

As was the habit of the Russian "public," they thought in terms of analogy with French revolutionary history. Since the French Revolution had begotten victorious armies that swept over Europe and great military leaders such as Carnot and Napoleon, they persuaded themselves that this revolution too would beget invincible armies, victorious generals, and glorious victories. They forgot that France was at peace and prospering when its revolution occurred and that its revolutionary wars did not begin until the third year of revolution, while Russia was in its third year of an exhausting and indecisive struggle that had worn out its human and material resources. The French peasant, as Lewis Namier has reminded us, went to the front to retain the land he had seized, while the Russian peasant in uniform deserted the front to go home and seize his share of the land.[1]

In order to illuminate the moment of anarchy when disobedient soldiers from the demoralized Petrograd reserves brought on the downfall of the tsar, I turn to a close and highly articulate observer, Vladimir Stankevich. His memoirs are particularly revealing on the relationship between the Provisional Government, the Soviet, and the *stikhiia*. He writes:[2]

Officially they celebrated, glorified the revolution, cried hurrah to the fighters for freedom, adorned themselves with red ribbons and marched under red banners . . . Every one said we, our revolution, our victory, and our freedom. But in their hearts, in solitary talks—they were terrified, trembled, felt themselves prisoners of a hostile elemental force [stikhiia] that was moving in some unknown direction. Bourgeois circles of the Duma who essentially had created the atmosphere that called forth the explosion were completely unprepared for such an explosion.

1. L. B. Namier, *Avenues of History* (London, 1952), pp. 6–7.
2. V. B. Stankevich, *Vospominaniia 1914–1919 g.* (Berlin, 1920), pp. 70–71. What follows is from pp. 71–77.

There follows a picture of Rodzianko, "that ponderous nobleman," striving to walk with dignity through the disorderly mob of soldiers filling all the corridors of the Tauride Palace, his face marked with suffering and despair as he went out to address fresh detachments of arriving soldiers as "heroes." "Officially this was supposed to mean that 'the soldiers have come to support the Duma . . . ,' but in fact the Duma was eliminated from the outset."

This is particularly interesting since Stankevich himself was the first officer to lead his own regiment in good order, drums beating and flags flying, to the Duma to offer it support, an event which so moved Chkheidze that he fell on his knees and kissed the banner that Stankevich presented on behalf of the regiment. Clearly, the Chairman of the Soviet (Chkheidze was a leading socialist in both bodies) feared the disorderly soldiery too and devoutly hoped that this first orderly act of an army detachment might be a portent of things to come.

Stankevich looked at the soldiers filling the corridors of the Tauride Palace, and into the dining hall where

All day and all night the soldiers were welcome to eat by turns without paying anything . . . The soldiers sat concentratedly chewing, not letting their rifles out of their hands, not even speaking to one another, not sharing their impressions yet herdlike seeming to possess some common feeling, thinking in their own individual fashion each in his own special way, incomprehensible, inaccessible to the understanding.

The officers themselves were demoralized by the sudden turn of events that had broken all rules of order and discipline appropriate to a modern army.

It was not a matter of Orders No. 1 and 2 or any other formal measures . . . It was the fact that the soldiers, breaking discipline, left the barracks not merely without their officers but even despite their officers, and in many cases against their officers, even killing some of them who tried to fulfill their duty. And now by universal, popular, official acclaim, obligatory for the officers themselves, the soldiers were supposed to have realized by this a great deed of emancipation. If this was indeed a heroic exploit, and if the officers themselves now proclaimed it, then why had they not themselves led the soldiers out onto the streets—for you see that would have been easier and less dangerous for them than for the soldiers. Now after the victory is won, they adhere to the heroic feat. But is that sincere and for how long? You see, during the first moments they were upset, they hid themselves, they changed into civilian clothes . . . Even though next day all the officers returned. Even though some of the officers came running back and joined us five minutes after the going out of the soldiers, all the same it was the soldiers who led the officers in this, and not the officers the soldiers. And those five minutes opened an impassable abyss cutting off the troops from all the profoundest and most fundamental presuppositions of the old army.

(Actually Stankevich is talking of himself in particular when he speaks of officers who hid themselves for only five minutes. When he heard that his soldiers had left their barracks he began to run toward the barracks, but a junior officer stopped him with the words, "Don't go there; dead officers are lying in the doorway and soldiers shoot at other officers as they appear." He hid then for a few minutes, but overcame his fear and went to his regimental mess hall. He found only a few soldiers drinking tea, the rest being out in the streets. He began by rallying those he found, and they formed the nucleus for the first march of a disciplined regiment to the Tauride Palace. But his regiment, too, had been out, and he had been away and had hidden himself for some five minutes, so that between his reconstituted regiment and the old army there was the same impassable abyss.)

Under what slogans had the soldiers gone out? They had gone out obeying some obscure mysterious voice, then with visible indifference and coldness they afterwards permitted to be hung upon them all possible slogans. Who led them when they conquered Petrograd? When they burned the district court? Not a political thought, not a revolutionary slogan, not a conspiracy, and not a mutiny. But an elemental movement that suddenly reduced the whole old regime to ashes with nothing left over: both in the cities and in the provinces, and the police power, the military power, and the power of self-government. Unknown, mysterious, irrational, welling up out of deepest layer of popular feeling, suddenly the street overflowed with a grey mass, bayonets sparkled, shots rang out, and bullets whistled. It was this mysterious unknown human force that was approached [by the leaders of the government, the Soviet, and the parties] to take control of it. And not being able to formulate objections nor knowing how to resist, the mass began to repeat slogans alien to it and words not its own, and permit itself to be inscribed into parties and organizations. Naturally, the least organized and the least demanding of organizations proved the most acceptable to the spirit of this mass. The Soviet, that meeting of half illiterate soldiers, appeared as their leader because it demanded nothing of them, serving only as a façade to cover up a complete lack of definite principles (beznachalie).

Over against these three forces and vague ideologies, we can from the outset see yet a fourth, that of Lenin's planned speculation with the *stikhiia*, its unrest, uncertainty, inexperience, and vulnerability to plausible, attractive demagogic slogans. It was precisely the *stikhiia* that he had always deeply detested, as he made clear in the period from 1902 to 1906 when he set forth socialist *soznatelnost'*—consciousness—as the polar opposite and determined opponent of the *stikhiinost'* of the masses, and again now in power when he declared the elemental uncontrollable spontaneity (*stikhiinost'*) of the "million-tentacled hydra" of the "petty bourgeois" peasantry, and the workers affected by their ideology, to be "the main enemy" and "more terrible than all the Denikins, Kolchaks, and Iudeniches put together." But Lenin, this sworn enemy of the *stikhiia*, saw in it in 1917 the dynamite that might be used to blow up the Provisional Government. His ideology in 1917 was a peculiar ad-mixture of utopian beliefs, ad hoc demogagic slogans to stir up the *stikhiia* against the Provisional Government, and the old Leninist centralist organizational predilections. He planned to use the *stikhiia* as the battering ram to smash his way to power, but in the back of his mind was clearly the determination to use that power according to the formula of 1918 in which he said, "We must organize everything, take everything into our hands."

In the Provisional Government and the Soviet we must note a sym-metrical opposite of Lenin's attitude, a planlessness toward the *stikhiia* and toward Lenin and his use of it. This planlessness is dramatized by the naming of the incompetent Tolstoyan, Prince Lvov, to be not only premier (a designation at least justified by the notion that his leadership of the *zemgor* and voluntary war organizations fitted him to run a country at war) but simultaneously Minister of the Interior. To name him Minister of the Interior meant that there would be no administra-tion, and no Department of the Interior. As a matter of fact, he never lifted a finger to set up a new administration and control after the old administration broke down, tore off its uniforms, and went into hiding. But this meant that the *stikhiia*, and Lenin's speculation with it as an explosive force, would go unchecked. Except for an occasional speech to a particular mob or mutinous regiment by some trouble shooter from the Government or the Soviet, there was no administration in Russia and no Ministry of the Interior.

Once in a radio interview I asked Kerensky, "Why did you not suppress the Bolsheviks after they openly declared their determination to wage war on what Lenin himself called 'the freest Government in the world,' and avowed his determination to overthrow it?" He an-swered, "What force did I have to suppress them with?" And, indeed, what did he have? But we must ask the further questions: from what ideology did it spring that there was no serious attempt to build up an administrative machine, and that a Lvov was appointed to the Ministry of the Interior, and then never once asked to report on what he was doing to set up a machinery or order an administration? Moreover, did not Lenin have the benefit of a self-paralyzing belief of other Social Democrats that he was just another, slightly more impatient type of Social Democrat? And did Lenin not have, as Mr. Anweiler has suggested, powerful protection within the Menshevik camp?

Martov, and not Ttseretelli, has always been glorified as the outstanding leader of Menshevism by the Mensheviks in defeat and exile. But it was the Martov "Internationalists" in 1917 that advanced the notion of the overriding solidarity of all socialists, the idea that socialists cannot disarm or suppress any organization calling itself socialist, nor any paramilitary formation calling itself an armed workers' Red Guard. From Martov to Kerensky there ran through the scarcely formulated ideology of both Provisional Government and Soviet the feeling that the only real danger was that of a counterrevolution from the right or a monarchist restoration. This was accompanied by the dangerous, indeed, fatal ideological delusion summed up in the formula *"pas d'ennemi à gauche."*

To be sure, Tseretelli and some of his friends urged the disarming of Lenin's workers' guard. But when they proposed this in the Soviet, Martov in his hoarse voice (he already had cancer of the throat), cried out, *Versaillets!* (Versaillan!) Since his voice was hoarse, the assemblage thought they heard him cry *Podlets!* (Scoundrel!). At this breach of the niceties of debate everybody was more shocked than by his real intention, which was to compare Tseretelli and his associates to the men of Versailles who had disarmed the Commune of Paris in 1871.

The proposal to disarm Lenin's paramilitary formations was voted down, or rather shouted down. *No enemy on the left!* And yet on the left stood anarchists and Bolsheviks and Lenin's impudent gamble on stirring up the *stikhiia* to undermine and destroy the nascent democracy embodied in the Provisional Government, the Soviet, and the forthcoming Constituent Assembly.

The Duma Committee sought to legitimate itself as best it could, but, as Mr. Schapiro has rightly said, it was self-appointed and lacked true legitimacy. It did not spring from the Duma, nor was it chosen by the Duma, nor did it report to the Duma, but it sought its legitimation precisely where there was none to be found, in the street and the barracks. But by so doing it gave a sort of legitimacy, not to its own existence but to the mutiny and the *stikhiia*. Thereafter, it could urge, plead, admonish, but not govern the turbulence nor build an administration.

Yet there was one sense in which it did lay the foundations for its own temporary legitimacy. This was not through its loyalty to the old government's promises to its allies, nor its attempts to continue the war with a no longer manageable army. These loyalties failed to take into account the new situation and served but to hasten the government's downfall.

The glory of the Provisional Government, as I see it, is the fact that it had the grace to call itself *Provisional*. Thereby it said what few governments arising out of revolution have said: "We do not regard ourselves as a permanent successor government to the one that has fallen. We do not set up our dictatorship. We regard ourselves as the temporary guardians of the power that has been entrusted to us (Alas, it could be asked, *by whom?*). We look upon ourselves as pre-legitimate, a pre-legitimate government whose chief task is to convoke an assembly representative of the entire people that will write a new constitution for Russia and thereby replace the monarchical hereditary legitimacy that has been ruptured with a new democratic legitimacy that will represent the will of the people of Russia, or the peoples of Russia." Whatever its errors, whatever its sins of omission and commission, this was the Provisional Government's grace and glory. I know that "grace" and "glory" are words bearing a moral connotation and I use them because in my judgment this is the acid test of a government that arises amid the discontinuities and chaos of revolution, namely that it recognize its provisional and pre-legitimate character and acknowledge as its first duty that of bringing into being a new legitimacy based on the consent of the governed, who have made the revolution.

It was the setting of a date for elections to a Constituent Assembly that led Lenin to set a precise date for his coup. The date he chose makes clear his keen sense of the realities of power in the midst of revolution. "Verily, verily," he said twice in his brief letter to the Central Committee on the date for an uprising, "Verily, verily, delay is like unto death." His preciseness in the setting of a date lay in the fact that the coup (it was not really an uprising) had as its function to forestall the consolidation of two potential loci of more legitimate power, to present two institutions with the *fait accompli* that power was already in the hands of his dictatorship and his party. The first institution was the Soviet itself in which he expected to have a pro-Bolshevik majority, but he knew that that majority was only nominal and was assured only by the fact that many of the "deputies" did not really know what he stood for. Had they realized that what he sought was a dictatorship by his party, which meant ultimately by Lenin himself, his majority would have melted away.

The second institution was the Constituent Assembly, which he knew would destroy his chance of taking power if it ever completed its work.

His quarrel with his Central Committee, even with his closest collaborator in the seizure of power, Leon Trotsky, turned on what seemed a hair-splitting difference between the seizure of power on October 24 and the sanctioning of "its own" power by the Soviet scheduled to meet on October 25. Lenin prevailed, so that the symbolic strongpoints were seized by his shock troops on the night of October 24, the night before the new Soviet was to assemble. From the actions of *Vikzhel*, the railwayman's organization, of the other parties, and even of the majority of his first body of People's Commissars, we can deduce that without the *fait accompli*, the new Soviet Congress might have voted for a government of all socialist parties or all Soviet parties but not for the single dictatorship of his party. From the actions of the one-day meeting of the Constituent Assembly before he dispersed it by force of arms, we can deduce that, meeting in freedom, they would indeed have adopted a new Constitution and created a new democratic legitimacy. Thus Lenin's sense of timing was proved right.

And thus was ushered in a period of dictatorship and chronic illegitimacy, a period that has now lasted fifty years. As we meet here to examine that revolution and the half century now coming to a close, we must recognize that in fifty years the regime thus founded has shown no signs of engendering a legitimacy. Indeed, it has not even worked out a legitimate mode of determining the succession. A French moralist has said that "hypocrisy is the tribute that vice pays to virtue." In that sense, the Soviet Government has the trappings of legitimacy: soviets that do not govern; elections in which the people do not choose or elect; parties (that is, parts of society) of which there is only one, and that one moribund and emptied of internal life; a constitution that might well choose as its epigraph: "Paper will put up with anything that is written on it."

Now at the end of a half century, we must recognize that this regime has no intention of creating such a legitimacy. At any rate, at this moment I cannot foresee any organized faction that might arise in the ruling party or oligarchy or in the discontented but unorganized yet overorganized body of the Russian people, that might publicly declare its intention of submitting to the judgment of the people of Russia the government's present actions, or its actions of the last fifty years.

Consequently, for me the great ideological divide of 1917 lies between those who accepted, as did both the Provisional Government and the first Soviet, the idea that the government was provisional and prelegitimate and must aim to establish a new democratic legitimacy, and those who were determined, following Lenin, to establish a dictatorship.

If this be so, and if this be the crucial nature of the ideological divide, then despite all the fashionable "convergence" theories and "models of an advanced industrial society," we stand about where we might expect: with a dictatorship that does not seek nor possess legitimacy in the sense in which I have defined it, but is ruled over by a series of "diminishing dictators," over the ultimate outcome of whose diminution we must puzzle at the present moment.

Discussion

Mr. Schapiro opened the discussion with the comment that Mr. Wolfe was right in pointing to fear—the soldiers' fear that they would be shot for mutiny unless they consolidated their position and the Duma deputies' fear in the face of the mob—as an important element in the development of the February Revolution. He then went on to clarify his views regarding the problem of legitimacy and the failure of the Provisional Government to consolidate its power.

In his opinion the Provisional Government had been a revolutionary government without legitimacy. As such it could have been overthrown very easily by anybody possessing more determination and greater skill at mobilizing the crowd. A different kind of government, conscious of this fact, would have left populism, Tolstoyism, romanticism, deliberation, and so forth, behind and would have made finding the means for keeping order its first aim; it would have relied on loyal troops or the police to get rid of mutinous soldiers. However, the possibility of employing force had not entered into the Provisional Government's thinking; the *intelligenty* who comprised the government never even saw the problem confronting them. They had not expected the revolution, they had not wanted it in the form and at the time in which it came, and in any event they had neither the equipment of political habit nor the experience which the situation required.

Mr. Anweiler agreed with Mr. Wolfe in regard to Martov's role in facilitating the position of the Bolsheviks in 1917. In general, the relationship between the Bolsheviks and left Mensheviks both before and after October was said to be an important subject requiring further study.

Mr. Rubel thought that it was misleading to say that Lenin's program undermined democracy; indeed, what Lenin had promised the Russian masses was precisely democracy. Mr. Wolfe replied that a close reading of Lenin's 1917 writings would reveal that they had not outlined any sort of comprehensive program; generally speaking, they probed trouble spots. In order to take advantage of the *stikhiia*, Lenin had proposed, for example, desertion by the soldiers and land seizure by the peasantry without waiting for village institutions to divide the land fairly or for the Constituent Assembly to determine the fate of the country. This could not be called democracy. On the contrary, democracy was precisely what Lenin sought to overthrow. The Provisional Government had not objected to the redistribution of land;

it had not promised peace, but then war was not inconsistent with democracy; it had granted literally all of the possible freedoms. Most important, it had the democratic grace to declare itself pre-legitimate or provisional pending the convocation of a Constituent Assembly. Mr. Wolfe repeated that to him this was the essence of democracy in a moment of revolution. In his published writings Lenin himself had referred to Russia no less than four times in 1917 as the freest country in the world. In view of all this it was not fair to say that Lenin was either starting or promising democracy.

Mr. Schapiro said that he had not understood Mr. Rubel to say that Lenin had introduced democracy. What he had said was that Lenin preached democracy, an opinion with which he was in full agreement. Mr. Seton-Watson added that Lenin had preached democracy but had done it in a way that ultimately undermined something which was a promise of democracy. Democracy had not existed either in the Provisional Government as Lenin saw it or in Lenin's subsequent acts. Winding up this exchange, Mr. Wolfe asserted that he could not agree that Lenin even preached democracy. To promise everything, he said, was not the same as preaching democracy.

Mr. Ulam made some observations on the significance of divisions within the Bolshevik Party in 1917. While he had no quarrel with Mr. Schapiro's comments on the lack of discipline and cohesion within the Provisional Government, the traditional view of the Bolsheviks as a tightly knit, iron-willed minority that seized power and then governed ruthlessly bore little correspondence to reality. Such documents as the published minutes of the Central Committee revealed that everything negative that could be said about the Provisional Government from the point of view of order and cohesion was equally applicable to the Bolsheviks. At the Sixth Party Congress, a considerable minority had argued that Lenin and Zinoviev should turn themselves in to the authorities so that their trial could be turned into a Dreyfus case. Observing that Dreyfus had spent a considerable period of time in jail and penal servitude, he concluded that this would have meant that Lenin would have been in a position to make a bid for power in 1930. The fact was that Bolshevik leaders had quarreled constantly and had been ready to resign at the drop of a hat. Even Lenin was not free of indecision, as his attitudes on such matters as the convocation of the Constituent Assembly and coalition with the Left SR's indicate. In view of this highly anarchistic setting the failure of people like Martov to take the Bolsheviks seriously was quite understandable.

The chaos and lack of discipline in the Bolshevik organization notwithstanding, Mr. Pipes felt that it was necessary to draw a distinction between the Bolsheviks and the Provisional Government in this respect. Referring to Lenin's promise to the Central Committee that if the party seized power no one would ever take it away, Mr. Pipes expressed doubt that anyone in the Provisional Government would have dreamed of saying such a thing. He asked Mr. Schapiro how he would account for the Provisional Government's outlook: whether its romantic, populist, slavophile belief in the primitive goodness and spontaneous organizational ability of the people were a result of Russian intellectual history, or of the conditions under which intellectuals lived, or of some other cause.

Mr. Schapiro responded that in a sense the immediate source of this attitude was the Liberation Movement and the failure of the Duma, the institution it had created. This had caused liberals to revert from the institutionalized party to a mass movement. However, behind this reversion was the intelligentsia's traditional belief that the *narod* was intrinsically right, that its failure was a consequence of the circumstances in which it lived, and that once the great weight lying on the *narod* was removed, everyone would return to his original virtue.

Mr. Ferro was not as confident as Mr. Wolfe of the Provisional Government's willingness to convene a Constituent Assembly. The ministers of the First Provisional Government had promised the convocation of a Constituent Assembly at an early date at a time when they believed that the Grand Duke Michael would be king. After this hope faded they had sought to postpone the assembly indefinitely.

Drawing a distinction between the February and October Revolutions, Mr. Seton-Watson pointed out that the former had witnessed the disintegration of the imperial regime, whereas in October the whole governmental apparatus collapsed. In this connection Mr. Seton-Watson raised a number of questions. He wondered how it happened that the Provisional Government had allowed the entire apparatus of power to fall out of its hands in the first place; what had been behind the Provisional Government's suspension of provincial governors; and why the Provisional Government did not try to employ the tsarist police or the army to maintain order. Mr. Seton-Watson tentatively suggested that part of the reason for the Provisional Government's behavior was its profound fear of the counterrevolution.

Mr. Seton-Watson then went on to make some comparisons between the development of the Russian and French Revolutions. The reason the Russian Revolution had reached a climax so much more quickly than the French, might lie in such factors as the war situation and the peculiar mentality of the Russian intelligentsia. Contrasting the greater negativism of the Russian intelligentsia with the outlook of the eighteenth-century French intelligentsia, Mr. Seton-Watson asked to what degree this might have been a consequence of the insufferable obstinacy of the tsars, the failure of the collapsing and incompetent elite to call on the services of the new elite, and the experience of the 1905 Revolution.

Mr. Katkov concurred with Mr. Wolfe's stress on the importance of fear in the development of the February Revolution. It was fear of the counterrevolution that had kept the pseudo-freemason group within the Provisional Government from coming out into the open. The same factor explained the failure of the Provisional Government to make use of the rather efficient tsarist administrative apparatus. This obsessive fear was a consequence of the fact that the leaders of the Provisional Government could not explain to themselves how the revolution had happened and who had made it. This uncertainty had served to reinforce their determination to destroy all vestiges of the old order.

To Miss Arendt the creation of a new legitimacy was the central question in any revolution. The Provisional Government's turn to the masses involved more than merely an appeal for mob support. It had been an aspect of the search for legitimacy. The soviets were organs of order and a potential source of a new legitimacy. The failure of the soviets was a consequence of the behavior of the parties, of the anarchy within each of the parties, and of the strife between all of the parties. Further contributing to the handicap under which the Soviets labored was the fact that the names of its leaders were not known. These weaknesses proved decisive at the moment when Lenin declared his determination to take power.

Mr. Rogger voiced disagreement with Mr. Schapiro's emphasis on the importance of the populist heritage in explaining the reluctance of the Provisional Government to exercise power forcefully. The Provisional Government leaders would probably have been more willing to exercise power had they thought they could get away with it. Apart from reasons of distrust, reluctance to employ the old organs of power was a consequence of the assumption, quite justified, that these discredited organs would not have been obeyed.

Reverting to the problem of legitimacy, Mr. Carr underlined the necessity of distinguishing between the legal basis for the existence of a government, generally a formula devised by lawyers, which was one form of legitimacy, and the nature of the support that enabled a government to maintain itself in power, which was another and more fundamental kind of legitimacy. Mr. Carr went on to challenge Mr. Wolfe's identification of freedom with democracy. Acknowledging that Russia was the freest country in the world in the first weeks after the revolution, he defined the prevailing situation as anarchism rather than democracy. Establishing a democratic system of government in Russian conditions had been an impossible task, and this had been the Provisional Government's fundamental weakness.

Mr. Wolfe made some final remarks on the problem of legitimacy. Lawyer's "formulas" notwithstanding, once hereditary legitimacy in Russia had been ruptured, the establishment of a democratic political system depended on the creation of a new democratic legitimacy. This legitimacy could not have been found in the streets because of the rapidly changing composition and demands of the mob; it required organized expression through decently supervised elections. The term "Provisional Government" implied the solemn obligation to bring into being a fresh expression of the will of the people in a Constituent Assembly. For his part Lenin never intended his government to be provisional and there was nothing provisional about it.

Mr. Wolfe agreed with Mr. Ulam that like other Russian political groups, the Bolsheviks had had their waverers, debaters, and people burdened by their past. However, Lenin was not among them. Lenin alone had absolute certainty. Among other things, Lenin wanted to displace the Constituent Assembly, to abolish the party system, and to exert total control over the press. Moreover, beginning very early in his rule, he attached the greatest importance to the use of terror. In Mr. Wolfe's view, this was the real Lenin.

Mr. Anweiler, addressing himself to Mr. Wolfe's remarks, suggested that the democratic system he had been describing was a parliamentary republic. This was not necessarily the only possible form of democracy. In revolutionary Russia a new form of democracy based on class lines was developing alongside such institutions of Western parliamentary government as the Dumas and the *zemstva*. The Bolshevik seizure of power had halted the development of the soviets. However, Mr. Anweiler expressed doubt that the soviets would ever have been capable of providing the basis for a viable political system in Russia.

Disagreeing with Mr. Rogger's argument in regard to the Provisional Government's reluctance to exercise power, Mr. Schapiro reiterated his conviction that another government might have made good use of the tsarist police, loyal troops, the more competent governors, and the imperial provincial administration. The Provisional Government might have taken advantage of the fact that in his final act of abdication the tsar had called on all administrative officials to obey the new government. That the Provisional Government did not do so was partly the result of fear and distrust; it was also in part a consequence of the ideological background of the Russian intelligentsia.

In a concluding observation, Mr. Schapiro echoed Mr. Pipes' criticism of the comparison made by Mr. Ulam of disorganization in the Bolshevik Party and the Provisional Government. Although he acknowledged the disorganization prevailing in Bolshevik ranks, he stressed that within this chaos there had always existed a hard core of determined individuals that was totally lacking in the Provisional Government.

The Aspirations of Russian Society — *Marc Ferro*

The success of the February Revolution was as unexpected as its outbreak. The Russian people had rid themselves of tsarism with a single blow, and for some time they were happy, being under the impression that they had at last attained freedom and adulthood. Now, the dream of Russian liberty had come true, and the people saw themselves as 130 million professional statesmen, each having in his pocket a proposal for changing and modernizing the country. Pictures in the film archives show them lining up at meetings, waiting to produce their own programs.

During the first weeks of the revolution thousands of telegrams and letters were sent to the Soviet and to the Duma. *Izvestiia* alone received 10,000 telegrams in a period of two weeks, copies of which were sent to Kerenskii, Rodzianko, and others. Everyone sent telegrams: coachmen, teachers, workers, Muslims, students, railwaymen, Jews, soldiers and so on.

During the first days of March, because the political parties and the local soviets were not as yet organized, these messages were spontaneous. This is illustrated by the many telegrams addressed to the Moscow Soviet inquiring what their demands should be.

I propose to study and classify these letters, telegrams, and motions emanating from the workers, the intelligentsia, the national minorities, and the soldiers, and to make a statistical study of the contents of some thousand messages that I have read in the Soviet archives.[1] From such

Note: All dates in this article are given in New Style.

1. This text is based on the examination of archive collections and the analysis of Russian newspapers which enabled us to draw up an inventory of over 4,000 letters and telegrams addressed to the government, the Soviet, and the Duma in the first few weeks following the fall of the monarchy. The following archives have been consulted: TsGAOR SSSR (Central Archives of the October Revolution, Moscow) Collections 3, 66, 398, 1235, 1244, 1978; GAORSSMo (State Archive of the

an analysis, it should be possible to learn what the different segments of public opinion wanted and expected. It will then be possible to compare these results with the programs of the political parties and to estimate the influence of each party on the population at the beginning of the revolution. Further, it will be interesting to compare the social and political aspirations of the population at large with the decisions of the soviets, the party organizations, and the Provisional Government. In this way, one should be able to understand the reasons for the failures of certain parties and for the success of others.

Allow me to make a preliminary observation before dealing with the specific aims of the working class, the peasantry, the army, and other groups. The perusal of the first 100 petitions or letters from each group furnishes one or several claims. One notes that in the messages dispatched by the workers, personal or private claims occupy a more prominent place than political or general ones—the proportion is more than two to one—whereas in the case of messages from the peasantry or the army, specific and general goals are evenly balanced. One could discuss this phenomenon at length and offer many interpretations, but I would now rather deal with the facts and leave interpretations for some other occasion.

Let us begin with the aspirations of the *workers*. By far the most frequent and insistent claim, requested in 51 percent of the petitions, is for the eight-hour day. This is the only claim the workers wished to have legalized. Fourteen percent indicated agreement to work overtime if paid at a higher rate and if the trade unions gave their approval. "We accept [overtime] for the sake of national defense" is often added to the petition. I will discuss this point later.

During the first two weeks after the outbreak of the revolution, salary claims were not very numerous—only 18 percent of the messages mention them. This relative indifference to salaries resembles the attitude of French workers after the Revolution of 1848, when many of them were prepared to sacrifice higher wages as a gift to the revolution. The figure changed as early as the third week of the revolution because so few concessions had been made during the first fifteen days of March; furthermore, the workers had to struggle for wages due them for the five days of the insurrection. Nevertheless, the initial salary demands

October Revolution, Moscow), Collection 66; GAORSSLe (State Archive of the October Revolution, Leningrad) Collections 47, 54, 55, 101, 151, 4592, 4598, 4601, 4602, 1000, 4600, 4605, 7384, 7389, 8878; TsGIAL (Central State Historical Archive, Leningrad) Collections 23, 1405, 1276, 1278.

were very moderate: in Moscow, on March 9, only 20 percent, and in Kursk on March 17, 50 percent of the messages allude to them. These figures acquire added significance if one bears in mind that the average salary was very low: something like the equivalent of 60 pounds of bread a month. Often, workers requested only trousers or shoes—one pair a year, thus incidentally revealing the extent of their poverty.

Finally, I may add that there was general hostility to standardization of salaries and that the workers favored more a reduction of the disparity between salaries than their equalization. However, just as important as the question of the amount of pay was that of salary stability (11 percent of the petitions) and sanitary conditions (12 percent). One must bear in mind the state of Russian industry in 1917: the difficulty of reconversion, the lack of understanding on the part of the employers, and later, before the lock-out in June, the shortage of raw materials that led to the dismissal of workers. All this explains the great gap between the economic aspirations of the workers, on the one hand, and the ability and intention of the employers to grant them higher salaries and greater security on the other.

Another important problem in the very first weeks of the revolution concerned the relations between workers and employers. To ensure fair employment practices, the workers wished to control the hiring procedure by placing it under the direction of a workshop committee. The workers frequently enumerated the powers of this committee, but only in 4 percent of the petitions did they express a desire to control the workshop itself. It became evident that the workers sought this right not under the influence of socialist or collectivist ideas, but because such control would enable them to check whether or not the employers were in a position to offer them higher wages and better working conditions. They wanted to check the books, the amount of raw material in the warehouses, and so on. When the workers took over the Ericson plant, for example, they organized a committee and granted higher wages but did not try to organize production. The workers of the big enterprises had no revolutionary plan of production as did the printers and bakers; the latter, however, were not a driving force in the labor movement.

Naturally, political demands run through about 50 percent of the worker petitions submitted after the outbreak of the February Revolution. The workers of the big enterprises and mines expressed four times more frequently their distrust than their confidence in the government, and the contrary is true of the railwaymen and artisans. The former tended to send their letters and telegrams to the soviets, and the latter wrote the Duma.

Among the first two hundred petitions, letters or telegrams emanating from the working class—including the railwaymen—14 percent asked for a "democratic republic." It is difficult to know exactly what they meant by this: whether it was universal franchise, the end of the monarchy, or perhaps a strong parliament. The miners of the Urals added: "A republic is really a democracy when it gives the people land and freedom." Twelve percent of the texts wanted a Constituent Assembly. For the Kadets and Octobrists these demands were an absurdity because they believed in the legitimacy of either a democratic republic or a Constituent Assembly but not of both. For the workers, there was no incompatibility between the two institutions: Nicholas II, having been overthrown, the republic was already a reality needing only to be legitimized. All groups, that is, soldiers, bourgeoisie, and Duma, felt themselves responsible for the change; Russia was henceforth a republic, and consequently there was no need for a Constituent Assembly to give it legitimacy. Moreover, they felt that even if there were such an Assembly, its sole purpose would be to proclaim the republic and to establish its rules and organization. From the outset, the workers felt that any delay in the convocation of the Assembly would be a trick played by the bourgeoisie, and so they demanded its immediate convocation. They were more perceptive in this respect than either the Socialist Revolutionaries or the Social Democrats, both of whom thought that the disorganized conditions of the political parties required a postponement of the Assembly.

On these points, all workers agreed. But, there is evidence of a cleavage in the attitude toward the government between railwaymen and artisans, on the one hand, and the more intransigent factory workers on the other. On the question of war, the disagreement was more marked, but not exactly the same: here, we have the greater part of the working class, including railwaymen and factory workers as opposed to a small minority of factory workers. Until the Soviet peace declaration of March 27, 1917, that is, during the first three weeks of the revolution, there was little mention of this problem in the petitions. Later, there was a great change. The workers were both lucid and cautious because, as the miners of Kuznets observed, war binds the working class to the upper classes. Many did not understand the cry "Down with the war!" so it was necessary to use discretion. In reports of the meetings, held in the first weeks, nobody dared to cry *Doloi voinu!* (Down with the war!) during the discussions; only later on, stealthily and as people were dispersing, did a minority raise their voice with that slogan. At the beginning of March, there were some meetings against the war, for example in the Moscow Kramer factories. As to the meaning of war in its class sense, a majority that condemned it existed only in the Urals. This was perhaps because in this area the ideological struggle involved a conflict among the workers themselves, while in Petrograd or Moscow the working class had to fight a coalition of the upper and middle classes. At any rate, even when some workers displayed unusual pacifist attitudes, most opposed a separate peace, not because of the sacred alliance with France or because of "solidarity with the German proletariat," but because peace seemed unlikely. It was believed that only the international action of the workers could bring about such a peace. There are twice as many texts expressing this international approach to the problem of peace as on any other issue. I did find some direct messages to Germany, not to its government but to its proletariat. It is noticeable that when workers or sailors wrote messages to the German workers, they employed a pacifist style, inviting the German workers to turn the imperialist war into a civil war. When writing to the workers of the allied countries, however, they made no mention of this move, but wrote merely: "Compel your government to conclude a peace, a reasonable peace." Even though they were not numerous, the pacifist workers were more advanced in their ideas than the political organizations, with the possible exception of the anarchists of *Rabochee Znamia*.

One is struck by the numerous similarities in the texts sent by the workers, which is not the case with telegrams and letters dispatched by the peasantry and the army. Even before the first political party meetings took place, the workers advanced claims in the same form and with the same topic sequence and although it clearly appears that the workers composed these texts spontaneously, one also senses the strong influence of the Social Democratic Party. For example, the workers of the little city of Alatry wrote to the Moscow Soviet: "If you want to know our desires, read the program of the Social Democratic Party."

However, one notes that three points of this Social Democratic program, omitted by the workers, were included in the motions of the soldiers and peasants. The first point—"graduated taxes and no others" —requires no comment. No mention of this exists, naturally, in the workers' telegrams. The other omissions are of greater interest: decentralization of government and universal franchise (point 2); independence and election of judges (point 2 of the SD program and point 3 of the SR Party).

By way of conclusion to the study of these aspirations of the working class during the first weeks of the revolution, I would like to add some observations. The word "socialism" appears very rarely, as does the word "communism" or the expression "classless society." The workers did not believe that they could transform their own condition, but hoped merely to improve their living standards. However, the behavior and opposition of the upper classes, as well as the demagogy of the political parties, were to lead to new objectives.

There is, in these worker petitions, a wide range between hopes and reality. For example, the demand for universal franchise appears in only 5 percent of the initial texts. Significantly, in the municipal elections that took place later, in May, 50 percent of the voters abstained. Even in the soviets, a large part of the working class was not represented: in Nizhni Novgorod, for example, or in cities such as Odessa and Baku where the lower categories of workers consisted of Muslims or other minority nationalities. I am not sure how democratic the workers were since they tried to expel the soldiers from many soviets. The initiative for such action was, of course, taken by the leaders of the soviets, but the workers did not protest. This is not without some significance and will be brought up later to explain other events. They were probably not yet convinced socialists, but they were very strongly class conscious.

Distrust of the Provisional Government was indicative of the distrust of any collaboration with the upper classes. This explains the surprise of the workers when the government and the soviet invited them to negotiate with their employers on March 6 in Petrograd. In their eyes, negotiation meant that they were only at the beginning of the revolution, and this attitude revealed the distance between the soviet's position and that of the workers. The latter wanted no cooperation with the upper classes: they sought either to be the power itself (inside the government) or the opposition. If they approved of the constitution of soviets and considered it as their own class organization, they wished to use it against the government rather than to secure any compromise settlement. For instance, on March 6 they refused to go back to work when their leaders in the soviet, under pressure from the soldiers, had to agree to their return. The soviet was forced to urge them to return to the factories three or four times. Nevertheless, from the inquiries of the Soviet of Moscow, it is clear that the political leaders of the local soviets (Ivanovo, Nizhni Novgorod, and so on) asked the workers whether or not they collaborated with the town institutions, knowing all along that there was general opposition to such collaboration.

From this, one can understand the roots of the cleavage between the workers, on the one hand, and the Mensheviks and SR's on the other, in this conception of class collaboration. Whether the soviet was right or not is another question. I only wish to suggest that between the soviet and the working class there had been, from the beginning, a misunderstanding that would continue to grow.

When we turn to the *peasantry*, the problem is different. Because of the Stolypin reforms and the great social and geographical diversity of the country, the ideal of peasant unity was more utopian than that of the working class. For this reason, common goals, other than political, were rare among them, and their petitions reveal a greater variety of claims.

The first striking observation is that the peasants were more violent than the workers. This is obvious from the style of the motions, even if there is doubt as to whether these texts were written by the peasants themselves. (I know of a few messages written on birch bark, composed by persons unused to writing. Also, in rural assembly reports, one reads very frequently that the muzhiks wanted to know exactly what the teacher or clerk was writing in their name, in order to correct him.) The violence of the peasants was expressed, for instance, in the claims they made against the tsar and the old administration or against the upper classes (31 times in 100 texts, compared to only 5 times for the workers' petitions).

At the same time, the peasants were unable to envisage any stages in the revolution, expecting everything to change at once: "Well, nothing has changed yet," they wrote from a village near Riazan, "and the revolution is already six weeks old."

As a rule, never having read party programs, the peasants had no idea of the differences between them and lacked a clear picture of the agrarian problems as a whole. A peasant assembly near Voronezh demanded the suppression of private property (point 2) and at the same time the equality of property (point 3). It also wanted a committee (point 9) to fix the workers' salaries and to specify their work, as well as that of the owners and farmers. Rarely in these texts can one find words employed in the programs of the political parties: socialization, nationalization, municipalization, collectivization, and the suppression of private property are mentioned only 7 times out of 100.

Here we touch upon one of the main problems: 51 percent of the peasant texts ask for land confiscation and 31 percent add "not only of the state land, but also of large private property." Fifteen percent of the texts ask for land free of charge—as a gift. The demand, therefore, was not for the suppression of private property but for its organization. Suppression of private property is demanded only 7 times in 100 petitions. This 7 percent came from areas near the big cities, where the socialist parties might have been influential. Seventy times out of 100, the peasants wrote: "Let the land belong to those who work it," often adding, "as much as they can plough." Great resentment was expressed toward the landowners who neglected to work their lands and this is where we feel the depth of the peasants' hatred.

I would like to call attention to two other problems: the attitude of the peasant towards the problem of collectivization; and the major opposition of the kulaks to the poor peasants. It is noteworthy that in only 2 percent of the peasant texts do we see that they wish to return to the *obshchina*, while in 15 percent of the texts some collective institution is proposed to organize the appropriated land. These are recommendations of the local committees whereas only twice is the state asked to organize land administration. Nevertheless, Russian peasants were less individualistic than the French, and proposed that every ten or twenty years an elected committee could and should supervise a new distribution of land.

The struggle between the large and small landowners is reflected very frequently in the communications, especially in regard to the use of prisoners of war or refugees. The peasants cared little that the big landowners could have twenty times as many prisoners to work their land, but they feared that this would enable them to cultivate a greater portion of their land and therefore make them eligible for a larger share in the new land distribution. Peasant owners of bigger properties preferred that decisions be taken at a higher level, that is, at the regional assembly, whereas the smaller farmers wanted them to be made at once and at the local level. They worried that at a regional level or even in a Constituent Assembly their interests would be ignored or badly represented.

From this evidence we may suggest that the relations between political parties and the peasants did not center on programmatic questions (nationalization or socialization, indemnity, organization of production, and so on). The peasants had only a vague knowledge of the various party programs and the party leaders had erroneous ideas about the desires of the peasants. Even the views of V. Chernov bore no relation to the peasant aspirations, and as soon as he stated that they would have to wait for the decision of the Constituent Assembly and obey that decision, the Socialist Revolutionaries lost a large part of the peasant vote, at least among the soldiers in the cities.

There is another reason for the peasants being more violent than the workers, especially the more specialized workers. The leaders of the revolution and of the new regime—in the Provisional Government and in the soviet alike—were city dwellers who paid little attention to the peasants' complaints. Although many books had been written on the agrarian problem, one finds nothing about it in *Pravda* or *Izvestiia* during the first weeks of the revolution. This indifference is flagrantly revealed in the letters of soldiers, as for example in a document from the 202nd Mountain Regiment: "In the government program, not a word on the agrarian problem. Be careful, the army could be used as a counter-revolutionary force if you do not introduce this topic into your resolutions."

There are two ominous points raised in the letters and petitions of the *soldiers*. Because they had already served two to three years, the veterans wished to have pensions for themselves or their families. There was also the problem of military discipline. This, we need not dwell upon at length because the history of Order No. 1 and Order No. 2 is well known. We also know that the soldiers were eager to introduce in the army more humane relations. These two points are an indication of the fact that the soldiers did not believe they would soon be discharged, or else they would have referred to other problems.

The above two points provide also an indirect indication of their attitude toward the questions of war and peace. In some texts one finds written: "For us, soldiers, a new government means the end of the war," but more frequently, in March and April, the soldiers were likely to treat advocates of immediate peace as supporters of the kaiser. This was particularly true in the trenches and in Petrograd. In a letter from the soldiers of the 6th Artillery Park, dated March 8, they asked the leaders of the Soviet whether they should not consider pacifists as *agents provocateurs*. There are many dispatches of this kind. In others, they were proud to show their officers that others did not have a monopoly on patriotism. They wrote to the Soviet: "On us lies henceforth a great responsibility."

Naturally, the soldiers would have liked to return home and they hoped that when the new government came to negotiate with Germany, it would find a revolutionary government installed there, too, which would be willing to conclude peace. In any event, they had confidence in the Provisional Government and were keenly disappointed when they realized that it followed the same foreign policy as the imperial regime.

It is worth noting that much as the workers tried, without any outside assistance, to solve their own conflicts with their employers (by means of strikes, and so on) and as the peasants tried vis-à-vis the property owners (by seizing the land, and so on), so the soldiers sought to solve the problem of discipline by simply disobeying their officers. However, some soldiers also thought of ending the war by fraternizing with the enemy. The failure of fraternization indicated that the government alone could achieve peace. We can, thus, understand the mounting fury of the soldiers at their own futile attempts to end the war and the inactivity of the government.

Now, allow me to bring up a link between the problem of war and peace and that of military discipline. As I mentioned, the question of discipline was the principal issue. When the soldiers grasped that the war offensive called for by the army staff was connected with that of discipline required by the officers, their outlook changed. At the beginning of the revolution, they had not opposed military operations and revealed even considerable patriotism, but later, seeing that the officers clung to the old form of discipline, the soldiers began to suspect all their plans and particularly their offensive operations. Here, in the stubborn insistence of officers on discipline, we see a connection between the passive, unexpressed, but normal and general desire for peace and the active pacificism of the coming months. Bolshevik propaganda contributed to this change of mood, but the real difficulty lay in the behavior of the officers: "They understood nothing about this revolution," wrote the soldiers of the fortress of Kiev to the Moscow Soviet.

Thus, aspirations in Russian society in the first weeks of the revolution were often conflicting. One may add that in the case of the workers, the employers did not oppose their claims in a merely defensive manner. We have the speeches of Riabushinskii, Kutler, and others who exhorted the workers to make a greater effort than before the revolution. The employers also wanted to be more independent of the state. They soon developed the attitude of the bourgeois conquerors in England at the beginning of the Victorian era or in France after June 1848. Believing that they would be in power for fifty years, they did not behave as a so-called class "condemned by history." This explains the twofold difficulty of the Provisional Government: the desire to transform Russia into a modern country like liberal England or France and the belief that too much time had already been lost made them impatient to act. On the other hand, the government had to fight the opposition from the left. There was a similar situation in the countryside in addition to antagonism in the army.

Nevertheless, the question remains: why did the government and the SR-Menshevik majority in the soviets use the same scale to evaluate the opposition of the left and the resistance to the right? I would suggest three answers: they received as many ultimata from the right as from the left; they had precedents in mind (the history of the French Revolution, for instance); and a great majority of the professional revolutionaries underestimated the will for reform and self-government of a large number of citizens. They forgot that although they were a majority within this group, they were a minority in the country. At the beginning of a revolution, the more violent leaders are not always specialists in the techniques of revolution.

Between the aspirations of some and the aims of others, there were not only deadlocks but often situations which permitted no immediate solution. I am speaking not only of the problems of war and peace. Allow me to present some examples.

First, one cannot ignore the national minorities who sent some hundred telegrams and letters during the first five days of the revolution. Two hundred messages were sent by the Muslims alone in March and April. Their desires were known to all, and in March 1917 all the political organizations were aware of them. One finds many references to this problem in the programs of the Russian parties. In March, the government granted political rights to the minorities—an individual gift to each of the members of these communities—making them full-fledged citizens. However, the minorities considered this measure a result of the revolution against tsarism and in no way a gift or reform, or even a recognition of their national identity.

On this latter point, Russian political leaders were surprised to discover that the aims of the national minorities and their own were not necessarily identical. They were even rather annoyed by this situation and really did not care to know the desires of the minorities, so busy were they with their own revolution! This point is corroborated by the testimony of Ukrainian and Finnish leaders. The Muslims wrote: "The new Russia does not pay any more attention to our problems than the old pre-revolutionary Russia." And this, in spite of party programs and declarations of friendship.

There were, however, other even more significant facts. In the worker soviets, only Russian citizens were elected in Baku, Kazan, Helsingfors, and other cities. In Reval, Moscow, and the Russian garrison of Kiev, the soldier soviets refused to permit the minorities to form their own regiments. There was thus more than a gap between the political party programs and the realities of Russian society. Those very citizens who sent heartbreaking messages to the government on the necessity of organizing a new society based on justice and equality were also responsible for organizing pogroms. Between the goals of the revolution and the collective psychology there was a structural incompatibility.

Second, another incompatibility existed between the economic demands of the workers and the possibilities of the Russian economy. This is not the place to speak of the highly interesting problem: whether the Russia of this period (1913–1917) was a kind of new America or the first of the underdeveloped countries. In any event the Russian bourgeoisie, as much as it might have desired, did not dispose of large financial resources.

Still a third incompatibility existed between the political conceptions of the parties and their leaders, on the one hand, and the political reactions of Russian society on the other. We noted above that the workers neglected to demand universal franchise and that abstentions were numerous in the municipal elections. In the south, when the army was polled on the principle of electing a president of the future Russian republic, 90 percent of the soldiers voted negatively. Elsewhere, as is well known, disintegration of the state apparatus and of the many soviets was proof that the Russian people were secretly hostile to representative power: they wanted not a better government, but no government at all. This point needs stressing in order to show the gap between the daily acts of society (such as disobedience to the government or the soviet) and the abstract goals and dreams of the party leaders.

Until the revolution, soldiers, peasants, minorities, and workers had been treated as pawns in the struggle against tsarism. Now suddenly, they wanted to deliberate and comment upon each law, each sentence, each opinion. Henceforth, the specialists of political action, that is to say the professional politicians, the artists, the writers, would lose their influence. They were once again afraid, as they had been in March. Gorky, Chkheidze, Gippius, the white-collar workers, the professors, the lawyers, and others, no longer knew whether they had reason to rejoice or to grieve. Caught in the contradiction of war and peace and class conflict, they imagined that because of their position as "old revolutionaries," they might and could say "no" to the overwhelming aspirations of the Russian people. They thought that Russian society would turn to them as the new leaders of the country. It was, however, too early to stop the rising tide, and they disappeared in the turmoil.

Table 1. Working class aspirations (covering the first 100 motions voted between March 3 and March 28, 1917, among factory workers).

Demand	Percent of motions making reference
General policies	
Take measures against the tsar	2
Take measures against the former administration	3
Establish a democratic republic	14
Introduce universal suffrage	5
Confidence in the government	3
Lack of confidence in the government	11
Decentralize	0
Hasten the convocation of the Constituent Assembly	12
Provide free education	3
Introduce a graduated tax and no other	0
Proclamations in favor of the war	3
Proclamations in favor of peace, without annexations or contributions	3
Abolish the professional army	1
Workers' problems	
Introduce the eight-hour day	51
Abolish overtime hours (7 percent with this provision: "unless they are better paid")	14
Assure social and wage security	11
Raise salaries	18
Questions concerning hiring	7
Allow choice of foremen	2
Improve sanitary conditions	15
Questions concerning the role of the factory committee	12
Questions concerning the workers' administration	4
Internationalist sentiments	7
Give land to peasants	9
Wait for salary increases and other advantages; show patience	1

Sources: Izvestiia: 20 motions, *Pravda* and *Sotsial-Demokrat,* 20 motions. Archives: 60 motions. The regional breakdown is as follows: Petrograd: 40 percent; Moscow: 25 percent; other cities: 35 percent.

Later on, there were other claims: that prisoners of war receive a salary equivalent to that of the Russian workers, otherwise they will unintentionally play the role of strike breakers. Especially toward the end of March, petitions on the question of war became more and more numerous.

Table 2. Aspirations of the peasantry.

Demand	Percent of motions making reference
General policies	
Take measures against the tsar	4
Take measures against the former administration	16
Establish a democratic republic	24
Introduce universal suffrage	9
Confidence in the government	10 (7 in March)
Lack of confidence in the government	10 (in April)
Decentralize	12
Hasten the convocation of the Constituent Assembly	17
Provide free education	10
Introduce a graduated tax and no other	6
Proclamations in favor of the war	4
Proclamations in favor of a quick and just peace	23
Abolish the professional army	3
Take measures or precautions against the big land owners	11
Agrarian questions	
Decrease land rents	17
Prohibit the sale of land until the Constituent Assembly meets	13
Prohibit spontaneous occupation of land	4
The Constituent Assembly should fix the terms for granting land and solving the agrarian question	15
Undertake seizure of state lands	20
Undertake seizure of state lands and the lands of the big owners	31
Undertake land seizure without compensation, free of charge	15
Abolish private property	7
Socialize or nationalize land	12
Place the land under the *obshchina* (commune)	2
Give land to those that work it, according to their number (without paid help)	18
Introduce land norms	8
Entrust land management and distribution to the municipalities, soviets, and so on	15

This table summarizes the first hundred motions among the 300 documents which Soviet historians have assembled, on the agrarian question, for the months of March and April 1917. This sample is as good as any other for there is a definite connection between the selection made here and the agrarian troubles in February and March. However, one is struck in the documents published in 1959 and 1960 by an over-representation of the Moscow and Vladimir (near Moscow) areas because of the greater development of historical studies in the capital.

Setting aside this distortion, the provinces of Tula (9 motions), Riazan (6 motions), Kaluga, Pskov, and Smolensk are represented on the table by five or more motions. These are just the areas where agrarian troubles were to be the most numerous. (Cf. TsGAOR SSSR, 3, 1, 302, docs. 2 and following.) Half of the hundred motions listed here cover the areas which knew the most serious agrarian troubles. The rest cover a very varied number of provinces: 33 provinces are represented of a total of 50 in European Russia.

Thus, one can consider that this sample gives an indication of the aspirations of the Russian peasantry during the first months of the revolution.

A comparison of the two tables, point by point, is suggestive. Still, one must bear in mind that the peasants were slower in sending in their petitions. The delay was approximately a fortnight. For this reason, it would not be sound to draw unqualified conclusions on attitudes to the question of war which was not raised in the first days of the revolution.

Comment by John M. Thompson on — "The Aspirations of Russian Society" by Marc Ferro

The research undertaken by Mr. Ferro is unique, as far as I know, and many of his conclusions are both revealing and iconoclastic. Before turning to the results of his study I wish to raise two questions, one concerning the scope of his work, a second pertaining to the materials themselves.

As the paper itself makes clear, the petitions, telegrams, and letters that Mr. Ferro is dealing with data primarily from the first month, six weeks, or, at most, two months of the revolution. This was a period of great euphoria, and the changes that occurred in the demands of the masses as the summer progressed, as the first elation of revolutionary victory passed, as the elemental aspirations of the people remained largely unfulfilled, are as significant as, if not more important than, this first outburst of rather naive expressions of dreams and hopes. If similar materials are available for the period from May to October 1917, it would be extraordinarily interesting and useful for Mr. Ferro to continue his analysis in order to see whether, as is commonly assumed, the goals of the masses became increasingly more radical and maximalist as the revolution proceeded.

I disagree slightly with Mr. Ferro in regard to the spontaneity of the materials. Certainly they were written in a spirit of great enthusiasm; everyone was excited and happy at the fall of the tsar. The appeals also were undoubtedly drafted hastily and without a great deal of consideration. Nevertheless, their content often reflected a history of political thought and action that went back at least as far as 1905, and popular demands, even in that revolutionary moment, were largely based on fairly well established programs of organized parties and groups. Thus, the petitions and telegrams probably embodied to a greater extent than Mr. Ferro suggests ideas that had developed and crystallized in the preceding decade and that were known to and articulated by individuals and groups primarily through the instrumentality of some political or social organization. Moreover, I suspect, following from this hypothesis, that the influence of "activitists" and intellectuals in the initiation and composition of these "spontaneous" appeals was probably greater than it might appear on the surface. To some extent these doubts concerning the spontaneous nature of the materials might be tested by comparing the content of the petitions to that in other kinds of evidence: contemporary letters, memoirs, the press, and public statements of social and political leaders or groups.

Three of the conclusions reached by Mr. Ferro seem especially important to our understanding of the revolution. First, the evidence he presents clearly indicates that the demands of the workers at this stage in the revolution were predominantly *economic* not political in nature, a fact often overlooked by historians of the revolution, particularly Soviet authors. The main objective of the proletariat in the beginning was potently a rapid and tangible improvement in their immediate situation, in their personal working and living conditions. The larger issues seem to have mattered little to them at this juncture. To a considerable extent, of course, self-interest and the desire for direct benefits dominated the aspirations of all groups, but it is particularly striking in the case of the workers, who were presumably the most politicized element of the general population.

Second, it is significant, as Mr. Ferro has clearly pointed out, that at this point the demand for "workers' control" did not at all involve socialization of industry or actual direction of production by the workers. The proletariat had no desire to own or run the factories. They wanted "control" simply to guarantee that they would in fact obtain the economic gains they were most interested in and to ensure provision of conditions of employment that they considered satisfactory. This point also has been considerably obscured by Bolshevik historiography.

Third, the relative absence of antiwar sentiment indicated by Mr. Ferro's findings is most revealing. In the earliest period of the revolution there seems to have been general support for the war, or at least, with the exception of a few petitions, little opposition to it. Here it would be especially important, in continuing the research chronologically, to trace the change in this situation, to see when revulsion against the war began to develop and what form it took. As with the two previous interpretations, this conclusion of Mr. Ferro provides a welcome and instructive corrective to much writing about the revolution, in which it is generally assumed, even by Western authors, that the war issue was a key one right from the beginning.

I would also like to raise some questions about certain aspects of the paper. For example, I am not convinced that the claims of the peasants, as Mr. Ferro has presented them, were in fact more generalized, less personal and self-interested, than those of other groups. The chief demand of the peasants was for land and, although this could be expressed in general terms for the whole society, its realization would have provided direct immediate gain for the individual peasant, just as fulfillment of the workers' demands would have given them concrete economic benefits. Thus, I do not fully understand Mr. Ferro's categorization of peasant aspirations as half general and half specific or private.

Mr. Ferro argues that in this early stage of the revolution the workers were already reflecting considerable class-consciousness and articulating demonstrably anti-bourgeois sentiments. This may well be so, but the evidence to substantiate this interpretation seems largely lacking in the paper. Mr. Ferro does not fully indicate what sort of statements or petitions led him to this conclusion.

As regards the general political attitude of the workers, I find the paper somewhat confusing. On the one hand, Mr. Ferro suggests that the calling of a Constituent Assembly was a vital issue for the proletariat. They wanted it convened right away, and when it was not, they took this as some sort of a "bourgeois" trick. On the other hand, he maintains that the workers were not interested in questions of the franchise and political representation and that they were perhaps even anti-democratic or anti-representative in organizing certain soviets. This may well be an accurate reading of what is contained in the telegrams and petitions, but the obvious contradiction between these two attitudes of the workers calls for further explanation.

There are also two of Mr. Ferro's conclusions that I wish to challenge. They may be quite correct but they do not seem persuasive to me. One is that the bourgeois were aggressive in taking advantage of the revolution and that they actively blocked fulfillment of the workers' demands. There is insufficient evidence presented to support this assertion. It seems to me that the war and the inherent weakness of the economy were far more important than the active resistance of the industrialists in making it impossible for the economic claims of the workers to be met.

Second, the link Mr. Ferro makes between the problem of discipline in the army and the growth of antiwar sentiment among the soldiers is not convincing. His evidence certainly indicates that in the beginning the rank and file were concerned primarily about the "democratization" of the army and that they were not attempting to exert control over military operations or even over war aims to any great extent. But he then goes on to suggest that when the soldiers were not satisfied with changes in the organization and disciplining of the army, they transferred their frustration on those issues to a general opposition to the war. This may well be, but it does not necessarily follow that the one attitude led to the other. It seems more logical to look for other reasons for the growing disenchantment of the soldiers with the war. For example, as the summer progressed and rumors spread that a "black repartition" of the land was taking place in the villages, many peasant soldiers may have decided that participating in the division of land was more important than staying in ranks to fight a war they did not understand. Moreover, the spread of the idea of defensism and the continuing defeats suffered by the army, most notably in the July offensive, may have done more to foster antiwar sentiment than any resentment at inadequacies in "democratizing" the army.

Finally, I would like to raise three points concerning the aspirations of the masses that Mr. Ferro did not deal with. First, what were the aims and hopes of the nonworker urban population? This element is not represented in the petitions discussed by Mr. Ferro. Perhaps they did not form sufficiently homogeneous groups to submit representative views, or perhaps their opinions were subsumed in those of the political parties or other existing organizations; but one wonders what the industrialists wanted, what the white-collar workers and those in retail and service enterprises aspired to, what the students or lawyers or doctors or engineers dreamed of? Did any of these elements send in petitions, and if so, what did they ask for?

Second, is there a trace of anti-foreign or xenophobic sentiment anywhere in the petitions? Some observers have argued that as the revolution developed, it contained growing undertones of anti-Westernism, of a revulsion against Russia's inferiority, of a resentment against Russia's military and economic subservience to the West, of a hatred of foreigners as being chiefly responsible for the debacle of the war and, in fact, for all of Russia's woes. Apparently none of this is reflected in the letters and telegrams studied, but it would be interesting to know if, for example, any of the petitions from workers railed against the role of foreign capital in Russia, or if soldiers spoke out against being killed to benefit primarily foreign interests.

Third, despite being generally couched in fairly concrete terms, did not the claims of the masses amount in essence to a common yearning that was more psychological than practical? Behind all the petitions was there not a general striving for dignity and integrity, what Mr. Seton-Watson has called "a passion for justice?" Mr. Ferro himself has suggested this indirectly near the end of his paper, and although it is difficult to pin down, it is a point worth exploring further. To be sure, there were immediate "private" gains that both workers and peasants wanted, but underlying these claims can one not detect a more elemental concern, a plea for an end to generalized oppression and misery? Related to this, do not the petitions also reflect an attitude that goes beyond self-interest and borders on negativism or even anarchy? Were not the petitioners rejecting the old order and system as much as any order or system? They talked of the new freedom and how they were going to exercise it but by implication were they not also denying all restraints, all responsibilities, everything that was constructive and positive? As Mr. Ferro points out, people puzzled over each word and phrase, they were determined to make their own decisions, and the result may have been, as Professor Von Laue suggests in his *Why Lenin? Why Stalin?*, that Russia was not yet ready to cope with the liberating effects of the revolution.

Discussion

Mr. Ferro opened the discussion by responding to some of the points raised by Mr. Thompson. He agreed that a passion for justice, although difficult to assess quantitatively, was strongly reflected in the letters and telegrams he had analyzed. Although he detected no signs of xenophobia, the spirit of internationalism on the part of the Russian people in the immediate aftermath of the February Revolution was far stronger than he would have supposed. To his surprise he had come across more than one hundred letters protesting the conviction of Friedrich Adler for the murder of the Austrian Minister of Justice.

Elaborating on the connection between opposition to the reinstitution of military discipline and antiwar attitudes within the armed forces, Mr. Ferro explained that prior to initiating his study he had read everywhere that the foremost desire of the soldiers was for land and that their greatest fear was that the land would be redistributed before they returned home. However, there was very little evidence of such a mood in the materials which he had analyzed. As far as he could tell antiwar sentiment was not very pronounced in March and April, and the number of authentic desertions during this time was quite low. Many of the soldiers who hurried home after the fall of the tsar returned to their posts soon afterward. A change in the soldiers' attitudes toward the war came about after the April crisis and the beginning of preparations for the resumption of offensive operations on the eastern front.

Turning to the reservations expressed by Mr. Thompson in regard to the attitudes of the bourgeoisie toward the aspirations of the workers, Mr. Ferro indicated that these could not be studied in the same way as the views of workers, peasants, and soldiers because, generally speaking, the bourgeoisie did not record their views in letters and telegrams. However, he expressed the conviction that although the bourgeoisie was willing to grant limited economic concessions to the workers, it objected to such fundamental changes as, for example, factory committee control of accounts.

Mr. Ferro noted the difficulty in reaching any conclusions regarding the views of the intelligentsia but indicated that he was able to observe a significant difference between the attitudes of professional men and academics. Professional men tended to be more antagonistic to the government than professors, although even so their attitudes corresponded more closely to the views of the bourgeoisie than to those of the left.

On the importance of the Constituent Assembly to the workers, Mr. Ferro commented that in the first two or three weeks after the February Revolution workers, influenced by whatever they could recall from the Social Democratic program, were impatient for its convocation. However, by May the workers tended to ignore not only the Constituent Assembly but the Soviet as well. By that time the factory shop committees dominated the workers' movement.

In evaluating the class consciousness of Russian workers after the February Revolution, Mr. Ferro drew a distinction between the attitudes of factory and nonfactory workers. He noted that factory workers tended to be more violently antagonistic toward the government and the bourgeoisie and less concerned with general Russian interests than were the railroad workers, for example. He attributed this difference to the fact that the isolated factory workers were alienated from the rest of the urban population to a far greater degree than were the more integrated railroad workers. He added that in their political attitudes craftsmen were well to the right of even the railway workers. Mr. Ferro concluded that in discussing the aspirations of the workers in the first weeks after the revolution he had not meant to imply that their demands were mainly economic. The desire for such things as personal dignity and a greater degree of influence were of crucial importance.

Mr. Roberts pointed out that Mr. Ferro's implied thought that the traditional categories of "political" and "economic" aspirations did not convey the subtlety of what the workers were seeking corroborated impressions he had gained from study of the strike wave in Russia immediately preceding the war. His conclusion was that the primary drives motivating Russian workers were more psychological than political or economic in nature. The desire for justice, dignity, and decent treatment was the factor that carried real force.

Mr. Kennan pointed out that Russian railroads were the first sector of the Russian economy to be taken over and administered with considerable vigor by the Provisional Government. The more conservative attitudes of the railway workers might be attributed in part to the fact that in the immediate aftermath of the February Revolution railway workers alone had a workable means of communication and maintained better contact with the center and the Provisional Government. Mr. Kecskemeti interpolated to say that also shaping the attitudes of the railwaymen was the fact that they were in a much better economic position than factory workers.

Mr. Kennan went on to comment on the irresponsibility of the soldiers, workers, and peasants. The soldiers wanted to fight a war but did not want any discipline or orders from officers. The workers wanted control of such matters as hiring practices but they did not want financial responsibility for the conduct of the enterprise. The peasants were only interested in getting land, and what happened in the rest of Russian society was apparently a matter of total indifference to them. These attitudes, said Mr. Kennan, made him much more sympathetic to Lenin's elitist opinions because neither the soldiers, nor the workers, nor the peasants were in a frame of mind that could have supported a constructive political program.

Mr. Rogger wondered whether the apparent absence in the armed forces of ideological opposition toward the war meant that the soldiers actively opposed the conflict only in so far as it involved risk to life and limb. Mr. Ferro disagreed, remarking that the opposition of the soldiers to the war crystallized when early hopes for a negotiated peace were unfulfilled.

Mr. Schapiro asked whether it was possible to perceive differences in the attitudes of the soldiers at the front and those in the garrison. Mr. Ferro replied affirmatively, stating that the attitudes of soldiers stationed in Petrograd were more extreme and partisan than were those of the men in the trenches.

Miss Arendt drew attention to the similarity between the evidence contained in the materials studied by Mr. Ferro and information regarding popular aspirations contained in recently published documents on the French Revolution. Along with a passion for justice the French documents revealed an anarchistic, anti-hierarchic attitude, and perhaps the same held true of the situation in Russia. In regard to the euphoria prevailing in the initial stages of the revolution, the significance of this feeling should not be underestimated simply because letters and telegrams suggest that it dwindled fairly rapidly. The mood persisted in France for a year, and it might have lasted in Russia for a longer period than the documents actually show.

In reply to Miss Arendt, Mr. Ferro said that euphoria was great after the February Revolution but that it was not general. The mood did not prevail among the intelligentsia and among many workers who were acutely aware of the fact that the February Revolution was not their revolution.

Mr. Anweiler took issue with Mr. Ferro's seeming conclusion that the Russian people did not want to be governed at all. The great problem of the immediate post-February period was that of finding the means by which the awakening civic consciousness of the workers could be expressed at a time of growing anarchistic feeling among the masses.

The Bolshevik Insurrection in Petrograd

— Dietrich Geyer

The subject to be discussed bears many names, none of which entirely covers it: coup d'état, uprising, insurrection, the Great October Socialist Revolution, conspiracy of a minority (*zagovor*), "ten days that shook the world," *action directe*, carried out by a group of determined men. These terms differ widely and can no longer be employed as equivalents. Fifty years after the event, its history resides in the nuances, and the interest of the historian transcends the bare facts that seem to tell "how it really was."

The October days of 1917 have often been described,[1] and yet we never cease to reexamine them. This probably would not be the case if these events had been no more than a mere coup d'état of which it could be simply said: "The Bolsheviks did not seize power. They picked it up."[2] Without doubt more was at stake: the history of Russia and much of our own history as well. This may explain why we can no longer separate the consequences of the revolution from its mere chronology. The events and their historical results have merged, and our controversies possess a history of their own.

It is perhaps possible to say that there is agreement on at least one point: no one will deny that the transfer of power during October was the result of an uprising, of a violent effort to overthrow the Provisional Government—an action relying on the support of the armed forces of the Petrograd garrison, of the Baltic Fleet, and of the working class— organized and directed by the Bolshevik Party. But if we go but one step

1. This paper does not attempt to give a bibliographical review of the sources now available or an account of research done on the subject by Soviet and Western historians. Footnotes are confined to a minimum. All dates are given in Old Style.

2. Adam B. Ulam, *Lenin and the Bolsheviks: The Intellectual and Political History of the Triumph of Communism in Russia* (London 1966), p. 314. The fullest narrative of the events published so far is S. Melgunov's *Kak bol'sheviki zakhvatili vlast': Oktiabr'skii perevorot 1917 goda* (Paris, 1953).

beyond this simple assertion, the event quickly ceases to be unequivocal. The term "uprising" (*vosstanie*) is ambivalent, and no description of it is possible that is not at the same time an evaluation. It raises the question of the character of the insurrection, and it is at this point that opinions begin to diverge.

It is well known that controversy over the uprising did not originate with historians. Among the first to doubt the rationality of the uprising were the men who eventually made the revolution. Lenin, as we know, first mentioned the controversial subject in two letters written from Finland in the middle of September 1917 after the defeat of the so-called "Kornilov Revolt."[3] "The Bolsheviks," he declared, "must take power at this very moment." In his opinion, only an "armed uprising" in Petrograd and Moscow, "an insurrection . . . treated as an art," would assure victory.[4] The laconic minutes of the meeting of the Central Committee on September 15 reflect the embarrassment of those who had to deal with Lenin's demands: Stalin pleaded for consultations with the most important party organizations; other participants wanted to make sure that no copies of the letters would be allowed to circulate; and Kamenev requested a rejection of Lenin's proposals and tried to persuade the Central Committee to pass a resolution "declaring all street actions to be for the moment inadmissible." The Committee finally decided to take measures "to prevent any actions in the barracks and in the factories."[5] This thinly veiled rejection of his proposals caused Lenin two weeks later to tender his resignation from the Central Committee, reserving for himself "freedom to campaign among the rank and file of the party and at the Party Congress."[6] Not until October 10, after Lenin had moved back to Petrograd from Finland, did the Central Committee consent (against the votes of Zinoviev and Kamenev) to place "the armed uprising on the order of the day," considering "that an armed uprising is inevitable and that the time for it is fully ripe."[7] But even then opposition persisted within the innermost circle of the party. The conflict had not been resolved.

3. "Bol'sheviki dolzhny vziat' vlast'. Pis'mo Tsentral'nomu Komitetu, Petrogradskomu i Moskovskomu komitetam RSDRP (b)" (September 12–14, 1917), *Polnoe sobranie sochinenii*, 5th ed. (Moscow, 1962), XXXIV, pp. 239–241; "Marksizm i vosstanie. Pis'mo Tsentral'nomu Komitetu RSDRP (b)" (September 13–14, 1917), *ibid.*, pp. 242–247.

4. *Ibid.*, pp. 240, 246–247.

5. *Protokoly Tsentral'nogo Komiteta RSDRP (b). Avgust 1917–fevral' 1918* (Moscow, 1958), p. 55.

6. "Krizis nazrel" (September 29, 1917), *Polnoe sobranie sochinenii*, XXXIV, p. 282.

7. *Protokoly Tsentral'nogo Komiteta*, p. 86.

The review of these facts, the correctness of which is not denied by Soviet historians, leads us to the core of the problem. Until October, the concept of an "armed uprising" or "insurrection" has been extremely vague and ill-defined for all. Those who spoke of an insurrection, whether to support it or reject it, saw before their eyes the scenes of the July 1917 days in Petrograd: street demonstrations by workers and soldiers, meetings with banners and placards, strikes and bloody clashes, the incitement of the masses against legal authority. These were the fruits of agitation in which organization and planning had played no major part. The Bolshevik leadership had shown itself incapable of channeling the underlying force of the movement, and instead of being a prelude to the seizure of power, the uprising had ended in defeat. Nevertheless, it corresponded to that classical type of insurrection that, since 1789, had been firmly established in the tradition of the European revolutions. Barricade fighting in 1848, the 1871 Paris Commune, the December 1905 revolt in Moscow, all followed the same basic pattern, which lost nothing of its fascination despite invariable failures.

In 1905, not even the Mensheviks had managed to avoid the prospect of an uprising.[8] In *Iskra*, their military experts discussed the best methods of erecting barricades, the place of artillery in street fighting, and the pros and cons of armed mass demonstrations. The insurrectionary formula was in no way binding. It committed the Social Democrats neither to a certain course of action nor to a conspiratorial activism. The term *vseobshchee narodnoe vosstanie* (general mass insurrection) had by 1905 become a substitute for everything that seemed to denote the climax of the revolution, even in the ranks of the liberal Kadets. The insurrection presupposed the action of the masses, of the overwhelming majority of the people. It was understood as a kind of revolutionary plebiscite, as an elementary event in the revolutionary process, as unpredictable as the processes of nature. Consequently, the legitimacy of the popular uprising could never be questioned.

As a matter of fact, as long as the tsarist regime remained firmly in the saddle, the controversies within the socialist camp centered on other issues. The debate was not whether a mass uprising should be welcomed or not but over the role of the party in the revolution. It is over this question that the well-known conflict between the Mensheviks and the Bolsheviks became irreconcilable. The Mensheviks had always rejected the idea that the rebellion, as they conceived it, could be planned, organized, let alone "made" by the Social Democrats. Not the party but the masses would have to launch it. The party, with its agitational ap-

8. For a recent analysis of the discussions in 1905 see Alexander Fischer, *Russische Sozialdemokratie und bewaffneter Aufstand* (Wiesbaden, 1967).

paratus, should serve only as a regulating force. To contemplate planning or directing the uprising was considered adventurism, conspiratorial mentality, a betrayal of the revolution. Certainly, Lenin, too, had never thought of an armed insurrection in any other way than in connection with an uprising of large parts of the population, of the proletariat as well as of the peasantry. But unlike his Menshevik opponents, he considered insurrection a central part of the revolutionary strategy of his party. Since 1901, he had demanded again and again that preparations be made for a popular uprising. To prepare an uprising meant to organize the party. The task was to arm the party for the hour when the mass uprising had broken out. This was the basis of the conspiratorial organization of the Bolsheviks.[9] The professional revolutionaries were to assume the hegemony, the leadership of the movement, they were to fight as the advance guard of the rebellious masses, they were to determine the political aims of the uprising and to deliver the decisive blow. Should the party falter when the people were ready for the insurrection, it would lose, in Lenin's view, its right to exist. By the beginning of 1905, this policy had long been formulated. The London Congress of the Russian Social Democratic Party held in 1905 had discussed the practical aspects of this idea,[10] but the events of 1905 proved that the revolutionary situation as anticipated by Lenin would not come about unaided. The seizure of power, the victory of the "revolutionary democracy" could not be achieved by the barricade fights of Presnia in December 1905.

In September 1917, when Lenin demanded that armed insurrection be treated as an art, the political scene had changed completely, but the idea of the uprising occupied the same position in his revolutionary thought:

> To be successful, insurrection must rely not upon conspiracy and not upon a party, but on the advanced class. That is the first point. Insurrection must rely upon a revolutionary upsurge of the people. That is the second point. Insurrection must rely upon that turning point in the history of the growing revolution when the activity of the advanced ranks of the people is at its height, and when the vacillations in the ranks of the enemy and in the ranks of the weak, half-hearted and irresolute friends of the revolution are strongest. That is the third point . . . Once these conditions exist, however, to refuse to treat the insurrection as an art is a betrayal of Marxism and a betrayal of the revolution.[11]

9. See Dietrich Geyer, *Lenin in der Russischen Sozialdemokratie* (Cologne, 1962), pp. 318–346.

10. *Tretii s"ezd RSDRP (b). Aprel'–Mai 1905: Protokoly* (Moscow, 1959), pp. 98–160, 450–451.

11. "Marksizm i vosstanie," *Polnoe sobranie sochinenii*, XXXIV, pp. 242–243.

The controversies in the Central Committee of the party were not primarily concerned with whether such an interpretation of the uprising was compatible with the principles of Marxism, or whether by adopting Lenin's definition the party would become guilty of "Blanquism." The argument lay elsewhere: it was over the analysis of the revolutionary situation as given by Lenin and over the question whether the political course of the party and the struggle for power should really be tied to an insurrection. Lenin's first thesis stated that now (September 1917), as a result of the defeat of Kornilov, all the conditions he had mentioned as necessary for the uprising were at hand: the support of the class representing "the vanguard of the revolution," "a countrywide revolutionary upsurge of the masses," "vacillation on a serious political scale among our enemies and among the irresolute petty bourgeoisie," and "the turning point in the history of the revolution." There were, of course, no real guarantees that these assertions were correct. But Lenin went even further: "It would be naive," he declared, "to wait for a 'formal' majority for the Bolsheviks. No revolution ever waits for that."[12] Lenin's view of what a majority was had a quality of its own, for it had nothing to do with elections or votes. From the fact that the Bolsheviks had obtained a majority in the soviets of Petrograd and Moscow, he drew the conclusion that "we have the following of a class, the vanguard of the revolution"; because the Mensheviks and the Socialist-Revolutionaries had rejected a coalition with the Kadets after the Kornilov revolt, he inferred that they "clearly lost their majority among the people"; since Chernov proved incapable of solving the agrarian question, he saw a confirmation of the statement that "We have the following of the majority of the people. Our victory is assured, for the people are close to desperation, and we show the people a sure way out."[13] It is obvious that Lenin's deductions (a majority in the soviets of both capitals equals a majority of the vanguard of the people equals a majority of the people equals victory in revolution) were not immediately intelligible to his comrades. The degree of reality inherent in this optimism remained questionable. Not until the very moment of armed action did the top echelons of the party become convinced that the insurrection would succeed. These doubts persisted as late as the meeting of the Central Committee on October 16.[14]

Apart from Lenin's assertion that "the time for the insurrection is fully ripe," it was undoubtedly the political consequences of his theses that met with strong opposition. In September 1917, for the first time since the fiasco of the July days, the party saw itself fully rehabilitated

12. *Ibid.*, p. 241.
13. *Ibid.*, p. 244.
14. *Protokoly Tsentral'nogo Komiteta RSDRP*, pp. 93–104.

in the eyes of "revolutionary democracy." During the fight against the Kornilov Revolt, its following had grown, and its political program, promising the masses peace and land, met with an increasing response among soldiers and workers. The Bolshevik majority in the soviets of Moscow and Petrograd and the catastrophic losses of the Mensheviks in the municipal elections were unmistakable signs of the dynamic growth of the Bolshevik party. From the beginning of September, the party had, with Lenin's approval, again taken up its old slogan: "All power to the Soviets"—the appeal with which they now planned to confront the Democratic Conference during its meeting in Petrograd. Chances for a radicalization of soviet democracy semed not too bad during those days, and it was not absurd to hope that the pressure of the masses would in the foreseeable future compel the replacement of the Provisional Government by a Soviet government, that is, by a coalition in which the Bolsheviks would assume a decisive role. In accord with these views, the Bolsheviks declared to the Democratic Conference: "Our party . . . has never striven and does not now strive for the seizure of power against the will of the organized majority of the working masses."[15] Seizure of power on the basis of the Soviet democracy—compared to this, the course advocated by Lenin had to appear as risky, even adventurous.

It is worth noting that Lenin in his contributions to the September issues of *Rabochii Put'* did not preclude alternatives to insurrection and civil war. In the event that power should be transferred to the soviets one should not rule out "a peaceful development of the revolution," compromises with the Mensheviks and the SR's, and a non-Bolshevik Soviet government with a Bolshevik opposition party—"under a really complete democracy." On September 16 appeared an article by Lenin that stated, "Only an alliance of the Bolsheviks with the SR's and the Mensheviks, and an immediate transfer of all power to the Soviets would prevent civil war in Russia."[16] Even as late as September 27, two days before Lenin had tendered his resignation, the party organ carried the following lines by him: "By seizing full power the Soviets could still today—and this is probably their last chance—ensure the peaceful development of the revolution, peaceful elections of deputies by the people, a peaceful struggle in the Soviets . . . and power should pass peacefully from one party to another."[17]

What is hinted at here is only superficially inconsistent with Lenin's

15. "Deklaratsiia fraktsii bol'shevikov, oglashennaia na Vserossiiskom Demokraticheskom Soveshchanii" (September 18, 1917), *ibid.*, p. 51.
16. "Russkaia revoliutsiia i grazhdanskaia voina," *Polnoe sobranie sochinenii*, XXXIV, p. 222.
17. "Zadachi revoliutsii," *ibid.*, p. 237.

demand that preparations be made for an insurrection. The alternative between civil war and a peaceful revolution presupposed the fall of the Provisional Government; it was valid only under the condition that power was transferred to the soviets. But in Lenin's mind, the method by which this power was to be gained was irrevocably linked with an armed insurrection. In this respect, the perspectives of a "Soviet democracy" that Lenin drew up had an agitational function only in the struggle for power. Last but not least, his reflections also had the aim of forcing the Bolshevik party into his line of thinking. He had to deal with a party whose top echelons did not concentrate their energies on an insurrection, but on political activities: on September 21 the Central Committee acquiesced to the vote of the Bolshevik faction at the Democratic Conference favoring participation in the Pre-Parliament.[18] This "peaceful" and "parliamentary" procedure Lenin violently attacked. There can be no doubt that compromises had become unacceptable to him.

It is probably correct to say that from September 1917 Lenin's position rested on the dialectic combination of three axioms: (1) those who support the Bolshevik slogan "All power to the soviets" must break with the parties which up to then had been the pillars of "revolutionary democracy"; (2) those who want a Soviet regime in this sense have to decide in favor of the insurrection; (3) those who decide in favor of the insurrection pronounce themselves for a Bolshevik Soviet regime.

Already in his first letters dealing with the uprising, Lenin had demanded that the Bolsheviks confront the Democratic Conference with a sharply worded ultimatum and demand the unconditional adoption of the Bolshevik program. Without waiting for an answer, the Bolsheviks were then to leave the Conference, and appeal immediately to the masses, to the factories and barracks: "*There* we must explain in passionate speeches our program and put the alternative: either the Conference adopts it in its entirety or else insurrection. There is no middle course. Delay is impossible . . . In putting the question in this way . . . we shall be able to determine the right moment to start the insurrection."[19] The passion with which Lenin strove to induce the party to act is clearly reflected in his brusque letters to the Central Committee and in his energetic appeals to party organizations and conferences. With growing aggressiveness, he pursued the boycott of the Pre-Parliament and condemned the "utter idiocy," the "sheer treachery" of those who wanted to wait for the All-Russian Congress of Soviets to convene. With arguments that acquired an emotional coloring he de-

18. *Protokoly Tsentral'nogo Komiteta RSDRP*, p. 65.
19. *Polnoe sobranie sochinenii*, XXXIV, p. 247.

manded again and again that the insurrection be treated as an art, as a problem of technique and organization. For guidance in these matters Lenin drew on the experiences recorded in Engels' pamphlet, *Revolution and Counterrevolution in Germany,* and he never wearied in presenting these terse reflections on the insurrection as Danton's and Marx's great legacy to which the party had to conform.[20]

It is impressive to see how unshakable Lenin was in his belief that no time must be lost. Now or never, he thought, was the moment to seize power and to assure its permanent possession. "It is my profound conviction that if we wait . . . and let the present moment pass, we shall ruin the revolution" (September 29).[21] Success seemed a certainty. His analysis of the revolutionary and military situations assured victory. The attack was to be opened simultaneously in three places: Moscow, Petrograd, and Finland. This time, he said, the army would not march against the insurgents; the wavering attitude of the government, the disintegration of the Mensheviks and the SR's, the agitation for peace and the distribution of land would assure the Bolsheviks of a majority in the country.[22] These judgments, however, should not be considered in isolation. The battle Lenin had to fight within his own party ranks became the driving force behind his argumentation and his analysis of the situation became a function of his polemics. This explains the excessive exaggeration of Lenin's political diagnoses. The fact of agrarian unrest led him to the prognosis that an enormous uprising of the peasants was at hand and that the Bolsheviks would betray democracy and the idea of liberty if they failed to take action in support of the peasants. By repeated references to symptoms of crises in the belligerent countries, Lenin placed the insurrection within the context of an international revolution. He interpreted reports about mass arrests of socialist party leaders in Italy and about the beginning of mutinies in the German navy as "indisputable symptoms," and as proof of the fact "that a turning point is at hand, that we are on the eve of a worldwide revolution."[23] Here reemerged the old idea that it was the destiny of the Bolsheviks to act as the vanguard of the international proletariat: "They will save the world revolution . . . and the lives of hundreds of thousands of people at the front."[24]

20. "Sovety postoronnego" (October 8, 1917), *ibid.,* p. 383; Lenin's quotations are from Engels' brochure, which he mistook for a work written by Marx: *ibid.,* p. 335.

21. "Krizis nazrel," *ibid.,* p. 283.

22. *Ibid.,* p. 282.

23. *Ibid.,* pp. 272, 275.

24. "Pis'mo v TsK, MK, PK i chlenam Sovetov Pitera i Moskvy-Bol'shevikam" (October 1, 1917), *ibid.,* pp. 340–341.

The basis of Lenin's astonishing assurance, the question of how he gained such unswerving confidence in the validity of his theses cannot be discussed here in full. Any answers have to take into account the psychological constitution of this man. But even psychology does not excuse us from looking for a rational explanation. It is certain that Lenin saw the military problems of the insurrection in closest connection with the political problems of the revolution. "Events compel us . . . History has made the military question now the fundamental *political* question" (September 27).[25] The insight implied here Lenin may have found in Clausewitz: "Armed uprising," he wrote, "is a special form of political struggle," that is, "politics with other means." Added to this was (with reference to Marx), "Insurrection is an art quite as much as war."[26] Everything that was military or technical became incorporated into the political strategy of the revolution. Thus, Lenin's thesis that "to wait is a crime" could be detached from the specific moment and continually absorb new arguments from the changing situation. These were: that a separate peace among the imperialists was impending, that Kerensky schemed to deliver revolutionary Petrograd into the hands of the Germans, that a second Kornilov coup was at hand, and that "the success of both the Russian and the world revolution depends on two or three days' fighting."[27]

By October 10, Lenin had, as we know, succeeded in his attempt to secure within the top committee of the party a majority for his policy of insurrection. The decision of the Bolshevik faction to walk out on the Pre-Parliament during its opening session on October 7 was an important step in that direction. On the same day, Lenin returned from Finland and took lodgings on Vasilevskii Ostrov in Petrograd. Three days later the Central Committee voted in favor of his thesis that the time was ripe for an insurrection. The situation justified this resolution. At the beginning of October, the government was undoubtedly headed for a new and serious crisis; it rapidly lost authority. The military situation on the northern front was catastrophic. In the capital, one had every reason to doubt the loyalty of the strong garrison stationed there. Because of the continuous shortages of fuel and food, prices soared uncontrollably.[28] The lethargic attitude of the working people

25. "Pis'mo I. T. Smilge," *ibid.*, p. 264.
26. "Sovety postoronnego," *ibid.*, pp. 382–383. See Werner Hahlweg, "Lenin und Clausewitz," *Archiv für Kulturgeschichte*, XXXVI (1954), pp. 30–59, 357–387.
27. *Polnoe sobranie sochinenii*, XXXIV, p. 384.
28. New information, based on archival sources, is given by Z. V. Stepanov, *Rabochie Petrograda v period podgotovki i provedeniia Oktiabr'skogo vooruzhennogo vosstaniia* (Moscow-Leningrad, 1965).

in the suburbs and in the factories could easily turn into unrest and riots. The pathos of the speakers at the Council of the Republic could not conceal the general misery. The Executive Committee of the All-Russian Congress of Soviets, consisting of prominent Mensheviks and SR's, was no less isolated than the Provisional Government. It was to be expected that the Second All-Russian Congress of Soviets, scheduled for October 20, would consolidate the Bolsheviks' gains. The Soviet of Petrograd was dominated by Trotsky, the exponent of the Bolshevik majority. The Left SR's seemed ready to support the Bolsheviks. At a Congress of the Soviet Deputies of the Northern Region, held on October 11 at the Smolny Institute, the animosity toward the government led to manifestations approaching a formal declaration of civil war. Lenin hoped that this congress could be transformed into an organ of the uprising and that the Finnish troops and the Baltic fleet could be induced to march on Petrograd.[29] It appeared that the Central Committee had chosen the right moment for its decision to prepare the insurrection.

Upon closer inspection, however, it appears that on October 10 the Bolshevik Central Committee still avoided making a clear commitment. The technique of the uprising and the strategy of the power seizure had not been discussed. Instead, the old controversies flared up again because of Kamenev and Zinoviev, who protested that the insurrection would end in defeat and force the petty bourgeoisie into the camp of the Kadets, that a proletarian government would be unable to carry on a revolutionary war against the German imperialists, and that the mass of the soldiers would turn away from the Bolsheviks. They rejected Lenin's thesis that the majority of the people and the international proletariat had already been won over. In their view, the best chances for the party lay not in an insurrection but in the utilization of the impending All-Russian Congress of Soviets and in concentrating the party's efforts on elections for the Constituent Assembly.[30] In view of this opposition, Lenin was compelled to intensify his struggle for the acceptance of his strategy.[31] The polemics of his opponents became entangled in arguments that, no doubt, carried a certain historical

29. "Pis'mo k tovarishcham bol'shevikam, uchastvuiushchim na Oblastnom S"ezde Sovetov Severnoi Oblasti" (October 8, 1917), *Polnoe sobranie sochinenii*, XXXIV, pp. 385–390.

30. G. Zinoviev, Iu. Kamenev, "K tekushchemu momentu" (October 11, 1917), *Protokoly Tsentral'nogo Komiteta RSDRP (b)* (Moscow, 1958), pp. 87–92.

31. See Lenin's "Pis'mo k tovarishcham" (October 17), "Pis'mo k chlenam partii bol'shevikov" (October 19), "Pis'mo v Tsentral'nyi Komitet RSDRP (b)" (October 19, 1917), *Polnoe sobranie sochinenii*, XXXIV, pp. 398–427.

dignity, but had little practical relevance. Lenin's opponents had difficulty keeping in touch with the actual situation.

As a matter of fact, the controversy had little effect on the course of
events in Petrograd. The call for an insurrection could be dispensed
with as soon as a method for the overthrow of the Provisional Government had been found. There is much evidence to indicate that Trotsky,
the chairman of the Petrograd Soviet, had a large share in the solution
of this problem. On October 6, a rumor concerning a "counterrevolutionary conspiracy" was discussed in the Soldiers' Section of the Soviet.[32]
The rumor was that the government was preparing its flight from
Petrograd and intended to abandon the "citadel of the revolution" to
the approaching Germans. Trotsky made a momentous decision when he
resolved immediately to take advantage of this rumor. In the Bolshevik
declaration to the Pre-Parliament he painted a grim picture of the
"deadly danger" that now threatened the capital. Kerensky, he wrote,
planned the transfer of the government to Moscow with the view of
transforming that city into a stronghold of the counterrevolution and
breaking up the Constituent Assembly. The garrison, he continued, was
soon to be evacuated, which meant the abandonment of the city to the
German army and the smothering of the revolution.[33] Trotsky had
obviously recognized the usefulness of this charge. If the alleged danger
could be rendered credible, the Soviet of Petrograd would obtain a
powerful and highly effective instrument for the organization of a
broad line of resistance. It could also determine the nature of the appeal
that was to be addressed to the garrison and to the workers. These were
to be called upon to protect the capital from its external and internal
enemies; to defend it against the counterrevolution, personified by
Miliukov and the Kaiser. This strategy made the appeal for an insurrection superfluous. In the slogan "Petrograd in danger" the Bolsheviks
had a formula capable of affecting the masses in a very fundamental
way. Their agitation received a uniform direction, and the practical
measures were given a concrete aim. The object was to paralyze the
authority of the Military Staff of the Petrograd garrison, to put the
troops under the command of the Soviet, and to enable the workers to
arm themselves and to support the troops.

The Petrograd Soviet lost no time in realizing the chances thus offered. Already on October 9 the regiments were asked to increase their

32. "Rezoliutsiia Soldatskoi Sektsii Petrogradskogo Soveta" (October 6, 1917),
L. Trotsky, *Sochineniia* (Moscow, n.d.), vol. III, pt. 1, p. 321.

33. "Deklaratsiia fraktsii bol'shevikov na zasedanii Demokraticheskogo Sovesh-
chaniia" (October 7, 1917), *ibid.*, pp. 321–323. See also *Protokoly Tsentral'nogo
Komiteta RSDRP (b)*, pp. 77–79.

combat readiness.[34] Two days later, Trotsky's addresses before the Congress of Soviets of the Northern Region gave the appeal for the active defense of the capital wide resonance, far beyond Petrograd itself.[35] The immediate concern of the Bolshevik leaders was to incorporate the forces on the periphery of the city into the general plan for action, especially the troops of the northern front and of the Baltic fleet.[36] It was to the advantage of the Bolsheviks that they could operate behind Soviet legitimacy. They carried out their preparations publicly and in an orderly manner. Already on October 15, the readers learned from their Sunday papers that the Bolsheviks planned action against the Provisional Government.[37] On the following day Trotsky declared before the plenum of the Soviet: "We are told that we prepare a staff for the seizure of power. We make no secret of it."[38] The Military-Revolutionary Committee, founded on October 11 as an operational center,[39] was, as a matter of fact, not a club of conspirators, but a formally elected institution of the Petrograd Soviet. This meant that it had many channels open: it had its own press and official contacts with the soviets in all districts of the city,[40] with the trade unions and the factory committees, the workers' militia and the Red Guards as well.[41]

34. "Rezoliutsiia Petrogradskogo Soveta o vyvode voisk iz Petrograda" (October 9, 1917), L. Trotsky, *Sochineniia*, vol. III, pt. 1, p. 327.

35. *Ibid.*, vol. III, pt. 2, pp. 5–14

36. On the role of the Baltic fleet in October 1917 see recent Soviet documentations sponsored by the Historical Institute of the Academy of Sciences and the Central Archives of the Soviet fleet: *Baltiiskie moriaki v podgotovke i provedenii Velikoi Oktiabr'skoi revoliutsii* (Moscow-Leningrad, 1957); *Protokoly i postanovleniia Tsentral'nogo Komiteta Baltiiskogo flota, 1917–1918* (Moscow-Leningrad, 1963).

37. *Delo Naroda*, no. 181, October 15, 1917, quoted in R. P. Browder and A. F. Kerensky, eds., *The Russian Provisional Government 1917: Documents* (Stanford, 1961), III, pp. 1764–1765. On October 14, the Menshevik leader Dan drew attention to the Bolshevik preparations for an uprising during a session of the Central Executive Committee of the All-Russian Soviets. See *Izvestiia TsIK*, no. 198, October 15, 1917, quoted in *Velikaia Oktiabr'skaia Socialisticheskaia Revoliutsiia. Khronika sobytii*, IV (Moscow, 1961), p. 429.

38. L. Trotsky, *Sochineniia*, vol. III, pt. 2, p. 15.

39. Important material has been collected in *Petrogradskii Voenno-Revoliutsionnyi Komitet: Dokumenty i materialy*, 3 vols., (Moscow, 1966–67); compare, *Velikaia Oktiabr'skaia Sotsialisticheskaia revoliutsiia. Dokumenty i materialy: Oktiabr'skoe vooruzhennoe vosstanie v Petrograde* (Moscow, 1957).

40. See *Raionnye Sovety Petrograda v 1917 godu: Protokoly, rezoliutsii, postanovleniia obshchikh sobranii i zasedanii ispolnitelnykh komitetov*, I–III (Moscow-Leningrad, 1964–66).

41. V. I. Startsev, "Voenno-revoliutsionnyi Komitet i Krasnaia gvardia v Oktiabr'skom vooruzhennom vosstanii," in *Oktiabr'skoe vooruzhennoe vosstanie v Petrograde: Sbornik statei* (Moscow-Leningrad, 1957), pp. 106–141.

The government saw its sphere of power systematically diminished without being able to arrest the process of its isolation.

The wisdom of this tactical concept was proved by the fact that the Bolshevik Central Committee now began to concern itself with practical questions connected with the planned power seizure as well. On October 16 the Bolsheviks resolved to attach a permanent delegation to the Military-Revolutionary Committee.[42] Long discussions had again given rise to a multitude of doubts. Many members still tended to recall the fiasco of July whenever talk of an insurrection came up. The reports of local Bolshevik representatives gave no basis for any definite opinions concerning the chances for success. In the end, the impression that gained hold was that the seizure of power was conceivable only if it developed from active resistance of the garrison, as a defensive action against measures of the government directly affecting the fate of the troops. This corresponded to the course chosen by the Soviet. Thus, Trotsky found himself justified even before achieving any success. The seizure of power had to start with the seizure of the garrison, with the gradual emasculation by the Military Revolutionary Committee of the Military Headquarters. In the days that followed, the task became one of provoking the enemy, as a means of setting off the process of the transfer of power.

There was so little resemblance between these tactics and the common idea of an insurrection, that Trotsky could exploit the general confusion to conceal the further preparations. The government, the bourgeois press, and even the Mensheviks expected that, as in July, the action of the Bolsheviks would again erupt into armed mass demonstrations. On October 18 Maxim Gorky expressed his fears, "An organized mob will pour out into the streets, . . . and adventurers, thieves, and professional murders . . . will begin to 'make the history of the Russian revolution.' "[43] Trotsky declared on the same day that no decisions had been taken which were not publicly known: If the Soviet—"this revolutionary parliament—finds it necessary to call a demonstration, then it will do so . . . We have still not set a date for the attack."[44] All the actions of the Military-Revolutionary Committee, including the arming of the workers' militia, were still declared to be purely defensive measures. Not the Soviet, Trotsky continued, but the bourgeoisie provoked the

42. *Protokoly Tsentral'nogo Komiteta RSDRP (b)*, p. 104.

43. Novaia zhizn', no. 156, October 18, 1917, quoted in Browder and Kerensky, *The Russian Provisional Government*, III, p. 1766.

44. L. Trotsky, *Sochineniia*, vol. III, pt. 2, pp. 31–33, for a second version of Trotsky's speech, see Browder and Kerensky, *The Russian Provisional Government*, III, p. 1767.

conflict; the counterrevolution was about "to mobilize all forces against the workers and soldiers." Trotsky announced that any plot against the forthcoming Second All-Russian Congress of Soviets and any attempt to clear Petrograd of its garrison would be answered "with a ruthless counteroffensive carried to its end."[45] Declarations of this kind seemed to leave it to the enemy to begin hostilities.

Bolshevik agitation was now entirely concentrated on the slogan: "The All-Russian Congress is in danger." Trotsky could not dispense with this formula if he wanted his concept of the gradual seizure of power to succeed. He declared that the deputies to the Congress must be enabled to fulfill their task without hindrance. This task was "to pass resolutions transferring power to the All-Russian Congress of Soviets, concluding an immediate armistice on all fronts, and transferring all land to the peasants."[46] The procedure of having the organization of the coup d'état sanctioned by the soviet institutions of Petrograd remained unaltered. The Bolsheviks were thus obliged to observe the rules of the Soviet. Success was assured by the steady increase of the authority of the Petrograd Soviet, rather than by pressure on the Bolsheviks to start an insurrection. For Trotsky "insurrection as an art" meant treating Soviet legality as an art. Even some members of the Military-Revolutionary Committee may have believed that they worked exclusively to safeguard the forthcoming Congress of Soviets and to defend the garrison against counterrevolutionary pogroms. As late as October 24, Trotsky, Kamenev, and Balashev entered into negotiations with the Socialist-Revolutionaries on the basis of this formula.[47]

We know that even Lenin was deceived by the rationality of these moves and misinterpreted Trotsky's intentions. It was unacceptable to him that the seizure of power should be tied to the resolutions of the Congress; this seemed "a disaster, a sheer formality." The Congress had interest to him only if the insurrection anticipated its resolutions, thus reducing the function of the deputies to applauding the Bolshevik triumph. On the evening of October 24, shortly before taking the streetcar to the Smolny, he wrote in a state of extreme excitement: "We are confronted with problems which are not to be solved by conferences or congresses . . . , but exclusively by peoples, by the masses, by the struggle of the armed people." He categorically demanded a decision "at any cost, this very evening, this very night."[48] Little remained to be done

45. *Ibid.*
46. *Ibid.*
47. *Golos soldata*, October 25, 1917, reprinted in *Petrogradskii Voenno-revoliutsionnyi Komitet*, I, p. 99.
48. *Polnoe sobranie sochinenii*, XXXIV, pp. 435–436.

in this respect. The Provisional Government had become a mere shadow; practically speaking, it had already lost its power. Its security depended on a few hundred rifles; its hope rested with the fiction that troops were marching to its relief. On October 21 the Petrograd Soviet had already set off the mechanism of the transfer of power. Consistently with the general tactics, the first move was to confront the District Head-quarters under Colonel Polkovnikov with an ultimatum.[49] The Soviet demanded that the commissars it had appointed should be recognized and that henceforth all military orders obtain the sanction of the Revolutionary-Military Committee. The capitulation act thus had already been formulated. It was realized on October 23 when the Soviet claimed for itself the sole power of command over the garrison.[50] The bulk of the regiments placed themselves under the command of Smolny; the Cossacks remained neutral; the citizens of the capital were asked to maintain a state of absolute calm and self-control.

What followed resembled a mere police action. The insurrection was not formally proclaimed, nor were the people called out into the streets, nor was the fighting quality of the workers put to test. The decisive signal for the seizure of power was finally given by the government itself when it tried to shut down the Bolshevik press on the morning of October 24. The final episode was insignificant. Macabre scenes took place in the Mariinskii Theater when Kerensky informed the Council of the Republic of the insurrection in the capital.[51] Before the sailors of Kronstadt went ashore on the following day and before the cruiser "Aurora" had readied its guns, the victors had already advertised their success: "The Provisional Government has been deposed. State power has passed into the hands of . . . the Revolutionary-Military Committee which heads the Petrograd proletariat and garrison."[52] The martial impressions left by the event of October 25 were mainly due to the simple fact that the cabinet continued its session in the Malachite Room of the Winter Palace, although the Prime Minister had left.

Kerensky's fall was undoubtedly a result of the brilliant technique of power seizure as developed by Trotsky. But the very fact that this could be performed so easily points to something beyond the mere technical aspects. The regiments of the garrison that followed the Bolshevik slogans formed no potential capable of sustaining the burden

49. *Petrogradskii Voenno-revoliutsionnyi Komitet*, I, p. 59.
50. *Ibid.*, pp. 67, 97–98.
51. *Rech'*, no. 251, October 25, 1917, in Browder and Kerensky, *The Russian Provisional Government*, III, pp. 1772–1774.
52. "K grazhdanam Rossii" (October 25, 10:00 A.M.), *Petrogradskii Voenno-revoliutsionnyi Komitet*, I, p. 106.

of a military contest. The military effectiveness of the workers' militia and the Red Guards is also doubtful. It became evident that the secret for success did not lie in the military means that the Military-Revolutionary Committee had at its disposal. The transfer of power in Petrograd was rather the result of the victory that the Bolsheviks previously achieved in the *political* sphere on the basis of that very Soviet Democracy whose principles they rejected, but whose apparatus they could not dispense with.[53] The coup d'état in Petrograd could be organized only after the Soviet had been conquered. It was possible to disarm the enemy physically because he was already disarmed politically. Power could not have been captured as long as it was not secured politically. The art of insurrection was a product of the art of politics; it was the result of a policy whose plebiscitary quality can hardly be contested. At the last moment even the Mensheviks and SR's seized Bolshevik formulas in order to avoid being crushed between the Scylla of the counterrevolution and the Charybdis of a Bolshevik dictatorship.[54] Armistice and distribution of land—there was, in October, no plausible political alternative to this emergency program. This situation had a compelling force and not only the Provisional Government fell a victim to it, but soviet democracy as well. Lenin remained in power because he dared to do what had become a necessity.

53. Oskar Anweiler, *Die Rätebewegung in Russland 1905–1921* (Leiden, 1958), pp. 180–241.
54. See Browder and Kerensky, *The Russian Provisional Government*, III, pp. 1778–1784.

October in the Provinces — John Keep

In the foreword to his classic study of the October Revolution in
Petrograd and Moscow, S. P. Melgunov remarks that the story has yet
to be told of "how the rest of the country reacted to the act of violence
perpetrated in the capitals."[1] There are two principal reasons why this
has not been done. One is the centralist bias common among students
of Russian history, who have in the main viewed developments in the
provinces as no more than a reflection of events in the capital cities—
even in a period of revolutionary *Sturm und Drang.*[2] The other is the
lack of adequate documentation. A satisfactory account would require,
as Melgunov points out, "a fairly detailed and painstaking study of the
local sources,"[3] most of which are unhappily difficult of access. Even
the Moscow libraries are reputed to have important deficiencies. The
local newspapers appeared irregularly, and the central ones contain a
curious amalgam of fact, rumor and trivia.[4] Much valuable information
was collected and published in the 1920's by the local sections of
Istpart, but these volumes are bibliographical rarities. In the era of high
Stalinism little appeared, and the flood of information released since
1957 has in a sense aggravated the problems facing the independent
investigator because of the strict rules that currently govern the publication of documents from Soviet archives.[5]

Note: All dates in this article are given in Old Style.

1. S. P. Melgunov, *Kak bol'sheviki zakhvatili vlast'* (Paris, 1953), p. 7.

2. With the important exception of R. Pipes, *Formation of the Soviet Union:
Communism and Nationalism, 1917–1923*, 2d rev. ed. (Cambridge, 1964). Another
useful work is O. Anweiler, *Die Rätebewegung in Russland 1905–1921* (Leiden,
1958); the provincial soviets in 1917 are ably analyzed on pp. 241 ff. He agrees that
studies of this subject are "still in their infancy" (p. 248n).

3. Melgunov, *Kak bol'sheviki*, p. 272.

4. As noted by Professor W. E. Mosse, whom I thank for kindly lending his
valuable collection of extracts from the central newspapers for the immediate post-
revolutionary period.

5. It is interesting that these rules have recently come under attack by Soviet
historians. A. I. Gukovskii has condemned what he calls "the illustrative method of

Any study of the subject can therefore be little more than an introductory survey. Many of the most fundamental questions cannot yet be answered adequately. To what extent and in what ways did the "social geography" of the various regions affect the popular response to Bolshevism? How important was the proletarian element vis-à-vis that of the soldiers and of the intellectuals? How far was the central apparatus of the Bolshevik party in control of events and, conversely, how far did local leaders, activists, and rank-and-file members act in response to pressures from below? How important was the use or threat of violence in enabling the party to attain its ends? On any reading of the evidence, the element of political manipulation is of considerable significance, and more needs to be known about the role played in the transfer of power by the soviets and their executive committees (*ispolkomy*) as well as other bodies—whether those primarily of working-class appeal, such as factory committees (*fabzavkomy*) and trade unions, or public organizations (cooperatives, professional unions and societies), or organs of public administration (municipal dumas and *zemstva*). Similar questions might be asked with regard to the extensive hierarchy of military committees and soviets, ranging from the All-Army Committee at Mogilev to those within the humblest detachment in the armed forces.

It should be emphasized that a study of the provincial materials cannot of itself explain why the Bolsheviks won. For this, reference must be made to a broader range of data: to the political struggle in Petrograd and to the intellectual history of the Russian Left. But this is fairly well-trodden ground, and it is as well to shift our gaze away from the capital cities—all the more so since developments in the provinces were by no means merely a pale copy of events at the main centers. There is little validity in the stereotyped image of a "triumphal march of Soviet power."[6] On the contrary, a striking feature of the

selection," exemplified by the ten-volume documentary series on the 1917 Revolution published under the editorial supervision of A. L. Sidorov (Moscow-Leningrad, 1957–). He commends the procedure followed in the 1920's and suggests that entire archival series should be reproduced as they stand, that is, without regard to the ideological rectitude of their contents (*Voprosy istorii*, no. 5, 1966, pp. 65–76). Among the useful materials that deserve publication in full are the Central Committee's journals of outgoing and ingoing mail, referred to by V. V. Anikeev in *Voprosy istorii KPSS*, no. 9 (1963), p. 99, and the archive of TsIK, quoted in selection by K. Riabinskii in the compilation *Revoliutsiia 1917 g.: khronika sobytii*, V (Moscow-Leningrad, 1926). For a brief description of relevant materials in the Central Party Archive, see Anikeev's article in *Voprosy istorii KPSS*, no. 11 (1966), pp. 122–127.

6. D. A. Chugaev and others, eds., *Triumfal'noe shestvie sovetskoi vlasti*, 2 pts. (Moscow, 1963).

provincial scene is the degree to which local leaders, cut off from their accepted sources of political guidance and control, arrived at their own practical solution to the problem of power—one which often failed to commend itself either to the old rulers of Russia or the new.

At this point the term "provinces" needs to be defined more closely. We are not concerned here with Bolshevik agrarian policy and so may exclude the purely rural areas; similarly, the nationalities question deserves more extended treatment and only one minority area (the Ukraine) will be considered. We may also omit from discussion the areas in the immediate vicinity of both Petrograd and Moscow, the fate of which was closely bound up with that of these two metropolitan centers, the focal points of the insurrection. We are left in effect with the country towns—in most cases a *gubernskii gorod*, sometimes a large industrial settlement, occasionally a backwoods township reminiscent of Saltykov-Shchedrin's Glupov, where the tale is one of half-hearted fumbling and compromise rather than of a clash between titanic political forces.

We may first examine the condition of the local Bolshevik organizations on the eve of the seizure of power.

The basic unit of party organization was the city committee (*gorkom*), of which 288 are known to have existed at this time.[7] Usually this body was a fairly recent creation, which owed much to men who had arrived in the area since February 1917. As these leaders' local contacts grew, so did the number of committee members. To prevent their authority from becoming too diluted, the leaders would frequently form an inner nucleus, usually a triumvirate (*troika*), and would submit important decisions to a full meeting of the committee whenever they thought this expedient.

The committeemen were sometimes differentiated socially from the party rank and file. In Saratov, we are told, "the most active people were nonworkers,"[8] that is, intellectuals. In Kiev "the workers from the masses stubbornly refused to stand as candidates [for the *gorkom*] as they considered themselves unfit for committee work."[9] But these social differences were less obvious now than in less turbulent eras of party history, and shared experiences, hopes, and fears created an emotional bond between the leaders and the led.

7. V. V. Anikeev, "Svedeniia o bol'shevistskikh organizatsiiakh s marta do dekabria 1917 g," *Voprosy istorii KPSS*, no. 2 (1958), p. 132.

8. V. P. Antonov-Saratovskii, *Pod stiagom proletar'skoi bor'by: otryvki iz vospominanii o rabote v Saratove* . . . (Moscow-Leningrad, 1925), p. 119n.

9. E. B. Bosh, *God bor'by: bor'ba za vlast' na Ukraine s aprel'ia 1917 g. do nemetskoi okkupatsii* (Moscow-Leningrad, 1925), p. 38.

The committee was divided both functionally and geographically. The military section (*voennaia sektsiia*), which was concerned with agitation among the troops, often enjoyed considerable autonomy. In Kazan it had an office conveniently located beneath that of the soviet but took care to keep itself organizationally distinct.[10] According to recent Soviet research a total of 40 party organizations had military groups attached to them.[11] The nonfunctional divisions, in the first instance the city ward (*raion*) committees, could serve as a useful reserve base should the *gorkom* prove unable to act. Thus in Kiev, the Pechcrski ward organization played an important role in the October days, after the *gorkom* had been arrested.[12] In some smaller towns (Kaluga, Tambov) the *gorkom* itself was of small significance compared with the powerful party organizations that existed in the outlying industrial areas.

These lower-echelon groups in the factories were the main driving force behind the *fabzavkom* movement, which despite its inherently anarchic and disruptive character had by October developed a sizeable apparatus of its own, culminating in a Central Council in Petrograd.[13] There was some tension between these bodies, with their overtly political purpose, and the trade-union branches, which felt that they had a responsibility to safeguard their members' economic interests. But this conflict could be contained without too much trouble. The trade-union movement was structurally still very decentralized, and it was relatively easy for the party to win the support of the local union branches, especially at the factory level. It was more difficult at the city and regional level; nevertheless, in Kiev the three individuals who specialized in this kind of work won control of the regional trade-union organization and one was elected chairman of the (regional) metal-workers' union.[14]

Another type of grass-roots organization on the periphery of the *gorkom* was the combat squad of armed militants (*boevaia druzhina*), sometimes known as Red Guards. Such groups might be formed on the initiative either of the men themselves or of the local leaders. The latter was the case in Saratov, where P. Lebedev—who rather incongru-

10. K. Grasis, "Oktiabr' v Kazani," *Proletarskaia revoliutsiia*, no. 33 (1924), p. 125.

11. V. V. Anikeev, "Dokumenty Tsentral'nogo Partiinogo Arkhiva," *Voprosy istorii KPSS*, no. 11 (1966), p. 126.

12. Bosh, *God bor'by*, pp. 45, 49.

13. The First All-Russian Conference of these bodies, held from October 17 to 22, was an important sounding board for Bolshevik policy. See P. N. Amosov et al., *Oktiabr'skaia revoliutsiia i fabzavkomy: materialy po istorii fabrichno-zavodskikh komitetov*, 2 pts. (Moscow, 1927), pt. II, pp. 141 ff.

14. Bosh, *God bor'by*, p. 14.

ously was a lawyer by profession—decided to follow the example set in the capital.[15] In some other areas, such as the Urals, the leaders had a strong local tradition of violence to draw upon. At Ufa, combat groups came into existence spontaneously and in secret early in the year; in June, V. P. Artsybashev, an old party activist, raised the matter in the *gorkom* (which at that time still included the Mensheviks) but was defeated, whereupon he and his supporters simply disregarded the ban and proceeded to help form such squads "under the guise of organizing a town militia."[16] According to statements by Bolshevik delegates to the Second Congress of Soviets in October, each of the following six provincial cities had more than a thousand men enrolled in *druzhiny*: Astrakhan (3,500), Kiev (3,000), Odessa (2,000), Omsk (1,500), Kharkov (1,000), Nikolaev (1,000).[17] Curiously enough, only one of these towns, Omsk, was a Bolshevik stronghold.

The chief arena of Bolshevik activity, of course, was the local soviet. The party had most success with soviets that were worker-based, rather less with those that jointly represented workers and soldiers (although there were significant exceptions), and relatively little influence in independent peasant soviets. These were informal and extremely fluid organizations, with ill-defined structure and powers. Their claim to represent a particular social group was often shadowy. Delegates' mandates were seldom thoroughly verified, and they could easily be swept off their feet by the highly charged emotional atmosphere in which the proceedings were generally conducted. Each left-wing group sought to maintain its own "fraction" in the soviet and on its executive, and much time was consumed in complying outwardly with democratic procedures. In some remoter places, however, matters might be arranged more casually: in Murom, for example, the Bolsheviks did not formally organize their soviet followers into a "fraction" until November 4, one week after the seizure of power.[18]

The Bolsheviks' greater sense of discipline gave them a powerful advantage over their rivals, which far outweighed any numerical inferiority. Practical experience soon taught them many manipulative

15. Characteristically, he first suggested this idea to the *fabzavkomy*, not to the Soviet controlled by moderates, because he realized that the latter would regard the move as a threat to its own security. P. Lebedev, "Fevral'–oktiabr' v Saratove," *Proletarskaia revoliutsiia*, no. 10 (1922), p. 250.

16. I. Podshivalov, *Grazhdanskaia bor'ba na Urale 1917–1918 gg.: opyt voenno-istoricheskogo issledovaniia* (Moscow, 1925), pp. 55–56, 101.

17. A. F. Butenko and D. A. Chugaev, eds., *Vtoroi s"ezd sovetov rabochikh i soldatskikh deputatov: sbornik dokumentov* (Moscow, 1957), pp. 229–385 (replies to question 20).

18. *25 let Muromskoi organizatsii RSDRP(b)—VKP(b): sbornik* (Murom, 1928), p. 67.

techniques, which they used to considerable effect. If they could not bring their adversaries to the point of schism by propaganda pressure, they would seek to play off one element in the soviet organization against another. Factory meetings would be called to protest against the line taken by the assembly and to demand a reelection of the delegates; more simply a vociferous part of the assembly might declare that the executive had forfeited its confidence and force it to resign. Alternatively, an executive, or a bureau speaking in its name, might appeal to the electors against a recalcitrant assembly. The choice of tactics depended largely upon the distribution of political power. If Bolshevik influence were stronger among workers than among soldiers and the former were in a majority, expediency would dictate a merger between the two bodies; conversely, if such a merger entailed a risk that the radical element might be swallowed up by the moderates, then the two would be kept apart and counterposed to one another. The aim was always simple: to win and maintain control of the organizations in their entirety, thereby enhancing and legitimizing the authority exercised by the local party militants in the name of the "revolutionary masses."

It was the Bolsheviks' good fortune that most members of the soviets were concerned primarily with local issues. In the soviet hierarchy, provincial (*guberniia*), regional (*oblast'*, *okrug*), and national deliberative assemblies proliferated, but there was a notable dearth of executive bodies capable of effectively coordinating their policies. During the summer and fall regional bureaus of soviets came into existence, but these were somewhat ephemeral creations, since the energies of their members went fully into local affairs.[19] The Central Executive Committee (TsIK) elected in June lost authority by its association in the popular mind with the cunctatory Provisional Government, especially after the abortive revolt of General Kornilov. In many provincial centers like Petrograd and Moscow, this was the turning point in the struggle between the Bolsheviks and the moderate socialists for control of the soviets. In Saratov, as one Bolshevik leader notes, the Kornilov affair "with one stroke returned us the sympathies of the masses, which we had almost lost"; the Bolsheviks overcame their rivals' suspicions as to their patriotism and soon found themselves with a slender majority in the soviet.[20]

Although the soviets played a conspicuous role in Bolshevik theory and practice, they were supplemented, and in some cases supplanted, by other channels of contact between the *gorkom* and the mass of the

19. Bosh, *God bor'by*, pp. 26, 62.
20. Lebedev, "Fevral'," p. 249.

population. An important function often fell to organs of local self-government and other public bodies, official and semi-official, in which there were party members or sympathizers, not infrequently occupying positions of control. Such allies clearly had a vital function to play, particularly in the military apparatus: at Orsha, for example, the Bolshevik agent in the town commandant's office transmitted to his comrades in the *gorkom* information about troop movements through this key railway junction, on which they acted.[21] In the civilian administration, sadly ill equipped for its superhuman tasks, such men could often rise to leading positions. At Ufa, A. D. Tsurupa, an old party activist and *zemstvo* employee, was appointed successively chairman of the *guberniia* supply committee, a deputy to the reformed *zemstvo* at district and provincial level, and chairman of the municipal duma—offices he combined with his functions in the local soviet and the party organization.[22] Another well-known Bolshevik, V. V. Kuibyshev, who led the party's forces in Samara, was elected mayor of the city on October 16; after the transfer of power it was a natural transition from this post to that of chairman of the provincial executive committee.[23]

The party's success in the municipal elections raised problems for the local leaders. First, tenure of important office could discredit them either by association with unpopular policies of the central government or by demonstrating their inability to cope with urgent administrative tasks. Second, it could lead to loss of revolutionary élan among party members. At Ivanovo-Voznesensk, for instance, where in August the Bolsheviks won four fifths of the seats in the town duma and its executive committee, the latter body eclipsed the soviet, which was temporarily reduced to insignificance.[24] There was ample scope for local Bolsheviks to penetrate white-collar organizations. This was as much of a risk as an opportunity, however, for the party's discipline was lax by later standards and the idea of a peaceful compromise with the "bourgeois" parties, so abhorrent to Lenin, was attractive to many of his supporters.

The importance of this issue will become clear if we consider relations between the local party committees and the center. Soviet his-

---

21. I. Dmitriev, "Oktiabr' v Orshe," *Proletarskaia revoliutsiia*, no. 10 (1922), p. 410.

22. B. Eltsin, "Dni oktiabr'skogo perevorota na Iuzhnom Urale i v Ufe," *Proletarskaia revoliutsiia*, no. 10 (1922), p. 352. This resulted from the "left bloc" policy adopted by the Bolsheviks, Mensheviks, and SRs in the municipal elections, which gave them 72 percent of the vote. Butenko and Chugaev, *Vtoroi s"ezd*, p. 359.

23. Riabinskii, *Khronika*, p. 104.

24. I. Firger, "Oktiabr'skaia revoliutsiia v Ivanovo-Voznesenske," *Krasnaia letopis'*, no. 6 (1923), pp. 279–80. Cf. E. Kviring, "Ekaterinoslavskii sovet i oktiabr'skaia revoliutsiia," *Letopis' revoliutsii*, no. 1 (1922), p. 64.

torians have recently striven to build up a picture of a smoothly functioning *apparat*, which transmitted the decisions taken in Petrograd to the grass-roots organizations through a well established hierarchy of regional and provincial committees. This image bears little relationship to the realities of a revolutionary epoch. Scholars have identified 13 *obkomy*, 32 *gubkomy* and several other intermediate groups whose existence often had been previously unknown,[25] but the extent of their power is not easy to assess. Many of them seem to have existed largely on paper. In other cases (Ufa, Nizhni Novgorod), the *gubkom* appears to have exercised responsibilities that elsewhere fell to the *gorkom*, and the membership of the two bodies may well have overlapped. V. V. Anikeev states that on September 1, according to the incomplete statistics available, the Central Committee was in contact with 640 organizations and individuals; these he classifies by region, but does not attempt a breakdown according to their status in the hierarchy.[26] His findings support the commonsense view that there was little systematic about Bolshevik party organization during this period. Sverdlov's makeshift office seems to have welcomed virtually any and all connections that came to its notice.[27]

One suspects that the regional executive bodies, where they existed, were a good deal less important than the deliberative organs to which they nominally owed their authority—that is, to the party conferences at the regional and provincial level. Materials collected in the 1920's mention five of these as having met between October 1 and 25; the geographical distribution is haphazard and suggests lack of central direction.[28] Such gatherings seem to have had a low priority in the local leaders' program of engagements. An attempt to call a party conference in Kursk province failed when only two delegates appeared.[29]

The relative weakness of the links between the provincial organiza-

25. F. G. Zaikina, "Organizatsionnaia perestroika KPSS posle pobedy Oktiabria," *Voprosy istorii KPSS*, no. 11 (1966), p. 52, note 8; cf. V. V. Anikeev, *ibid.*, no. 2 (1958), p. 132.

26. "Nekotorye novye svedeniia po istorii oktiabr'skoi revoliutsii: obzor otchetnykh i finansovykh dokumentov TsK za 1917 g.," *Voprosy istorii KPSS*, no. 9 (1963), p. 102.

27. This impression is fortified by a reading of *Perepiska Sekretariata TsK RSDRP(b) s mestnymi organizatsiiami* (Moscow, 1957). For a non-Bolshevik view of Sverdlov's activities in this field, see W. E. Odom, "J. M. Sverdlov: Bolshevik party organizer," *Slavonic & East European Review*, no. 103 (1966), pp. 421–443.

28. Regional conferences were held in the Caucasus, northwest, and Latvia; provincial conferences in Viatka, Novgorod, and Smolensk. Riabinskii, *Khronika*, pp. 7, 35, 41, 47, 86. This list is not exhaustive.

29. I. Kolychevskii, "Literatura ob oktiabr'skoi revoliutsii," *Proletarskaia revoliutsiia*, no. 33 (1924), p. 222. This article (pp. 200–239) contains valuable bibliographical references to early Soviet publications.

tions and the center was due in part to technical reasons: as postal services were uncertain, communication was maintained chiefly by couriers (*khodoki*).[30] But the main reason was political: the local bodies wished to manage their affairs without too much interference by the top. Some *gorkomy* actively resisted the formation of a regional link. In the lower Volga area no *obkom* could be created owing to rivalry between Antonov's committee at Saratov and Kuibyshev's at Samara; Antonov's relations with Minin at Tsaritsyn were also strained.[31] Apparently both these leaders thought that Antonov tended too far to the right.

Much more fully documented is the conflict among the Bolsheviks of the southwest. In April, a regional committee embracing seven provinces was formed, with a militant lady secretary, Evgeniia Bosh, who saw it as her main task to eliminate Menshevik influence from the organizations within her purview. She and her colleagues also adopted an intolerant line towards the Ukrainian nationalists. This antagonized the Kiev committee, headed by the brothers Iurii and Leonid Piatakov, who recognized that in a politically sophisticated milieu the adoption of sectarian policies would fatally damage the party's chances. On September 24 Madame Bosh persuaded an all-city conference to condemn Iurii Piatakov for his reformist line, but he checkmated the move by setting up a three-man "conciliation commission" with his brother as chairman. The upshot was that the leftists won formal control of the committee but the rightists had the stronger following.[32] The dispute had wider implications, since the *gorkomy* in at least three other major Ukrainian cities—Odessa, Nikolaev, and Ekaterinoslav—sympathized with the Kievans; the first two wanted an *obkom* of their own, a request granted on October 2.[33]

The local committees were often most reluctant to accept Lenin's demand that they break with the Mensheviks, particularly where the latter took a left-wing, "Internationalist" line. In Saratov, for example, the rank-and-file party members favored unity and could not understand why their leaders were quarrelling; although the Bolsheviks brought about a schism already in April, relations with the Mensheviks con-

30. Of the 75 couriers who reported to the Central Committee after the historic meeting of October 10, a few came from areas as far distant as Transcaucasia. Anikeev, "Nekotorye novye svedeniia," p. 103.

31. Antonov-Saratovskii, *Pod stiagom*, pp. 119, 135 ff.

32. Bosh, *God bor'by*, pp. 21, 23, 39–41.

33. *Ibid.*, p. 25; O. S. Pidhainy, *The Formation of the Ukrainian Republic* (Toronto-New York, 1966), p. 176; V. Averin, "Ot kornilovskikh dnei do nemetskoi okkupatsii na Ekaterinoslavshchine," *Proletarskaia revoliutsiia*, no. 70 (1927), p. 151.

tinued to be amicable, and only one committeeman stoutly refused to have any personal dealings with them.[34] Such conciliatory tendencies existed in other Volga towns as well.[35] In general they persisted longer in the outlying and minority regions—the Ukraine, Siberia, and Central Asia; the Urals were also affected, but to a lesser extent. Of fifteen *gorkomy* in Siberia, eight did not split up until after the Sixth Party Congress (July 26–August 3), and five until October or even later.

This organizational weakness explains why many local committees were not adequately informed about the impending insurrection in Petrograd and as a consequence were ill prepared to take similar action themselves. Even in the Central Industrial region, which was in fairly close contact with the Moscow Regional Bureau, the machinery creaked badly. On October 15–16, a member of the Bureau addressed a congress of soviets at Ivanovo, urged the need to "adopt a course for a rising," and secured an appropriate resolution; yet a local committeeman, F. Samoilov, relates that he and his colleagues were waiting daily for directives from the center.[36] At nearby Kineshma the Bolshevik chairman of the soviet brought back the news of the revolutionary plan early in October and a *revkom* (revolutionary committee) was elected; "but it must be said that this troika did not do much in practice" and its attention was monopolized by more peaceful activities.[37] A committeeman in Voronezh complains, "we received absolutely no information from our party centers . . . [and] were left completely in the dark," whereas the local Socialist Revolutionaries were well informed of events in the capital.[38] Equally outspoken is Antonov of Saratov: "Our party committee, which was closely following the approaching dénouement, impatiently awaited the guiding instructions promised by the Central Committee. Alas! None came."[39] It was the same plaintive cry at Kazan: "We received no instructions of any kind [and] were left to our own devices."[40] On the other hand, at Nizhni Novgorod, a committeeman

34. Antonov-Saratovskii, *Pod stiagom*, pp. 114, 125–128; Lebedev, "Fevral'," pp. 241, 253.

35. D. Kin, "Bor'ba protiv ob'edinitel'nogo udara v 1917 g.," *Proletarskaia revoliutsiia*, no. 65 (1927), pp. 47 ff.

36. F. N. Samoilov, "Oktiabr'skaia revoliutsiia v Ivanovo-Voznesenske," *Proletarskaia revoliutsiia*, no.33 (1924), p. 196, and "Oktiabr' v Ivanovo-Voznesenske," *ibid.*, no. 71 (1927), p. 99.

37. N. Evreinov, "Iz vospominanii o podgotovke Oktiabria v Kineshme," *ibid.*, no. 70 (1927), p. 188.

38. I. [Ia.] Vrachev, "Oktiabr'skaia revoliutsiia v Voronezhe," *ibid.*, no. 33 (1924), p. 164.

39. Antonov-Saratovskii, *Pod stiagom*, p. 146.

40. Grasis, "Oktiabr' v Kazani," p. 129.

was summoned by telegram to Moscow and informed of Petrograd's decision, which he then reported back to his colleagues.[41]

Of course, a good deal of improvisation was only to be expected, and information will have been frequently transmitted informally through nonparty channels. Yet the prevailing impression given by the sources is that the provinces were expected to fend for themselves, and that "organized preparations" for the rising, where they were made, took a surprisingly casual form. In most cases the impulse to action was given by the news that the Bolsheviks had struck in the two capital cities.

From this survey two conclusions follow: first, that Bolshevik organization was more efficient at the lower levels of the hierarchy than at the summit—curious though this may seem in a party that stressed centralization and discipline; second, that if the local authorities had taken timely precautionary measures, the transfer of power in the provinces would have been a much more difficult operation than it proved to be in fact. Or to put the matter more starkly: the October Revolution was not so much won by the Bolsheviks as lost by their opponents.

We may now pass from the party's organization to its tactics. Bolshevik activities in October took a variety of forms, ranging from peaceful propaganda to warlike measures by armed combat troops. It was the latter that made the greatest impression upon most contemporary observers, who frequently looked on their movement as purely anarchical and destructive, a *pogromnoe dvizhenie* devoid of any rational purpose other than the gratification of the desires of those who participated in it. Such a view was, however, superficial. There was in fact very little violence, even where military units were the principal force involved. Such fighting as occurred was usually the result of misunderstanding or panic: for example, random firing by trigger-happy soldiers might be interpreted as the signal for an impending offensive.

Almost invariably the elements actively involved were small, and the bulk of the opposing forces tried to avoid conflict for as long as they could, ultimately giving their support to whichever side deemed to have the advantage locally. A few individuals suspected of counterrevolution were lynched or shot; many more were arrested and imprisoned, although usually for a brief period; a much larger number were subjected to arbitrary searches, robbed of their property, and insulted or humiliated in various ways. But there was as yet no wholesale terror. The

41. *1917–1918: god proletar'skoi diktatury: iubileinyi sbornik* [Nizhni Novgorod (Gorkii), 1918], pp. 11–12.

young Konstantin Paustovskii, who was put up against the wall by a band of Red Guards in Moscow and narrowly escaped death, comments on the good humor of his captors.[42] What counted in October was not force but the threat of force, psychological pressure rather than outright physical violence.

The most important action the Bolsheviks took was of an organizational nature: measures designed to eliminate non-Bolshevik influence from the soviets and other mass bodies and to bring them under the party's full control. Their problem was not so much to overthrow the existing regime as to establish in its place a viable new order—one whose outlines they themselves perceived but dimly.

The campaign for the immediate convocation of the Second Congress of Soviets gave local Bolshevik leaders an excellent opportunity to mobilize mass opinion and to prepare the ground psychologically and organizationally for the transfer of power. Even in soviets that had no Bolshevik majority there was considerable sympathy for the congress, and it was seldom very difficult to secure the passage of a resolution endorsing the principle of "soviet power," and to elect as delegates Bolsheviks or their sympathizers armed with an appropriate mandate. An extensive selection of these somewhat repetitive resolutions has since been published.[43] But it would be rash to conclude from this that, even in Bolshevik-controlled soviets, the deputies' intentions coincided with those of Lenin and Trotsky. Fairly typical was the resolution adopted on October 7 by the Soviet at Ekaterinodar in the Kuban, in which the Bolsheviks formed the largest fraction. This resolution called for "the immediate formation of a government composed of members of the Congress of Soviets pending the Constituent Assembly, responsible only to the soviets," and in the next breath demanded immediate convocation of the Assembly; it imposed no party-political restrictions upon the composition of this "Soviet government."[44] This was in conformity with the line taken by Kamenev and other "soft" members of the Central Committee, who sought to combine elements of "soviet" and "bourgeois" democracy.

Moreover, the campaign was not entirely authentic but owed much to the Bolsheviks' organizing talent. It was they who were primarily responsible for calling the regional congresses (or conferences) of soviets, which provided them with a valuable agitational forum. Historians

42. "Povest' o zhizni," *Sobranie sochinenii* (Moscow, 1957), III, pp. 591 ff.
43. Butenko and Chugaev, *Vtoroi s"ezd*. They were first published in *Krasnyi arkhiv*, no. 84 (1937), pp. 18–132.
44. Butenko and Chugaev, *Vtoroi s"ezd*, pp. 148–149.

of the revolution have rightly underlined the importance of the Northern Regional Congress of Soviets, convoked in Petrograd on October 11, which set up a Regional Committee and a seven-man bureau with F. F. Raskolnikov as chairman.[45] Even more important were the similar gatherings held in many provincial centers, where there were fewer alternative platforms available to the party. The right to call such meetings lay with the regional soviet executive (*obispolkom*), but in view of the insubstantial nature of these bodies this was a formality that could be bypassed in practice. Not every regional congress ran smoothly; nor did every local soviet endorse mechanically the line which these gatherings set. Two congresses at least are known to have rejected Bolshevik proposals: one at Irkutsk, embracing the soviets of eastern Siberia, and the other at Kharkov, covering those of the Donets–Krivoi Rog area. In the former case 34 Bolshevik and 15 Left SR delegates faced 23 United SDs and 45 Right SRs; when their resolution was defeated, the leftists walked out and transferred their hopes to a rival assembly, the First All-Siberian Congress of Soviets, which met in the same city five days later; this had 64 Bolsheviks and 35 Left SRs to 11 Mensheviks and 50 Right SRs; it duly adopted a declaration endorsing Soviet power and chose a presidium of 3 Bolsheviks, 2 Left SRs, and 2 others.[46] In the latter case the local Bolsheviks reacted less firmly, perhaps because they had no obvious alternative. The conference (as it called itself, observing constitutional proprieties) passed by 51 votes to 46 a Menshevik resolution on "the current moment," and there matters rested.[47]

Other examples of resistance may be quoted. The line set by the Northern Regional Congress was challenged by the soviet executive of Novgorod, which was under moderate leadership. On October 9 it voted to recall its delegate, and on the fifteenth, having summoned a provincial congress of its own, rejected Raskolnikov's appeal to join his Regional Committee, declaring itself in favor of a socialist coalition government.[48] Similarly, the soviet of the little town of Bobruisk refused to take part in the Bolshevik-controlled conference of soviets of the Western region at Minsk or to send delegates to the Second Con-

45. Riabinskii, *Khronika*, pp. 63, 71, 86.
46. *Ibid.*, pp. 66, 79, 104.
47. *Ibid.*, pp. 66, 74. The claim that the Bolsheviks had the strongest "fraction" at this congress (Butenko and Chugaev, *Vtoroi s"ezd*, p. 264) seems dubious in view of the fact that the regional committee that it set up contained three members from each of the three parties, Bolsheviks, Mensheviks, and SRs.
48. *Ibid.*, pp. 53, 97; cf. Butenko and Chugaev, *Vtoroi s"ezd*, p. 392.

gress of Soviets.[49] However, such cases were the exception rather than the rule. The overwhelming impression these meetings give is of a strong leftward movement with which the moderates were hard put to keep pace. Those soviets that they still controlled did not make their influence felt on a national scale, and the Central Executive Committee of the Soviets did nothing effective to coordinate their opposition. Meanwhile the Bolshevik Central Committee pressed on with its final preparations for insurrection.

We may now examine the various regions in turn, endeavoring to ascertain the actual distribution of power between the Bolsheviks and their rivals at the moment of the Petrograd rising and to discover the reactions of the local leaders to the situation that faced them.

The general pattern of events was that, where thc Bolsheviks controlled the soviets, they formed from their leadership a Revolutionary Committee or Military Revolutionary Committee (*revkom* or *voen-revkom*) to effect the actual seizure of power, with the aid of Red Guard detachments or sympathetic military units, and then called a meeting of the soviet at which the transfer of authority was formally proclaimed. Where the soviets were under moderate control, the *revkomy* based themselves directly upon lower-echelon pro-Bolshevik elements and confronted the soviets with a demand that it either endorse the transfer of power or authorize new elections, on the grounds that they allegedly no longer represented popular opinion. Some soviets complied with this request or accepted dissolution without resistance; but the majority split. The more resolute non-Bolshevik elements rallied around "public safety committees" that were set up under the auspices of the municipal duma to coordinate action by all democratic parties and groups; these sometimes acted in concert with the local military and civil authorities. The salvation committees (as we shall call them) were in many cases suppressed fairly rapidly, but in the remoter areas they continued to function for several weeks, in uneasy coexistence with the *revkom*. At a number of places the pattern was rather different: here the local Bolsheviks collaborated with the moderates in the salvation committees or their equivalents—bodies whose task was as much to maintain order as to make revolution—and external pressure was required to effect the transfer of power.

Naturally each locality witnessed some modification of this scheme. Where so many variable factors are involved, any attempt at categorization is bound to be arbitrary. Nevertheless, we may usefully divide provincial Russia into five zones, which differ according to the form

49. Riabinskii, p. 103.

that the revolution took in each. They are distinguished not just by geography but by several criteria—socioeconomic, political, and military; to insist on any one of these factors as decisive is to distort the picture.

Category A

This zone comprises the Central Industrial region and the Urals. Both these are areas of technologically lagging or even declining industries (respectively, textile manufacture and mining and metallurgy), with a homogeneous and socially predominant labor force, living for the most part in isolated settlements and proud of its militant traditions. The workers have been won over to radicalism early in 1917, as have the few garrison troops located in this area. Their activism expressed itself in the formation of lower-echelon organizations (*fabzavkomy* in the Central Industrial region, combat squads in the Urals) rather than in soviets. From the party's point of view they were strong in morale but weak in discipline.

Thus in Ivanovo-Voznesensk the Bolsheviks achieved their objectives "in the most painless manner . . . without firing a single shot or shedding a single drop of blood."[50] The news of the Petrograd coup was announced to an enthusiastic meeting of the town duma, leading to the formation of a five-man "revolutionary staff." Yet despite their numerical preponderance, the local Bolsheviks at first acted cautiously, as though anxious to minimize the extent of their breach with the old order. On October 27, perhaps under the impact of the fighting in Moscow, they decided to expand the "staff" formed two days earlier "to give it more authority in the eyes of the population." Among the new members were representatives of three other parties, the soviet executive, and the local garrison. But their role was conceived as purely decorative, for on the following day a three-man presidium was formed consisting exclusively of Bolsheviks. On November 4 the defensists were expelled on the grounds that their presence was no longer fitting and we hear of a seven-man team in control. After a month the staff could be disbanded as superfluous and its functions passed to the soviet and duma, both of course firmly Bolshevik.[51]

A similar picture could be observed elsewhere in the region. Although a few bands of enthusiasts went to help their embattled comrades in Moscow, most adopted a temporizing attitude. At Kineshma the initial

50. Firger, "Oktiabr'skaia revoliutsiia," p. 279.
51. Samoilov, "Oktiabr'," pp. 102–103; I. N. Liubimov, ed., *Revoliutsiia 1917 g.: khronika sobytii*, VI (Moscow-Leningrad, 1930), pp. 6, 77; *Pravda*, November 4, 1917.

reaction was to set up a "district people's council" together with representatives of the *zemstvo* and other political parties; only when their leader returned did the local Bolsheviks take a firmer line.[52] A similar coalition *revkom* existed in Kostroma. It undertook "to fight counter-revolution *in all its forms* and to ensure that elections to the Constituent Assembly were carried out peacefully."[53] In some of the less industrialized centers there were anarchic outbreaks by drunken mobs and the transfer of power was delayed by several days. At Iaroslavl it was the soldiers who were radical and the workers who were moderate; the two groups were evenly balanced in the soviet. On October 27 the Bolsheviks stiffened the soviet with *fabzavkom* and soldier delegates and passed a resolution on the transfer of power; the moderates demonstratively walked out.[54]

In the Urals the news of the Petrograd insurrection fell upon well-prepared soil, since the Bolsheviks controlled over half of the town soviets.[55] At Cheliabinsk and Ekaterinburg they took over speedily but then accepted a compromise imposed on them by, respectively, the Cossacks and the Left SRs. In the latter town a "committee of people's power" was set up on October 31 consisting of 6 Bolsheviks, 5 SRs and 5 others; it lasted until November 22 when it was dissolved by its Bolshevik element.[56] At several centers there were strong SR and Menshevik organizations that had to be broken or won over. At Zlatoust, Bolshevik and SR influence is described as "roughly equal" and armed resistance

52. Evreinov, "Iz vospominanii," p. 189. *Pravda*, November 13, gives the membership as 5 Bolsheviks and 1 Left SR to 3 United SDs, 1 Right SR and 1 nonparty member.

53. *Novaia zhizn'*, November 10 (report of October 31, our italics); V. Leikina, "Oktiabr' po Rossii," *Proletarskaia revoliutsiia*, no. 49 (1926), p. 203. The latter is a valuable source. The article is divided into three sections: no. 49, pp. 185–233, no. 58 (1926), pp. 234–255, and no. 59 (1926) pp. 238–254.

54. Butenko and Chugaev, *Vtoroi s"ezd*, p. 371; Leikina, "Oktiabr'," p. 203; *Novaia zhizn'*, November 4 and 9.

55. According to the latest research, 88 soviets out of 145: F. P. Bystrykh, "Bol'sheviki Urala vo glave mass . . . ," *Voprosy istorii KPSS*, no. 4 (1967), p. 54. He puts the party's total strength here at 34,200, of whom half were in the central Urals. The orientation of the regional (*okrug*) committee seems doubtful. The Bolsheviks had 86 out of 120 delegates at its congress on October 13, but the resolution adopted by the Ural *okrug* soviet favored coalition government (Riabinskii, *Khronika*, p. 79; Butenko and Chugaev, *Vtoroi s"ezd*, p. 396). By October 27, however, it had joined with the party *obkom* in nominating a Bolshevik troika: Liubimov, *Khronika*, p. 8.

56. Liubimov, *Khronika*, pp. 35, 194; *Pravda*, November 5, 25; *Rabochaia gazeta*, November 5; N. K. Lisovskii, in D. A. Chugaev, ed., *Ustanovlenie sovetskoi vlasti na mestakh v 1917–1918 gg.*, pt. II (Moscow, 1959), p. 397.

continued until March 1918.[57] At Izhevsk the Bolsheviks shared power with the Maximalists, the Mensheviks, and the Right SRs forming a sizable minority. Here, admittedly, the soviet had not been reelected since August, but at Nizhne-Tagilsk, where elections had been held as recently as early October, the Mensheviks still had more than half the members of the joint soviet.[58] At Perm the conventional institutional alignment was reversed: the Bolsheviks controlled the town duma, the Mensheviks the soviet. The latter voted for coalition government; the surrounding factories, aided by the Regional Committee (nothing is said in the sources about the duma!), organized a *revkom* to combat it, but this "soon turned against Soviet power, transformed itself into a salvation committee, and then collapsed."[59] The resistance was eventually overcome by external pressure.

A rather similar pattern occurred at Ufa, at the southern end of the Ural chain. The duma here was Bolshevik-controlled, but Tsurupa proved unable to make it a firm *point d'appui* for Bolshevism: on October 30 its members revolted against their chairman, although without agreeing on any alternative. According to one report, a *revkom* was formed that attempted to assert control over the city's institutions but, on meeting resistance, resigned and was replaced by another "which set itself the task not of seizing power but of controlling the activities of governmental bodies and ensuring the speedy convocation of the Constituent Assembly";[60] there may, however, be an element of wishful thinking here. The soviet apparently played little part, possibly because it was overshadowed by the more representative body. In any case the *revkom* had to fall back on the lower-echelon organizations in the city and more particularly on the militant miners of the vicinity. "When the Ural workers descended from their mountains into the valley, they straightened the line of the town soviet and raised it to a revolutionary height." It was not until November 27 that the Mensheviks left the soviet and it could adopt "a course of militant Bolshevism."[61]

Throughout this region the main political factor was the equivocal relationship between the Bolsheviks and the SRs, whose latent differences could be bridged temporarily by their common attraction to maximalism, but were bound to widen as soon as the Bolsheviks began

57. Butenko and Chugaev, *Vtoroi s"ezd*, p. 272.
58. *Ibid.*, pp. 274–275, 312–313.
59. Leikina, "Oktiabr'," p. 221; Butenko and Chugaev, *Vtoroi s"ezd*, p. 393; Liubimov, *Khronika*, p. 55.
60. *Novaia zhizn'*, November 17.
61. Eltsin, "Dni," p. 355; Liubimov, *Khronika*, pp. 8, 223.

to penetrate into the villages, where a virtual state of civil war prevailed by the spring of 1918. This strained the centralist loyalties of the combat squads, which began to operate independently, committing anarchistic excesses more evocative of the *Pugachovshchina* than of a Marxist revolution.

Category B

This category comprises fairly large centers with less industrial development, a mixed labor force, often consisting largely of communications workers, and a substantial middle class with its own cultural and political traditions. It embraces such middle and lower Volga towns as Nizhni Novgorod, Samara, and Saratov, as well as those on the Trans-Siberian railway (Krasnoiarsk, Irkutsk). Their population was swollen by the influx of workers in new industries, often catering for defense needs, and of wartime evacuees, which intensified the pressure on scarce resources of food and accommodation.[62] The military situation here was much the same as in Category A. The workers formed powerful soviets, which sooner or later came under radical control, but autonomist tendencies were strong. The middle-class groups were also relatively well organized; their outlook too was predominantly local. The October days here took the form of a brief confrontation, often marked by violence. Despite the rapid achievement of Soviet power conciliatory tendencies survived.

One may note first the case of Kazan, exceptional in that here the transfer of power occurred as a military coup by the pro-Bolshevik garrison. The town soviet seems to have been under Bolshevik control, whereas the provincial one was split; more important than either, however, is the military regional committee. On October 19 the army authorities arrested a certain Lieutenant Drozdov (Gvozdev?); this incident, together with the threat of dispatch to the front, led to protests and armed clashes; a Military Revolutionary Committee was set up in the headquarters of the 164th Infantry Regiment, and on October 24 an officer of this unit, Captain Mosalskii, aided by an artillery colonel and some young Bolshevik ensigns, took over the town without re-

62. According to the census of June 1917 the urban population of Saratov *guberniia* was 678,500, and of Nizhni Novgorod *guberniia* 393,600, whereas normal growth projected from the 1897 census data would have given figures of 442,000 and 198,000 respectively. L. S. Gaponenko and V. M. Kabuzan, "Materialy sel'skokhoziaistvennykh perepisei 1916–1917 gg. kak istoricheskii istochnik," *Istoriia SSSR*, no. 6 (1961), p. 114.

sistance. Only after this action did the soviet assemble to endorse it by a majority vote and to form a (civilian) Revolutionary Committee. At this point the moderates walked out.[63]

If in Kazan the Bolsheviks won by timely military action, in Nizhni Novgorod they faced a tougher problem. The soviet was controlled by moderates and adopted by a large majority (105 votes to 62, with 9 abstentions) a resolution condemning the Petrograd rising. A strong salvation committee had been set up by the provincial commissar already on October 23. This obliged the Bolshevik Revolutionary Committee, appointed by the party's provincial committee,[64] to rely upon such lower-echelon groups as combat squads, trade unionists and *fabzavkomy*. It came into being relatively late, on the night of October 27/28, but soon won for itself a strong position vis-à-vis the salvation committee. The two organizations entrenched themselves in different public buildings and engaged in a war of nerves, settled on November 1 by a *coup de main* that deprived the moderates of the military cadets on whom they had depended for their defense. But it is characteristic of the half-hearted attitude of the combatants that, when the reconstituted soviet met, it voted almost unanimously for a socialist coalition government (admittedly, with a Bolshevik majority) and speedy convocation of the Constituent Assembly. Not until November 21 did the Executive Committee of the Soviet claim full power over the province.[65]

In the other large Volga towns the pattern of events was generally similar, although here the Bolsheviks were the strongest force in the local soviets. In Samara, which had sent an all-Bolshevik delegation to the Second Congress of Soviets, the executive at first played a cautious game: on October 26 it still voted to support the Provisional Government, but on the 27th, swamped by *fabzavkom* and trade-union representatives introduced into the hall, it passed a resolution in favor of Soviet power and elected a *revkom* under Kuibyshev. This *revkom* then had to be broadened to include non-Bolshevik representatives in order to make it acceptable to the garrison. Fresh elections to the soviet gave the Bolsheviks slightly less than a majority (155 places out of 309), but

63. Grasis, "Oktiabr' v Kazani," pp. 124, 133–134; V. Povolzhskii, "Pered Oktiabrem i v Oktiabre: po Kazani i Kazanskoi gub.," *Proletarskaia revoliutsiia*, no. 10 (1922), p. 343–344; Leikina, "Oktiabr'," p. 212; Kolychevskii, "Literatura," pp. 216–7; Butenko and Chugaev, *Vtoroi s"ezd*, p. 390; *Rabochaia gazeta*, November 9.

64. The source of this information is none other than L. M. Kaganovich. *1917–1918 gg.: god bor'by*, p. 5; cf. Pisarev in *ibid.*, p. 14.

65. *Ibid.*, pp. 19–20; Liubimov, *Khronika*, pp. 62, 189; *Rabochaia gazeta*, November 9.

this was a minor embarrassment, since they controlled the executive.[66]

In Saratov, too, there was initial hesitation in the soviet, despite the numerical preponderance of the Bolsheviks (320 deputies as against 103 SRs and 76 Mensheviks). One Bolshevik member of its military section rashly agreed to participate in the salvation committee, for which he was reprimanded by his senior party colleagues. Fear of an adverse vote in the soviet led the Bolshevik caucus to decide on an extraordinary session, packed by *fabzavkom* and trade-union representatives. At this meeting the moderates walked out, amidst emotional scenes, and the two sides prepared to do battle. Their operations had a strong element of make-believe, but the shooting lasted for 24 hours and caused a number of casualties. (The spirit of the affray is perhaps best rendered by the story that, when the Bolsheviks eventually approached the barricades around the duma, they could nibble away the barricades because they were constructed in part of sacks of fruit.) After their surrender the members of the salvation committee were roughly treated by angry crowds but were soon restored to liberty.[67]

In Siberia it was harder for the Bolsheviks to establish their authority. These towns were far removed from the main revolutionary centers; their social makeup was different, as were the problems confronting the peasantry; and among the intellectuals there was a weak regional separatist movement to contend with. Moreover, the Bolsheviks' main strength was concentrated in distant Krasnoiarsk, with its important railway repair shops. They met no opposition in taking over the town, where they controlled both the soviet and duma;[68] but they faced adversaries to the east and to the west. Irkutsk was still under moderate control, despite the maneuvers that had gone on over the regional soviet, and the cadets of four military schools provided support. Not until mid-November did the Bolsheviks manage to call another All-Siberian Congress of Soviets, which elected an executive body known as *Tsentrosibir*, under B. Shumiatskii; this helped the party to win control of the Irkutsk city soviet (November 19). On December 8, however, their adversaries rose in revolt, and it was ten days before their resistance was quelled by reinforcements from central Siberia.[69] Further

66. Liubimov, *Khronika*, pp. 8, 120; Kolychevskii, "Literatura," p. 218; Leikina, "Oktiabr'," p. 214.
67. Antonov-Saratovskii, *Pod stiagom*, pp. 147–175, 188; Lebedev, "Fevral'," pp. 252–261; Leikina, "Oktiabr'," pp. 217–218; *Novaia zhizn'*, November 9; *Delo naroda*, November 21; *Saratovskii vestnik*, November 5.
68. M. Frumkin, "Fevral'–oktiabr' v Krasnoiarske," *Proletarskaia revoliutsiia*, no. 21 (1923), p. 144; Liubimov, *Khronika*, pp. 17, 27; *Pravda*, November 5, 12.
69. Leikina, "Oktiabr'," pp. 228–229; *Novaia zhizn'*, November 12, 14.

east, too, in Nerchinsk and Chita, extraneous forces (returning front-line soldiers and miners) proved decisive in securing victory for the new régime.

In western Siberia, by contrast, there was less trouble. Omsk was under strong Bolshevik influence. In Tomsk the garrison was pro-Bolshevik, but the railwaymen followed the Menshevik-controlled soviet. A coalition *revkom* was set up that allowed the existing local government bodies to continue for several days, until the executive of the soldiers' soviet persuaded the *zemstvo* to accept a "renovation" of the *revkom* whereby it came to consist solely of Bolsheviks.[70] As one early Soviet historian comments with some justice: "By skilful practical maneuvers the Bolsheviks were able to subordinate the majority by the expenditure of relatively small means, without any notable shocks or sharp changes."[71]

Category C

This category comprises smaller towns, less developed industrially and more isolated, where the surrounding countryside often made its presence forcibly felt. Here social tensions were less acute because the well-to-do and the poor were both linked to the peasant world, whose interests indeed they largely existed to serve. In such towns as Tambov, Tula, Voronezh, or Kursk the political conflict was subdued and the local soviet's formal assumption of power brought little change; violence came later and was introduced from without—by bands of militants from the larger centers who disturbed this rustic somnolence. In brief, the factors noted in Siberia were here magnified in significance.

In the Black Earth belt the SRs, although now deeply divided, were by far the strongest party. The only center where the Bolsheviks controlled the local soviet was Belgorod, and in Orel they had "an exact half-share"; both these towns were in the west, within the area subject to military control.[72] Elsewhere the Bolsheviks often exerted an influence upon the soviet leadership disproportionate to their numerical strength: thus in Voronezh they had only 24 deputies out of some 120 to 140, and only 4 executive members out of 45, but on the presidium 2 posts out of 6, including those of deputy chairman and secretary.[73] In Kursk, however, according to one account, their supporters were numbered in dozens, and in Tambov there were precisely 3 of them,

70. Leikina, "Oktiabr'," p. 226.
71. Kolychevskii, "Literatura," p. 224.
72. From data in Butenko and Chugaev, *Vtoroi s"ezd*, pp. 239, 326.
73. Vrachev, "Oktiabr'skaia revoliutsiia," p. 162.

who appeared in town just before the October insurrection.[74] In the latter province such strength as they had was concentrated in smaller places that had undergone industrial development. Eleven miles from Tambov was a defense establishment, "Factory No. 43," employing 8,000 men; after winning control here, the local Bolshevik leaders endeavored to recruit support in the provincial capital. The salvation committee set up in Tambov on October 27 had no Bolshevik representation. On November 14 the soviet was asked to dissolve it on these grounds; when it refused, the Bolsheviks took the matter to the garrison, where they also met with a rebuff.[75] But the soldiers did agree to reelect their officers, and by the end of November the soviet had met the same fate. The Bolsheviks now had a majority, but only in coalition with the Left SRs, who seem to have been very strong since the transfer of power was not formalized until January 30, 1918.[76]

In Kursk "the revolt in the capitals found no response until February 1918 and even for long after that an anarchist-SR group continued to make mischief."[77] At first, power lay with a salvation committee representing all local institutions and parties, the Bolsheviks not excluded, and its legality was formally recognized by the local courts.[78]

Where conditions were less idyllic, the military were responsible. Their action could have very different results, as the following two examples show. In Voronezh the Bolsheviks twice, on October 28 and 29, decided against an insurrection in the face of what appeared to be strong measures by the local army authorities and the moderate majority in the soviet, which on October 27 had voted 51 : 46 in favor of a salvation committee rather than Soviet power. But almost immediately they found themselves caught up in a movement that had begun spontaneously among the soldiers, who feared they were about to be disarmed. Leadership was provided by an energetic individual named Moiseev, whose party affiliation is uncertain, and at the price of a few casualties they captured the military headquarters and the main points in the town. Only *after* this coup did a *revkom* come into being, which on November 2 (or 3?) called a meeting of the soviet to endorse the

74. Kolychevskii, "Literatura," pp. 222, 223, quoting local Istpart materials.
75. Liubimov, *Khronika*, pp. 139, 146.
76. Kolychevskii, "Literatura," p. 223; Leikina, "Oktiabr'," p. 207; Butenko and Chugaev, *Vtoroi s"ezd*, p. 395. Cf. the fair picture given in the recent work of P. N. Sobolev et al., *Istoriia velikoi oktiabr'skoi sotsialisticheskoi revoliutsii* (Moscow, 1962), p. 223.
77. Kolychevskii, "Literatura," p. 222.
78. Leikina, "Oktiabr'," pp. 206–207; Liubimov, *Khronika*, p. 62; *Rabochaia gazeta*, November 10.

fait accompli. Most moderates boycotted this gathering, which proceeded to replace its former executive by a Bolshevik-dominated bureau.[79]

In Kaluga, by contrast, it was the provincial commissar, Galkin, who imposed his will upon events. The situation here was much as one might expect, the Bolsheviks having only a small group in the soviet but a commanding position in the garrison. In response to a call from the municipal duma, Galkin sent in a force of Cossacks, arrested the soviet executive (October 19), and dispersed the mutinous troops. The duma and soviet were induced to approve these measures, and on receiving news of the Petrograd insurrection they set up a strong salvation committee, which arrested the remaining Bolshevik activists. But here matters rested. Kaluga, a small town close to Moscow, was a poor base for an anti-Bolshevik crusade, even if the city fathers had wished to launch one. At the end of November, bands of armed workers arrived from Moscow, Tula, and elsewhere, who dissolved the salvation committee and disarmed the shock troops who had provided it with armed support.[80]

Category D

These two episodes, and also that of Kazan, indicate plainly enough the importance of military morale in any town where sizable forces were stationed. This was, of course, the dominant factor in the situation throughout the area behind the four fronts in western Russia, a predominantly rural region where industrial workers were in any case not plentiful. Here, and also in areas with a semi-military sociopolitical organization (that is, the territories of the various Cossack *voiska*), the pattern of events was distorted by the presence of large bodies of men in uniform. The main impetus to political action came, not from the Bolshevik takeover in Petrograd, to which they were largely indifferent, but from the "peace decree." Seen geographically, the bolshevization of the army was a slow surge from north to south; seen organizationally, it somewhat resembled the crumbling of an old-fashioned trestle-bridge, as the vast structure of army committees collapsed, the lowest units generally yielding first. Military intervention in local politics was most helpful to the Bolsheviks in the north, somewhat less so in the center and southwest, and positively detrimental (for a time) in the south.

79. Vrachev, "Oktiabr'skaia revoliutsiia," pp. 169–181, 187–189, summarized in Leikina, "Oktiabr'," pp. 208–210; Liubimov, *Khronika,* pp. 7, 16, 26, 62, 86; *Novaia zhizn',* November 9; *Pravda,* November 17 (a good account).
80. Kolychevskii, "Literatura," pp. 220–221; Leikina, "Oktiabr'," pp. 204–205; Melgunov, *Kak bol'sheviki,* p. 273; Liubimov, *Khronika,* pp. 84, 139, 146, 151.

On the northern front the First, Fifth, and Twelfth Army committees were neutral, and of the junior organizations a slender majority favored continuation of the war. Most senior commanders, notably Generals Cheremisov, Boldyrev, and Iuzefovich, saw it as their prime duty to avert armed conflict among their men, and for this reason they refrained from bold political initiatives. All the local soviets (except those at Fellin in the forward zone and at Pskov, Velikiie Luki, and Vitebsk in the rear) were under Bolshevik control, and the transfer of power encountered relatively feeble resistance. On November 9 the Twelfth Army endorsed the new regime by a narrow majority, 248 votes to 243. A new soldiers' executive committee was set up, ostensibly on a parity basis but purged of those members who had served before the rising. It was charged with preparing an extraordinary army congress. This met at Venden on November 15; two thirds of the delegates supported the Bolsheviks or Left SRs.[81]

On the western front (Second, Third, and Tenth Armies) the situation was somewhat less favorable to the insurgents. Although they had captured the soviet at Minsk, where the headquarters was located, the moderates controlled the front and army committees, Mogilev (the site of the General Headquarters), and in the rear Borisov, Orsha, and Smolensk. Yet in all these places some military units were sympathetic to the Bolsheviks, and the local *revkomy* were encouraged to act with an energy and determination that, as one might infer, reflected creditably on their army training. Thus at Minsk the soviet presidium, acting at the behest of a former front-line soldier, Miasnikov, already proclaimed the transfer of power at 2 P.M. on October 25, two hours after the news from Petrograd had reached him by army radio, without waiting to call a plenary meeting of the soviet.[82] Two thousand men under arrest for revolutionary activity were released, supplied with arms from a depot under party control, and paraded complete with red banners within a matter of hours. Confronted by this display of force, General Baluev accepted the commissars nominated by the soviet (that is, by its presidium). On the next day Miasnikov set up a flamboyantly titled "Military Revolutionary Committee of the Western Region,"

81. Leikina, "Oktiabr'," pp. 186 ff; Liubimov, *Khronika*, pp. 152, 159.
82. A. Kirzhnits, "Oktiabr'skie dni v Belorussii," *Proletarskaia revoliutsiia*, no. 71 (1927), p. 109. It is worth noting that the seven-man presidium of the soviet was all-Bolshevik, although the assembly elected on October 9 had 155 Bolsheviks to 44 SRs and 41 Mensheviks or Bundists, and the executive had only a narrow majority of Bolsheviks: 23 out of 40. This was because the moderate parties refused to participate in the vote when the presidium was reelected on October 14 as a gesture of protest. Riabinskii, *Khronika*, pp. 51, 87; Butenko and Chugaev, *Vtoroi s"ezd*, p. 294.

which in fact contained no representatives from centers other than Minsk. The moderates do not appear to have challenged its credentials. Instead they negotiated a compromise, which in effect if not in intention favored the insurgents. By its terms no troops were allowed to leave the front for Moscow or other centers where the issue was still in doubt, but the Second Army (which had since declared for the Bolsheviks) was able to send to Minsk an armored train with reinforcements. When it arrived on November 2 the moderates were overawed, the salvation committee disintegrated, and the soviet fell into Bolshevik hands. Within a few weeks Miasnikov emerged as the new front commander.[83]

An element of bluff also helped turn the scales at such rear bases as Orsha. There are said to have been only fifty Bolsheviks in the town, but the local military authorities, who had five regiments at their disposal, wildly exaggerated their strength. The *revkom* employed astute *ruses de guerre*—for example, stationing pieces of artillery around the town square even though they had no one who knew how to fire them. No sooner had the salvation committee met on October 27 than it was dispersed by a handful of soldiers; the soviet executive had been voted out of office already on October 24 over the protests of the moderates, and the assembly itself seems to have died a natural death. A Bolshevik writer comments that their opponents "were pitiful, for they did not realize that they could have 'combed us out' in a moment with a couple of Cossack machine guns, since we were holding on only by psychological effect and by taking desperate risks." Gradually, the *revkom* built up its strength until it was in a position to send advice (over the military telegraph) to colleagues in other towns of the region, such as Vitebsk and Gomel.[84]

Characteristically, in most places further to the rear a more cautious line was adopted because the Bolsheviks here belonged not to the fighting but to the supporting branches of service (transport, supply, ordnance, and so on). In Gomel, they were cut off for several days and only proclaimed the transfer of power on October 30, when they had learned of events elsewhere; the *revkom* bore a coalition character.[85] In Smolensk a *revkom* was set up on October 25, and it seized the arsenal but then adopted a defensive posture, awaiting the outcome of the struggle in Moscow and at the front; on October 30 these activists

83. Kirzhnits, "Oktiabr'skie dni," pp. 111–124; Leikina, "Oktiabr'," p. 109 f.; *Rabochaia gazeta*, November 4.

84. Dmitriev, "Oktiabr' v Orshe," pp. 408–424, esp. 413–416; Riabinskii, *Khronika*, p. 173. *Novaia zhizn'*, November 7, prints a protest by the soviet against Bolshevik usurpation of its powers.

85. Kirzhnits, "Oktiabr'skie dni," p. 136; Kolychevskii, "Literatura," p. 236.

successfully beat off an attack by Cossacks and then took the offensive, whereupon resistance speedily collapsed. One source describes the attitude of the large garrison as neutral.[86] In both towns a salvation committee tried to maintain control, but with little success, apparently because of its largely civilian composition.

In the last resort the outcome of events in this region depended on the General Headquarters. Initially the All-Army Committee and the Mogilev soviet took a strong line against the insurgents, but by November 1 their attitude had changed, partly because of the influence of certain politicians who had come to the Headquarters from Petrograd and who talked incessantly but fruitlessly in an effort to hammer out a common policy. There was an unbridgeable gap between those right-wing leaders like the SR Gots and the Menshevik Skobelev, on the one hand, men who wanted to preserve the front, reconstitute the Provisional Government, and oppose Bolshevism by force if necessary, and those like Chernov, who thought it sufficient to exert nonviolent pressure against the "adventurists" in the hope that they, sensing their isolation, would agree to a socialist coalition government. The latter group gained the sympathy of the All-Army Committee, which on November 7 invited other military organizations to support a coalition headed by Chernov. The response was cool and earned the committee the displeasure of the Gots faction. This failure, coupled with growing pressure by local pro-Bolshevik forces, then pushed it further to the left. The ground was thus well prepared for Ensign Krylenko: as he approached the town on November 18, the soviet executive, relying on its military supporters, proclaimed the transfer of power; a *revkom* was set up, which on the following day dissolved the All-Army Committee and arrested the commander-in-chief, General Dukhonin.[87]

On the southwestern front (Eleventh, Seventh, and Special Armies) the Bolsheviks had to face potential or actual opposition from Ukrainian troops, who were undergoing regroupment on national lines. The Rada government's efforts to bring these men back to its territory were obstructed by the Bolsheviks. This issue was one cause of the rupture between Kiev and Petrograd in December. From a local point of view it meant that as late as November 18–24, when an extraordinary front congress was called at Berdichev, the Bolsheviks and their Left

86. Kolychevskii, "Literatura," p. 235; *Novaia zhizn'*, November 7; *Rabochaia gazeta*, November 7; N. V. Andreev, *Pobeda velikoi oktiabr'skoi sotsialisticheskoi revoliutsii v Smolenskoi gubernii* (Smolensk, 1957), pp. 45–49.

87. Melgunov, *Kak bol'sheviki*, pp. 250–254; O. H. Radkey, *The Sickle under the Hammer: the Russian Socialist Revolutionaries in the Early Months of Soviet Rule* (New York-London, 1963), pp. 73–91; Leikina, "Oktiabr'," pp. 191–195.

SR allies still commanded less than half the votes: 322 votes were cast in favor of the transfer of power and 232 against, and 138 delegates were absent or abstained. The Bolsheviks secured 18 out of 35 places in the new front *revkom*, but it soon transpired that their forces were weaker than those of the Rada, which by the end of December were able to arrest many of their most active Bolshevik opponents.[88]

On the Romanian front the process of dissolution was delayed and complicated by the greater national diversity of the troops concerned. In the Eighth Army, based on Mogilev-Podolsk, it was a Great Russian (Siberian) Cossack corps that first succumbed to bolshevism; but before the movement reached the army *revkom*, Ukrainian and other Cossack elements regained the initiative and briefly arrested the Bolshevik leaders before allowing the army to evacuate at the end of the year.[89] The other armies further south had Romanian forces to contend with as well. One consequence of this was that the (Great) Russian left-wing groups tended to close ranks for their own protection. The support which the Left SRs in particular gave to the Bolsheviks proved crucial to their ultimate success.

In early December these two parties won control of the Ninth Army, stationed in the Bukovina, which was evacuated in December and January, although not without a certain amount of fighting.[90] The Fourth Army, based on Roman (Bessarabia), lost to bolshevism successively a division (the 48th) and a corps (the 24th), whereupon an army congress was held (December 1–4) and elected a Left SR, I. Kondurushkin, as its commander; but on December 11 he was arrested by Ukrainian and Romanian troops.[91] Finally, the Sixth Army, stationed in the Danube delta and the furthest removed from the centers of revolutionary influence, held an army congress in late November at which the Bolsheviks had some 200 out of 450 delegates. In the new army committee that it elected, the Bolsheviks and their Left SR allies had a slight advantage over the other parties and a Left SR, L. Degtiarev, was chosen as army commander. These troops only extricated themselves with great difficulty, as on December 9 serious fighting broke out with Romanian forces, culminating in their occupation of Bessarabia.[92]

---

88. Leikina, "Oktiabr'," *Proletarskaia revoliutsiia*, no. 49, p. 195 and no. 58, pp. 236 ff. Liubimov, *Khronika*, pp. 172, 202, 209. Anweiler, *Die Rätebewegung*, p. 254, has surely overlooked the abstainers.

89. Leikina, "Oktiabr'," *Proletarskaia revoliutsiia*, no. 58, p. 237.

90. *Ibid.*, pp. 238–239.

91. *Ibid.*, pp. 239–241; I. Kondurushkin, "Velikii Oktiabr' na rumynskom fronte," *ibid.*, no. 10 (1922), pp. 425–442.

92. Leikina, "Oktiabr'," *Proletarskaia revoliutsiia*, no. 58, pp. 241–249. L. Degtiarev, "Oktiabr' rumynskogo fronta," *Krasnaia letopis'*, no. 6 (1923), pp. 207–278.

It was in the shadow of these events at the front that bolshevism came to Odessa. The local soviet, which was under Bolshevik influence, expressed support for the insurrection but was soon obliged to accept a compromise settlement. The most powerful force in the city was the so-called *Rumcherod*,[93] a military-naval organization under moderate control. On November 28 a regional *revkom* was set up on which this and other local bodies were represented; the presence of the military district commander, General Marks, served to stiffen its resolve. It saw its task as the preservation of order pending the establishment of a socialist coalition government. Its authority was challenged by supporters of the Ukrainian Central Rada and more significantly by the soviet, which made two unsuccessful bids for power (November 15 and 30). In an effort to contain the opposition, *Rumcherod* broadened its membership to include an equal number of Ukrainian representatives, but by December 10 the pro-Bolshevik elements were able to call a congress, which decided to hold new elections to *Rumcherod*. This gathering, which claimed to represent all workers' and soldiers' soviets in the region, was in fact an overwhelmingly military affair, with over 800 of the 1,100-odd delegates from front-line or garrison units. The reelected *Rumcherod* was under effective Bolshevik control and preparations at once began for a showdown with the Ukrainians. This came about in mid-January, by which time the Rada's power had been undermined by events elsewhere; even so, a three-day battle (January 14–17, 1918) had to be fought before the Bolsheviks won control of the city.[94]

Category E

A similar triangular struggle developed elsewhere in the Ukraine, the military element decreasing in importance as one moved eastwards. On the right bank of the Dnieper the Bolsheviks were very weak, except in such military base areas as Vinnitsa. In the larger cities, Ekaterinoslav, Nikolaev, and Kherson—as in Odessa—united *revkomy* were established that pursued basically nonrevolutionary ends. The Bolsheviks participated in these mainly because their weakness left them no real alternative. Other factors that facilitated rapprochement were the Internationalist sympathies of the local Mensheviks, the experience of fruitful collaboration in previous months, and common opposition to Ukrainian claims. The compromise was in truth something of a shotgun

93. "The Executive Committee of Soviets of Workers' and Soldiers' Deputies of the Romanian Front, Black Sea Fleet and Odessa Military District."

94. Leikina, "Oktiabr'," *Proletarskaia revoliutsiia*, no. 58, pp. 249–255; *Novaia zhizn'*, November 9, 18; *Rabochaia gazeta*, November 5, 7; Pidhainy, *Formation*, pp. 253–259.

marriage, from which the Bolsheviks profited most. They won time to gather strength in lower-echelon organizations and to conquer the soviets from below and from within. In Ekaterinoslav they did not establish themselves until December 28 and in Nikolaev until January 7, 1918. In both these centers power slid fairly smoothly from one Russian group to another, that is, from a coalition *revkom* to a Bolshevik-dominated one. The main opposition came from Ukrainian elements, whose loyalties were, however, divided between the local "soviet" forces and the Rada in Kiev.[95]

The nationalist challenge was for obvious reasons greatest in Kiev itself. The Bolsheviks comprised the largest faction in the workers' soviet and its executive, but neither was under their effective control. There was also a joint workers' and soldiers' soviet that seems to have been torn by divided counsels. More important than either of these was the Mala(ia) Rada, a 27-man council dominated by Ukrainians but with some Jewish and Russian members. When news of the Petrograd insurrection was received, the soviet, under pressure from troops, declared its support, but was soon forced on the defensive. Both the Bolsheviks and the Malaia Rada set up what were in effect rival *revkomy*, but of the two, the Ukrainian organization was clearly the stronger.[96] Three Bolsheviks—Piatakov, Zatonskii, and Kreisberg—joined it and also the Malaia Rada, but on October 26 they withdrew in protest when the Rada condemned the Petrograd rising. On the same day fighting broke out between the Bolsheviks and forces loyal to the Provisional Government; the Ukrainians, who took a neutral stand, emerged three days later as *tertius gaudens*. At their behest the workers' soviet was now merged with that claiming to represent both soldiers and workers, the latter being less sympathetic to Bolshevism. Piatakov did not consider

---

95. E. Kviring, "Ekaterinoslavskii sovet," pp. 63–73; Ia. Riappo, "Bor'ba sil v oktiabr'skoi revoliutsii v Nikolaeve," *Letopis' revoliutsii*, no. 1 (1922), pp. 81–103; Kolychevskii, "Literatura," p. 231; Riabinskii, *Khronika*, p. 198; Liubimov, *Khronika*, pp. 9, 27, 195; Averin, "Ot kornilovskikh dnei," p. 153; S. Volin, *Men'sheviki na Ukraine, 1917–1921* (Inter-University Project on the History of the Menshevik Movement, Paper no. 11, N.Y., 1962), p. 18—where it is claimed that *right*-wing Mensheviks helped collaboration with the SRs—and pp. 27–28; Pidhainy, *Formation*, pp. 213, 236, 267–268.

96. Pidhainy throws doubt on the Bolshevik claim to have set up a *revkom*, but does not discuss Bosh's statement (*God bor'by*, pp. 44, 56, 63) that there was such a body, whose members were arrested along with the *gorkom* on October 25 (the date rightly adjusted by Liubimov to October 28; *Khronika*, p. 17). M. Rafes, *Dva goda revoliutsii na Ukraine* (Moscow, 1920), p. 46, states that the *revkom* was set up on October 22, and I. Kulik, "Oktiabr'skie dni v Kieve," *Letopis' revoliutsii*, no. 1 (1922), p. 40, gives the date of October 26.

that these reverses ruled out further collaboration with the Ukrainians—a view that smacked of liberalism and was to cause him trouble within the party. Accordingly on November 1 the Bolsheviks entered the area committee (*kraevoi komitet*), as the Malaia Rada now called itself. But relations remained strained and there was no real cooperation. The Bolsheviks endeavored to build up their support among lower-echelon groups, although for the moment to little effect, and launched preparations for an area (*kraevoi*) congress of soviets. This was a direct challenge to the Rada. When the delegates to this gathering assembled on December 3, they met a display of force by the nationalists, who swamped the hall with their men. Tension was now mounting over the Soviet government's ultimatum to the Rada. The local Bolsheviks decided to transfer their congress to Kharkov, where the political situation was more favorable to their designs. Here they set up an All-Ukrainian Congress of Soviets and a Central Executive Committee (TsIK), which claimed all authority in the Ukraine on behalf of the Council of People's Commissars in Petrograd.[97]

In Kharkov the Russian element in the population was stronger than in Kiev; there was also a long tradition of independent Social-Democratic activity. Unionist tendencies were marked, and there was no violence during the October days. In the soviet a well-known Bolshevik activist, F. Sergeev ("Artem"), was elected chairman, but the main political influence belonged to the Menshevik-Internationalists; the SRs, too, exceeded the Bolsheviks in numbers.[98]

One might have expected the Bolsheviks to turn toward the Ukrainians, but it seems that after some initial vacillation anti-Ukrainian sentiments gained the upper hand among both Bolsheviks and Mensheviks. The Russian parties in the soviet set up a coalition *revkom* comprising 5 Mensheviks, 2 SRs, and 2 Bolsheviks, but no Ukrainians. It pursued a moderate line; so, too, did the soviet, which called for an all-socialist coalition government. Local affairs were administered by a coalition "communal council." Such an arrangement could only be provisional. The Bolsheviks mobilized grass-roots support until on November 24 they were able to bring about a re-election of the soviet

97. *Novaia zhizn'*, November 3; *Rabochaia gazeta*, November 4; Bosh, *God bor'by*, pp. 63–64, 75–80, 85–88; Pipes, *Formation*, pp. 70–73; Leikina, "Oktiabr'," *Proletarskaia revoliutsiia*, no. 59, pp. 241–246; N. I. Suprunenko, "Ustanovlenie sovetskoi vlasti na Ukraine," *Voprosy istorii*, no. 10 (1957), pp. 57–60; Rafes, *Dva goda*, pp. 44–49; Volin, *Men'sheviki*, pp. 14–22; Liubimov, *Khronika*, pp. 9, 42–43, 70; J. S. Reshetar, *The Ukrainian Revolution* (New York, 1952), pp. 82–84.

98. The SRs and the Bolsheviks each had 120, the Ukrainians and Mensheviks 40 deputies. Butenko and Chugaev, *Vtoroi s"ezd*, p. 360.

executive. This gave them 19 seats to 11 for the SRs and 4 each for the Mensheviks and Ukrainians. It was now the Mensheviks' turn to withdraw to their lower-echelon base, the trade unions.[99]

Elsewhere in the eastern Ukraine the Mensheviks likewise managed to hold their own for some time. In the Donets regional soviet the Bolsheviks reported that they were "living amicably" with their Internationalist colleagues. At Iuzovka, where elections to the soviet were held on October 14, the two groups' numerical strength was roughly equal, but a motion endorsing the Petrograd insurrection secured only 36 votes, 69 being cast in favor of the formation of a joint "strike committee." On November 19 even the lower-echelon organizations of the region, meeting in conference, declared for a socialist coalition regime.[100] This may seem surprising, in view of the relative weakness of Ukrainian nationalism in this area; but the threat posed by the Cossack forces of General Kaledin had the same effect of driving Bolsheviks and Mensheviks together.

On October 25 Kaledin announced that his army (voisko) government was assuming full power and sent troops to disperse the soviet at Makeevskaia, northwest of Rostov; other detachments occupied individual Donets mines. But after a few days they were obliged to withdraw and Kaledin sought to consolidate his strength before attempting another offensive. On November 6 the conservative All-Russian Cossack Congress, which had moved from Kiev on the outbreak of the revolution, resumed its labors at Novocherkassk and one week later agreed on the basic provisions of an anti-Bolshevik government. Troops were promptly moved into Rostov-on-Don, where the local soviet had adopted a challenging attitude and after five days of fighting occupied the city. The writ of the new regime ran lightly in the city, and it soon became apparent that the Cossacks were deeply divided over political and social issues. In fact, Kaledin could rely only upon those elements closely identified with the Don region who had most to lose from revolution. The former front-line soldiers in particular were sympathetic to the Bolsheviks, who could also appeal to the underprivileged non-Cossack groups in the rural areas. In addition there was tension between the Cossack leaders and those of the "Volunteer Army" now being formed on their territory. For all these reasons, when the Red forces mounted

99. N. Popov, "Ocherki revoliutsionnykh sobytii v Khar'kove ot iiunia 1917 g. do dekabria 1918 g.," Letopis' revoliutsii, no. 1 (1922), pp. 16–34; S. Buzdalin, "Oktiabr'skaia revoliutsiia v Khar'kove," ibid., pp. 35–38; Delo naroda, November 5, 22; Novaia zhizn', November 7, 12; Liubimov, Khronika, pp. 27, 98, 120.

100. Rabochaia gazeta, November 12; Volin, Men'sheviki, pp. 17, 26; Liubimov, Khronika, pp. 43, 178; Butenko and Chugaev, Vtoroi s"ezd, p. 368; Riabinskii, Khronika, p. 174.

an offensive Kaledin's support disintegrated, although Rostov-on-Don was not evacuated until February 24, 1918.[101] These events were in effect the first round in the Civil War that was to wrack Russia for the next three years, as the anti-Bolsheviks vainly sought to recover the ground they had surrendered so readily in the crucial October days.

The historian F. Grenard remarks that the population of Petrograd showed "an astonishing indifference" to the Bolshevik assumption of power.[102] The same was true, broadly speaking, of the provinces. Events had moved so fast, and the normal pattern of political life had been so distorted, that most people were utterly confused. Relatively few seem to have felt that this was a decisive turning point in history or that a moment had come when they must fight and die for their beliefs; it was a matter of avoiding what one feared or hated most, rather than of affirming deeply held aspirations. Such negative attitudes were common among supporters of all the contending parties, but the anti-Bolshevik forces in particular seemed to suffer from a curious paralysis of the will. Those groups that might have been expected to rally against the threat of left-wing extremism were divided by a gulf of distrust so wide that it has scarcely been bridged even today.

The army leaders, to whom the conservative and liberal politicians looked as the potential nucleus of a strong government able to "regenerate" the country, had no tradition of intervening in civilian affairs; their first effort to do so, under General Kornilov, had ended in utter failure. Few senior professional officers could resist a feeling of *Schadenfreude* at the overthrow of the Provisional Government, which, as they saw it, had been to blame for this disaster. They had no desire to burn their fingers again. Generals Cheremisov, Baluev, and others were reluctant to commit any large body of troops to Kerensky's support at a time when such action could have proved decisive. The general tendency was to minimize the significance of the Bolshevik take-over. At First Army Headquarters, only a few hours' rail journey from the capital, staff officers had no reliable news of the insurrection:

Just a few tales by casual visitors, week-old newspapers, and the white telegraph tapes with the usual laconic instructions . . . As for the messages from Petersburg, "to all, all, all!" nobody took them seriously; we had grown used to them as part of the daily round and, I must admit, underestimated their new resolute tone.[103]

101. *Rabochaia gazeta*, November 2, 4, 12; *Novaia zhizn'*, November 17; *Pravda*, November 3, 12; Riabinskii, *Khronika*, p. 199; Liubimov, *Khronika*, p. 93.

102. *La révolution russe* (Paris, 1933), p. 285.

103. D. G. Fokke, "Na stsene i za kulisami Brestskoi tragikomedii," *Arkhiv russkoi revoliutsii*, XX (Berlin, 1930), p. 6.

The argument that the commissar and committee system in the army frustrated any attempt at action should be treated with caution. Many units preserved a modicum of discipline, but their commanders showed little initiative. At Mogilev, Dukhonin allowed the politicians to bicker among themselves, taking only an indirect interest in their deliberations. This inactivity could be explained in part by democratic scruples and respect for the will of the impending Constituent Assembly, but a far more powerful motive was the desire to recover for the army its traditional nonpartisan image and to leave the democratic politicians saddled with the responsibilities of government. It was characteristic that one general who decided that the only alternative to Bolshevism was a military regime should have mooted the idea in private with great diffidence and sworn his interlocutor to secrecy.[104] It took a year of civil war before the notion of a military regime became really respectable in regular army circles.

Some Cossack leaders seem to have had a rather more realistic view of the country's problems, but they lacked the physical means to implement their ideas, except on a very limited scale; the position that the Cossacks occupied in Russian life was too exceptional for them to take the lead in building a viable military regime.

The Achilles' heel of Russian conservatism at this time was its rigid attitude towards the war. It should have been obvious that the armed forces were no longer capable of significant action against the enemy (in the European theater, at least), yet senior officers insistently opposed any serious step toward a negotiated peace. The irony was that soon after the Bolshevik overturn some of them reluctantly concurred in the Soviet government's efforts to secure an armistice and within a few months actively contributed to the buildup of the Red Army. Only after that did they gradually realize how fallacious had been the assumption, prevalent in army circles in the latter half of 1917, that the Bolsheviks were little more than enemy agents and that concern for the national interest was a monopoly of the right. In 1917 illusion held sway, preventing the conservatives from analyzing correctly the nature of their opponents and devising rational methods of combating them.

It must be acknowledged that the element of illusion was as great, if not greater, in the camp of "revolutionary democracy." Large elements in both the main socialist parties, anxious to win popular favor, were willing to overlook significant differences of principle that separated them from the Bolsheviks. They regarded Lenin and his followers as

104. W. S. Woytinsky, *Stormy Passage: A Personal History* (New York, 1961), p. 365.

misguided comrades who would soon be brought by history to see the error of their ways; the task of the moderates, they thought, was to persuade them to renounce their unreasonable "maximalist" tendencies and to revert to an objective scientific view of the revolutionary process. It was axiomatic to all those with a Marxist upbringing—and the SRs too had been deeply influenced by Marxism—that premature "adventuristic" actions could lead only to isolation from the masses, the defeat of the revolution, and a conservative restoration. Once the results of the elections to the Constituent Assembly were known, the Bolsheviks' relative weakness would be apparent and they would be obliged to seek a compromise.

This reasoning invited the comforting conclusion that it was unnecessary to use coercion against the "usurpers," who were in any case doomed; it was enough to make a gesture of moral defiance. The demonstrative protest, the walkout from the council chamber, became the symbol of the democratic left's response to triumphant bolshevism. As one sympathetic critic puts it:

All over Russia the same phenomenon was repeated: wherever the SRs and Mensheviks had a fairly significant majority in the soviets, instead of staying in them to fight the Bolsheviks . . . they voted to withdraw, voluntarily abandoning the battlefield. The Bolsheviks did not fail to take advantage of this decision and very quickly replaced the right-wing socialists with their own supporters. Thanks to this the Communists or their Left SR sympathizers soon had a majority of votes in almost all soviets and executives. Within a few months the right-wing socialists realized their mistake, but by then it was too late to undo it.[105]

This attitude also accounts for the poor showing generally put up by the salvation committees—although it should be pointed out that, owing to the state of the sources, very little hard information is available about the way in which these bodies functioned. It is not certain, for instance, to what extent the debates in them were conducted and decisions arrived at along party-political lines. The municipal and *zemstvo* representatives will doubtless have often put their practical skills to good use in maintaining essential supplies and performing similar tasks, whereas the inclusion of soviet and trade-union representatives will have provided an invaluable channel of communication with the masses. Even the presence of Bolsheviks on some of these bodies, which at first sight seems to suggest unpardonable naiveté, could be defended on the

105. N. Voronovich, "Mezh dvukh ognei: zapiski zelenogo," *Arkhiv russkoi revoliutsii*, VII (Berlin, 1922), p. 57.

grounds that at the provincial level there was a good deal of conciliatory and localist feeling among them.[106] However, the non-Bolsheviks made no very systematic effort to exploit these sentiments, and the fact remains that the salvation committees collapsed in a matter of days, or at least weeks. It is reasonable to attribute this collapse primarily to the defective vision of the democratic politicians.

One result of this débâcle was that the burden of passive resistance to bolshevism fell upon the shoulders of the infant trade unions, some of which, all things considered, stood up for their principles remarkably well. In the case of the industrial unions, which were overwhelmingly under Bolshevik control, only branches in areas remote from the capital could attempt resistance, and they sometimes did so if the political climate was favorable to their designs. Somewhat better placed were the semi-professional unions, particularly in the communications. It is well known that on October 29 Vikzhel, the railwaymen's union, threatened to call a general strike unless its demand for a socialist coalition government were met and unless in response to this pressure certain Bolshevik leaders entered into negotiations with the opposition.[107] Eventually this resistance was broken by the standard political maneuver: when a national congress (December 29) failed to give the Bolsheviks control, they called a gathering of their own adherents (January 5, 1918), who dissolved the union and formed a rival body, Vikzhedor.

The role played by the postal workers' union, Potelsoiuz, which was under SR control, deserves more attention than it is generally given. It too opposed the Bolshevik insurrection as a challenge to the authority of the Constituent Assembly and called for a socialist coalition government. In post and telegraph offices throughout the country union members and other employees withdrew their labor, sometimes taking obstructive action. On November 18 the union met in congress at Nizhni Novgorod and a week later adopted a resolution reaffirming its support for democratic institutions, calling upon the authorities to respect the inviolability of the mails and setting up a committee to plan further strikes if its demands were disregarded.[108] In most cases the local Bolsheviks were able to restore essential services within a few days by

106. It is interesting that Liubimov's collection of sources contains only two resolutions from Bolshevik gorkomy openly critical of the vacillating tendencies in the party's Central Committee. Khronika, pp. 103, 146.

107. L. B. Schapiro, The Origin of the Communist Autocracy: Political Opposition in the Soviet State: First Phase, 1917–1922 (London, 1955), pp. 70–74; J. Bunyan and H. H. Fisher, The Bolshevik Revolution 1917–1918: Documents and Materials (Stanford, 1934), pp. 155–160. The union branches' political sympathies were divided on geographical lines, the Bolshevik strength lying mainly in the north and the south supporting the leadership in its search for a compromise.

108. Liubimov, Khronika, pp. 170, 213.

employing blackleg labor (such as military telegraphists), threatening strikers with dismissal, and arresting the most recalcitrant elements. Nevertheless, this "sabotage movement," as it was misleadingly termed, caused them no little embarrassment. The breakdown of communications added considerably to the Bolsheviks' problems in organizing a smooth transfer of power in many provincial centers and helps explain the uncoordinated nature of much of their activity at this time. But such opposition, limited as it was by the organizational weakness of the Russian trade-union movement, could not prevail against the armed might of the "proletarian dictatorship."

To understand fully the reasons for the Bolsheviks' success in October it would be necessary to undertake an excursion into the familiar field of Russian *Geistesgeschichte*. Here it must suffice to note that, over a broad spectrum of political opinion, there was a firm conviction that, if the Bolsheviks took power, their rule would be of short duration. Joseph Gessen, a widely respected jurist whose contacts extended into all reaches of Russian society, recalls in his memoirs: "I never met anyone who doubted that the overthrow of the Bolsheviks was imminent. The only question was how and when."[109] Obviously this view underestimated Lenin's resourcefulness and his tactical skill in the manipulation of political power. If even Lenin asked himself whether his party could successfully administer a modern state, it is hardly surprising that his opponents did likewise and that they should have arrived at the wrong answer. They were after all faced with an unprecedented situation: few as yet foresaw that a single-party dictatorship could create the prerequisites for its own survival.

The anti-Bolshevik forces, with few exceptions, based their conduct on moral principle rather than on considerations of *Realpolitik*. The psychologist might say that they did so in order to rationalize their own physical weakness, of which they were subconsciously aware but which they could not afford to admit. There is some truth in this, but it is not the whole story. Their failure to make use of such physical strength as they possessed was a conscious intellectual decision, taken by men who had experienced the abuses of power committed by the *ancien régime* and who were determined to avoid similar temptations themselves. Hence their ideological cast of thought, their distaste for precise juridical concepts, their romantic idealization of the people (*narod*), of freedom and democracy, and other abstract notions sanctified by generations of usage among the intelligentsia. The myths of nineteenth-century Russian radicalism still exerted a powerful fascination.

109. I. V. Gessen, "V dvukh revoliutsiiakh: zhiznennyi opyt," *Arkhiv russkoi revoliutsii*, XXII (Berlin, 1937), p. 382.

The Bolsheviks, too, were a product of the same radical tradition. But they had leaders able to blend the determinist certainties of revolutionary Marxism with their own voluntarist drive for power and to inspire their followers with the same modes of thought and conduct. The more activist elements on the left were irresistibly drawn to the Bolsheviks (and their allies) because they seemed to possess the will to translate ideals into practice. This was why thousands of individuals who had only the vaguest idea of Lenin's organizational and tactical doctrine could apply its essential precepts in their own environment, by simply joining in the struggle for power with boundless enthusiasm.

The distinction between moderates and radicals did not follow class lines. It was essentially a psychological, emotional barrier that defies exact analysis. One provincial Bolshevik leader puts the point well in his record of a conversational exchange with a Menshevik colleague, who asked him why the Bolsheviks were so fanatical and self-confident. He replied: "I can't really say: we're convinced, that's all. And if you're convinced of something, then for some reason you can't be unsure of yourself. That's all there is to it." He then made a bow to current political orthodoxy, claiming, "We are men of the proletarian mass," to which the Menshevik objected—correctly, but as it happens irrelevantly —that they were in fact all intellectuals, as was Lenin himself.[110]

This ideological élan, linked to a well articulated philosophy of organization, gave the Bolsheviks the edge over their rivals and enabled them to turn the transient popular mood to their party's account. Once Soviet power had been achieved, the ideals of the propagandists were soon obscured by the harsh realities of dictatorship and the revolution lost much of its romantic allure. But by then a machine had been built powerful enough to keep dissent in check and, with time, even to reshape men's memories of the cause for which they had fought in October 1917.

Comment by Merle Fainsod on — "The Bolshevik Insurrection in Petrograd" by Dietrich Geyer and "October in the Provinces" by John Keep

Let me begin with Mr. Geyer's admirable paper. Its general thesis is one with which I find myself in agreement. Mr. Geyer does not undertake

110. Antonov-Saratovskii, *Pod stiagom*, p. 126.

to add to our knowledge of the events of October. What he has done is to put them in an interpretative framework. Before addressing myself to his interpretation, I should like to call your attention to a very recent, late 1966, publication of documents, *Petrogradskii Voenno-Revoliutsionnyi Komitet,* which helps significantly in filling out details on the actual seizure of power. The first part of the first volume, on which Mr. Geyer has drawn, is particularly illuminating in the way in which the Military Revolutionary Committee of the Petrograd Soviet organized its activities and developed its network of contacts with the garrison units and the factories. A review of this material, however, only serves to reinforce Mr. Geyer's thesis that the actual seizure of power was the expression of a political victory the Bolsheviks had already won when they achieved a majority in the Petrograd Soviet and acted in its name.

One of the points Mr. Geyer stresses is the importance of the Soviet as a shield of legitimacy for the seizure of power. In the given circumstances, short of the Constituent Assembly, the Soviet institutions represented the nearest approximation to a symbol of legitimacy available. In effect, the Bolsheviks subordinated their own role and operated under the cover of the Soviet and its Military Revolutionary Committee. The seizure of power was justified as a defensive action. The revolution was allegedly in danger; the bourgeoisie wanted to disarm the workers and the garrisons and turn Petrograd over to the Germans. The Bolsheviks operating through the Military Revolutionary Committee purported to defend the forthcoming Congress of Soviets, and even the Constituent Assembly. They ostensibly favored a coalition of socialist parties and were forced to govern alone only because the other parties refused to cooperate. Actually, the Military Revolutionary Committee functioned as an instrument to mobilize a wide array of popular support that would not have been available to the Bolsheviks had they made their bid for power in their own name.

Actually, as Mr. Geyer points out, victory was won as early as October 21, when the Military Revolutionary Committee made good its demand that its commissars control the issuance of arms and that no military orders be issued by district army headquarters without the sanction of the Military Revolutionary Committee. Operating through the Soviet, the Bolsheviks maintained their defensive posture to the last. The actual seizure of power took place only after the Provisional Government tried to shut down the Bolshevik press. In effect, October was not a revolution in the name of bolshevism, but in the name of the soviets and soviet democracy. The party remained in the shadows, manipulating the symbol of legitimacy that had the broadest worker and soldier appeal.

Let me now turn to Mr. Keep's paper on October in the provinces. Given all the difficulties of assembling accurate information on developments in the localities, it seems to me that he has done a remarkable job. As he rightly points out, his subject has been neglected, and there has been some tendency to assume that events in the provinces were merely a mirror of developments in the center, instead of the chaotic and confused improvisations which in fact they were.

Again, I should point out that the documents of the Petrograd Military Revolutionary Committee help fill out many details, although they do not affect the main conclusions that Mr. Keep has reached. They do, however, make clear the efforts of the center to impose direction on events in the localities. There are many documents of authorization designating this or that person to serve as a commissar or emissary of the Petrograd Military Revolutionary Committee to work in one or another military unit or region. There are also many reports from these commissars or emissaries that undertake to report on the activities in which they have taken part. Some of these, such as the report on developments in Minsk, provide a slightly different version of events from that contained in Mr. Keep's paper, but it is a tribute to the thoroughness of his research that I was able to discover very few such disparities indeed.

Perhaps the most striking impression that emerges from his paper and the newly available documentary sources is the confusion that attended the transfer of power in the provinces. The following report of a delegate of the Tiflis 15th grenadier regiment, dated November 9 (OS) conveys the chaotic flavor of the post-October days:

> On the 29th of October we received a telephone message from the corps committee with the following content: that in Petrograd and Moscow there is taking place a rising of Bolsheviks. Kerensky is leaving with troops from the front to suppress it. Some time afterwards, another telephone message signed "Military Revolutionary Committee" arrived with the following content, that all power has passed into the hands of the Soviet of Workers, Soldiers, and Peasant Deputies, and that we should take strictest measures to prevent [Kerensky] from reaching Petrograd. Some time after that we received a telegram signed by Kerensky and the Minister of Internal Affairs, Nikitin, with the following content: that Kerensky had occupied Petrograd, that the Bolshevik uprising had been suppressed, and that order had been reestablished in Petrograd. A short time after that we received a telephone message with the following content, that a Military Revolutionary Committee had organized itself in Petrograd, which called on all military units not to fulfill Kerensky's orders. Immediately after that message we received a telegram from the front committee signed by a Committee for the Salvation of the Revolution of the Western Front which cancelled the

order of the Military Revolutionary Committee and called on us only to fulfill the orders of the Committee for the Salvation of the Revolution and the commander of the Southwestern Front, General Valuev, without whose approval no order was to be fulfilled. When we turned for an explanation to the division committee, they answered us that just as you can't make anything out of it, neither can we. Then the regiment committee assembled and resolved that, in view of the receipt of such different tendencies of messages, which we could make nothing of since up to that time we had not received any news from the papers which could explain to us all that had happened in Petrograd, and in order not to do harm to the revolution, and in order to find out what the Committee on Salvation of the Revolution represents and what the Military Revolutionary Committee represents, we decided to send representatives to Petrograd and Moscow for an exact elucidation of events and to find out in whose hands power finds itself.[1]

Pending a clarification of developments, the regiment decided to remain "passive." What emerges from this and many similar accounts is a picture of utmost confusion in which passivity and apathy played a much larger role than is commonly assumed. Strikingly evident is the lack of local initiative, the tendency to wait for a signal from the center, and the reluctance to embark on any course of action which would be out of phase with developments in Petrograd.

Why then did the Bolsheviks triumph? The Bolsheviks, unlike most of their opponents, were willing to take the initiative and, for all their own disorganization, they represented a relatively disciplined force. They were greatly aided by division among their opponents, by the general assumption, which all their opponents shared, that the Bolsheviks could not possibly consolidate their authority. The complete disillusionment of the military and the more conservative forces with Kerensky and their refusal to rally around him redounded to the advantage of the Bolsheviks. The cleavages among the non-Bolshevik socialist parties weakened resistance on the left. Finally, the ability of the Bolsheviks to cloak their seizure of power in the legitimacy of Soviet institutions and to make their appeal in terms of such powerful rallying cries as peace, land, and bread provided the political leverage which enabled them to march to power.

Discussion

Mr. Pipes began the discussion by asking what the term "Bolshevik" conveyed to Lenin's supporters at the time of the October Revolution. In reply,

1. *Petrogradskii Voenno-Revoliutsionnyi Komitet,* II (Moscow, 1966), p. 315.

Mr. Geyer said that the term was rarely used in Bolshevik declarations. Mr. Keep added that in the prevailing situation, with conditions changing rapidly and with political parties dividing, merging, and fragmenting all the time, even relatively educated and literate elements of the urban population had difficulty keeping abreast of party politics. In general, people simply identified the Bolsheviks with hard policies; among political groups of the time the Bolsheviks appeared to be the most revolutionary, the most radical, and the most effective. The bulk of Bolshevik supporters probably had no understanding of the factors underlying the emergence of their party.

Mr. Fainsod expressed agreement with this interpretation. Insofar as people had any sense of what bolshevism stood for, it probably meant the slogans of the moment: peace, land, and bread. Mr. Geyer added that an understanding of the reactions caused by the July days accusations against the Bolsheviks and by the Kornilov affair, although difficult to obtain, would be helpful in answering the question posed by Mr. Pipes.

In trying to understand the Bolshevik victory in October, Mr. Rogger wondered what role was played by simple fatigue on the part of Lenin's opposition. He thought it significant that despite their policy differences, the Bolsheviks seemed to have possessed greater determination and willingness to take risks than the other parties. Mr. Keep interjected that the Bolsheviks had not needed very much determination to get an edge over the Mensheviks.

Mr. Wolfe pointed to the irony in the fact that in 1917 Lenin had abandoned his earlier emphasis on revolutionary war. Believing that the peace issue provided the key to the seizure of power, Lenin had made peace his central slogan. To the Petrograd garrison bolshevism meant an end to the war and no removal from the capital; this attitude was what had enabled Trotsky to neutralize, if not win over, the garrison in October.

Mr. Wolfe further commented on why army chiefs and provincial leaders had done so little to prevent the Bolsheviks from consolidating their power. The actions of the generals were influenced by their feeling of having been ignominiously deceived by the Duma leaders at the time of Nicholas II's fall. When they saw the consequences of the February Revolution, the generals regretted the role they had played during and after the tsar's abdication. In October they were still isolated from the center and disinclined toward further precipitate action. Mr. Wolfe stressed as well that the black mark received by the army as a whole at the time of the Kornilov uprising and the conviction that the maintenance of the front would be best served if they abstained from politics also helped determine the policies pursued by the military.

Mr. Erickson observed that the passivity and confusion of the army at the time of the October Revolution are usually explained by developments in the highest and lowest echelons. But the significance of attitudes and changes in the middle echelons of the armed forces should not be underestimated; the officer corps had become divided as a consequence of war losses. There was conflict not only between professional and wartime officers, but between officers stationed in the field and those at headquarters. Consciousness of these divisions and the realization that the army was rocking helped to impart a sense of caution to military leaders.

Mr. Wolfe cited two factors in explaining the actions of both generals and provincial leaders in the fall of 1917: the habit of unquestioning acceptance of direction from the capital (a heritage of Russia's autocratic past) and the total lack of any rallying center for bolshevism's scattered opponents. Only someone possessing Lenin's overpowering will and certitude would have been capable of effectively coordinating this opposition.

Returning to Mr. Pipes' question about the popular image of the Bolsheviks, Mr. Anweiler spoke of the need to distinguish between differing conceptions of bolshevism held by various elements of the Russian population. Bolshevism did not mean the same thing to troops in the garrison, soldiers at the front, peasants in the village, and workers in the factories. However, the Bolsheviks had successfully utilized these varying conceptions as well as the picture of Soviet legality conjured by Trotsky in effecting their seizure of power.

Mr. Anweiler pointed out that the Left SR's and anarchists played important roles in the development of the revolution in some areas and wondered why this factor was missing from Mr. Keep's analysis.

Mr. Ferro remarked that although attitudes toward the Bolsheviks in liberal circles were strongly affected by the July days, mass public opinion was most of all influenced by the Kornilov affair. In the aftermath of that event, soldiers, workers, and peasants viewed the soviets as the last bastion of the revolution. And in October, believing that the soviets were threatened by the counterrevolution once again, the masses were prepared to support the Bolsheviks in their defense. The precise nature of Lenin's goals was unclear not only to Lenin's supporters generally, but even to many Bolshevik leaders.

Responding to a question by Mr. Avineri in regard to the view of Lenin prevailing in the provinces at the time of the October Revolution, Mr. Keep stated that Lenin appeared more as an image than as an individual. This was at least partly because the Bolsheviks had always been careful to use vague organizational terms and to avoid specific commitments about individual leaders.

To Miss Arendt, the image of Lenin's personal authority within the Bolshevik party was a very important matter. She asked whether it was not in fact so well established both among party members and the population at large that an appeal or slogan issued in Lenin's name carried a special element of authority. Mr. Geyer's response was that, although Lenin's authority within the inner circle of the Bolshevik party was surely great, the popularization of his image did not occur until much later.

Mr. Katkov questioned Mr. Geyer's view of the role and importance of the Military Revolutionary Committee in the seizure of power in Petrograd. The activities of the Military Revolutionary Committee were merely a front behind which the work of forming a new government was going on. The appointment of a new government, Lenin's Council of People's Commissars, came as a complete surprise when it was announced at the Second All-Russian Congress of Soviets. Referring to Lenin's frenzied correspondence with the Bolshevik Central Committee in September–October 1917 Mr. Katkov speculated on Lenin's mental state during this period. The evidence of "very peculiar thinking" could be found in Lenin's writings as early as 1915, and already at that time Lenin might have been afflicted by the brain disease which was to take his life in 1924. Because of this Mr. Katkov saw the need for psychiatric analysis in explaining Lenin's behavior in 1917.

Mr. Geyer admitted to lack of competence to provide a medical diagnosis of Lenin's mental health. However, he pointed out that the impatience, frenzy, and excitement that Lenin exhibited in September–October 1917 could probably be explained by his extended period of isolation in Finland. Mr. Ulam remarked that Mr. Katkov suggested one of the reasons for the complacency of the Bolsheviks' opponents in 1917, that is, their conviction that Lenin was mad and that most other Bolshevik leaders were reasonable men. He added that this erroneous assumption had given the Bolsheviks an advantage, for as Churchill put it, madness is a quality which confers on its possessor the ability to stage a surprise.

Turning to a different subject, Mr. Kecskemeti noted that the necessity for a popular uprising appeared frequently in Lenin's writings and, indeed, that Mr. Geyer had shown that for Lenin revolution was synonymous with an uprising of the people. However, what occurred in October was a coup d'état, that is, the seizure of power without mass action. A more minute theoretical differentiation than the traditional breakdown between popular uprisings and coups d'état was necessary to explain modern revolutions. Speaking only of the popular uprising, he distinguished two types: the victorious revolutions from below of February 1848 and February 1917, which were spontaneous and unorganized, and the events of July 1848 and July 1917, in which one party set itself apart from other groups in calling for an uprising. He added that historically the former type of revolution was more successful than the latter.

Mr. Geyer recognized the value of this kind of differentiation. However, bearing in mind the confused nature of the Bolshevik role in the July uprising, he questioned whether it fitted into the category Mr. Kecskemeti had described. Moreover, it was questionable whether the term "coup d'état" was fully applicable to October. Bolshevik faith in a popular uprising was to all appearances sincere, and Lenin, right up until October 24, continued to hold that the seizure of power was entirely related to a popular insurrection.

Mr. Schapiro referred to the need to bear in mind that there were really two things happening at the time of the October Revolution. At one level there was the perfectly organized seizure of the critical points of power on the night of October 24–25. At another level, there was the symbolic vote on the new Provisional Government by the Congress of Soviets on October 25. As regards the latter development, the questionnaires filled out by the Congress deputies showed that the idea of a Bolshevik monopoly of power never crossed the minds of the overwhelming majority. Indeed, in their questionnaires, the deputies spoke again and again of the replacement of the inefficient Provisional Government by a broad coalition government of all parties of the left. Thus it appeared likely that the only people who had thought very much about the acquisition of power by the Bolsheviks were a narrow circle of Lenin's followers.

In his closing comments Mr. Fainsod reinforced the remarks made by Mr. Schapiro about the events of October 25 having proceeded on two rails. At one level Lenin had worked to consolidate power in his own hands without reference to other parties. However, the attainment of this objective was greatly facilitated by developments at the other level, the Congress of Soviets. There the emphasis was on revolutionary legality and the convocation of a Constituent Assembly; at this point this was what Lenin's seizure of power meant to those who took his words seriously.

Referring to remarks by Mr. Ferro, Mr. Keep speculated about why rank-and-file Bolsheviks seemed to have paid so little attention to what Lenin had said and done during the summer of 1917. They tended to view Lenin as just another democratic leader, perhaps a bit harder than the rest but not fundamentally different. Ignoring Lenin's scathing attacks on the Mensheviks and his demands for a complete break with them, Bolsheviks at the local level had gone on collaborating with Mensheviks throughout 1917. Acknowledging the difficulty of explaining this phenomenon, Mr. Keep wondered whether the unrealistic, semi-mythical world in which all political groups seemed to have been operating did not have something to do with it.

To Mr. Wolfe, Mr. Keep commented that although the problem of Bolshevik slogans had already been virtually exhausted, a question meriting further study was whether or not local leaders had made any important amendments to the slogans that they received from the center. For example, how far had they gone in adapting slogans to the particular problems which they were facing? Had they used only those slogans which were relevant to their own situation and discarded the rest, or had they merely published them as handed down and let events take their course? Mr. Keep suggested that Western historians, influenced by the later Bolshevik obsession with efficient organization and by Soviet historical studies, tended to assume that the Bolshevik party apparatus functioned much more efficiently than it ever could have in a revolutionary situation.

The Origins of the Red Army — *John Erickson*

Whatever the triumphs of the battlefield, the original Worker-Peasant Red Army, the *Raboche-Krest'ianskaia Krasnaia Armiia*, presently transformed into the Soviet Army, has suffered defeat after defeat at the hands of the historian, an opponent more wily, more persistent and more intractable than any it encountered elsewhere. Acting at the behest of the party, or operating under the monstrous rigor of the "cult of personality," Soviet historians inflicted very distinctive damage of their own, burying the early, inevitably frantic days of the Red Army under a massive slab of mythology, twisting the military history of the Civil War into grotesque shapes and bizarre contexts, pressing every convolution of strategy and each peculiarity of tactics into a Stalinist mold, obliterating leading military personalities and outstanding field commanders from the record, or else assisting that transmutation which turned loyalty into treason, efficiency into doltishness, and integrity into baseness.

Like its latter days, the very earliest months of the Red Army's existence have suffered considerably from the historian's malpractices. The nature of the subject itself—the imprecision of time and place, the bewildering admixtures of terminology, the loss or unavailability of records, the imperfections of memory—contributes even now to making the task of extricating historical reality formidable in the extreme. Valuable contemporary accounts of these early days there are—but these are inevitably incomplete and filled with the inaccuracies of the moment.[1] The post-Civil War literature, memoir and monograph alike,

All dates in this article are given in New Style.

1. G. Lindov, *O politicheskoi rabote i politicheskikh rabotnikakh na fronte* (Samara, 1918; also Kharkov, 1919); E. Iaroslavskii, *Krasnaia Armiia* (Moscow, 1919); V. I. Samuilov, *Ustroistvo vooruzhennykh sil Respubliki* (Petrograd, 1919); R. I. Berzin, *Etapy organizatsii i razvitiia Krasnoi Armii* (Kharkov, 1920).

the first-hand accounts and the studied compilations,[2] although adding new information, was certainly a part of the search for the bubble reputation, a part of the anti-Trotsky (and pro-Trotsky) campaign, and a part of that retrospective reconstruction common to all military history, which seeks to tidy the battlefield. The Stalinist mortmain obliterated the relics of facts, facts that are now being most diligently unearthed by recent Soviet scholarship.[3]

The question of "the origins" of the Red Army is from the outset beset by problems of chronology. Properly speaking, from its initial formation to the achievement of a stable organization there extended a period of almost a decade. But in a more restricted context of actual origins, the investigation can limit itself to the period beginning with the first serious debates about an "army" (November–December 1917) through the abandonment of the volunteer system and the organization of the eastern front as a "front" in a recognizable sense, to the deployment of the first Red divisions (June 1918). Such an inquiry must spread inevitably much beyond the confines of purely military questions. It involves looking into most nooks and crannies of the state, into the crevices of the party, into the relationship between the center, the regions, and the periphery, into much early Soviet administrative practice, into idealism, utopianism, and a brutal realism, the ugly business of waging civil war.

If chronology is one hazard, then the complexity and widely ramified contexts of "the origins" is another. To launch out on a discussion of

2. Some principal works include: A. S. Bubnov, *Grazhdanskaia voina, partiia i voennoe delo* (Moscow, 1928); S. I. Gusev, *Grazhdanskaia voina i Krasnaia Armiia. Sbornik voenno-teoreticheskikh i voenno-politicheskih statei (1918–1924 gg.)* (Moscow, 1925; reprinted 1958); V. Antonov-Ovseenko, *Stroitel'stvo Krasnoi Armii v revoliutsii* (Moscow, 1923) and *Zapiski o grazhdanskoi voine* (Moscow-Leningrad, 1924–1933); N. Kakurin, *Kak srazhalas' revoliutsiia*, I (Moscow-Leningrad, 1925); S. Ventsov, *Ot Krasnoi Gvardii k vooruzhennomu narodu* (Moscow-Leningrad, 1927); A. S. Bubnov, S. S. Kamenev, M. N. Tukhachevskii, and R. P. Eideman, eds., *Grazhdanskaia voina 1918–1921*, I-III (Moscow-Leningrad, 1928–1930). See also *Oborona SSSR i Krasnaia Armiia-Katalog knig* (Moscow-Leningrad, 1928), 242 pp.

3. V. I. Startsev, *Ocherki po istorii Petrogradskoi Krasnoi Gvardii i Rabochei Militsii (Mart 1917–Aprel' 1918 g.)* (Moscow-Leningrad, 1965), 310 pp.; E. N. Gorodetskii, *Rozhdenie Sovetskogo gosudarstva 1917–1918 gg.* (Moscow, 1965), chap. V, pp. 353–428; A. L. Fraiman, *Revoliutsionnaia zashchita Petrograda v Fevrale–Marte 1918 g.* (Moscow-Leningrad, 1964), 323 pp.; S. M. Kliatskin, *Na zashchite Oktiabria—Organizatsiia reguliarnoi armii i militsionnoe stroitel'stvo v Sovetskoi Respublike 1917–1920* (Moscow, 1965), 475 pp. This work wholly supersedes N. I. Shatagin's, *Organizatsiia i stroitel'stvo Sovetskoi Armii v period inostrannoi voennoi interventsii i grazhdanskoi voiny (1918–1920 gg.)* (Moscow, 1954), 247 pp.

the earliest days of the Red Army without more detailed knowledge of the final months of the Imperial Army—for the two lived in brief but significant symbiosis—means missing relevant detail about early Soviet military units. To concentrate on the center means displacing the relevance of the regions and bypassing the chaos of the periphery. Nor is there simple salvation in tracing the development of institutions. The proliferation of offices, the splitting of organizations into sub-groups and self-appointed committees, the diversity of names used in the provinces for functions carried out in rudimentary centralized fashion, the grandiloquent style of "staffs" and "divisions" (or even armies) for proconsular commands and private military ventures—all these encrust the documentation and confuse the narrative.

Much in recent Soviet writing is both scrupulous and admirable in its careful turning over of files and records, yet the attention to detail precludes the wide view. The myths are only partly overturned.

Similarly, the overly strident claims or the mere repetitive assertions that here was (and is) "an army of a new type"[4] do justice neither to the complexity of contemporary problems nor to the findings of history. The Red Army did indeed incorporate singular features. It was certainly conceived as the sword and shield of the revolution and as a "revolutionary army." It had forebears, not least the French revolutionary armies whose origins have been exhaustively depicted in Richard Cobb's monumental, *Les Armées Révolutionnaires*.[5] The comparison bears some weight. As a model, Cobb's study has twin advantages. First, the abundance of source material at his disposal—central and regional records, personal dossiers, the records of individual formations, and so into the mountain of material—presents an almost ideal picture of what is needed to probe the early stages of a revolutionary army, an army in the making. Second and perhaps even more significant is the relevance of parallel problems, such as the arming of an elite against the arming of the *sans-culottes*, the debates between proponents and adversaries of a "revolutionary army," the issue of the subordination of powers, the controversy over establishing a single "army" or countenancing an array of regional armies, the originality of the institutions, the administrative control of this new force, and the discovery that administration was a much less formidable problem than that of command. All this had a familiar sound in early 1918, even as it crackled in the fiery atmosphere of 1793.

In one important respect, however, the "model" drawn from 1793

4. N. I. Shatagin and I. P. Prusanov, *Sovetskaia Armiia—armiia novogo tipa* (Moscow, 1957), 277 pp.

5. Richard Cobb, *Les Armées Révolutionnaires: Instrument de la Terreur dans les Départements, Avril 1793–Floréal An II*, I (Paris-The Hague, 1961), 364 pp.

and from Mr. Cobb's study must be reversed. Whereas *Les Armées Révolutionnaires* is deliberately concerned with "the army" as a corrective to the profusion of studies on individual French armies, the "Red Army"—the central institution—is well enough known even if present studies are incomplete. On the other hand, the individual armies, the regional formations and the forces on the periphery conspicuously lack their complement of serious investigations, though the "biographies" of these armies can be partially assembled through histories of particular divisions and special brigades, or from accounts that range more freely over separate "fronts." But even the fronts, major entities that they were, pose very serious problems of research. Dating for example, "the origin" of the eastern front, the one on which the Red Army first really went to war to learn as well as to fight, is fraught with all the discrepancies between contemporary accounts and retrospective recording. Although Soviet historians (very properly) regard the establishment of the eastern front as a "turning point" in the evolution of the Red Army, there can be little exactitude in this matter.[6]

Sources, therefore, constitute and will continue to constitute the gravamen here. *Les Armées Révolutionnaires* was built out of a plenitude of source material: there is no such *embarras de richesse* available for an investigation of the Soviet revolutionary armies.[7] If there is a critical lack, it lies in the unavailability of material concerning personnel, particularly officers. Nevertheless, notwithstanding the paucity facing the non-Soviet historian, the available or accessible source material forms a certain coherency:

(a) *Newspapers*, a source of primary information and acknowledged as such by Soviet historians, in particular, the 74 issues of *Rabochaia i Krest'ianskaia Krasnaia Armiia i Flot*,[8] as well as the regional press.

(b) *Decrees and regulations*, both the contemporary editions[9] and supplementary materials published recently.[10]

6. For a recent survey of previous periodization of the early history of the Red Army, and a criticism of published and dissertation work, see A. P. Nenarokov, "K voprosu o nachal'nom periode stroitel'stva Krasnoi Armii," in *Oktiabr' i grazhdanskaia voina v SSSR—Sbornik statei k 70-letiiu Akademika I. I. Mintsa* (Moscow, 1966), pp. 433–444.

7. For a discussion of Soviet archives, see Kliatskin, *Na zashchite Oktiabria*, pp. 35–41.

8. First published as *Armiia i Flot Rabochei i Krest'ianskoi Rossii*, ed. K. S. Eremeev; after April 1918 as *Izvestiia Narodnogo Komissariata po Voennym Delam*. Eremeev edited *Krasnaia Armiia*, the Petrograd military newspaper.

9. For example, *Sistematizirovannyi spravochnik-ukazatel' dekretov, postanovlenii, prikazov i rasporiazhenii pravitel'stvennykh organov tsentral'noi sovetskoi vlasti po voprosam, otnosiashchimsia k vedeniiu Narodnogo Komissariata po Voennym Delam za 1917–1918* (Moscow, 1919).

10. *Dekrety Sovetskoi vlasti*, I-II (Moscow, 1957–1959).

(c) *Documentary publications*, relating directly to the Red Army, with *Grazhdanskaia voina—Materialy po istorii Krasnoi Armii* (Moscow, 1923) assuming great importance for the early period, materials relating to the central military institutions[11] and a voluminous set of regional records with materials relating to military questions.[12]

(d) *The earliest contemporary accounts*, Lindov, Samuilov, Berzin.

(e) *The memoirists*, Trotsky, Antonov-Ovseenko, M. D. Bonch-Bruevich, Kedrov, Aralov, Miasnikov, Podvoiskii.[13]

(f) *Formal military histories* (including divisional and unit histories), in particular Kakurin and the three-volume Civil War history published between 1928–1930.[14]

(g) *Recent Soviet monographs*, Fraiman, Gorodetskii, Kliatskin, Startsev.

(h) *Soviet doctoral dissertations.*

(i) *White records*, including Soviet publication of White materials. Newspapers remain the prime source, although following his appointment as People's Commissar for Military Affairs, Trotsky's archive impinges immediately upon part of this formative period, that is, from March to June 1918.

Nor is it entirely a question of soldiers: early Soviet military efforts relied to no small degree upon the Bolshevik sailors, tough fighting squads thrown into many a breach, though a prey to indiscipline and lawlessness (a failing by no means confined to the sailors, as events shortly proved). A rigorous investigation of the early Soviet military

11. Cf. "Kratkaia spravka o deiatel'nosti Narodnogo Komissariata po Voennym Delam v pervye mesiatsy posle Oktiabr'skoi revoliutsii," in *Istoricheskii Arkhiv*, no. 1 (1962), pp. 83–93.

12. Too numerous to list or even to sample, this type of publication is covered by region in E. N. Gorodetskii, ed., *Sovetskaia strana v period grazhdanskoi voiny, 1918–1920—Bibliograficheskii ukazatel' dokumental'nykh publikatsii* (Moscow, 1961), especially under VIII, pp. 179–254.

13. L. Trotsky, *Moia Zhizn'—Opyt avtobiografii*, I-II (Berlin, 1930), (*Ma Vie*, Paris, 1930); Antonov-Ovseenko, *Zapiski o grazhdanskoi voine*; M. D. Bonch-Bruevich, *Na boevykh postakh fevral'skoi i oktiabr'skoi revoliutsii* (Moscow, 1930, reprinted as *Vsia vlast' Sovetam* in 1957 and 1964); M. S. Kedrov, *Za sovetskii Sever* (Leningrad, 1927); S. I. Aralov, *Lenin i Krasnaia Armiia* (Moscow, 1959), also "Riadom byl Lenin," in *Nezabyvaemoe* (Moscow, 1961), pp. 3–24; N. I. Podvoiskii, "Ot Krasnoi Gvardii k Krasnoi Armii," in *Istorik-Marksist*, no. 1 (1938), pp. 3–38.

14. To N. Kakurin's *Kak srazhalas' revoliutsiia* and the three-volume *Grazhdanskaia voina, 1918–1921* published between 1928–1930, should be added A. Anishev's *Ocherki istorii grazhdanskoi voiny, 1917–1920 gg.* (Leningrad, 1925). In *Iz istorii grazhdanskoi voiny v SSSR*, I, covering May 1918–March 1919 (Moscow, 1960) there is also substantial material on the origins of the Red Army (pp. 99–186).

reorganization must include the provisions for the navy,[15] but here the fleets and the sailors will be treated only in terms of the manpower they contributed to Soviet land units. Finally come "the Internationalists," the ex-prisoners of war and the foreign Communists—Polish, Czech, Hungarian, Serb, German, the Chinese and Korean laborers—who took service with the Red Army, to form first the "Red Army International Legion," small in number but potent in influence, with Bela Kun at the head of the organization of Communist international detachments. Jaroslav Hašek, author of *The Good Soldier Schweik*, served in the International Section of the political administration of the Fifth Red Army, having already served for all practical purposes as the head of the Ufa Organization of Foreign Communist (Bolshevik) Parties.[16]

Latvian riflemen, Bolshevik sailors, the workers of Moscow, Petrograd and the Urals, volunteers from the old Imperial Army, ex-prisoners of war and peasants shuffling about in local militia units, all these milling about at the center or scattered about the provinces, or yet again organized into miniature, swaggering "armies," formed part of the kaleidoscopic elements of the Soviet armed forces, enjoining, for all the creation of the Red Army, a variety of local designations. As the Bolsheviks found, to incapacitate an army, the Imperial Army, was eminently feasible: to create one was agony.

On the morrow of the Bolshevik seizure of power the Second Congress of Soviets invested control of military affairs in the Military-Naval Committee (*Komitet po voennym i morskim delam*), consisting of Dybenko, Krylenko, and Antonov-Ovseenko, a body speedily expanded to include Mekhonoshin, Eremeev, Vasilev, Lazimir, Sklianskii, and Podvoiskii, the "military" Bolsheviks whose military activity nevertheless pertained more to the demolition of military organizations than to their consolidation.[17] Faced with their new-found responsibilities, these "military" Bolsheviks, cocksure and yet lacking any real military experience, set about at once reorganizing the military administration and speeding up the "democratization" of the Imperial Army. The ad-

15. A useful recent Soviet history is R. N. Mordvinov, *Kursom 'Avrory'—Formirovanie Sovetskogo Voenno-Morskogo Flota i nachalo ego boevoi deiatel'nosti* (1917–1919 gg.) (Moscow, 1962), 398 pp.

16. See Jaroslav Křížek, *Jaroslav Hašek v revolučním Rusku* (Prague, 1957), also N. P. Elanskii, *Yaroslav Gashek v revoliutsionnoi Rossii* (1916–1920 gg.) (Moscow, 1960).

17. A work that still retains its value is M. I. Akhun and V. A. Petrov, *Bolsheviki i Armiia v 1905–1917 gg.* (Leningrad, 1929). Much new material is incorporated in a forthcoming work by A. Rabinovitch, *Prelude to Revolution: The Bolsheviks and the July Uprising of 1917* (Indiana University Press, in preparation).

ministrative reorganization came within the competence of the Bureau of the Soviet of the People's Commissariat for Military Affairs (*Biuro soveta Narkomvoena*), a three-man body which promptly set up another organization, *Kantselariia Narkomvoena*, to handle the matter. While Krylenko rushed on with more "democratization" and ordered "a gradual reduction in military strength," with the arrest of War Minister Manikovskii and the Chief of the General Staff, Marushevskii, the immediate running of the military machine now devolved upon Podvoiskii, Legran, Mekhonoshin, and Sklianskii.

Throughout late November and December the old army underwent its drastic "democratization" with the Bolsheviks hacking out what Lenin called "the undemocratic institutions in the army," blows aimed at the authority of the officers—and designed to neutralize the internal military threat to the regime. Yet for all the scuffles and clashes at the time of the Bolshevik coup, no effective military intervention aimed at the Bolsheviks materialized.[18] "Saboteurs" (by Bolshevik definition) the senior Russian officers may have been, but *putschists* they were not: the great military axe never fell. After three years of a terribly wounding war, the Imperial Army had slowly withered from within, its senior officers sickened with the politicians and "intellectuals," and its officer corps diluted with the replacement officers brought in to make up for battle losses.[19] The men, if not demoralized, were plainly disaffected, a mood actively promoted by Bolshevik agitation. Indifference, disillusionment, indecision, and actual impotence were all part of the old army's extreme reluctance to mix in "politics." The only military consensus was "to hold the front," to keep the troops in the line, to fend off the armies of the Central Powers. Slowly, inexorably, and ironically, this problem too stole upon the Bolsheviks, intent after November on arranging an armistice. Meanwhile, the Imperial Army would be further dismantled. As for any "new" army, a draft decree from *Narkomvoen*, the Military Affairs Commissariat, insisted in early December (1917) upon the establishment of "a free army of armed citizens, an army of workers and peasants with broad self-government of elected soldiers

18. Cf. R. Pipes, "Communism and Russian History," in *Soviet and Chinese Communism: Similarities and Differences*, ed. Donald W. Treadgold (Seattle-London, 1967), pp. 21–22, for a discussion of the army's attitude.

19. On the Imperial Army, see General A. I. Dénikine, *La décomposition de l'armée et du pouvoir* (Paris, 1922). N. N. Golovine's *The Russian Army in the World War* (New Haven, 1931) retains still great value, as does N. Kakurin's *Razlozhenie armii v 1917 godu* (Moscow-Leningrad, 1925). The complexity of the problem and the need for further research is well illustrated in L. M. Gavrilov and V. V. Kutuzov, "Novyi istochnik o chislennosti russkoi deistvuiushchei armii nakanune Oktiabr'skoi revoliutsii," in *Istochnikovedenie istorii Sovetskogo obshchestva* (Moscow, 1964), pp. 131–152.

organizations," "a new army to secure the power of workers and peasants," "a revolutionary army of workers and peasants" drawn up as the old one was finally ground down.[20] "Instructions and regulations" on full, speedy "democratization" were now promulgated—the election of officers, the abolition of officer rank, the annulment of decorations and wholesale transfer of power to the Soldiers' Committees.[21]

It was not the decisions to "democratize," however, but the plans to demobilize that invested talk of a "new" military force with sudden, demanding relevance. "The army," a standing army, had an ugly ring about it. It was as ideologically odious as it was politically undesirable, yet the Soviet regime could not stand naked against its enemies. At Lenin's instigation, Podvoiskii convened in December a "special defense conference" (*Osoboe soveshchanie po oborone*) to look into "the mechanism" of any Soviet defense effort. According to an unpublished Soviet source,[22] in early December Lenin was urging the use of "military specialists," that is imperial officers, to work out a plan for the "military-technical supply of a revolutionary army" to fight the anticipated civil war: "It is not just one Vendée that is being raised against us, therefore we must be ready." Having so characterized the situation, Lenin went on to argue for the curtailment in the production of heavy weapons and heavy-calibre ammunition in favor of light guns, machine guns and rifles. Toward mid-December (1917), as preparations were proceeding for the forthcoming All-Army Conference on Demobilization, three possible methods of forming a new Soviet fighting force—the word "army" was still handled cautiously—were being hotly debated: the proposals of the "military specialists" to use part of the old army; the plans prepared by the General Staff of the Petrograd Red Guard to expand into two corps; and the "Socialist Guard" advocated by M. S. Kedrov (since December 5, a Deputy People's Commissar for Military Affairs in his capacity as Chief of the Army Demobilization Section).

The Red Guard plans[23] were quite unrealistic and the General Staff knew it. The Petrograd Soviet even denounced the scheme as a counter-

20. Kliatskin, *Na zashchite Oktiabria*, pp. 66–67.
21. The best single collection of material on this early period is *Grazhdanskaia voina—Materialy po istorii Krasnoi Armii* I (Vysshyi Voennyi Redaktsionnyi Sovet, 1923)—on "democratization," pp. 55–71. See also "Demokratizatsiia staroi armii," in Gorodetskii, *Rozhdenie sovetskogo gosudarstva*, pp. 355–381, emphasizing that "democratization" was meant not only to break the old machine but to bring forward "new military cadres."
22. P. A. Kozlim, "Pervye shagi t. Lenina v tekhnicheskoi podgotovke k grazhdanskoi voine," cited in Gorodetskii, *Rozhdenie Sovetskogo gosudarstva*, p. 417.
23. "Polozhenie o vseobshchei Krasnogvardeiskoi povinnosti": see V. Malakhovskii, "Perekhod ot Krasnoi Gvardii k Krasnoi Armii," in *Krasnaia letopis'*, no. 3 (1928), p. 6.

revolutionary plot designed to set the soldiers against the workers and the peasants. Meanwhile, the General Staff officers proper (from the Imperial Army) had first propounded their own ideas at the preliminary conference on demobilization held on December 10. Here Colonel Daller presented a report urging the use of the old army—cut to its prewar level of 1,300,000 men—to construct a new force. The detailed proposals emanating from the General Staff, nothing less than a plan for a "mixed military system" (elements of the old army being used to hold the frontiers and to form the core of a new "militia"), were debated on December 21 and 27, the very eve of the Demobilization Conference to which some proposal must be presented. The latter discussion (December 27) became vehement. All rejected the idea of using the old army as a "core" for a new Soviet army and now Kedrov interjected his plan for a "Socialist Guard" to be raised in the industrial districts, the peasantry being excluded.[24] Two days later Krylenko presented to the Council of People's Commissar a special report about transitional forms of army organization in the period of demobilization, but no decision was reached. To obtain the required information, Lenin circulated a questionnaire[25] among the Demobilization Conference delegates. The same day (December 30) Krylenko announced the decision to form a "People's Guard" (Narodnaia Gvardiia), one corps made up of "tested revolutionaries," each man to be a volunteer.[26]

The Council of People's Commissar instruction of December 31 (based on information acquired through Lenin's questionnaire[27]) stressed the danger arising from ruptured armistice negotiations, the need to "reorganize" the army and the advisability of agitation on "revolutionary war." At the same time the Soldiers' Section and a full plenum of the Petrograd Soviet gathered to argue the merits of the "old" army versus the "new." Under "reorganization," the General Staff envisaged cutting the army down to 100 divisions at war strength, pulling back as many units as possible to the rear and setting up base areas in the Moscow and Kazan Military Districts. The "new" army made up

24. "Kratkaia spravka o deiatel'nosti Narodnogo Komissariata po Voennym Delam . . ." (compiled by N. Potapov) in Istoricheskii Arkhiv, no. 1 (1962), p. 86 on Kedrov's plan.

25. V. I. Lenin, Polnoe sobranie sochinenii, 5th ed., XXXV, pp. 179–180. According to Gorodetskii (p. 406), Krylenko presented a report "O polozhenii na fronte i sostoianii Armii . . ." on the basis of information thus gained.

26. Grazhdanskaia voina (1923), pt. III "Sozdanie Krasnoi Armii," doc. no. 1, pp. 106–109 for the Instruktsiia.

27. Gorodetskii (p. 407) points out that the material itself, the replies, is lost; his reconstruction of the content is from Podvoiskii, "Ot Krasnoi Gvardii k Krasnoi Armii."

of soldier-volunteers would comprise 144 infantry regiments (36 divisions, each of 10,000 men) and would be organized in the Moscow region.[28]

The Petrograd Soviet had meanwhile come out unreservedly for a "new army," a "Socialist army" built "on elective principles, on the principles of mutual comradely respect and discipline." Yet what made the day of that declaration (January 4, 1918) decisive was not this sudden unanimity but signals coming into Petrograd from headquarters that the Romanian front was falling apart: desertion, which elsewhere clogged the railway system, had reached disastrous proportions far outstripping demobilization.[29] Somehow, new men would have to be rushed into the line. This problem was urgently debated by Lenin, Podvoiskii, Dybenko, Potapov, and Mekhonoshin in the Duty Officer's room of the Military Affairs Commissariat on January 4.

This tense meeting authorized the movement of all available Red Guard units from Moscow and Petrograd up to the front areas, with a new force—10 corps (300,000 men)—to be raised in the next 8 to 10 days. The soldiers' committees at the front were to provide instructors to impart some military training to this raw reinforcement. In retrospect, Podvoiskii would argue that this was not mere "reinforcement," but the proletarian leaven of a "new army" in the making. Whatever the truth of that assertion, the emergency urban mobilization was prompted not by the dangers of "the internal front" but by fear of German-Austrian divisions. Stalin, Lunacharskii, and Proshian labored simultaneously on the revision of a manifesto dealing with "socialist war," a document never published (and never found) but whose contents were communicated to Krylenko by Legran. With his imagination so fired, Krylenko issued his order of the day on January 11 calling for the establishment of a "Revolutionary National-Socialist Army," the first definite and authoritative summons to "a new army—the people in arms, the rudiments of which are to be found in the Red Guard."[30] The immediate work, however, had fallen to Podvoiskii, whose enthusiasm was inclined

28. Kliatskin, *Na zashchite Oktiabria*, p. 79.

29. "Kratkaia spravka o deiatel'nosti Narodnogo Komissariata po Voennym Delam . . ." in *Istoricheskii Arkhiv*, no. 1 (1962), p. 87. For the Romanian Front, there is much valuable information in M. S. Frenkin, *Revoliutsionnoe dvizhenie na Rumynskom fronte 1917–mart 1918 g.—Soldaty 8-i Armii Rumynskogo fronta v bor'be za mir i vlast' Sovetov* (Moscow, 1965).

30. Gorodetskii, *Rozhdenie Sovetskogo Gosudarstva*, pp. 410 and 412–413; "Kratkaia spravka o deiatel'nosti Narodnogo Komissariata po Voennym Delam . . . ," p. 87. Gorodetskii also refers to "Vospominaniia N. M. Potapova," a manuscript in the Institute of History, Academy of Sciences, as amplification of the "Kratkaia spravka."

to outrange his competence. In the wake of the January 4 meeting, instructions were sent out to raise the 300,000-man "army," and on January 8, after four days of frantic activity, the Military Organization of the Central Committee (together with representatives of the Military Affairs Commissariat and Red Guard staffs) argued out the implications and requirements of a "Socialist Army."[31] Five echelons (5,000 men) of the Red Guard had already been sent to the front; the additional 300,000 men, whom Podvoiskii was confident of raising before any German attack materialized, would then become "the cement and skeleton of a new army."[32] Dispensing for once with extra organization, this conference simply assigned to Podvoiskii, Mekhonoshin, and selected personnel of the Red Guard staff all and any duties connected with the raising of the new army. Five days later, Lenin, Podvoiskii, and Red Guard commanders attended the review and inspection of the first detachment of the "Socialist Army" presently forming in Petrograd.

Also at Podvoiskii's prompting, the Demobilization Conference accepted (by 153 votes) the idea of a "Socialist Army." By now, however, there were several agencies working hard to raise new forces. Krylenko urged the formation of the holding detachments, the special "Guards," as well as the new "revolutionary army." Headquarters, anxious not to weaken the front further, split the existing forces into "the regular army" and "National-Socialist Guards," the latter to form in the rear.[33] Front commands, with soldier committees and commissars in the lead, set about creating their own "revolutionary armies" like the "Revolutionary Red Army" of the northern front, instructions for which Pozern signed on January 5. With so many cooks at this military broth—the Military Organization (Central Committee), the Demobilization Conference, the headquarters, front commands—it is not surprising that a highly variegated product emerged: a "Socialist Army," "the National-Socialist Guard," "the National-Revolutionary Guard" (on the western front), "the Red People's Guard" or "the Revolutionary Red Army" (the northern front), and even "the Internationalist-Socialist Army" promoted by the Central Committee of the Field Army and Fleets. Diverse the names might have been, but the consciousness of building a "new" army—an army specially distinguished from the "militaristic armies"—ran deep through all the phrase making. The "new" army, based on the volunteer

31. "Protokol sobraniia voennoi organizatsii pri Ts. K. R.S.D.R.P. (bol'shevikov) v zale Armii i Flota . . . ," in *Grazhdanskaia voina* (1923), pp. 112–122.

32. *Ibid.*, p. 115.

33. "Obshchie soobrazheniia po sformirovaniiu armii na nachalakh dobrovol'chestva," and "Primernaia instruktsiia po formirovaniiu revoliutsionnykh batal'onov Narodno-Sotsialisticheskoi Gvardii . . . ," quoted in part in Kliatskin, *Na zashchite Oktiabria*, pp. 85–87.

system and "mutual comradely respect," was perceived as a clean break with the "old system," indeed the cleanest break of all. This was the "newness" of the proposed Soviet fighting force: the confusion was secondary. And the "Socialist Army" promised great things, as Podvoiskii affirmed: "The sooner we create this socialist army, the sooner we cement the front, the sooner peace will be concluded and the sooner the socialist revolution will come to the West."

"The Worker-Peasant Red Army" emerged out of the welter of names in the Declaration of Rights of the Toilers and the Exploited and was defined as the army of the dictatorship of the proletariat, the army composed of workers and toiling peasants. The draft decree on the Red Army was in preparation.

The first stage of demobilization was ushered in by the Demobilization Conference. The same Conference, by authorizing agitational and administrative procedures, breathed the first life into the Red Army as such.[34] This Agitational Collegiate, which came to replace the Demobilization Conference that had elected it, promulgated the original "Instructions" for the organization of the Red Army,[35] reviewed the draft decrees on the "All-Russian Collegiate for the Formation of the Red Army" (a body proposed by *Narkomvoen*) and proceeded to carve out of itself a "Provisional Bureau for the Creation of the Red Army," a subcommittee which lasted only for the second half of January.[36] The men of this remarkable Bureau (Grigor'ev, Iorgenberger, Litke, Mikosho, and Nikonov) went straight to the delegates for the front to the Third Congress of Soviets to present their plans for a new army, clasping the new decrees on "the Red Army" and on its proposed administration (the All-Russian Collegiate). The Bureau, in addition to suggesting agitation-organization sections, proposed the establishment of a "Provisional Supreme Staff" for the Red Army and an operations section.

Meanwhile, on January 25–26, the Third Congress of Soviets heard out Podvoiskii and Krylenko and approved Podvoiskii's plan to form the new army "in the rear" (as opposed to Krylenko's scheme to fashion it at the front), as well as the draft decrees on the Red Army and the

34. For the "Protokol" and the "Instruktsiia," see *Grazhdanskaia voina* (1923), pp. 131–137. Kliatskin, pp. 91–93, cites an archival source. There appears to be no disparity and we are in agreement over the importance of these proceedings and instructions.

35. "Instruktsiia organizatoram-agitatoram po organizatsii Raboche-Krest'ianskoi Krasnoi Armii," cited in *Grazhdanskaia voina* (1923) as "Iz materialov N. I. Podvoiskogo."

36. The minutes of the "Provisional Bureau" (*Vremennoe Biuro po Sozdaniiu Raboche-Krest'ianskoi Krasnoi Armii*) are printed in *Grazhdanskaia voina* (1923), pp. 144–160.

all-Russian Collegiate. The decree on "the Red Army" had yet to be submitted to the surgery of Lenin's pen, which was wielded with some prescience—eliminating, for example, the absolute insistence on voluntary enlistment.[37] On January 28, the decree was published. Three days later the "Provisional Bureau" liquidated itself, giving way to a grand new edifice, the "All-Russian Collegiate for the Organization and Administration of the Worker-Peasant Red Army," headed by Krylenko, Mekhonoshin, Podvoiskii, Trifonov, and Iurenev, with the defunct "Provisional Bureau" members providing its senior commissars and former officials of the old War Ministry its staff.[38] On paper at least the Red Army was steadily emerging, but very significantly its "apparatus" (the All-Russian Collegiate) did not include a Mobilization Section.

Armies feed and fatten themselves on men, not on phrases: early in 1918 there was a profusion of the latter, a dearth of the former. The volunteers failed to materialize; brisk desertion brought further enfeeblement. The All-Russian Collegiate in a great flurry of activity sent out orders to regional and local soviets to form "military sections" to recruit for and to administer Red Army units.[39] In front areas, armies and corps would set up "Red Army Staffs" as the catchments for men for the new force. Moscow set about organizing its "Central *Oblast* Commission for Red Army Organization," fitted out with five sections (induction, mobilization, inspectorate, supply, and organization-propaganda). Each volunteer would submit information on himself and on his family and be "recommended" by a "responsible political authority." He would agree to serve six months and to submit himself "to the Council of People's Commissariat, their agents, and their discipline." To encourage recruitment, the *Oblast'* Commission established a special induction bureau—*biuro po zapisi dobrovol'tsev*—branches of which were to be set up in all military units and regional soviets. The Inspectorate was intended to be "a reserve of instructors," ex-officers "recommended by

37. Pre-publication text with emendations, *Dekrety Sovetskoi vlasti*, I, pp. 352–355; published text, *ibid.*, pp. 356–357.
38. There is no specific study of this All-Russian Collegiate. Some detail is supplied in "Iz istorii formirovaniia Krasnoi Armii," *Voenno-istoricheskii Zhurnal*, no. 2/7 (1940), pp. 119–131 and in *Organizatsiia Krasnoi Armii—Sbornik dokumentov i materialov* (Moscow, 1943), 191 pp. Kliatskin in his note on Soviet dissertations (p. 18), mentions one devoted to the Collegiate, I. M. Volkov, "Deiatel'nost Vserossiiskoi Kollegii po Formirovaniiu Krasnoi Armii (dekabr' 1917 g.–mai 1918 g.)," presented in 1951, but Kliatskin's comments are doleful about the quality of this and other work.
39. "Instruktsiia dlia rukovodstva sovetam i komitetam na mestakh dlia sozdaniia upravleniia Krasnoi Armii," *Grazhdanskaia voina* (1923), pp. 180–184.

Bolsheviks or Left SR's."[40] The All-Russian Collegiate, trying to stagger to its feet (its offices undermanned and its structure never fully filled out), was able at the very most to keep a rudimentary check on European Russia. In February the Commissariat of Military Affairs had to send its own agents, a "special commission" under Kobozev, to investigate western Siberia and Central Asia. Out of 33 *guberniia* centers, 27 set up some kind of "military apparatus," but there was none in Kazan, Orenburg, Penza, Simbirsk, and Chernigov. Nor was the system scooping up men: in Samara, the *guberniia* commissar reported that 20 percent of the men were rejected on the first "sifting" (*filtratsiia*), in Irkutsk there were all of 50 Red Guards (and 2,000 troops on "guard duties"), in the Caucasus and Asiatic Russia only seven towns had local military sections of any sort. Nor did the fronts fare better. As the deserters galloped homewards, the northern front had culled only 7,500 volunteers by early February, and the western front could show nothing more impressive.[41] Each corps on the northern front was losing 500 men a week through desertion. The Petrograd area garrisons were down to 154,000 men in January (half the figure for November 1917). The Northern Twelfth Army reported that it could no longer hold on.

Like its organization, the elements of Soviet military power at this point were both diffused and enormously variegated. The Red Army as a force scarcely existed. The number of men was no real index—what counted was trained manpower, and the Soviet regime could command perhaps 50,000 trained men. There were the Bolshevik sailor-squads, ruthless fellows but scarcely an army. They were sought as volunteers for the "Naval Detachment" of the Red Army (*Morskii otriad Raboche-Krest'ianskoi Krasnoi Armii*).[42] It was the dour, highly disciplined Latvian riflemen, a corps of some 17,000 men, who played a vital part in sustaining Soviet power. At the beginning of 1918, the Latvians were fighting in the Ukraine with Antonov-Ovseenko. Two of their regiments had gone to the western front (to fight Dobor-Musznycki), while other

40. All-Russian Collegiate report on progress in the provinces, February 17, 1918: *Iz istorii grazhdanskoi voiny v SSSR* I (1960), p. 113.

41. All figures are relative, though far from useless. Most sources agree that this phase of volunteerism was a failure. Cf. Kliatskin, *Na zashchite Oktiabria*, p. 95; A. I. Cherepanov, *Pod Pskovom i Narvoi* (Moscow, 1957), pp. 25–32; M. S. Frenkin, *Revoliutsionnoe dvizhenie na Rumynskom fronte*, pp. 348–358 on the Eighth Army.

42. *Moriaki v bor'be za vlast' Sovetov na Ukraine—Sbornik dokumentov* (Kiev, 1963), doc. no. 83, p. 101. For the Navy, see "Dekret ob organizatsii Raboche-Krest'ianskogo Krasnogo Flota," *Dekrety Sovetskoi vlasti*, I, pp. 434–441. The naval forces were also organized *"na dobrovol'cheskikh artel'nikh nachalakh"* ("on voluntaristic *artel*-like principles").

238 – John Erickson

regiments were held in Petrograd, Moscow, Velikie Luki, and Bogo-lom.[43] (In April the Latvians were organized into the Latvian Soviet Rifle Division with three brigades.) Deployed as they were at strategic points or sent to stiffen difficult sectors, the Latvians nevertheless could not be everywhere.

Scattered throughout the regions were miniature armies and inde-pendent detachments, in addition to local Red Guards. Quite distinctive were the Urals "fighting squads," the *boevye organizatsii narodnogo vooruzheniia* (BONV) tracing their antecedents to the 1905 Revolution, whose first "regulations" were drawn up in December 1917 at the Ufa *guberniia* conference of fighting organizations. In March 1918 Ka-domtsev, chief of the Ufa *guberniia* Red Army Staff and Fighting Or-ganizations, issued a third set of regulations and very comprehensive they were, covering everything from sharp-shooting to basic hygiene—this was not only a war on landlords and the bourgeoisie, it was war against germs: *strich volosy—k volosam prilipaiut vsiakie mikroby* (shave your hair—all kinds of microbes attach themselves to it).[44] Early in February, workers' *druzhiny* captured Orenburg, thus dislodging Ataman Dutov whose stronghold this had been. With Soviet power more securely established in the north and in the central regions, how-ever, the main Bolshevik effort early in 1918 was directed to the south, the Don and the Ukraine. The "armies" here were miniscule, but the fighting took a savage turn from the start—little quarter, no prisoners. In December 1917 Antonov-Ovseenko had begun operations against General Kaledin, setting up his base in Kharkov and seeking to slice away the Don from the Ukraine. At most, Antonov-Ovseenko mustered some 7,000 men (sailors, ex-soldiers, and Red Guards) with a few score guns and machine guns.[45] As Antonov-Ovseenko turned finally against the Ukrainian Rada, his force was swelled with local recruits and with Red Guard reinforcement, though the latter proved to be an unruly bunch.

In Mikhail A. Muraviev, a former lieutenant-colonel of the Imperial Army, the Bolsheviks found a capable if ruthless commander, one who served them well until he turned traitor. From Kharkov, where refugee Kievan Bolsheviks had set up their "Ukrainian government" in exile, Muraviev launched his "Northern Army" against the Rada, and on

43. T. Ia. Draiudin, *Boevoi put' Latyshskoi strelkovoi divizii v dni oktiabria i v gody grazhdanskoi voiny (1917–1920)* (Riga, 1960), pp. 52–61; *Latyshskie strelki v bor'be za Sovetskuiu vlast'* (Riga, 1962), pp. 27–53.
44. I. Podshivalov, *Grazhdanskaia bor'ba na Urale 1917–1918—Opyt voenno-istoricheskogo issledovaniia* (Moscow, 1925), "Historical Documents," p. 208.
45. Cf. N. Kakurin, *Kak srazhalas' revoliutsiia*, I, pp. 172–175.

February 9 he took Kiev. None of the forces involved in these operations was large or even well organized. Muraviev moved his "army" on to Bessarabia and into the conflict with the Romanians.[46]

Antonov-Ovseenko's detachments were deployed in the Don. The Soviet Ukrainian government, so recently installed in Kiev, was in less than a month tumbled out in precipitate evacuation when German and Austrian divisions moved on the Ukrainian capital. The description of the state of Bolshevik "armies" pulling back out of reach of these German divisions is contemporary admission of parlous weakness and disorganization.[47]

There were other regional "armies," important less for their actual strength than for the fierce pride of possession they engendered and for a stubborn, almost ineradicable sense of military autonomy, the *partizanshchina* born of loyalty to the detachment or the local army. Such was the case with the "Southeastern Revolutionary Army," a force brought into being early in March on the orders of the Soviet Defense Staff at Tsaritsyn. This army, with Avtonomov named as commander, was to form up at Tikhoretsk, its men coming from Red Guard detachments and soldiers of the 39th Infantry Division. It was in fact an agglomeration of *otriady*, "detachments," scattered at Maikop, Taman, Batalpashinsk, and Novorossiisk. By mid-March Avtonomov had mustered some 20,000 men at Ekatorinodar, but he proved to be so stubborn and high-handed in handling them that sheer indiscipline on his part allowed the Volunteer Army to escape the trap meant to destroy it.[48] Insubordination finally cost him his command, but Avtonomov refused to take this lying down. He squabbled with the Extraordinary Defense Staff set up by the Central Committee of the Kuban and Black Sea Republic and at the end of May ordered the 154th Infantry Regiment to arrest the Staff, whereupon Avtonomov held his own army conference and there won over the Bolsheviks. All this belongs to the biography of the Eleventh Red Army.

The center could scarcely claim anything better. Added to the failings

46. The Eighth Army had meanwhile formed volunteer detachments and a "peasant Red Guard." Its *revkom*, in consultation with the "Supreme Autonomous Collegiate for Russo-Romanian and Bessarabian Affairs," authorized the movement of all Red Guards against the Romanians. In mid-March the Eighth Army was disbanded, its men sought as recruits for the Red Army, its stores being used to supply the "4th Donbas Worker Army": M. S. Frenkin, *Revoliutsionnoe dvizhenie na Rumynskom fronte*, pp. 348–349 and 356–357.

47. Cf. N. Kakurin, *Kak srazhalas' revoliutsiia*, I, pp. 140–142, on Remnev's army, Petrov's army and the "Novozybkovskaia gruppa."

48. V. T. Sukhorukov, *XI Armiia v boiakh na Severnom Kavkaze i Nizhnei Volge (1918–1920 gg.)* (Moscow, 1961), pp. 11–25.

of the volunteer system was the confusion brought about by organizing on "detachment" lines, the result being only "a conglomeration of occasional, improvised *otriady,* not held together by any command organization" in the words of one contemporary professional appraisal. The raising of the First Corps in Petrograd was a prime illustration of all the early shortcomings. The corps, decided upon in January, was meant to have six battalions, a machine-gun battalion, a cavalry regiment and an aviation unit. On February 26, it had a staff and three battalions (800 workers). All-Russian Flying Club was commandeered to form the aviation unit and 20 electricians of the Petrograd streetcar depot manned the technical unit. Partisan units, special guard units, Red Army units, and militias were all in the market for men and poached ceaselessly from each other. Government and party agencies, wholly unclear about organizational procedures and objectives, meddled and overlapped with each other.[49] But for the bosses of the bureaus and the masters of the private urban armies time had almost run out.

The resumption of the German advance on February 18 threw the cruelest daylight on the bareness of the military cupboard. Lenin was justifiably wearied with "phrase-mongering": the proponents of "revolutionary war" for all their passion and indignation showed little sense of military realism. In Petrograd the Military Affairs Commissariat set up the "Extraordinary Petrograd Military District Staff" with Bonch-Bruevich, Basilevskii, Eremeev, Lashevich, Mekhonoshin, and Iurenev as members. The Petrograd Soviet raised the Committee for the Revolutionary Defense of Petrograd, 15 men in all, chosen by plenary session of the Petrograd Soviet, with Sverdlov as chairman and Gusev as secretary (with five men co-opted from the Extraordinary Staff). The Committee had to look for men at once: orders went out to raise two detachments of 1,000 men to be deployed between Pskov and Reval. In the Twelfth Army some 5,000 to 6,000 volunteers had materialized (to form First and Second Red Army Infantry Regiments) but volunteerism had virtually failed.[50] Of the 30,000 Red Guards, 10,000 were in condition of "military readiness" though latterly discipline and order had broken down at a sharp rate.[51] The new defense staff for the city now proposed to form the volunteers "into a single powerful force."

49. A. L. Fraiman, *Revoliutsionnaia zashchita Petrograda,* pp. 137–144.

50. *Ibid.,* pp. 244–255 for detailed, tabulated discussion of volunteer strength. Fraiman also points out (p. 247) that volunteers did not necessarily "sign up" for the Red Army. This section of Fraiman's work is the best account of recruiting yet available.

51. V. I. Startsev, *Ocherki po istorii Petrogradskoi Krasnoi Gvardii i Rabochei Militsii,* pp. 241–243 on indiscipline. Startsev argues that serious breaches were "relatively rare," but the countermeasures were fierce enough. As for the strength of the Red Guards, Startsev's work is indispensable and a model of thoroughness.

Toward the end of February the All-Russian Collegiate and the Petrograd Defense Committee ordered the establishment in the city of "regional Red Army staffs" made up of a recruiting commission, two men from the regional soviet, two Red Guard representatives, and one from the All-Russian Collegiate. Men might sign up for the period of the emergency in Petrograd without signing up for service with the Red Army.[52] The "regional Red Army staffs," to which Red Guard leaders did not easily accede, represented the first real merger of the apparatus. Front units of the Red Guard were transformed into Red Army units, and by mid-March some 10,000 men were passed into the Red Army. In 13 regions, 14,768 men signed up for the Red Army.

Soviet historians have put Soviet manpower for mid-March 1918 at some 200,000 (or even 300,000) though the myth of massive volunteering is no longer propagated. The returns on recruitment for April 1 from Moscow, Petrograd, and seven regions, part of the statistics of the All-Russian Collegiate, give a figure of 114,678 men (with an additional 40,000 from the fronts), the grand total being 153,678.[53] Even more important were the changes at the top. In March the Petrograd Defense Staff was converted into the Supreme Military Soviet, *Vysshyi Voennyi Sovet*. Trotsky moved in as War Commissar and Krylenko lost his job. The creation of the VVS, manned by the "military specialists," and responsible for the "military" problems of the Soviet republic, ushered in what Soviet historians call the period of "parallelism" in the early history of the Red Army: two concepts of an army, two sources of command and two images of "the enemy." Who was to command whom and to what end?

The VVS, staffed as it was with senior "military specialists," was assigned to deal with the purely "military" aspects of defense. In this capacity, on March 14 it approved a "Campaign Plan for 1918" drawn up by the Petrograd staff officers, envisaging a fighting Soviet withdrawal and retirement behind the Volkhov River in the event of further German and Finnish advances.[54] By March 5 the VVS had drawn up plans and issued orders for "the screens" (*zavesy*), the covering forces on the western frontiers. The main "screens" were the northern and western, with defensive sectors earmarked for Moscow and Petrograd, each sector of such "screens" to be run by a Military Soviet manned by an ex-officer

---

52. A. L. Fraiman, *Revoliutsionnaia zashchita Petrograda*, pp. 139 and 247 (the latter giving the total strength of "volunteer detachments," 76 detachments of various kinds, as 18,356 men).

53. *Iz istorii grazhdanskoi voiny v SSSR* (1960), p. 122. (See tables on page 255.)

54. Fraiman, *Revoliutsionnaia zashchita Petrograda*, p. 270.

flanked with two commissars. This method of staffing a higher command agency was found to be both workable and suitable. While this military reconstruction went on, the Council of People's Commissariat ordered a special commission, to which Altfater, Algedorskii, and Danilov were attached as "professional military advisers." Its task was to produce no later than March 15 plans for a "militia army," a "Socialist militia" with a new "military center."[55] Within the VVS, however, the "specialists" under General Bonch-Bruevich were working on plans of their own for a new force. If Germany could field 1.5 million men, the Soviet government too must have 1.5 million at its disposal, an army consisting of all arms and backed by an organization to train the civilian population. This force was envisaged as consisting of three elements—a field army, garrison troops, and training units, all organized along conventional lines with companies, divisions, and so on, up to army level.

In scouting the militia idea, these "specialists" also proposed throwing out the principles of voluntarism and elective command. The latter proposal proved too much for those Bolsheviks who were prepared to go along with greater numbers and military orthodoxy, as did Podvoiskii. Lenin proclaimed the target of one million men, but in his office on March 25 he faced a great outburst of discontent and dissatisfaction over the growing use of "military specialists," the terms of military service, the role of Communists in the army, the place of commanders and commissars—a dress rehearsal almost to the day for the great outburst over military policy that was to occur at the Eighth Party Congress in March 1919. In March 1918 (as well as a year later) the most contentious issue was the use of the "specialists." The evidence pertaining to this vital meeting, in which Lenin's views prevailed finally, remains fragmentary in the extreme.[56] Nor apparently did it mark the end of attempts to block the advance of the "specialists." In fine orthodox style the ex-officers planned to reconstruct the military districts, new divisions being raised on the district basis. There would be four such main districts (White Sea, Iaroslavl, Moscow, and Orel) and two "internal" ones (Ufa and Samara). Trifonov, one of the luminaries of the Red Guard, protested bitterly but unavailingly that what General Bonch-Bruevich planned was wrong, that the Red Army should be raised "through our proletarian centers of organization and through the ideological direction for the foundation of the Red Army" and that there

55. Kliatskin, *Na zashchite Oktiabria*, p. 149. The decision to organize a "Socialist militia" was approved by the Fourth Extraordinary All-Russian Congress of Soviets.

56. No record was kept of the meeting. See A. F. Miasnikov, "Moi vstrechi s tovarishchem Leninym," *Vospominaniia o V. I. Lenine*, II (Moscow, 1957), p. 149, and S. I. Aralov, *V. I. Lenin i Krasnaia Armiia* (Moscow, 1959), pp. 7–11.

should be four such "proletarian centers"—the south, the Urals, Siberia, and the Volga.[57] The VVS, however, continued undeterred. As Trifonov's plans were simply thrown out, the VVS instructed the old Main Administration of the General Staff to work out a new plan for a regional and local military administration, sweeping away the "military sections" and the "Red Army Staffs," and in April instructions for military commissariats at *uezd* and *volost* levels, as well as for the *guberniia* and *okrug*, were formally promulgated.

With all its professionalism, the VVS thought almost axiomatically in terms of formal divisions, formal fronts and formal war: "the enemy" to be warded off was the German Army. Podvoiskii distrusted the "Allied orientation" of the VVS (although because the Soviet government was then toying with ideas of Allied aid in building up the Red Army, the VVS was hardly inconsistent). The internal fighting, the "civil war," came under Commissariat of Military Affairs with its own Operations Section (*Operod*), a body brought into existence in January as part of the Extraordinary Defense Staff of the Moscow District. *Operod* was originally formed to work with Red Guard detachments, but on April 11 under Order No. 351 it was formally combined with the War Commissariat as its official Operations Section, a body with which party authorities preferred to deal (as opposed to the VVS) for there was a strong party element in *Operod*.[58] "Parallelism" for Soviet historians comes to a close in early May when Trotsky set up the All-Russian Supreme Staff (*Vserosglavshtab*), a body which was meant to replace the All-Russian Collegiate. The General Staff Administration, the old "Glavnyi Shtab," subordinate staff organs and the Commissariat for Training Institutions were also closed down.

Podvoiskii had been entrusted with the Supreme Military Inspectorate, *Vysshaia Voennaia Inspektsiia* (set up on April 24), as a consolation prize. The Inspectorate was given authority to regulate disputes between the center and regional bodies over the formation of the Red Army, yet it had neither an establishment nor prescribed functions save that it would operate under "the general direction" of the party and the Soviet government. Three agencies, the All-Russian Collegiate, the VVS and the Supreme Inspectorate, were all involved each in their own way

57. Kliatskin, *Na zashchite Oktiabria*, pp. 165–166.
58. The origins of *Operod* (or *Operot*, according to S. I. Aralov) remain obscure, but that it was formed originally in the Moscow Military District seems established: see S. I. Aralov, "Riadom by Lenin," *Nezabyvaemoe* (1961), pp. 3–4. According to Aralov, *Operod* also dealt with the supply of weapons and ammunition and had a hand in partisan operations. The VVS-*Operod* dichotomy was bitterly assailed by Colonel Egorov in his paper of August 20, 1918 (doc. T-41, The Trotsky Archives, Harvard University).

244 - John Erickson

in forming the Red Army, a proliferation that Trotsky began to curtail in early May by putting the military build-up under the All-Russian Supreme Staff and by splitting the VVS on May 14 into two "administrations"—operations and organization—with sections for military communications, an economic inspectorate, field engineers, artillery, and medical organization.[59]

These were administrative rationalizations, all steps on the road to the great centralization of September 1918. Command was for the moment an obscure but potentially very divisive issue. Control, the subordination of military to party-governmental power, was to be managed through the political apparatus and the "military-political commissars," renamed "military commissars" on April 8, 1918. The actual status of the commissar—agent of government or party—remained somewhat obscure; nor were all the commissars Bolsheviks. In the "screens," the pattern of military-political deployment (one commander and two commissars) seemed to work. In formal terms the commissar had two functions: the maintenance of "revolutionary discipline" and the supervision of the "specialists." Under the regulations promulgated on April 8, 1918, the commissar was identified as "the political organ of Soviet power in the armed forces," the commissars themselves being "tested revolutionaries." This same regulation set up the All-Russian Bureau of Military Commissars over which Iurenev, former head of the Red Guard *Glavnyi Shtab*, would preside. The Bureau took over the Agitation-Educational Section of the All-Russian Collegiate and by the end of May the Bureau itself had filled out with its secretariat, administration, inspectorate, agitation and signal sections.[60]

In April the officers of the VVS were already pressing for systematic mobilization. This request was refused on "economic grounds" and out of a preference for extending the "breathing spell" to the men of military age for as long as possible. With that the "specialists" had to rest content, although their plans rested on an abundance of manpower. In the "screens," detachments were steadily grouped into divisions, seven each in the north and west, with four divisions cemented together in the Moscow defense zone. The Military Commissariat of the Petrograd Labor Commune promised one division (the Second Petrograd). The

59. *Iz istorii grazhdanskoi voiny v SSSR* (1960), p. 127 and Kliatskin, *Na zashchite Oktiabria*, pp. 175–176. On the Supreme Military Inspectorate, Kliatskin (p. 174) takes a modest view, one not shared by E. P. Tarasov's laudatory biography, *Nikolai Il'ich Podvoiskii* (*Ocherk voennoi deiatel'nosti*) (Moscow, 1964), pp. 83–85.

60. A. A. Geronimus, *Partiia i Krasnaia Armiia* (Moscow, 1928), and "Osnovnye momenty razvitiia partiino-politicheskogo apparata Krasnoi Armii," in *Grazhdanskaia voina 1918–1921*, II, pp. 110–129. See also *Partiino-politicheskaia rabota v Krasnoi Armii (aprel' 1918–fevral' 1919)* (Moscow, 1961), doc. no. 28, pp. 63–67 and no. 30, p. 77.

same commissariat also issued orders for the disbanding of all Red Guard units by May 1. Four other divisions were forming, identified by their territorial origins—Voronezh, Gatchina, Novorzhevsk, and Luga. The VVS plan called for 28 divisions at full war strength, requiring 720,000 men. Since the Red Army could only muster 450,000, the "specialists" had to settle for half-strength companies (36 men). Plans piled on plans: the main VVS target was 88 divisions (28 of them being raised in the western frontier districts), out of which the Soviet republic could fashion no less than ten armies, plus three cavalry divisions to be raised in the Orel, Moscow, and Turkestan areas. To defend the south, the VVS had ordered the establishment of the North Caucasus front.[61] All this expressed the soldier's view of the military priorities of the republic.

The outbreak of hostilities with the Czechoslovak Legion in May 1918 threw these plans into disarray, much as the crumpling of the front at the end of 1917 had swept aside the schemes for "militias" and paper armies. With Czech troops arrayed against the Bolsheviks, with the flimsy Soviet "armies" flung aside in the Ukraine and German divisions moving on to the Don, where White troops under Denikin and Krasnov were gathering, the simple symmetry and the orthodox assumptions of the VVS were exploded. Hitherto, Red units in the interior had grappled in clumsy style with hostile forces as weak and as poorly organized as themselves. The Rada succumbed out of sheer feebleness, and the early Volunteer Army, for all the experience of its veteran soldiers, mustered but a few thousand men. The experience of the eastern front in the early summer of 1918 worked upon the enthusiastic and conceited amateurs exactly as Brest-Litovsk had influenced Trotsky: it inculcated a sense of realism.

When the Czech troops struck in May, Bolshevik strength was minimal and organization marginal. The First Red Army (under Kharchenko) had a nominal strength of 10,000 men, but of these only 3,000 were fit to fight. Detachments too disorganized for use were disbanded, "regiments" and "companies" were short of officers, gun batteries were bereft of commanders or instructors, the guns lacked sights. The basic unit was still the *otriad*, anything from 700 to 1,000 Red Army men under "a commander" and his two assistants, all elected and usually without experience.[62] At the end of May, Miasnikov, the former Bol-

---

61. Kliatskin, *Na zashchite Oktiabria*, p. 190.
62. A. P. Nenarokov, "Obrazovanie Vostochnogo fronta i perekhod k massovoi reguliarnoi armii (mai–iiun' 1918 g.)," Nauchnye doklady vysshei shkoly, *Istoricheskie Nauki*, no. 4 (1961) for a recent and original investigation of the origins of the eastern front, derived from the author's dissertation, "Vostochnyi front letom

shevik commander of the western front and presently "chief" of the northwestern "screens," came east as the first "commander" of all troops operating against the Czechs and the Whites. Miasnikov assigned the ubiquitous Podvoiskii to take over the "eastern Czechoslovak front" (with its detachments under Malyshev, Berzin, and Blokhin). He himself took over the "western Czechoslovak front" (Ural-Orenburg), and the Troitsk Military Commissariat assumed responsibility for any forces in the Polietaevo-Cheliabinsk region. In Simbirsk the Party committee set up an Extraordinary Defense Staff, seven men in all, with Penevskii at its head and Freiman and Ismailov as his assistants.[63]

Miasnikov was recalled early in June and replaced by Muraviev, an appointment with Podvoiskii contested furiously in a telegram to Lenin,[64] Muraviev, with Blagonravov and Kobozev as his commissars, took over the new Revolutionary Military Soviet on June 13. Three days earlier Podvoiskii held a conference with the Urals *oblast* Party committee, *oblast* Soviet, and his Inspectorate officers to find some way to unify the command. Podvoiskii proposed to do so by creating a North Urals-Siberian front with R. I. Berzin in command. Meanwhile in Simbirsk there was more organization. By June 12 the "Military-Operational Staff of the Volga Detachments" had been set up, and the "Composite Detachment of the Samara fighting companies (*druzhiny*)" was pulled out and put under the Simbirsk command.

The VVS was apparently unimpressed by all this flurry over a few Czechs. General Bonch-Bruevich recorded somewhat laconically that "the Czech threat scarcely appeared real, while from the Germans we could expect anything."[65] Neither Rattel (former head of Military Communications in the Imperial Army and presently chief of staff to the VVS) nor anyone else issued any kind of operational order or directive to the eastern front before August. Nor did *Operod* do any better, in spite of or possibly because of the panic. In the field, out of what he had seen as "inspector" and as "commander," Podvoiskii confessed his change of heart over military organization. He had already prepared a detailed report, "The tasks of Soviet power in the struggle with the Czechoslovak revolt." Early in June, in a signal to Lenin, though he

1918 g. i voprosy stroitel'stva Krasnoi Armii" (Rostov-on-Don, 1962). On the "detachments" of the First Army, see V. V. Kuibyshev, "Pervaya revoliutsionnaia armiia," a 1920 essay reprinted in *Simbirskaia guberniia v 1918–1920 gg.—Sbornik vospominanii* (Ulianov, 1958), pp. 26–29.

63. *Simbirskaia guberniia v gody grazhdanskoi voiny (mai 1918 g.–mart 1919 g.) Sbornik dokumentov* (Ulianov, 1958), doc. no. 2, p. 28.

64. A. P. Nenarokov, "Obrazovanie Vostochnogo fronta . . . ," *Istoricheskie Nauki*, no. 4, p. 33.

65. M. D. Bonch-Bruevich, *Vsia vlast' Sovetam* (Moscow, 1957), p. 303.

confessed himself to having been earlier "the most fervid proponent of a volunteer army," he now learned from battle experience that "swift and decisive abandonment of the volunteer system" was essential.[66] At the Fifth Congress of Soviets Miasnikov came out with equal vehemence for the abandonment of the *otriad* system, for the institution of firm discipline and for "the organization of a powerful, well equipped, maneuverable regular army." The change of direction had also begun to register well beyond the confines of the eastern front. The Sixth Petrograd All-City Conference on the Red Army (June 9) proposed a unified administration of its own and confirmed the decision of the Petrograd Labor Commune Commissariat to amalgamate units. The Novgorod *guberniia* conference on the Red Army held in mid-June came out unequivocally in favor of abandoning the volunteer system. This, and similar affirmations, including the Fifth Congress of Soviets itself, was all retrospective acceptance and approval of the Central Executive Committee of the Soviets (VTsIK) decree of May 29 introducing compulsory military service for the working class.[67]

Trotsky approached this first mobilization very gingerly, and with good reason. Moscow, the seat of Soviet power, with its large contingent of workers and its relatively well developed local military apparatus, was selected for the first test. Convened at the beginning of June by Trotsky, a "Special Conference" selected on June 2 an "Extraordinary Commission" (with accredited members from the Military Affairs Commissariat, the Moscow Military District, and the Council of Trade Unions) to work out the full mobilization procedure. The next day this Commission, conscious that here was a crucial, experimental undertaking, decided on a target figure of 10,000 to 12,000 men drawn from workers (employed and unemployed) between 18 and 40 years of age. Exemptions would be granted to "specialist workers," those in essential industry, those maimed or seriously unfit, and criminals. Families whose only son or sole support was mobilized, received a promise of direct support. By June 8 the Commission had finished its draft regulations governing the mobilization of the Moscow workers.[68]

Such were the pressures on the eastern front, however, that there could be no waiting to prepare regional mobilization with any comparable care. The decree mobilizing five age-groups (1897–1893) of

66. Quoted by A. P. Nenarokov, "Obrazovanie Vostochnogo fronta . . . ," *Istoricheskie Nauki*, no. 4, p. 37.

67. *Dekrety Sovetskoi vlasti*, II, no. 183, pp. 334–335. For the Petrograd resolutions, *Iz istorii grazhdanskoi voiny v SSSR*, I (1960), p. 133 quoting *Petrogradskaia Pravda*, No. 122.

68. "Nastavlenie po prizyvu rabochego naseleniia Moskvy" in Kliatskin, *Na zashchite Oktiabria*, pp. 194–195.

workers and peasants in 51 *uezdy* of the Volga, Urals, and West Siberian Military Districts was rushed out on June 12. Within two days, the Military Affairs Commissariat had prepared a complicated code on administrative procedures, exemptions, and the like. The records of these early mobilizations must provide a great haul of social and economic information, but only a minute part of it is accessible. The basic document was the conscript's personal paper (*lichnaia kartochka*) with its 23 sections covering education, trade or profession, liability for or exemption from military service, previous military service and training— a variety of data but no record of "class origins" or political affiliations. That omission led inevitably to the induction into the Red Army of many men who did not properly belong there. Officers were screened by the Attestation Commission (set up in April). The "Provisional Regulations" (June 18) covering officers required the submission to the local military commissariat of a formal application from those seeking "command responsibility" in the Red Army, whereupon the commissariat was to publish in the local press details of the candidate's past service. The local citizenry had ten days in which to register observations and objections relating to the candidate-officer.[69]

The first mobilization in Moscow had been an unqualified success. For all the severity of their conditions, the workers had come forward readily enough to join the Red Army. The VVS investigation of July 15 set the tally of men raised in Moscow at some 10,000. The mobilization in the eastern regions, on the other hand, where the need for men was desperate and where it had been expected no less than 275,000 recruits would be raised, had gone badly. The fiasco in the east confirmed the VVS in its opinion that mobilization had to be aimed at the workers. On orders from the VVS, the All-Russian General Staff drew up a new mobilization plan, which was officially adopted on July 23. This revised plan proposed the mobilization of workers in the 1895–1893 age group in Moscow and Petrograd to produce 25,000 men. When this quota was filled, mobilization in these two cities would cease and be switched to the Moscow, Petrograd, Vladimir, and Nizhni Novgorod provinces. With these recruits the VVS planned to raise eight infantry divisions. Of the 15 mobilizations carried out between June 12 and August 29, 11 were confined to workers. Their fullest impact fell on Moscow and Petrograd. In addition, there was the special mobilization on August 2 of worker noncommissioned officers in the 1898–1895 age group. The Red Army acquired in all some 540,123 men and 17,800 noncoms.[70]

Of the four basic problems that creating the Red Army had raised—

69. Kliatskin, p. 203.
70. Figures from Kliatskin, p. 201, quoting V*serosglavshtab* data.

manpower, administration, command and combat capability (training, morale, and experience)—the first three were tackled more systematically after June 1918. The eastern front played a fundamental role in this, as it had done in teaching the Red Army how to fight. At the All-Russian Conference of Military Commissars held in Moscow between June 7 and 11, Trotsky argued that the hopes vested in the army had been realized "to the extent of 30 percent." After June that percentage began to climb slowly.

Whereas the defeats suffered in February–March 1918 had been incurred—for all the myth about the "birth" of the Red Army at this time—by units drawn from the old and ailing army, the early disasters in the east had befallen forces that were indisputably part of the new Red Army. The security and the self-assurance of the Bolsheviks were afflicted simultaneously. With agonizing slowness the first centralized military units of the Red Army made their appearance on the eastern front. In the field, Red regiments one by one sloughed off their "committees," their soldiers' assemblies, and their incompetent, self-appointed "commanders." Paradoxically, the desertions that hollowed out Soviet strength from within helped to boost the progress of reorganization, for in this fashion the useless and the shiftless were in large measure skimmed off. For all the overcrowding of the railway system, men were rushed to the east. The newly established military commissariats in the west (including those within the "screens") were ordered to send men castwards, while local mobilizations (though hampered by lack of personnel to operate them and shortage of supplies to fit out recruits) produced more men. Perm and Vyatka were especially successful in this respect. The report of the Ural district military commissariat for the period May–June (1918) underlined what fighting with bits and pieces meant:

The first period of the struggle with the Czechoslovaks might be called the otriad *period, then we conducted the war in primitive style, without any kind of previously worked out plan, with detachments of from 20 to 100 men. Of the more or less regular Red Army units at the front there were: 2nd Ural Regiment at Kyshtyma, 7th Ural Regiment at Zlatoust. The remainder of the troops consisted of separate, wholly unconnected detachments containing from 20 to 100 men, for the major part workers from this or that individual factory or plant.*[71]

By the end of June the strength of the eastern front had grown to 50,000 men (double the number obtaining at mid-June), 366 machine guns, and 133 field guns. Some supervision over a mass of local agencies

71. *Iz istorii grazhdanskoi voiny v SSSR*, I (1960), p. 349.

and authorities had been vested in the new North Urals-Siberian front, which was in the process of setting up a field staff and a front operational staff. Although without orders or instructions of any kind from Moscow, this front under Berzin made contact with Muravev's eastern front command and learned that the General Headquarters was now at Kazan and that all Soviet forces were to be deployed as four armies. One after another volunteer detachments and partisan units were squeezed into more orthodox regiments, and the regiments in turn concentrated in divisions. Units were forbidden to open up independent channels of communication with Moscow: signals were to go through the chain of command. They were to leave the railways free for armored trains and for the movement of senior staffs.

On June 27, Tukhachevskii, hitherto a military commissar of the Moscow region of the western "screens," arrived at Inza railway station to take command of the First Revolutionary Army (First Red Army: eastern front). The fashioning of the First Army into a fighting instrument is a miniature history of the Red Army; scores of detachments were combined into three rifle divisions (the Penza, Inza, and Simbirsk Rifle Divisions), the staff (consisting originally of five men) was expanded, effective discipline was introduced, the ranks were stiffened with Communist Party members and divisional, brigade, and regimental establishments were filled out with ex-officers, "military specialists." (The very first mobilization of ex-imperial officers was carried out by the First Army on July 4, 1918, through agreement with Vareikis of the Simbirsk provincial committee of the party.)[72]

The first fighting Red Army was not "born" in February but was hammered out on the eastern front. To many of its proponents it was rapidly and increasingly becoming a strange, not to say alien thing. In spite of all the theories, this army was largely worker-manned, officered by "military specialists," and stiffened with Communists. The earlier failures, military failures of the Bolsheviks, had been born of utopianism, ignorance, and conceit. Now the utopianism was stifled, the ignorance outflanked by bringing in "specialists," and the conceit went underground. The "new" Red Army was a compound of political preconception, basic, inescapable military orthodoxy, and an abrupt pragmatism. The military statistics of the VVS and All-Russian General Military Staff were as fundamental to the Red Army as the fierce *pronunciamentos* emanating from many a bureau of collegiate. On the

---

72. M. N. Tukhachevskii, "Pervaia armiia v 1918 godu," *Revoliutsiia i voina,* no. 4/5 (1921), pp. 190–206, reprinted in *Etapy bol'shogo puti—Vospominaniia o grazhdanskoi voine* (Moscow, 1963), here p. 42. Ex-imperial officers were mobilized in the Soviet republic by the decree of July 29, 1918: *Dekrety Sovetskoi vlasti,* III, pp. 111–113.

way to the salvation of realism, Brest-Litovsk was only one half the story; the eastern front was the other.

Amidst these freshly raised divisions and newly fused regiments, another force at once supplementary and complementary was in the making. It was made up of units as unique as they were assorted, the multinational droplets of men which congealed into the "First International Legion of the Red Army," the "International Brigades," the separate national "revolutionary regiments," the "International Proletarian Army," or yet again the "International Red Army" set afoot in 1919. The war had washed great waves of men into Russia: the prisoners of war from the armies of the Central Powers, cobelligerent troops (Serb, Polish, Romanian), over a million refugees, Chinese and Korean unskilled laborers brought in before 1914, and Finnish and Belgian skilled workers hired for the war industry. International "detachments" had already made their appearance in the autumn of 1917, such as the Polish Revolutionary Regiment,[73] the First Serb Soviet Revolutionary Detachment (set up by Serdić in Ekaterinoslav), two Romanian battalians in Odessa, and a detachment of Chinese volunteers in Tiraspol. By the end of 1917 prisoner-of-war organizations and "revolutionary organizations" sponsored by foreign workers sprouted from Petrograd to Omsk.

The "Legion" was intended to absorb the external, foreign proletariat and pro-Bolsheviks. Its appeal for volunteers in February 1918 went out in Russian and in English. The American Albert Williams was put in charge of signing up recruits. The All-Russian Collegiate for the Red Army organized it first as the "First Revolutionary International Detachment" in Petrograd. It moved to Moscow in March as the "Legion of the Red Army" and was put under the command of Ebengolts. Six months later, with 231 men from various nations in its ranks, the Legion marched off to the western frontier as part of the 413th Moscow Soviet Regiment.[74]

It was the bulging prison camps, however, that from the outset attracted persistent Bolshevik attention, much as they figured prominently in the preoccupations of the Allies and the German command.[75] Early in 1918 the responsibilities hitherto vested in several agencies for prisoners of war were turned over to the Section for Army Demobilization.

73. Aleksander Zatorski, *Dzieje pulku Bielgorodzkiego—1 Polskiego Pulku Rewolucyjnego w Rosji* (Warsaw, 1960), 279 pp.
74. *Boevoe sodruzhestvo trudiashchikhsia zarubezhnykh stran s narodami Sovetskoi Rossii (1917–1922)* (Moscow, 1957), pp. 51–52, 69–70, 100–101.
75. George F. Kennan, *Soviet-American Relations, 1917–1920*, II: *The Decision to Intervene* (Princeton, 1958), pp. 74–81. For *Auswärtiges Amt* records, see St. Antony's College, Oxford, Film Reels 127 and 128: captured German documents.

An All-Russian Bureau for Prisoners of War (attached to the Military Section of the All-Russian Central Executive Committee) was set up. The Moscow Committee of Prisoner-of-War-Internationalists was preparing after its December meeting to hold an All-Russian Congress of Prisoners of War. That Congress duly met in April, discussed the creation of an All-Russian Organization for Prisoners of War, elected a Central Executive Committee of Prisoners and—in closed session—established a "Central Collegiate for the Formation of the International Proletarian Army."[76]

Meanwhile "national Communist groups," many ex-soldiers or refugees, emerged in some profusion in the spring of 1918. Among them were the Hungarian Group of the RKP(b) in March, the Romanian Group in April, the German Group also in April, and the Yugoslav Group in May. To coordinate these "groups" Bela Kun took over the direction of the Central Federation of Foreign Groups attached to the Central Committee of the RKP(b), which in the summer of 1918 set up its own "Commission for the Organization of the International Groups of the Red Army" (transformed in the spring of 1919 into a full administration, the Administration for the Formation of the International Red Army).[77] These men of the "Federation" set about forming their various battalions and detachments, Czech, Hungarian, Yugoslav, and German. (To the relief of the German government, German prisoners responded only indifferently to Bolshevik blandishments.)[78] The Czech Communists organized a "Czechoslovak Red Army"[79] with some of the first units in Samara *guberniia* where "Yugoslav Soviet troops," the First Socialist Revolutionary Yugoslav Regiment, also formed in June 1918.[80] The "Central Collegiate" for the "proletarian army" also promoted the formation of Serb, Polish, Romanian, and German platoons and small companies after April, many of these men being sent south to join Antonov-Ovseenko in the Ukraine.

76. A. Klevanskii, "Voennoplennye Tsentral'nykh Derzhav v Tsarskoi i revoliutsionnoi Rossii (1914–1918 gg.)," in *Internatsionalisty v boiakh za vlast' Sovetov* (Moscow, 1965), p. 62.

77. *Internatsionalisty* . . . , *ibid.*, p. 3.

78. I. M. Krivoguz, "Germanskie voennoplennye-internatsionalisty v Rossii v 1917–1920 gg.," in *Noiabr'skaia revoliutsiia v Germanii* (Moscow, 1960), here p. 337, blaming "counterrevolutionary officerdom" and the "chauvinism" of many of the prisoners of war.

79. A. Klevanskii, *Chekhoslovatskie internatsionalisty i prodannyi korpus* (Moscow, 1965), pp. 229–254. On p. 243, the strength of "Cheshko-Slovatskaia Krasnaia Armiia" is put at 2,960 volunteers as of June 19, 1918.

80. *Jugoslovenski dobrovoljački korpus u Rusiji.-Prilog istoriji dobrovoljačkog pokreta (1914–1918)* (Belgrade, 1954), 197 pp. On the "First Yugoslav Regiment," see doc. no. 46 (Inspectorate of Infantry, Samara *guberniia*, May 31, 1918) in *Boevoe sodruzhestvo* . . . (1957), p. 79.

Internationalism was written into the decree on the organization of the Red Army, though it was as much the shortage of trained men as devotion to principle that prompted the Bolsheviks to cull the prison camps. The first "international units" were never large (although by the end of 1918 ex-prisoners had formed detachments at some 400 points within the Bolshevik perimeter) and they never played any significant military role. With the repatriation of the prisoners of war the great reservoir of manpower drained away. In March 1919 the "Commission" for international units set up by the Central Federation had assembled a series of units (predominantly Hungarian) with a combined strength of some 18,000 men. The history of these international units is still relatively unexplored, yet for all their lack of numerical and actual military significance the formation of these units lies intrinsically within "the origins" of the Red Army as a whole. The military aspect of "internationalism" is yet another question, and like the early military utopianism it too was speedily sacrificed in the interests of efficiency, professionalism, and centralization.[81]

Not all the conceit, inexperience, and somewhat vague utopian inclinations of the early "military Bolsheviks" could withstand the pressures of military necessity that squeezed the Soviet state from the first days of its existence. The revulsion against a regular army, the hereditary foe of socialism, was understandable but its substitute, a militia, straightway foundered when the Bolsheviks had to find an organized force and that quickly. Revolution had not abolished the need for military organization. On the contrary, it had intensified it. The shock discovery and reluctant realization of this fact injected considerable acrimony into the first serious debates over Soviet military efforts. The acceptance of a "new" army—new in the sense of being unexampled, in embodying the political principle of the new regime and in marking a definite break with the "old" army—was, for all the attendant confusion, decisive. It remained decisive in spite of the first compromise, which was incontrovertibly the worst one, a "democratic" army that merely proliferated anarchy. The professional soldiers, the "military specialists," whose aid was early enlisted were inevitably impelled through their anti-German passions and their professional inclinations to build along orthodox lines to fight an orthodox war. The indignation over this alien intrusion, as if the "new" army had not escaped the clutches of the "old" (which insofar as it was an army it had not and could not), knew few bounds. The bitter clash of March 25, 1918, registered the shape of

81. Cf. Bertram D. Wolfe, "The Influence of Early Military Decisions on the National Structure of the Soviet Union," *American Slavic and East European Review*, IX (1950), 170–179.

future conflicts with astonishing clarity. Brest-Litovsk for all its harsh-
ness completed only half the schooling of the naive. The other half
came with the first weeks of the eastern front, making every concession
toward a "powerful, well equipped regular army" unquestionable, though
fashioning that army took many months more.

During the first mobilization of the Red Army the issue of the
"newness" of the Soviet military establishment was embedded more
firmly in emotion than in ideology. There were limits, unsuspected by
the early "military Bolsheviks," upon the actual destruction of the "old"
state machine and upon the efficacy of the break with all "bourgeois
military tradition," whatever the longings for the accomplishment of
both. Only in the most general sense did ideology contribute here.
There had been no preparation for the Red Army, "not even in theory"
as Lenin subsequently admitted, so that improvisation was inescapable.
It was the actual dissolution of the "old" army, its men melting away
from the front, that forced a decision. Nothing in particular sanctified
the volunteer principle save the practical impossibility of simultaneously
demobilizing 8 million men and mustering them (or a part of them) by
compulsion to the new colors. Nor, as Lenin himself argued both precisely and correctly, was the option of "national war" and "national
resistance" open to the Bolsheviks in the spring of 1918. Nevertheless,
the sense of outrage, the feeling that historical and political gains were
being snatched from under their very noses, found free and forcible
expression on the part of the proponents of "proletarian" innovations
and autonomies at the crucial meeting of March 25.

Much as the desire for distinctiveness was part of the politics of the
mobilization of the Red Army, so was it an important element in the
plans for the demobilization of the army, discussed during and after
January 1920. Entrenched now within Vsevobuch (the administration for
Universal Military Training set up in 1918) Podvoiskii came out with
fresh militia proposals ("The transition to the class militia system") on
December 3, 1919. Six weeks later (January 18, 1920), at the Military
Revolutionary Council of the Republic, Vatsetis produced the official
report of his special commission, "Variant of a reform of the armed force
of the RSFSR with a transition to the militia system." The wheel had
apparently come full circle. The time limit on compromise had run out,
"a Red Army" was to give way to "the Red Army," an ideal system of
"the people in arms." But in the vital meeting of December 16, 1920,
the professional soldiers once more had their way: one staff (not two,
for the field army and militia respectively), a regular army, and as its
appendage, a militia. The compromise had passed from being time-fixed
and became permanent.

Appendix

Table 1. Red Army strength: recruitment of volunteers to April 1, 1918.

Region	Total
Petrograd	25,000
Central	
(a) Moscow	9,347
(b) Remainder	27,767
Northwest	20,378
North	802
South and Southwest	11,870
Northeast	5,338
Southeast	8,853
Siberia	900
Caucasus	4,423
	114,678

Fronts	
Northern	
(a) Narva, Kolpino Tsarskoe Selo	12,000
(b) Pskov	12,000
Western	15,000
Grand Total	153,678

Source: Uchetnyi otdel: Vserossiiskaia Kollegiia po formirovaniiu Raboche-Krest'ianskoi Krasnoi Armii.

Table 2. Red Army strength: no date, early summer, 1918.

Area	Infantry	Cavalry
White Sea Military District	8,831	419
Eastern Front (future 1st, 3rd, 4th Armies)	35,550	2,318
"Screens": Southern	17,502	2,318
"Screens": Western Sector	3,441	463
"Screens": Petrograd Sector	10,514	699
Moscow Military District: Moscow Garrison	32,297	1,723
Vitebsk *Gubvoenkomat*	7,902	–
	116,037	7,940
Estimated total allowing for other forces in the interior:	200,000	10–12,000

Source: N. Kakurin, *Kak srazhalas' revoliutsiia,* I (Moscow-Leningrad, 1925), pp. 143–144.

Table 3. Data of the all-Russian central staff on Red
Army strength: military districts, internal fronts and
"screens" for August 15, 1918.

Military districts	Number of men
Iaroslav MD (to August 1)	53,692
Moscow MD (to August 1)	50,288
Orel MD (to August 1)	13,080
White Sea MD (to August 1)	11,015
Ural MD (to August 1)	19,161
Volga MD (to July 1)	7,938
West Siberian MD (to July 1)	4,328
Central Siberian MD (to July 1)	2,093
East Siberian MD (to July 1)	1,053
North Caucasus MD (to August 15)	116,449
Turkestan MD (to July 1)	964
	280,061

Armies: internal fronts	
1st Army	12,857
2nd Army	No information
3rd Army	24,691
4th Army	24,270
5th Army	8,918
6th Army	10,056
Army reserves	1,306
	82,098

"Screens"	
Northern sector	13,089
Western sector	18,414
Southern (Voronezh) sector	17,800
	49,303
Total	411,462

Source: Iz istorii grazhdanskoi voiny v SSSR, I (Moscow,
1960), doc. no. 160, p. 150.

Discussion

Mr. Schapiro noted that Mr. Erickson's work illustrated once again how romantic revolutionary enthusiasm inexorably gives way to practical necessities. It was particularly remarkable that it was Trotsky, the great revolutionary romantic, rather than Lenin, who first asserted this principle.

To Mr. Pipes, Mr. Erickson's account confirmed the virtue of straight factual, chronological history. It was fascinating to learn that the Red Army had come into being in response to a very concrete situation—the protection of Petrograd from the Germans and the defense of the eastern front—whereas all the talk about the kind of army Communists should have led to nothing.

Mr. Thompson wondered what effect the international revolutionary aspirations of left elements in the Communist Party had upon the debate over the Red Army.

Mr. Erickson agreed that this was an important point. He explained that several schools of thought could be distinguished in the debate and that the influence of those who argued in internationalist terms was reflected in the decree on the Red Army. A group to which Mr. Erickson referred as "military innovators" believed very passionately in the feasibility of partisan warfare against the Germans. However, Trotsky realized that the attitudes of the military innovators were unrealistic.

Mr. Katkov noted that Mr. Erickson confined his analysis of the organization of the Red Army to developments relating to the defense of Petrograd and the eastern front. He asked for information on the organization of Muraviev's army in Kiev.

Mr. Erickson agreed with Mr. Katkov on the importance of including the Muraviev army in his analysis. He commented that Muraviev's force could not be classified as a partisan unit and, indeed, that it was the only proper army that existed at the time.

In response to a question raised by Mr. Kecskemeti, Mr. Erickson spoke of the difficulty of determining the effect which the cessation of war with Germany had upon the development of the Red Army. In a sense it had no significance at the top, the high command merely continuing to plan and prepare. However, the lack of materials made it very difficult to study such a question as the effect of Brest-Litovsk upon the proponents of revolutionary war and upon the morale of the army.

Mr. Rubel wondered whether Mr. Erickson would agree that in the last analysis the Red Army was patterned after the occidental model, and asked him to comment on the differences between the new and tsarist Russian armies and on ideological elements in the constitution of the Red Army.

Mr. Erickson replied that Soviet works on the Red Army written in the 1920's, when military authorities had little to do but theorize, greatly exaggerated the importance of Marxist ideology in the formation of the Red Army. Some of the first decrees of the Soviet Army were copied from French revolutionary decrees of 1793. Comparing the Red and Imperial Armies,

Mr. Erickson said that the two were similar in structure and military discipline, but that in the Red Army consciousness of newness—the sense of having created a model revolutionary force—was a factor of major significance.

Mr. Meijer asked whether it was possible to distinguish between party and military historians of the Red Army and whether there was evidence of a neutral school emerging.

Accepting the distinction between military and party historians, Mr. Erickson referred to the problems which he had encountered in conducting research in the Soviet Union. Noting that it was considerably easier to obtain data on the Soviet Army in World War II than on the Civil War period, he attributed the difficulty to the protectiveness of party historians. Despite pressure from military historians, party historians have yet to formulate a mutually acceptable interpretation of the Civil War and the origin of the Red Army. He expressed confidence that scholarly histories based on thorough study of the archives would be produced in the future, quite likely by younger civilian historians.

Town and Country in the Civil War

— Jan M. Meijer

The opposition between town and country may seem at the same time a promising and yet overly facile framework for the understanding of the Russian Revolution. It is promising because the anomaly of a proletarian revolution in an agrarian country has occupied many politicians and historians both before and after 1917. During several decades before the ascendancy of the Social Democrats, the revolution had been expected to start in the countryside. The Social Democrats, however, dismissed the peasantry as a factor in the revolution. To them, it was indeed a reactionary class. It required the successes of the Socialist Revolutionaries in the countryside to draw attention to the revolutionary possibilities that the peasantry offered. Lenin almost stole their agrarian program.

On the other hand, this demarcation is too facile. As categories, "town" and "country" seem attractively vague and more apt to confuse the issues than to clarify them. Class concepts and socioeconomic categories seem to offer a more solid basis for discussion. But they too present problems. It is difficult to determine exactly who was a proletarian; the subdivision of the peasantry into poor, middle, and well-to-do has given rise to much discussion; and class membership—an objective factor— can be complicated by subjective factors. All this by itself does not make the categories of town and country any more useful, but neither does it make them superfluous. If we can succeed in clarifying them, they may still be of service.

The subject of this paper is the difference between two basic attitudes: the attitude of the typical town dweller, who, convinced that the town is superior to the countryside, looks condescendingly at the countryman as less knowledgeable than himself; and the outlook of the countryman who feels at home only on the land and who, while wondering at the marvels of the city, maintains a deep distrust of townspeople and usually feels himself taken advantage of in his dealings with them. This attitude is the basis of what is known as "peasant cleverness."

If our inquiry is to have any significance, these fundamental attitudes must be shown to remain more or less constant and identifiable in a period of rapid change. Indeed, we think that they are. "The proletarian" had not only his class membership but also his town dweller's viewpoint, only partly conscious. The peasant acted not only true to class, but also true to type. In the eyes of a proletarian, the peasant was a peasant first—his class membership came second. Our principal question will ask whether these opposing attitudes of town and country exercised any influence on the course of events during the revolution, the Civil War, and the period immediately following. In other words, we will inquire to what extent these attitudes became political facts. One of our main problems will be paucity of materials. Because of this, our inquiry will in some respects accomplish no more than raise questions, without prematurely attempting to answer them. It has been pointed out that the history of the French Revolution has been only recently enriched with local and country material, which has contributed to a new view of it.[1] In the case of the Russian Revolution this stage may not be attainable for some time to come.

Without entering into the origins of the opposing attitudes with which we are dealing, let us say only that their discovery was one of the deep and traumatic experiences of the early revolutionary movement. The transition from populism to Social Democracy had been conditioned in large part by the realization that the workers, the town dwellers, reacted to propaganda more readily and with greater understanding than did the peasantry. Urban workers were to be trained as country propagandists on the assumption that they, recent arrivals from the villages, would make better propagandists in those villages. This policy did not work, and the assumption that there was little difference between town and country proved faulty. Intended to radiate into the countryside, socialist teachings found an unexpected echo in the town. One would not exaggerate much if one were to state that Social Democracy came into existence with the discovery of the divergence in outlook between town and country.

This echo often manifested itself as a thirst for knowledge. The idea *znanie-sila* (knowledge is power) was strong in Social Democracy everywhere. Liebknecht's pamphlet bearing that title has been very popular throughout the Social Democratic movement. But in Russia this thirst was perhaps stronger than elsewhere because of its backwardness. (Later, *Znanie-sila* became the motto of the Soviet State publishing house.) In the countryside, distrust of the townspeople proved the stronger ele-

1. "When to translate," *Times Literary Supplement*, January 12, 1967, pp. 17–18.

ment. More often than not the propagandists were denounced to the authorities.

It is no wonder then that the whole Social Democratic view was colored by this experience, and that it was some time before the successes of the Socialist Revolutionaries demonstrated the revolutionary potentialities of the countryside. Marxism, of course, reinforced the town attitude. Peasants had in it no place of honor. They were *petit bourgeois* at best. It was when the urge to get things done began to overcome ideological purity that the revolutionary potentialities of the countryside were first seriously considered. It was a kind of breakthrough of the town attitude to acknowledge Lenin's position that the peasantry was not a homogeneous class. One wonders, however, how far Lenin's followers accepted this reversal of position. If Russian Marxism did not look down on the peasantry as such, nothing in it could counteract a condescending attitude on the part of its younger adherents. Just as the populists had shown an aversion to city work—as opposed to the real work in the countryside—so now the Marxists did not care to engage themselves in the countryside. This field was, in the main, left to the Socialist Revolutionaries. There was the danger that the conflict in attitude between town and country would unconsciously instill *petit-bourgeois* traits into the outlook of the urban Marxists. The attitude of superiority toward the village could be an expression of social insecurity and of an urge to "belong." But as long as most of the party activities were illegal, the selection of members was sufficiently severe and the intellectual tradition was sufficiently strong to control any *petit bourgeois* tendencies in it.

All the same, for the Russian *intelligent*, the peasantry was traditionally the embodiment of Russia's immobility. To the intelligentsia, the great majority of the peasantry belonged to the exploited, but their world view classified the peasantry as would-be exploiters. The distinction between the proletarian and *petit bourgeois* was so much less clear in the countryside than in the town that the intellectuals accepted much less critically the traditional views of the countryside than those of the town. There was nothing to force the Marxists to analyze their attitude toward the peasantry with regard to these traditions and it is safe to assume, therefore, that they were influenced by them. They did not differentiate between the view of the peasantry moving in the "right" direction, even if passively, and the view that peasants would turn exploiters if they had the opportunity. If the average Marxist before 1917 did not think often of the countryside, he could be excused. The town, after all, was his first concern and the enormity of the tasks confronting him in the towns was such that little time was left for the country. His heart was not in it.

The attitude of the peasantry toward the city must be distinguished from their attitude toward the imperial government. The latter attitude was determined by a desire to be left alone as much as possible, a desire natural enough in a people that could expect from above nothing but demands. The peasant knew the local authorities and distrusted them; his mistrust of them was as strong as was his trust in the tsar—and equally unshakable. The attitude toward the landlord was also clear. The local authorities acted on his behalf. But there was a group in between, that did not know and did not trust: they were the people from the cities. Peasant cleverness, against the city, as against the landlord, was a defensive weapon. The countryside never felt superior to the city.

Perhaps the attitude of the peasantry toward the city crystallized only after 1861. Before that time, the peasants were the "people," and it seems that they hardly distinguished the town as such, from governmental authority. Outbursts of hate, when they occurred, were directed at the landlord, not at the city. And when the city began to enter into the picture, in the course of the nineteenth century, it became not an object of hate, but an object of wonder and suspicion. Which of these would prove the stronger depended on circumstances, among others, of economic necessity. If the peasant attitude toward the town was a defensive one, that of the cities toward them was not necessarily offensive. Such fundamental attitudes are not conditioned entirely by economic factors. It is not that the town knew the countryside better than the countryside knew the town. There was prejudice on both sides. But one can say that lack of basic knowledge was part and parcel of the peasant attitude. The peasant was less prepared than the worker for a movement in which knowledge was power.

For a long time propaganda directed towards the peasant took the form of stories. One of the most popular of those was entitled *Khitraia mekhanika*; a justification of peasant distrust based on their exploitation by the state. Early peasant sympathizers were partly ethnologists. Men like Shchapov and Khudiakov discovered an almost foreign people, and Bervi-Flerovskii destroyed the rosy-colored view of the countryside. Knowledge of the other side was hard to acquire for the city and for the countryside because, for one thing, their own problems took up all their time. It would have seemed natural for the intelligentsia to assume the role of mediator, but the countryside hardly accepted it as such. It is understandable, therefore, that the intelligentsia turned more readily to the workers in the towns, than to the countryside. The countryside would be chosen as a field of action only on the basis of previously determined convictions, as was the case of the Socialist Revolutionaries who claimed to be the inheritors of the populists. The intelligentsia as a whole did not rise above the opposition of town and country and by 1917 was divided along the same lines.

It might be objected that in contrasting the town to the countryside we are concentrating on a secondary aspect of the peasant outlook, the first and foremost ingredient of which was hatred of the landlord; that the city was over the horizon; and that the peasant's first concern was for more land. This is true enough. The town came relatively late within the peasant's purview. But even if we concede that the peasant outlook was conditioned exclusively by economic factors, that is, by the desire for more land and for a better exchange rate for his products, it must be recognized that in this exchange he still dealt with people from the cities. From 1861 onwards, the city became increasingly important to the peasant as an economic partner, and the landlord less so.

Another reason for questioning the validity of the opposition between town and country attitudes might be peasant inertia. It can be argued that the peasantry, the essential and timeless Russia, lived its quint-essential life without interference from or concern for the city. This argument has a Rousseauistic and slavophile ring. In its own time the argument may have seemed convincing to a person so conditioned and one who thought of the "city" exclusively in terms of the two capital cities. Even so, it would probably not have withstood closer examination. By 1905 and certainly by 1917, this argument was outworn. One cannot say that either 1905 or 1917 provided demonstration of peasant inertia, nor that the town was outside the range of peasant consciousness.

There can be no doubt that by 1917 town and country were well aware of each other: the town dweller, in particular the *petit bourgeois*, looking down his nose at the peasantry, and the peasant wary of and wondering about the town. They were not each other's enemies because both saw the cause of their troubles in the government. Collaboration between town and country did not seem impossible. Such collaboration had been proposed by the *Krest'ianskii Soiuz* in 1905, and it was now offered by the proletariat under its own leadership. To what extent did the respective attitudes affect such collaboration?

The short *Dekret o Zemle* (Land Decree) was perhaps the single most important lever of the 1917 Revolution. Even though its provisions began to be put into effect before its promulgation, this decree directed the process and legalized it. "The dream of black repartition, dreamt of for so long by the Russian people and sanctioned by the progressive intelligentsia, has been realized before our eyes to the extent that an ideal is at all capable of realization," an observer wrote in the 1920's.[2]

2. B. Brutzkus, *Agrarentwicklung und Agrarrevolution in Russland* (*Quellen und Studien*) (Berlin, 1925), pp. 156–157.

With one stroke, the antagonist of the countryside had been destroyed and his land taken. Now town and country faced each other directly and had to learn whether they could cooperate. The decree seemed to have proven that they could. It brought the peasantry to the side of the proletariat and kept it there as long as there was any chance of the landlord's returning. As a result of Civil War and intervention, town and country were virtually compelled to cooperate.

The first thing the peasant experienced from the town was that it fulfilled his main wish and made him, so to speak, more of a peasant than he had been before. It would be natural to expect that his distrust of the city would therefore disappear and give way to a new spirit of collaboration. But what the Land Decree essentially did was to leave the peasantry for the first time in centuries to its own devices. This was not a *quid pro quo* between two parties, groups, or classes, arrived at for a common end out of common interest. The peasants were grateful, there was no doubt about that, but they had no way of expressing their gratitude other than by seizing the land—fully 96 percent of what was available for the taking. They looked favorably upon the government that had permitted them to take the land and they defended it against attempts to unseat it. But a decree to leave the peasantry to itself could not be repeated. The Soviet government was the heir of the imperial regime, and it soon began to interfere just as previous governments had done. The landlord's power also was now transferred to the cities, that is, that part of power that had not been done away with. Orders would still be issued.

The government that claimed to speak for the proletariat realized the peasant's backwardness and the need to explain to him its actions. It believed in propaganda, but it was so preoccupied with its natural allies in its efforts to build up its power and realize its dictatorship, that it had little time left for the peasantry. When the government had to interfere it was unable to explain itself adequately and thereby awakened the old distrust. The Whites had been opposed without the need for explanations. As long as the other parties (that is, mainly the Socialist Revolutionaries) had been active in the countryside, some propaganda had been necessary to counteract their influence. But from the moment the dictatorship of the party became effective, propaganda in the countryside virtually ceased. The Communists were all townspeople, in spirit if not actual origin. With the rapid influx of new members into the party after October 1917, the town outlook, including its *petit-bourgeois* ingredient, was bound to be strengthened. The little explaining of the government's actions that was done in the countryside was accomplished by local Communists, the least sophisticated element of the party, who could be expected to share both the Marxist's dim view of the peasantry and the townsman's prejudice against peasant backwardness. No sustained effort was made, in areas where Soviet power was not disputed, to develop the revolution in the countryside except to organize and consolidate the organs of power. And it was precisely this that made the new government, in the eyes of the peasants, increasingly similar to the old one and engendered among them the same old reactions. The traditional distrust of the towns found justification every day.

In its agrarian measures, the Soviet government acted on the assumption that there was no homogeneous peasant attitude. It sought support among the most untypical peasants, the rural proletarians, the *bednota*. To the extent that the peasantry was in effect one, it was by definition a class enemy. The urban Communist in the country had to convince the poorest and least educated layer of the peasantry that the cities were justified in opposing the peasants he knew. The *Kombedy* (Committees of the Poor) were, as an institution, short-lived, but not ineffective They were useful in that they showed the government forces where to locate grain. In the summer of 1918 this was of overriding importance, so much so that the search for grain undid the agrarian policy. If a *bedniak* (poor peasant) gave help in finding grain, he did so not from any urban or rural attitude but for his own profit.

In effect, however, he dissociated himself from most of the village and crossed the front in what has been called the war between town and country.[3] He was bound to go all the way with the Communists or stop informing. His function presupposed an elevated view of communism and of his own position in the party that the townspeople whom he had assisted did nothing to instill or entertain. More often than not, the members of the Committees of the Poor fell back on the village, largely as a result of the agrarian revolution that had given them land (or rather the use of it). Lenin was only partially right when he said that the revolution in the countryside began with the Committees of the Poor. If he were fully right, the membership of these committees would have been larger, but the choice before the individual member would not have been essentially different. The *bedniaki* did not constitute the absolute majority of the village even before 1917. The Committees of the Poor then either had to disappear or assume full power in the countryside. This latter course would have antagonized and consolidated the countryside, so the risk was not taken.

3. E. Zamiatin, *My* (New York, 1954), p. 21: "I am speaking of the Great Two-Hundred Years' War—the war between town and country."

It could be argued that attitudes had nothing to do with the episode of the Committees of the Poor: their existence can be adequately explained by economic necessities and interests. Against this it should be pointed out that the abolition of these committees was the result neither of changed circumstances nor of their having accomplished their objective—for the village after the committees was often socially more homogeneous than it had been before. They were ultimately abolished because they had been based on an incorrect estimate of peasant attitudes. The peasant found his traditional attitude to the city confirmed both by the Committees of the Poor and by the grain requisitioning. The grain was confiscated in the name of solidarity that the requisitioning squads did everything to destroy. The instructions of the central government were often ill-adapted to local circumstances, so that the behavior of the requisitioners became all the more important.

There is little doubt that they went out in support of the revolution against a peasantry that in its majority was reactionary. But their attitude partook of a certain dualism that was inherent in official policy also. On the one hand, there was the belief that the majority of the peasantry was reactionary; the poor and, later, the middle peasants, had to be won over, while the rest had to be fought. On the other hand, it was the revolution of Russia, that had started in the capital and then spread through the country in widening circles. This view implied that the country equalled the town plus inertia; the revolution in the country came later, but it was not really very different. This same view applied to the other nations in Russia. It was, in fact, sometimes applied to the Ukraine.[4] One consequence of this latter view, unexpressed but acted upon, was the notion that what was good for the town was good for the countryside as well. The requisition squads were often met with arms in hand. Their actions were far more convincing than any official policy to the contrary. And the dualism in official agrarian policy was translated on the local level into pure expediency. The peasant was antagonized as before, but no longer officially. A "middle" or "poor" peasant who concealed grain would be considered a *kulak* by the requisition squads who found him out, whatever his objective class status might be. The peasant, in turn, would rise in arms and cut down his sown acreage. If there were fixed prices, there was also *meshochnichestvo*. All Russia engaged in it and in this case the rate of exchange definitely favored the seller.

As a result of hunger in the towns during the Civil War, the proletariat began drifting toward the countryside. This fact seems to argue

4. For example, by Trotsky, in document 199 of the *Trotsky Papers*, vol. I (The Hague, 1964).

against the existence of two different viewpoints. But the economic situation sometimes left no alternative. The entire proletariat did not consist of class-conscious elements, and temporarily becoming a peasant again did not necessarily give a person a peasant outlook. The horizon of those who thus went to the villages remained urban. There are examples of town dwellers who chose to remain in the country once the emergency was over. This incidental migration did little to change basic attitudes. The hungry proletarian, migrating temporarily to the village, did not come as a representative of the town. He would be, as a rule, a *kozhanaia kurtka* (leather jacket), the name by which the new people became known.

If there was one thing that could have been expected to bring about a meeting of minds, it was the Red Army. The large majority of its recruits were peasants. They were taught the ways of the town to defend the country against the landlord. They answered the call. Units were probably not intentionally mixed, but at the fronts peasants were bound to come into close contact with proletarians. They learned many new words and things. In several cases, a conscious effort at schooling was made. The horizon of the soldiers was widened, but their allegiance did not become proletarian; it continued to be directed toward their units, as with soldiers everywhere and, finally, to the land. They now remained at the front for the same reason that they had left it in 1917. Bogdanov complained that proletarians would lose their class consciousness through soldiering.[5] This was not the case with the peasants. Normal life was shelved for the time being. But it was for a normal peasant life that they fought, and not for the towns, however much they might sympathize with individual proletarians.

As soon as the main danger from the landlord had passed, numerous peasant risings demonstrated this to have been the case. We do not yet have a history of peasant uprisings during the Civil War period, and this article can only call attention to their importance.[6] The subject certainly deserves closer study. The risings can be divided into peasant, worker, and national movements, of which peasant risings were by far

5. In his article "Nasha kritika" in: *Proletarskaia kul'tura*, no. 3, (August 1918), pp. 12 ff.

6. Only a few examples are mentioned in the Appendix for which information happens to be available. It should be further investigated how far the *atamanshchina*, in which also Tiutiunnik and Petliura should be included, is essentially a peasant movement. Mutinies also may be a form of peasant rising.

Our list may be introduced here by two quotations, of 1918 and 1922, that indicate how common a phenomenon they were. First Lozovskii, speaking in December 1918 at the Congress of Economic Councils [*Trudy II Vserossiiskogo s"ezda sovetov narodnogo khoziaistva (19 dekabria–27 dekabria 1918 g.)*, Stenograficheskii otchet (Moscow, 1919)], p. 110: "If we take what is in the counterrevolutionary risings

the most numerous. The difference between peasant and national movements is not always clear.

A rising that occurred in early 1919 in the areas of Syzran and Sengilei showed both typical and untypical traits. It had expert military leadership, which was not common and which indicated to Gusev, who reported on it, links with the Whites.[7] The story he tells does not prove this, but he does mention the presence of a count among the leaders. He also speaks of a *shtabskapitan*, of *kulaks* who converted part of the middle peasantry to their cause, and of some deserters. *Kulaks*, middle peasants, and, to a somewhat lesser degree, deserters, are common features of these peasant uprising. Typical also is the sequence of events. In places taken by the insurgents, a peasant conference (*skhod*) was organized, an act of condemnation formulated, and the local Communists taken prisoner or killed. The arms of the military training unit (*vseobuch*) were seized and the requisitioning squads were dispersed. The center of this particular rising was Novodeviche, a village with more than a thousand households. There were *kulaks* in the local soviet before the rising occurred. This remained so even after the rising had been crushed and a new soviet elected.[8] The slogans for this election were pro-Soviet and not anti-Communist; the latter were rare, Gusev adds. As causes of the rising, he mentions: fear that free trade in grain, still existing in the area, would be stopped; inconstancy of the middle peasant; crimes perpetrated by individual Communists; the "obscurantism" of the countryside; everyday actions, such as the refusal of the local authorities to accept grain delivery after closing time; and a "*kulak*-White guardist" conspiracy. The last named cause is the least important. This and the change of participation by Social Revolutionaries were stock in trade— risings by definition had to be caused by one or the other. These generic explanations, fitting any anti-Soviet activity, expressed conviction and attitude rather than fact. The story of the uprising actually showed that the *kulak* stood for the village and the village for the *kulak*.

---

in the village, and ignore for a moment Cheka views, looking at them as Marxists should, then we see that in the village there are only 2 percent *kulaks*, and that these are risings of toiling peasants, who could not but rise out of self preservation. [In what has been published] we find the clear admission that all the risings occurred because of the absurd, idiotic measures of the local powers." And Lenin speaking to the Fourth Congress of the Comintern: "The peasant risings which earlier, before 1921, were, so to speak, a general phenomenon in Russia, have almost completely disappeared. The peasantry is content with its situation." (V. I. Lenin, *Polnoe Sobranie Sochinenii*, XLIV, p. 285.)

7. *Voennaia mysl'* (Izdanie Rev. Voenn. Soveta Vost. Fronta), no. 3 (April 30, 1919), pp. 11–16.

8. See also Iu. Larin, *Sovetskaia derevnia* (Moscow, 1925), p. 13.

Among the causes of this particular disturbance, we have not mentioned the main cause of most of the peasant uprisings—*prodrazverstka,* (food requisitioning) or, rather, its unpredictable methods. The drawbacks of *prodrazverstka* became clear to everyone by 1921, but before that date it had caused widespread violence. The city had nothing to offer the village in exchange for its grain. But was there no alternative to food requisitioning? The notion that it could have been replaced immediately by a tax in kind deserves at least further investigation. Has it been really established that *prodrazverstka* was anything more than the expression of urban attitude toward the countryside? How often is the blame for the peasant risings laid at the door of the local Communists who overstepped their authority? This authority was vague enough to give full scope for their feelings for the countryside. The occasional taunt levelled at Communists as *beloruchka* (white-hand), people who did not work themselves but ordered others about,[9] is a clear indication in that direction. The total effort required to raise a tax in kind would hardly have equaled that involved in the requisitioning and might have established a clearer line of authority in the village. It might have required more effort at the center and less locally, but the total effort would perhaps have been no greater.

Another characteristic of the peasant risings was their local character, however much their causes may have in common. Among their first victims were often the local Communists, whether or not they had exceeded their authority; requisitioned food would be taken back and redivided or destroyed; arms were seized. But in general, although there was no program, there were grievances, and once these had been vented or assuaged for the time being, the rebellion tended to peter out (unless it came under the influence of political or military organizers, which was not often). Fear of reprisals sometimes induced the insurgents to seek support in the neighborhood, but this did not make their organization more effective. Outsiders naturally had no sympathy for the insurgents, who furthermore had to be fed as well, thus becoming one more burden. Insofar as there was a political element, it was mostly Socialist Revolutionary. SR's were always mentioned in Soviet reports, but the Bolsheviks, on past experiences, tended to overestimate SR influence in the countryside. A number of risings, in fact, revealed an anti-intellectual bias, and the *intelligenty* who offered help were refused.[10] It is natural that when Socialist Revolutionaries were present, they tried to influence

9. L. S. Sosnovskii, *Dela i liudi,* II (Moscow-Leningrad, 1925), pp. 8–9.
10. This applies to the risings in Siberia in February 1921 listed in the appendix. The same is reported after the Civil War in L. Grigorov, *Ocherki sovremennoi derevni,* I (Moscow, 1926), p. 47.

the course of the rising. It is equally understandable that what political ideas there were were mostly of SR origin. But there is scant evidence of any organized Socialist Revolutionary guidance in local risings. Sometimes such risings were pure jacqueries. Where there were *skhodki* (peasant meetings), as often as not, the soviets remained in tact.

Sometimes deserters gave a certain military backbone to a rising. Because of their large numbers, deserters constituted a special problem for the central authorities. Both the carrot and the stick were used to keep them down. But it was easy for them to disappear in the countryside. Uncertainty about home and the family were a common cause of desertion. The deserters often took their arms with them. Obtaining arms was not a serious problem for the insurgents, particularly in places engulfed by the Civil War. Trotsky at one time complained of Ukrainian well-armed *kulaks* poking fun at badly clad and badly armed Soviet troops.[11] Special expeditions had to be organized to retrieve hidden arms. One source speaks of a wave of deserters' risings in 1919 and gives an example of a small one.[12] It would have to be studied further, to see whether they differ essentially from peasant risings, as does not seem likely.

Risings could also be organized around a person, or find themselves taken in hand by one. This phenomenon occurred particularly in the Ukraine, where it received the name of *atamanshchina*. These showed more coherence than purely local risings and sometimes spread over a larger territory. After their direct objectives were attained—and these were no different from those of ordinary peasant risings—these groups easily dissolved into bands that roamed the countryside. Their allegiance was to a person, and they might even change sides with it. The *atamanshchina* marks the transition from peasant to national risings, and in the Ukraine it is hard to say where peasant risings ended and national risings began. This difficulty is increased by the scarcity of programmatic documents. Such risings essentially broke out to reestablish a situation that was considered normal, not to establish anything new. The labels attached to these risings reflected either Bolshevik prejudices or the sympathies vaguely felt by people who wanted to explain for what cause they went to prison or before the firing squad.

Although collaboration between workers and peasants did take place, it was rare. The mutiny of a food requisitioning regiment in Viatka was perhaps such a case,[13] but the documentation is too incomplete to per-

11. *Trotsky Papers*, vol. I, doc. no. 360.
12. A. M. Bolshakov, *Derevnia, 1917–1927* (Moscow, 1927), p. 123.
13. It occurred in August 1919. *Oktiabr' i grazhdanskaia voina v viatskoi gubernii* (Viatka 1927), pp. 120–121.

mit conclusions. Idealists are a minority in any party, but they must be taken into account. Solidarity with the peasantry for some Communists, at least, must have been a genuine commitment, and such people in a requisitioning squad could come to the conclusion that peasants were maltreated by bad Communists. They would rise, not against communism as such, but to redress the wrongs committed by bad Communists. Such cases, of course, were exceptional.

The strike movement falls outside the scope of this paper. There was hardly a strike in which the issue of town and country played a role. The hunger strikes, especially frequent in February 1921 do not express the antagonism between town and country but fall in a category of their own.

Demobilization deserves particular emphasis. The risings of early 1921 have received more attention than the earlier ones and among their causes historians have singled out demobilization. But the best known rising, that of Kronstadt, involved men on active military service. Antonov's rising had been under way throughout 1920 and broadened its scope by the end of that year. And Makhno carried on much as before. The ranks of the insurgents were probably often swelled by demobilized Red Army men. Demobilized men may have actually started uprisings or provided foci for incipient risings. Hunger was, of course, an important factor. It should perhaps be investigated further to what extent the famine caused and to what extent it dampened risings. Whatever the case may have been, the risings of 1921, apart from sheer numbers, introduced no new elements into the picture. Kronstadt was not the only mutiny. Its striking quality lay in the fact that it was the sailors, the mainstay of the regime, who were involved. Perhaps it was under the impression of Kronstadt, that Lenin suggested to Trotsky to do away with the navy. But a mutiny of the troops that had been the first to come over to the Bolsheviks had also occurred in the case of the Kamenka Cossacks.[14] The slogan of "soviets without Communists" was not new either—it could have been heard in the countryside before. It could even have come from the countryside, as did many sailors. The slogan can be interpreted as an acceptance of the revolution but rejection of its (local) management.

Thus, the early months of 1921 appeared to be a second judgment on the revolution on the part of the countryside, but in fact the judgment had been in the making from 1918 onward. The form it now took did not in any essential respect differ from earlier manifestations. It only

14. *Leninskii sbornik*, XI, p. 22; V. A. Antonov-Ovseenko, *Zapiski o grazhdanskoi voine*, I (Moscow-Leningrad, 1924), pp. 198 ff.

assumed a somewhat wider scope and was more clearly defined because there no longer was danger from the Whites. What decided a man to become an insurrectionary was the return home to a hungry family, robbed of the necessities of life.

The introduction of the tax in kind took the wind out of the insurgents' sails, as it might well have done so had it been instituted two years earlier. Both town and country now went back to work—insofar as work could be found. Red Army soldiers turned again into either workers or peasants. During the war they had gotten to know each other and each other's territory, but they cooperated as soldiers, not as workers and peasants. Now both turned back and inward once more. The revolution had come to an end. The town had not become more village-oriented; perhaps it was even more town-conscious than before. The peasant had not become more town-oriented. This was the big chance that had been missed. It would have seemed possible even then to organize a truly representative peasant union. The idea was broached by Osinskii, but Lenin turned it down.[15]

With the transition to the NEP, the Soviet regime took a closer look at the countryside and at last took note of what was really occurring there. At the Tenth Party Congress, Skvortsov-Stepanov spoke of the urge of the rural Communists to move into town.

I have the impression that our [urban] centers have grown enormously and that they attract all workers from the smaller places. The province has become deserted. You often see that the countryside is afraid to send somebody to the center, for as soon as this happens the comrade in question goes to the Central Committee, there delivers himself of his views on how necessary it is for him to remain in the center, and stays there. In this manner the center pumps the living forces out of the countryside. It cannot go on like this.[16]

Further on in the same speech he expressed the view that "not Soviet power, but the *kulaks* are the defenders and representatives of the common interest of the villages."

Gradually it became clear how little the countryside was really known, and efforts were made to change this situation.[17] Early in 1923 Iakovlev

15. *Trotsky Papers*, document of May, 1921. Reviewing the course of the revolution, it becomes less and less understandable, from the historian's safe distance, why the Whites did not try to come to terms with the countryside. This is the clearest evidence that they were in fact *ancien régime*.

16. *Desiatyi S"ezd RKP(b)—Stenograficheskii otchet* (Moscow, 1933), p. 72; see also Grigorov, *Ocherki*, p. 201.

17. Besides the literature mentioned in the other notes, see also questionnaire on the agrarian question of the Eleventh Party Congress (Protokoly XI S"ezda RKP(b), Moscow, 1961, pp. 711–713); A. Gagarin, *Khozhiaistvo, zhizn' i nastro-*

assembled a party of specialists and with them went out to see "the countryside as it is," the title under which he published their findings.[18] When they organized a *krestianskii skhod* and announced that the Central Executive Committee (VTsIK) wanted to know their needs, no one asked any questions. "They continued to stare at us with the same dark distrust. Evidently they suspected in us some new Communist trick." But once the distrust was dispelled, the visitors learned many interesting things. They heard of a Communist cell that went to the priest to be blessed. They saw that the schools were run down, and sometimes used for stables. They met a former miner who had gone to the country because of the famine. He had heard that things were better again but had decided to remain there. "The countryside had already poisoned him," Iakovlev commented. What enraged the peasants was not so much the amount of the tax, but the number of different taxes they had to pay, often with arrears because the collection date had been made arbitrarily retroactive. Another peasant, a former tailor, also had definitely broken with the town and become a convinced middle peasant (*seredniak*). Few of the former soldiers had joined the party. "There is no section of the party that transmits the influence of the working class onto the peasantry,"[19] Iakovlev wrote, adding that for the preceding two years not a single Moscow publishing house had brought out anything for the village. A village chairman complained of the lack of support in the village—"*a prikazy iz volosti tak sypliutsia*" ("and the local administration keeps on pouring orders").

From another source comes the story of the former peasant who had risen to the rank of divisional commissar. After his demobilization in May 1921 he returned to the village but did not receive any ploughland. When he succeeded in growing something on the poor land he had received, the peasants plowed it under. It took him two years of suffering, in which he lost two children, before he was accepted by the village. The author comments: the peasants see in Communists idlers, administrators who give orders and do no work themselves.[20]

The fact that the authorities took a closer look at the village at the end of the Civil War attested to a certain change in the town's attitude toward the village. In some circles the previous feeling of superiority

---

enniia derevni (Moscow-Leningrad, 1925); and N. Rosnitskii, *Litso derevni* (Moscow-Leningrad, 1926). The list is far from complete.

18. Ia. Iakovlev, *Derevniia kak ona est'* (*Ocherki Nikol'skoi volosti*) (Moscow, 1923).

19. He makes the same point in his *Nasha derevnia—novoe v starom i staroe v novom* (Moscow-Leningrad, 1925), an elaboration of the things he had said in the earlier work.

20. See note 8, above.

now yielded to fear of the countryside. This change in attitude reflected a change in the economic relationship between town and country. The countryside could no longer be taken for granted; the discovery of 1921 was brought home in the following years. The resurgence of the country-side, it was felt, threatened to undo what communism had achieved. The question also had ideological aspects: did capitalism have to be acted out by every class separately, that is, did the peasantry have to go through a full capitalist phase?[21] The question What, after all, had the revolution accomplished? now presented itself not unnaturally as a cultural problem. A new culture was essentially what the revolution had been about, and this aspect now received due attention. From 1922 onwards a debate on culture got under way that raised a number of searching questions.

In 1918 the spokesmen for "Proletarian Culture" had been intent on keeping it free of peasant taints. In order to fulfill its task of developing the creative activities of the proletariat, the *Proletkul't* organization had to shed all the debilitating consequences of the political alliance with the peasantry.[22] The organizing principle of Proletarian Culture was collectivism, as against the individualism and property instincts of the peasantry. Though the term *petit bourgeois* originally referred to town dwellers, it truthfully expressed the basic leanings of the peasantry. Soldiering was a troubling factor because the majority of the soldiers were peasants, and that lowered its proletarian character. The *Proletkul't* people were "immediate socialists," who wanted to create socialist forms, thoughts, and feelings at once.[23]

Proletkul't as an organization lost its impetus after its efforts at or-ganizational monopoly had been thwarted by Lenin. But when the problem of culture reemerged after the Civil War, the underlying issues were essentially the same: proletarians, peasants, and *meshchanstvo* (petty bourgeoisie). The proletariat was now perhaps less exclusive than in 1918, but no more peasant-oriented. The idea that the dominant culture would be the culture of the dominant class, and therefore prole-tarian, was sound Marxism and enjoyed wide support. *Kul'turnichestvo*, in the sense of furthering culture on a nonpolitical level, was still re-jected on principle, even if accepted in fact.[24] *Meshchanstvo* was now found to infect the proletariat also. If at first the *kul'turniki* had been petty bourgeois, for example, when they introduced a coat rack in a

21. I. A. Teodorovich, *Istoricheskoe znachenie partii Narodnoi Voli—Sbornik pervyi*, (Moscow, 1930). The problem figured prominently in the discussion of the *Narodnaia volia* in 1930.
22. V. Polianskii, in *Proletarskaia kul'tura*, no. 1 (July 1918), pp. 3 ff.
23. A. Bogdanov, *ibid.*, no. 3 (August 1918), pp. 12 ff.
24. Lenin, "O kooperatsii," *Sochineniia*, 1st ed., vol. XVIII, pt. 2, pp. 144–145.

Communist youth club in Kiev; now the policy was reversed, and people were even told they should learn from the West.[25]

Trotsky rejected the concept of "proletarian culture" as too limited. The proletariat had made a revolution for a new all-human culture. If it remained solely a proletarian culture, it would fail in its objective. But if he cautiously accepted the fellow travelers—for one thing because they showed what the revolution had done in the countryside—he rejected the Soviet populism that some of them adhered to. He did not expect any cultural initiative to come from the countryside. The spread of culture had to start with basic things.[26] The proletariat should take the initiative, but it was not really ready to take on the countryside. Things really remained *stikhiino* (spontaneous), and the active spread of culture boiled itself down to education.

The thinking about culture during those years reflects a fundamental dichotomy toward tradition. Roughly, two attitudes can be distinguished. There was the newness, the urge to show what the proletariat could do, how much better and more humane than capitalism it was. But this approach provided no criteria for the acceptance or rejection of cultural forms. The other approach, tinged with a feeling of inferiority, wanted to show that the new culture could behave as properly as the old had done. It was much more ready to accept traditional elements. But neither of these approaches would accept the village as a positive cultural force. Both wanted to teach the village. Of the two, the traditionalist attitude was bound to win out. The "proletarian" approach overestimated the conscious element in culture. What was taught were the ways of the town, not proletarian ways. Proletarian distrust of the countryside narrowed the scope of cultural policy to teaching. The unconscious part of culture therefore could fully preserve itself. As between town and proletarians, it was the former that won. The new culture was more urban than proletarian. Between town and country, the matter is more difficult to ascertain. One can say that the countryside did not lose unequivocally, but a further inquiry into this question transcends the scope of this paper.

Our emphasis on such subjective things as attitudes by no means implies a denial of the importance of other, more objective factors. The question of attitudes perhaps raises more questions than it answers, as in a way it was meant to. But it is hoped that this paper indicates that an inquiry into attitudes can eventually contribute to a fuller understanding of the Russian Revolution.

25. Kostrov, "Kul'tura i meshchanstvo," in *Revoliutsiia i kul'tura*, no. 3–4, (1927), pp. 20–23.

26. Both his *Literatura i Revoliutsiia*, in which he discussed proletarian culture, and his *Voprosy Byta* were published in 1923.

Appendix
Some peasant uprisings during the Civil War.

Rising led by	Location	Dates	Number of participants	Source
	Tambov	June 17–19, 1918		J. Maynard, *The Russian Peasant*, (New York, 1962), p. 127.
	47 uprisings	July 1918		*ibid.*, p. 129.
	Vesegonsk	1918		Todorskii, *God s vintovkoi i plugom*, (Moscow, 1927).
"Kulaks"		end of 1918		Peters, in *Izvestiia*, Dec. 27, 1918.
	Simbirsk and adjacent provinces	March 1919		*Trotsky Papers*, vol. I, docs. no. 157, 159.
	Kostroma province and Povolzhe	March 1919		*VIII s"ezd RKP(b)*, Moscow, 1933, no. 86. (See also note 7 in the text.)
	Orel, Briansk, Smolensk, Astrakhan	March 1919		*Ibid.*, no. 74.
Cossacks	Donbass	March 1919	30,000	*Trotsky Papers*, vol. I, doc. no. 182.
Grigorev	Kherson-Ekaterinoslav	May 1919	15,000	*Ibid.*, no. 216.
Cossacks		June 1919		*Izvestiia*, June 19 and 21, 1919.

Makhno	Guliai-Pole	1919–1921	15,000	*Trotsky Papers*, vol. I, doc. no. 199.
Mironov	Poshekhon	Summer 1919		*Pravda*, September 10, 1920.
	Don	August 1919	5,000	*Trotsky Papers*, vol. I, doc. no. 379.
	Behind the Ukrainian Front	August 1919		*Ibid.*, no. 348.
	Moscow province	May 1920		*Izvestiia*, May 1, 1920.
Sapozhkov	Buzuluk	July–August, 1920	Division	*Trotsky Papers*, document dated August 2, 1920.
Antonov	Tambov	1920–1921	25,000	*Trotsky Papers*, document dated July 20, 1920.
Krest'ianskii Soiuz	Siberia	1920–1921 (mainly February 1921)	20,000–60,000	*Ibid.*, document dated February 21, 1921.
	Saratov	February–March 1921		*Ibid.*, documents of that period.
	Simbirsk	February–March 1921		Latsis in *Izvestiia*, March 6, 1921.
Popov	Saratov	March 1921		*Trotsky Papers*, document dated March 23, 1921.
	Ukraine	March 1921		*Pravda*, March 9 and 23, 1921.
Maslakov	Samara and Saratov provinces	March 1921		*Trotsky Papers*, document dated March 18, 1921.

Discussion

To Mr. Pipes it seemed that Mr. Meijer had somewhat exaggerated the hostility of the populists and early Russian socialists to the city. Even when the proletariat in Russia was still quite small, the anarchists had published for it a special newspaper, *Rabotnik,* and in general had pioneered in the conduct of propaganda among workers. Then, in 1879, *Narodnaia volia's* program had specifically declared that the industrial proletariat would be the carrier of the revolution, with the peasantry providing the elemental force behind it. Similarly, all through the 1880's the *narodovol'tsy* had placed the greatest faith in the urban proletariat; as the proletariat grew, that faith intensified. Hence, if the very early *narodniki* concentrated so much on the peasantry, it was primarily because the peasantry was then still virtually all there was to the *narod,* because it was the "people."

Mr. Meijer agreed that *Narodnaia volia* had a certain feeling for the workers. Nonetheless, opposition to the city did exist and in fact it was to this circumstance that the Social Democratic movement owed its rise. Reiterating his belief that Russian Social Democracy was strongly anti-countryside, Mr. Meijer stressed the enormous effect that the personal experiences of former *narodovol'tsy* had upon the formation of this attitude.

Mr. Kecskemeti raised a question regarding the impact of Lenin's views on the alliance with the peasantry upon relations between town and country. From the time of *What Is to Be Done?* Lenin had consistently recognized the need for cooperation with the peasantry despite its petty bourgeois character.

Mr. Meijer acknowledged the validity of this point. However, he pointed out that after October 1917 the realization of the revolution in the countryside was dependent on the least sophisticated elements in the Bolshevik movement, elements which often did not share Lenin's confidence in the role of the peasantry.

To Mr. Anweiler, Mr. Meijer's sociopsychological approach to the study of town and country in the revolution and Civil War seemed very valuable. His own research on Soviet education indicated that the great gulf separating the two was the main problem confronting Bolshevik educational policy until the 1930's. Mr. Anweiler asked whether or not Mr. Meijer would agree that the real turning point in the social history of Russia was the period of the First Five Year Plan rather than the October Revolution.

Mr. Meijer disagreed with this suggestion. Although fundamental changes in attitude did not come until much later, the revolution in the countryside actually began with the Land Decree. In his judgment World War II had a greater effect on the attitudes of town and country than either the Civil War or the events of 1930–31. Only with World War II did hostility between town and country approach an end.

To Mr. Carr, it seemed, Mr. Meijer had underrated the importance of taxation in engendering hostility to the town in the country. For a long time representatives of the party hardly ever penetrated into the more remote parts of the country; the only contact the peasant had with the town was with the tax collector. During the Civil War and industrialization periods, when the town was trying to suck resources from the peasants, the wedge between town and country widened further.

Mr. Meijer agreed that this was correct. He had not intended to suggest that the impact of taxes was not great but only that the peasants often appeared to have resented more the arbitrary, haphazard manner in which taxes were collected than the taxes themselves.

Mr. Wolfe returned to the problem of Marxism and the countryside. Although it was no doubt true that Marx was consistent in his opposition to the peasantry, Engels, if only for tactical reasons, had viewed something analogous to a peasant war as necessary for the success of any socialist revolution. Lenin's position vis-à-vis the peasant was significantly more complex than Mr. Kecskemeti had suggested. There could be found in Lenin's spirit a deep distrust and antipathy toward the peasantry. This attitude was strikingly reflected in an early memorandum from Lenin to his *Iskra* colleagues, in which he said that Russian Social Democrats should prepare to treat the peasants with courtesy, but that as soon as it was found that the peasants opposed socialist ideas, force would have to be used against them. Later, Lenin's attitudes toward the peasantry underwent a succession of interesting tactical swings. In the course of the struggle for power came the pillaging of the SR program. The Civil War period witnessed requisitions, the guerrilla warfare of the Committees of the Poor, and the shooting of bagmen, that is, Lenin's war on the village. And this was followed by reconciliation with the peasant under the NEP. The result of these tactical shifts was that although for propaganda purposes Lenin unhesitatingly described the Soviet Union as a peasant and proletarian dictatorship, in regard to the policy to be pursued toward the peasantry, he left his followers with several different strands which they interpreted for themselves. Bukharin developed one strand; his attitude toward the peasantry was both tactical and humanistic. On the other hand, Piatakov said in effect, "Loot the village, and that is how we will industrialize." For his part, Stalin used both Bukharin and Piatakov as ideologues, returning finally to Lenin's *Iskra* memorandum.

Mr. Meijer replied that he had purposely kept ideology out of his paper. However, he expressed the conviction that the policies toward the peasantry pursued by the Communists during the Civil War were motivated by economic rather than ideological factors. Moreover, he disagreed with some of Mr. Wolfe's comments in regard to Lenin's hostility to the village because much of the anti-peasant violence of the early Soviet period was inflicted by local Communists without direct inspiration from Lenin.

Mr. Rubel declared that Mr. Meijer had been justified in omitting ideology from his analysis because the revolution marked the failure of every ideology. He asked if any of the Russian revolutionary ideologies expected that the peasants would take the land. In his own mind none had, and in this sense Mensheviks, Bolsheviks, and SR's alike were bad Marxists.

Mr. Meijer disagreed. It was the expectation of precisely this development that had caused Lenin to change his policy toward the countryside before the revolution. Lenin had realized the revolutionary potential of seizing the land and that is what he adapted himself to.

Mr. Kennan prefaced some general comments on the plight of the peasantry under Soviet rule with the remark that Mr. Meijer's paper had aroused feelings in him that might sound a bit sweeping and emotional. He was aware that the early Soviet leaders had tried very hard to find theoretical rationalizations for their outlook that would allow them to think they had something worth while to offer the peasantry. However, he could find no reality whatsoever in these efforts. The Bolsheviks lacked any proper understanding of the agricultural process, and their ideology was insufficient to explain what went on in the village; they had no sympathy for the peasant as a human being or for the disciplined life that made him what he was, with the result that they had nothing to give the peasantry except the 28 percent of the land that still remained in the hands of the landlords. After that, the best the Bolsheviks could have done for the peasant would have been to permit him adequate terms of trade with the city. In the twenties the Communists moved in that direction, but then they thought better of it. Apart from that brief interruption, the revolution had made the peasantry an exploited, disenfranchised, and conquered class. This was a very heavy moral responsibility for the Soviet regime.

Mr. Epstein asked Mr. Meijer whether the town's fight against the village was not in part the result of Communist hostility toward the Orthodox church.

Mr. Meijer replied that there was evidence that this was the case. In this connection, Mr. Treadgold observed that we still do not know much about the immediate effect of the revolution on Russian Orthodoxy and on the religiosity of the Russian people. However, he had been struck by a statement in a Soviet study to the effect that during the Civil War the Communists found it wise in a number of units to concede to demands for priests by soldiers of peasant origin. Further study of the whole question of the revolution and the church was needed, particularly from the standpoint of the impermeability of the still partially religious village to a much wider range of ideas than those properly labeled Communist.

Mr. Seton-Watson wondered whether the source of Bolshevik hostility to the peasantry could not be pinpointed a bit more precisely. Did the hostility come from the working class? The working class in the cities was, after all, of very recent peasant origin. Did it perhaps stem from a tendency on the part of the intelligentsia element in the Bolshevik party to think of peasants as idiotic, brutish characters? Or did it come from a sort of *chinovnik*, bureaucratic attitude that Bolsheviks acquired when they became administrators?

In reply to Mr. Seton-Watson, Mr. Meijer said that the attitudes of intelligentsia, worker, and *chinovnik* elements all contributed to the general Bolshevik feeling of hostility toward the peasant, though in varying degrees.

Bearing in mind that the problem deserved further research, Mr. Meijer expressed the belief that for many of the most convinced Bolshevik intellectuals, the feelings of guilt that had characterized intelligentsia attitudes toward the peasantry throughout the nineteenth century had apparently given way to an almost managerial attitude bordering on contempt. Among workers recently arrived from the countryside, antagonism toward the peasantry appears to have been a consequence of their feelings of general uncertainty. It was precisely these petty bourgeois elements within the proletariat, which flocked to the party and were sent into the countryside to carry out Bolshevik policy there; much more than the intelligentsia, they carried with them anti-peasant feelings. As for the *chinovnik* attitude, almost from the start the lower bureaucracy in the villages and smaller cities fell into the hands of people who were not so much good Bolsheviks as local men who got things done. Their outlook was also primarily one of uncertainty and thus they also served as conveyor belts for petty bourgeois attitudes toward the peasantry.

Mr. Dallin commented that the urban-rural dichotomy was a phenomenon which could be found in virtually all developing countries and expressed the hope that Mr. Meijer and others would continue studies along these lines.

A Historical Turning Point: Marx, Lenin, Stalin
— E. H. Carr

The idea of progress and belief in history as a meaningful process, issuing from the Enlightenment and consecrated by the French Revolution, were a dominant creed of the nineteenth century. Marx fortified the belief in progress and the belief in history with the belief in revolution as "the locomotive of history" and, in so doing, created the first theory of revolution. It was appropriate that his name and doctrine should serve as the beacon for the next great revolution. In the interval between the final elaboration of Marx's system and the next revolution of 1917 much had changed, but much also had survived, so that, when we consider the historical significance of the Russian Revolution, we see the interaction of a Marxist or pre-Marxist revolutionary tradition and a neo-Marxist or post-Marxist revolutionary environment. One thing that had not changed—or, rather, that had been greatly intensified —was the emphasis on productivity. Marx stood on the shoulders of the Enlightenment thinkers and of the classical economists in treating production as the essential economic activity, to which all other categories were subsidiary: and he was in essence right when he saw the key to the future in the hands of the industrial worker and treated the individual peasant cultivator of the soil as an obsolescent unit of production. The Russian Revolution for the first time explicitly proclaimed the goal of increased production and identified it with socialism: Lenin's remark that socialism meant electrification plus the Soviets was the first primitive formulation of this idea. It was repeated over and over again by Lenin and other Bolsheviks that the test of socialism was that it could organize production more efficiently than capitalism. One of the few glimpses afforded by Marx of the Communist utopia was that there the springs of wealth would flow more abundantly. The success of the Soviet campaign for industrialization, which in 30 years, starting from a semi-literate population of primitive peasants, raised the USSR to the position of the second industrial country in the world and the leader in some of the most advanced technological developments, is perhaps the most significant of all the achievements of the Russian Revolution. Nor can the achievement be measured purely in material terms. In the time span of half a century, a population almost 60 percent urban has replaced a population more than 80 percent peasant; a high standard of general education has replaced near illiteracy; social services have been built up; even in agriculture, which remains the stepchild—or problem child—of the economy, the tractor has replaced the wooden plough as the characteristic instrument of cultivation. It would be wrong to minimize or condone the sufferings and the horrors inflicted on large sections of the Russian people in the process of transformation. This was a historical tragedy, which has not yet been outlived, or lived down. But, however the reckoning is made, it would be idle to deny that the sum of human well-being and human opportunity is immeasurably greater in Russia today than it was fifty years ago. It is this achievement that has most impressed the rest of the world and has inspired in industrially undeveloped countries the ambition to imitate it.

The world in which the USSR embarked on industrialization was, however, a very different world from that of Marx. It was not only technology that had advanced. Man's attitude to nature and his conception of his place in the economic process had also radically changed. The neo-Marxist world was a world of self-consciousness. The Russian Revolution was the first great revolution in history to be deliberately planned and made. The English revolution received its name *ex post facto* not from the politicians who made it, but from the intellectuals who theorized about it. The men who brought about the French Revolution did not want to make a revolution; the Enlightenment was not in intention or in essence a revolutionary movement. The self-declared revolutionaries appeared only after the revolution had begun. The revolution of 1848 was a conscious imitation of the French Revolution: this is presumably why Namier called it a "revolution of the intellectuals." Its one positive achievement was to extend to some parts of Central Europe some of the results of the French Revolution. The Russian Revolution was also a revolution of intellectuals, but of intellectuals who not only sought to make a revolution, but to analyze and prepare the conditions in which it could be made. It is this element of self-consciousness that gives the Russian Revolution its unique place in modern history.

The nature of the change can be analyzed in terms of the differences between Marx and Lenin, of the transition from Marxism to Leninism. Although nearly everything that Lenin wrote can be supported by quotations from Marx, the differences between them were profound and significant. The differences are sometimes explained as being due to the transplantation of Marxism to Russian soil: Leninism is Marxism adapted to Russian needs and conditions. There is much truth in this view. But it is more fruitful to think of the differences as the product of a difference in time: Leninism is Marxism of the epoch no longer of objective and inexorable economic laws, but of the conscious ordering of economic and social processes for desired ends.

The growth of consciousness begins in the economic sphere. So long as the individual producer and the small entrepreneur predominated, nobody seemed to control the economy as a whole, and the illusion of impersonal laws and processes was preserved. Marx's world picture was firmly grounded in the past. He learned from Adam Smith that individual entrepreneurs and owners of capital were the essential agents of production in bourgeois society; and he followed Adam Smith and Hegel in believing that the activity of individuals, acting in their own interests, led in virtue of objective laws—the counterpart of the "hidden hand" or the "cunning of reason"—to results independent of their own will and purpose.

Although Marx rejected the providential harmony of interests, he did believe that ultimate harmony would result from the economically motivated action of individuals: this absolved him from any deliberate planning for the future. All economic thinkers from Adam Smith to Karl Marx believed in objective economic laws and in the validity of predictions derived from them. This was the essence of "classical economics." The change came when technological advance gave birth to large-scale capitalism. With the arrival of the mammoth manufacturing corporation and trading cartel, the economic scene was dominated by what, in a masterly understatement, was described as "imperfect competition." Economics had become instrumental—a matter not so much of scientific prediction as of conscious manipulation. Spontaneous price adjustment through the law of supply and demand was replaced by price regulation for specific economic ends. It was no longer possible to believe in a world governed by objective economic laws. The hidden hand that pulled the strings was barely concealed by the velvet glove of the great corporations.

These developments made quite unrealistic the old conception of the "night-watchman" state, mounting guard to ensure fair play between a host of small independent competitive producers. The socialists, though they appear to have invented the term "planning," were far behind German industrialists, bankers, and academic economists in their recognition of the direction and the inevitability of the processes at work. The first more or less fully planned national economy in modern times was the German economy at the height of World War I, with the British and French economies lagging not far behind. When the revolution proved victorious in Russia, the case for planning rested both on socialist precept and on the example of the German war economy. The first long-term plan to be formally adopted in Soviet Russia was the plan of electrification in 1920. The first "five-year plan of the national economy" was adopted for the period 1928–29 to 1932–33. Since then the USSR, except in the war period, has never been without its five-year plan; and five-year plans (or sometimes six- or seven-year plans) have proliferated around the world. If one wishes to assess the historical significance of the Russian Revolution in terms of the influence exercised by it, productivity, industrialization, and planning are key words.

The transition from economic *laissez faire* to economic management (whether management by corporations or management by the state), from spontaneity to planning, from the unconscious to the conscious, had corresponding repercussions on social policy. The *Communist Manifesto* had accused the bourgeoisie of "naked, shameless, direct, brutal exploitation" of the worker. Yet, so long as poverty or bad housing or unemployment could be attributed to the operation of objective economic laws, consciences were appeased by the argument that anything done to remedy these misfortunes would be done in defiance of economic laws and would therefore in the long run only make things worse. Once, however, everything that happened in the economy was seen as the result of a deliberate human decision, and therefore avoidable, the argument for positive action became irrefutable. Compassion for unavoidable suffering was replaced by indignation at unnecessary suffering. The concept of exploitation acquired a new dimension. For Marx exploitation was not an incidental abuse of which individuals were guilty, but an essential characteristic of the capitalist system, ineradicable so long as that system lasted. Exploitation now became a misdemeanor that could be prevented or mitigated by remedial action. A perceptive English conservative writer in the last volume of the Cambridge Modern History, published in 1910, diagnosed the change of climate and defined by implication the character of the next revolution:

> The belief in the possibility of social reform by conscious effort is the dominant current of the European mind; it has superseded the belief in liberty as the one panacea . . . Its currency in the present is as significant and as pregnant as the belief in the rights of man about the time of the French revolution.

The Russian Revolution of 1917 was the first revolution in history committed to establish social justice through economic controls organized by political action.

The reassertion, due to the advance of technology and economic organization, of the need for political action to direct and control the economy, was reflected in a change of emphasis in Marxist doctrine. Marx's nineteenth-century belief in the primacy of economics over politics had been cautiously qualified, after his death, by Engels' famous remarks about the mutual interaction of base and superstructure. The change fitted readily into Russian conditions. At the turn of the century, the controversy between the orthodox Russian Social Democrats and the Economists, who wanted to give priority to the economic demands of the workers, helped shape and influence early Bolshevik thinking and encouraged Lenin, in *What Is to Be Done?* and elsewhere, to stress the primary need for political action. The Russian trade unions were too feeble to play any role in Bolshevik schemes of revolution. The Russian Revolution was a political revolution in an economically unripe country. Lenin, in a remarkable *obiter dictum* of May 1918, observed that one half of socialism—the political half—had been realized in Russia, the other half—a planned economy—in Germany. Political action, the dictatorship of the proletariat, was needed to promote an economic result, the building of a socialist economy. The assumption that, once the political revolution had triumphed, the economic consequences would look after themselves was, however, falsified. After the political episode of war communism, the introduction of NEP in 1921 meant a partial reinstatement of economic forces; and throughout the 1920's the battle went on between the market principle as the guiding force of the economy and the principle of planning. In theory everyone accepted the assumption that it was preferable to achieve the socialist goal through economic rather than through administrative action. In practice market forces proved unable to carry the strain of intensive industrialization, and by 1929 had completely broken down. The use of direct and conscious political means to bring about economic ends has been since 1929 a persistent leitmofif of Soviet history, scarcely modified by the play-acting of so-called "market socialism."

The dichotomy between economics and politics characteristic of Western nineteenth-century thought was reflected in the familiar issue of society versus the state. When the Physiocrats in France sought to free trade from the frustrating restrictions of state power, when Adam Smith had his vision of a vast economic process working independently of the state for the greatest benefit of all, when Hegel set "bourgeois society" over against the state and made this dichotomy the foundation of his political theory, the distinction between economics, which meant bourgeois society, and politics, which meant the state, was clearly established. Bourgeois society was the realm of economic man. Throughout the nineteenth century the argument proceeded about the desirable and practicable relation between society and the state, but not about the reality of the distinction. In the English-speaking world, in particular, the opposition between society and the state, and the natural priority of society, became a fundamental category of political thinking. But Marx fully shared the same view: "Only political superstition [he wrote in *The Holy Family*] today supposes that social life must be held together by the state, whereas in reality the state is held together by social life."

In nineteenth-century Russia an embryonic bourgeois society was too weak to withstand the hypertrophy of state power; and after the revolution of 1917 a paradoxical situation developed. In Western countries the persistence of the nineteenth-century liberal democratic tradition continued to encourage a negative attitude toward the state and an eagerness to denounce "bureaucratic" abuses of its power, even while the constant encroachments of that power were recognized and accepted. In the USSR the Marxist tradition also embodied a deep-seated hostility to the state, enshrined in Lenin's *State and Revolution* and in widespread denunciations of "bureaucratism." But here the worldwide strengthening of the role of the state and its officials was reinforced by the Russian tradition of an absolute power, and, in a period where the state was everywhere extending its function and its authority, the critics of bureaucracy fought a losing battle. What is happening everywhere today is not so much the assertion of the primacy of the state, by way of reaction against the nineteenth-century assertion of the primacy of society, as a gradual obliteration of the distinction between them. The state becomes predominantly social and economic in character. Society identifies itself with the power of the state. The dividing line between economics and politics that was the essential feature of bourgeois society ceases to exist. These changes are strikingly illustrated by the way in which Soviet thought and practice has turned away from the Marxist attitude to the state.

Here we come to Lenin's most distinctive innovation in revolutionary theory and practice—the substitution of party for class as the motive force of revolution. Lenin once again found himself in verbal agreement, at any rate with the earlier Marx. The *Communist Manifesto* foresaw "the organization of the proletarians into a class, and consequently into a political party"; and Lenin, of course, constantly spoke of the class of which the party was the spearhead or vanguard. But the change of emphasis was marked and corresponded to the shift from the world of objective economic laws to the world of political action designed to mold and modify the economy. A class was a loose economic group without clear definition or organization or program. A party was a closely knit political organization defined by a common conscious purpose.

Both for Marx and for modern sociologists, class remains an elusive concept. A class, for Marx, was an economic and social group bound together by a common relation to the means of production. It had no legal existence and no institutions. Its common action was the unconscious product of innumerable spontaneous actions of individuals pursuing their particular interests. It was these unplanned and unconscious common actions that determined the policies of bourgeois governments and constituted "the dictatorship of the bourgeoisie." This view of class fitted into the *laissez-faire* conceptions of economic action and thought, and of the sharp dichotomy between society and state, that were dominant in the advanced countries throughout the nineteenth century and was scarcely comprehensible in any other context. The embarrassments of attempting to apply the concept of class to earlier historical periods or to other continents are notorious. The only class that really comes to life in Marx's writings is the bourgeoisie; nearly everything written by him about class in general relates, consciously or unconsciously, to the bourgeoisie in particular. The proletariat as a class was envisaged by Marx on the same model. Increasingly intolerable economic conditions would drive the workers to take action in defense of their interests. The workers of the world would spontaneously unite; and this common action would bring about the overthrow of the bourgeoisie and the dictatorship of the proletariat. Marx made it clear that this did not imply consciously planned action: "The question is not what this or that proletarian, or even the whole proletariat at the moment, *considers* as its aim. The question is, *what the proletariat is*, and what, consequent on that *being*, it will be compelled to do."

Marx knew well that only a small proportion of the proletariat was as yet class-conscious (though, living in England, he may have tended to exaggerate this proportion); and he recognized the existence of a *Lumpenproletariat*, an unorganized and unreliable mass of low-grade workers. At the other end of the scale, Engels noted the birth in England of what he called "a bourgeois working class," of a stratum of workers who showed signs of making common cause with the capitalists. But Marxists as a whole were not troubled by these threats to the international solidarity of the proletariat. It was assumed that time would correct these anomalies, and that at the right moment the workers would play their historical role, like the bourgeoisie before them, as a unified class. The contradictions of the capitalist system and the pressures engendered by it would sap its progressive and expansive capacities and provoke a revolt by an increasingly numerous and increasingly impoverished pro-letariat. This would be the last revolution, which would overthrow the last ruling class, the bourgeoisie, and usher in the classless society.

When Lenin surveyed the scene—and the Russian scene in particular —at the turn of the century, the prospect was obscure. In the countries of the Second International, although few signs had appeared of an imminent proletarian revolution, the organization of the workers had made giant strides; and everyone appeared to agree that this was an encouraging token of their growing solidarity and revolutionary poten-tial. In Russia, workers' organization was primitive, and revolutionary hopes seemed infinitely remote. Logically, Lenin set to work to create a party to galvanize the Russian workers into action; and in Russian con-ditions the work of a party on Russian soil was necessarily secret and conspiratorial. These preparations seemed in no sense a departure from the Marxist tradition or from the models created by the great Social Democratic parties of the West; they were merely another desperate Russian attempt to "catch up" with the West. What was bewildering and decisive was what happened in 1914 and 1917—the negative and positive sides of the same medal. The outbreak of war in 1914 struck a crucial and long-awaited blow at the nineteenth-century capitalist sys-tem and found the workers of the advanced countries rallying to its defense in their respective national uniforms; the traumatic effect on Lenin of this incredible experience is well known. The Revolution of 1917 put in power the first government professing allegiance to Marxism and dedicated to the overthrow of capitalism; and this occurred in an economically backward country with a small, undeveloped, and rela-tively unorganized proletariat. This reversal of the expected order of events confronted the Bolsheviks with the task of maintaining and de-fending the victorious Russian Revolution in a hostile environment with woefully inadequate resources, human and material, at their disposal.

This crisis evoked a response already familiar in Russian revolutionary history. For the best part of a century, the Russian intelligentsia—a group without precise counterpart elsewhere—had provided the leader-ship and the inspiration for a series of revolutionary movements. Lenin's *What Is to Be Done?*, published in 1902, was a plea for a party of pro-fessional revolutionaries under intellectual leadership to spearhead the proletarian revolution; and Trotsky, in a famous polemic two years later, accused the Bolshevik party of attempting "to *substitute* itself for the working class." When therefore the survival of the revolutionary regime was placed in jeopardy by the inadequacy, quantitative and qualitative, of the proletariat, the party, led and organized mainly by intellectuals, stepped into the gap. The Russian Revolution was made and saved not by a class, but by a party proclaiming itself to be the representative and vanguard of a class. It was a solution consonant with the Russian revolutionary tradition. But, more important, it was a solution that marked the distance traveled since the days of Marx. It belonged to an age in which effective force was thought of as the product, no longer of the spontaneous action of mass of individuals, but of conscious political planning.

The *Communist Manifesto* recognized the role of leadership exercised by Communists as the only fully class-conscious members of the proletariat and of proletarian parties. But it was a condition of the proletarian revolution that Communist consciousness should spread to a majority of the workers. Marx attributed to Blanqui, and rejected as heretical, a belief in the revolutionary seizure of power by a disciplined minority. Lenin's conception of the party as the vanguard of the class contained *elitist* elements absent from Marx's writings and was the product of a period when political writers were turning their attention more and more to the problem of *elites*. The party was to lead and inspire the mass of workers; its own membership was to remain small and select. It would, however, be an error to suppose that Lenin regarded the revolution as the work of a minority. The task of leading the masses was not, properly understood, a task of indoctrination, of creating a consciousness that was not there, but of evoking a latent consciousness; and this latent consciousness of the masses was an essential condition of revolution. Lenin emphatically did not believe in revolution from above. His fullest account of what created a revolutionary situation was given in the pamphlet *The Infantile Disease of "Leftism,"* which he prepared for the Second Congress of Comintern in 1920.

Only when the "lower layers" (nizy) are not willing to put up with the old, and the "top layers" (verkhi) are not able to go on in the old way, only then can the revolution triumph. In other words this truth can be expressed as follows: revolution is impossible without a general national crisis affecting both exploited and exploiters.

Some critics have found an element of political casuistry in this attempt to combine an elite leadership with mass consciousness. The embarrassed and sometimes contradictory utterances of the Bolshevik leaders about class contrast with their precise and rigid conceptions of party. After Lenin's death, Lenin's successors lacked the capacity or the patience to evoke that measure of mass consciousness and mass support that Lenin had had behind him in the period of the revolution and the Civil War and took the short cut—always the temptation that lies in wait for an elite—of imposing their will, by measures of increasingly naked force, on the mass of the population and on the mass of the party. Stalin's once famous short history of the Communist party called the collectivization of agriculture "a revolution from above, on the initiative of state power, with direct support from below"; and, although the phrase "revolution from above" has since been condemned as heretical, it was symptomatic of the Stalinist epoch.

These developments were due in part to the peculiarly exacting nature of the problems that the revolutionary regime in Russia had to face and in part to the peculair conditions of a country where primitive peasants formed more than 80 percent of the population, and the number of trained and politically conscious workers, comparable to the organized workers of the West, was infinitesimally small. But they were also, and more significantly, a product of the period. The French revolutionary slogan of equality was a necessary and effective protest against privilege in a highly stratified society. For Marx this problem, like every social problem, was a problem of the relations of production. Capitalist society was based on the exploitation of man by man; the principle of inequality was built into the capitalist division of labor. The Marxist utopia contemplated the breaking down of the differentiation between different forms of labor—notably between manual and intellectual work. Lenin's State and Revolution, with its vision of the work of administration performed by ordinary workers in rotation and the initial experiments of the Bolshevik revolution in workers' control in the factories were the last and most famous tributes to this conception. Their failure heralded the advent of a new epoch. In the mass industrial society of today, the old stratified society against which nineteenth-century radicals of every complexion protested may have disappeared or be obsolescent. But a new kind of stratification has entered into every branch of administration and production. The need for technological and administrative elites declares itself at every level—in government, in industrial organization, on the factory floor, and on the farm—and is likely to increase with the increasing complexity of administrative and productive processes. When Stalin shocked the world in June 1931 by denouncing egalitarianism or "levelling" (uravnilovka) and remarked that "every industry, every enterprise, every workshop" had its "leading groups," and later accused supporters of egalitarianism of "petty bourgeois views," he struck a shrewder blow than was realized by his critics at the time. But this does not dispose of the difficulty of reconciling the need for administrative and technological elites with the egalitarian aspirations that mass democracy inherited from the French Revolution. The fact that many of these elites would call themselves nonpolitical does not mean that they do not wield decisive political power. "Bureaucracy" and "technocracy" are not empty words. The autocrats of the past have been replaced by anonymous Kafka-like figures, whom we cannot control and often cannot identify. The need, with which Lenin wrestled and which Stalin contemptuously dismissed, of reconciling elite leadership with mass democracy has emerged as a key problem in the Soviet Union today. Nor is the problem, though spotlighted by the sequel of the Bolshevik revolution, of exclusive significance to a single country. It would be rash to dismiss the Russian experience as irrelevant to our own or to be unduly complacent about our own solutions.

The educational function of the elite was strongly emphasized by Lenin in *What Is to Be Done?* Marx, like Adam Smith and Hegel, believed that individuals conformed to, and were the agents or victims of, objective social and economic laws of which they were, nevertheless, unconscious. "The conceptions formed about the laws of production in the hands of the agents of production and circulation will differ widely from these real laws"; and, *a fortiori*, "The workers are enslaved to a power which is unknown to them." These conceptions, which did not correspond with reality, were what Marx called "ideology." Ideology for Marx was necessarily false consciousness—the false idea of their motives formed by men who were unconscious of the real laws governing their actions. Marx did not consider it his function to issue positive injunctions—much less to propound a new ideology. His aim was to unmask error and illusion. Marx, following Hegel, identified the historical process with the growth of consciousness, and the growth of consciousness with the growth of freedom. Thus the final revolution leading to the Marxist utopia of the classless society would also mean the ending of the rift between reality and ideology and the realization of true freedom and true consciousness.

Lenin remained in one respect rooted in the nineteenth century. While Lenin proclaimed the need to instruct and influence the masses, he continued to believe in instruction by rational persuasion or by force of experience. By the middle of the twentieth century this belief had lost much of its validity both in the Soviet Union and elsewhere. This was perhaps the fundamental difference that marked the transition from Lenin to Stalin. Lenin regarded persuasion or indoctrination as a rational process in the sense that it sought to implant a rational conviction in the minds of those to whom it was directed. Stalin regarded it as a rational process only in the sense that it was planned and conducted by a rational elite. Its aim was to induce large numbers of people to behave in a desired way. How to achieve this aim was a technical problem, which was the object of rational study. But the most effective means to employ in achieving this aim did not always, or not often, appeal to the reason. It would be erroneous to suppose that this transition from rational persuasion to technical indoctrination was peculiar to the USSR, or to any particular form of government. A similar development in Western democratic countries has often been attributed to the influence of commercial advertising, the practices of which, and sometimes the practitioners who apply them, are transferred from the commercial world to that of politics. The candidate is sold to the voter by the same means used to sell patent medicines or refrigerators. The enormous expansion of media of mass communication has clearly fostered this process. But deeper underlying causes have been at work. The professional, politically neutral, public relations consultant, setting out to create a favorable image for his clients and to mold opinion, by every known technical and psychological device, in the sense desired by them is a now familiar phenomenon, difficult to reconcile with the principles of Lincoln or Gladstone, but apparently inseparable from contemporary mass democracy. The future of democracy, in any part of the world, is today a disturbing problem. Here, as in other respects, the transition from liberal democracy to mass democracy in the Western world has reflected the experience of the Russian Revolution.

The problem has been further complicated by the course of revolution since 1917. Had the Russian Revolution been quickly followed—as the Bolsheviks at first expected—by revolutions in Western Europe, its priority would have been no more than a chronological anomaly in the total scheme. But when the cause of revolution, having proved barren in the West, flourished in the fertile soil of Asia, the shape of things to come changed radically. Much more was involved in the change than a mere geographical transposition.The Marxist revolution reached the peoples of Asia and Africa in its Leninist incarnation. Industrialization had to be pursued in these countries in conditions far closer to those experiences in the Soviet Union than to those envisaged by Marx. More significant still was the weakness, or sometimes total absence, of a bourgeoisie or of any of the concepts of a bourgeois society. In these countries, the bourgeois revolution, still unfinished in the Russia of 1917, had not even begun. Here the Russian problem was reproduced in an extreme form, and could be met only by the Leninist solution of a small intellectual elite to assume the leadership of the revolution. Many of these new leaders had received their education and made their first acquaintance with Marxism in Western countries or under Western auspices. But, in practice, local conditions made Marxism applicable only in its Leninist transformation. The absence of a bourgeoisie and of an established bourgeois tradition meant rejection, in practice if not in theory, of bourgeois liberal democracy and a return to Rousseauistic or Jacobin conceptions of democracy.

It is perhaps too early to attempt to place these ambiguous events in historical perspective. What is clear is that the Russian Revolution has triggered off a revolutionary movement of revolt against the nineteenth century capitalist order, in which the challenge is directed not against its exploitation of the industrial workers of the advanced countries, but against its exploitation of backward colonial peoples. It never occurred to Lenin, and was never admitted later, that a revolution under these auspices, although it might be directed against capitalism and have aims that could be described as socialist, had moved far away from the Marxist premises. The post-Leninist reorientation of the socialist revolution on neo-Marxist or non-Marxist lines implied that the final overthrow of capitalism would be the work not of its proletarian victims in the advanced countries (who had somehow become its allies), but of its colonial victims in the undeveloped countries, and that it would be the work not of an economic class, but of a political movement. The era of the French Revolution ended in 1917, and a new revolutionary epoch opened. Historians of the future may debate whether that epoch ended in 1949, when the Asian and African revolutions effectively began, or whether these events can be interpreted as a slightly unorthodox prolongation of the Russian Revolution. Such debates are not very fruitful, and it is unnecessary to anticipate them. But so long as man is interested to explore his past, nobody will doubt the credentials of the Russian Revolution as one of the great turning points in his history.

Comment by Henry L. Roberts on — "A Historical Turning Point" by E. H. Carr

I find Mr. Carr's paper particularly challenging and difficult, in the sense of my being able to comment appropriately upon it, in the fact that he has here quite properly dealt with some enormously complex and general historical categories. My comments cannot be those of one dealing with a specialized monograph. We are confronted not only with the Russian Revolution as one of the great turning points in history but also with our conception of the historical process itself and, more particularly, with developments in the world during the period since Marx's day. Confronted with this formidable challenge, I can do little more than record certain points of personal agreement and affirmation, points that Mr. Carr has expressed with his expected felicity, and also raise a few questions concerning which my sense of the historical process, especially in the Russian setting, may differ somewhat from his.

I should say at the outset that I read his paper with truly mixed feelings—of strong agreement with a number of his points combined with a feeling of malaise that there existed, too, some important differences that I should try, to the best of my ability, to set forth for further discussion, perhaps here or perhaps as a stimulus for subsequent examination.

To take first a point of agreement, I fervently agree with Mr. Carr's statement that it is the element of "self-consciousness that gives the Russian Revolution its unique place in modern history." Beyond that, I would agree that the shift from the mid-nineteenth century to the mid-twentieth of this sense of "consciousness" is one of the most profound trends of the times. The belief that man's fate is not the product either of mysterious, or of recognizable but ineluctable, laws but is subject to conscious, purposive action does, I think, constitute a major change over the last century or so.

In a rather different connection, I have come to notice what has struck me as three rather distinct stages one can similarly perceive with respect to illness on the personal plane—and I believe they bear some relation to the question of social ills. Early on, the outcome of illness in a person was thought of largely as a product of God's will—and the attitudes toward death, the funeral ceremonies attending death, the existence of a certain callousness toward suffering, were in correspondence. Then, it seems to me, there was a middle stage, when medicine was in its infancy but capable of some real and demonstrable achievements—much of the nineteenth century—a period when one gets a curiously mixed picture, as in so many Victorian novelists, of a combination of science struggling to win (often expressed in bathos) but with death defeating man's efforts not infrequently. A whole cluster of pictures and literary scenes comes to mind. More recently, I should say in the last three decades or so, in our "mythology," about illness and death, we have the sense that science—which I would here equate with consciousness—is seen to be on the brink of real mastery, with a corresponding handling of the awkward but continuing problem of the deceased.

I have brought up this rather morbid subject, not merely to confirm, as I trust it does, one facet of Mr. Carr's argument, but also to illustrate with reference to the ultimate human situation, man's mortality, what I feel to be certain problems in Mr. Carr's historical outlook.

Some serious problems are raised by two of the concepts that Mr. Carr has advanced in his paper: first, the identification of progress with the belief in history as a meaningful process; and second, his phrase "If one wishes to assess the historical significance of the Russian Revolution in terms of the influence exercised by it, productivity, industrialization, and planning are key words." I would rather doubt, myself, whether the influence, and I would include the influence in the underdeveloped parts of the world, of the Russian Revolution, the attraction it has exercised, is necessarily to be explained by its economic attractiveness and presumed effectiveness. The appeal of power and control—some very illiberal attractions—have also played a significant role in the spread of Leninism outward into the non-European world. I would also question, parenthetically, the necessity of history being a meaningful process only in company with the idea of progress; a clock can unwind in a "meaningful," if disastrous, way. But beyond this, both these concepts encounter, as they did in the case of the Russian Revolution, the ambiguity of the transition from "objective laws," or the "hidden hand," to self-consciousness and the belief in the efficacy of control and purposive design. These concepts run ultimately into the situation of man's condition as a mortal being, a subject that I have felt Marx did not deal with adequately, that Lenin felt but suppressed, and that Stalin simply overrode brutally.

Thus, I would entirely agree with Mr. Carr's observation, as a historical statement, that "Once, however, everything that happened in the economy was seen as the result of a deliberate human decision, and therefore avoidable, the argument for positive action became irrefutable. Compassion for unavoidable suffering was replaced by indignation at unnecessary suffering." From this follow the concepts of purposive action, planning, and of the elites required to carry out such action and planning. From this, too, follows the move away from the "idiocy of rural life," with existence subject to the cycles of the seasons, to the rational operations of mechanized production.

And yet, as I have intimated, this does not take care of the full dimensions of the human situation—nor would it have to except for the all-encompassing pretensions of the Marxist-Leninist tradition, which purport to provide a general answer to man's problems, not only in society, but as a being. Here I think there is a real peril in the impulse toward purposive action, conscious control: of trying to extend them to solve too many problems. There are social problems, questions of social justice, of a depth and complexity that may well lie beyond the scope of "political means," and the effort to solve these politically can too easily lead to the "administrative" means of a Stalin, a point that Mr. Carr has so well pointed out.

Next, I would entirely agree with Mr. Carr that the nineteenth-century picture of the distinction between *society* and the *state* has been in the course of obliteration, and not in Russia alone, and that parties and elites (as against classes) have increasingly taken over. This strikes me as a sound and important historical observation.

I would, however, query his statement that Leninism is not simply Marxism adapted to Russian needs and conditions, but also a product of times: "Leninism is Marxism of the epoch no longer of objective and inexorable economic laws, but of the conscious ordering of economic and social processes for desired ends." I would suggest that Leninism is a product not just of Russian conditions, or of the times, but of Lenin, because it seems to me it was his singular genius precisely to develop, or at least to advance and crystallize, formulas with respect to conscious-ness, party vanguard, and the like as solutions to these admittedly objective problems emerging at the end of the century that were by no means something everybody else was picking up as an answer. Otherwise, it is hard to explain the peculiar difficulty the European and the Russian Left, both before and after the revolution, had in grasping what Lenin meant and intended. I would stress the personal quality of Lenin's solutions. Leninism strikes me as a quite special, individual response to the problems of the time, which in turn, when ultimately formulated in his writings and realized, in a manner, in the revolution, did *then* certainly find sympathetic echoes throughout the world, and especially in the underdeveloped world. In a word, I would lay very great stress upon Lenin's particular answer to these undoubtedly general problems of the late nineteenth century.

It is the singularity of Lenin's solution that would lead me to query Mr. Carr's emphasis that Lenin's aim was not one of indoctrinating the masses, of creating a consciousness that was not there, "but of evoking a latent consciousness." Although Lenin did not operate in the crass, revolution-from-above manner that one finds defended in Stalin, I would not subscribe to the statement that Lenin's "profession to learn from the masses was never an empty pretense." Perhaps not, but I would read into it rather a willingness to ascertain "what the traffic will bear." I am skeptical of Mr. Carr's sense of Lenin's relation to the "latent conscious-ness of the masses," except as something to be aware of, something not to be destroyed by, a feel for the limits beyond which it is not safe to go, and also a recognition, as in 1917, of the point at which it is possible to move rapidly and violently. But to "learn" in the meaning of gaining intellectual insight and instruction—I am rather doubtful of this. It seems to me that Lenin's own inner vision was much too strong.

Finally, I would entirely agree with Mr. Carr, and this extends well beyond the Russian Revolution, that we *are* confronted with the vital problem of reconciling the need for administrative and technical elites (I assume that we do not in the future plan to do without IBM, penicillin, or jets), and the aspirations we have inherited from the French Revolution. I rather question that Lenin, although he may consciously have regarded persuasion as a rational process, actually achieved his impact at that level (elsewhere I have suggested that his real effectiveness lay on a sub-literary level of which he himself may not have been wholly aware), but he certainly wrote "seriously," and the problems do remain with us and are constantly expanding.

I can only conclude with the hope that the third term of the French revolutionary triad can be brought into its necessary position: *fraternité*, without which the other two are always in danger of becoming antagonists. And finally, that we can—possibly through technology itself— restore our social units and activities to a more human scale. For these problems I personally find that the Russian Revolution and its aftermath have little positive to teach us. But certainly the Russians, too, and I think there is mounting awareness of this, must cope with these basic issues, in their factories, on their farms, and in their whole society.

Discussion

Mr. Carr's paper raised a number of questions in Mr. Lipson's mind. With regard to the statement that a political revolution was necessary in Russia in order to make a system of large-scale rational planning possible, Mr. Lipson asked whether Mr. Carr meant that Lenin had thought so, or that he himself also shared this view.

Mr. Lipson took note of Mr. Carr's explanation that the differences between Marxism and Leninism were the result not only of the adaptation of Marxism to Russian conditions but also of changes in the climate of the time. He asked whether the problem posed by the holding of power was not another factor that ought to be taken into consideration.

Mr. Lipson went on to comment that Bolshevik doctrine placed a great deal of emphasis upon stages in history and periodization, but that little attention had been given to the problem of transition. Noting that Mr. Carr had mentioned that, thanks to urbanization, the peasantry in Russia were an obsolescent group, Mr. Lipson asserted that this raised the question of how the Bolsheviks had assisted the peasantry to obsolesce.

Finally, Mr. Lipson observed that Mr. Carr had dealt at length with some of the universal aspects of the Russian experience. Thus, Mr. Carr had indicated that the cost of progress was great in the Soviet Union, but that the price of large achievements was high throughout history, that the spread of planning and some of its associated problems and the problem of reconciling elite leadership and mass democracy were not unique to Soviet society, and that Stalinist indoctrination bore similarities to subliminal commercial advertising. Bearing this in mind, Mr. Lipson suggested that had time allowed, Mr. Carr might have discussed the differences in degree of the common aspects of the Soviet and non-Soviet experience.

Mr. Wolfe criticized the tendency to "take refuge in abstraction from difference" in general and the "convergence theory" in particular. The mere magnitude of modern political, social, and economic problems did necessitate great expansion in the role of contemporary national governments. However, this very fact made more crucial than ever before in history such questions as whether the state existed for society or society for the state; whether a galaxy of nonstate organizations in a given society exerted pressures upon the state or whether the party-state controlled all organizations; and finally, whether or not a people retained ultimate power to rebuke or remove officials. Although a primary goal of the imperial Russian state from Peter the Great to Count Witte was, like that of the Soviet state, rapid industrialization, the imperial Russian government, unlike the Soviet state, did not seek to become coexistent with society. He cited the key role of technology in increasing the power and control of the state in the twentieth century. Yet there was a distinct difference between contemporary advertising and persuasion by an all-powerful government. An understanding of exactly these kinds of differences between societies was what made it possible to defend that which was precious in one's own heritage.

Mr. Wolfe went on to discuss the reasons for Lenin's admiration of the German wartime economy. What most attracted Lenin was Germany's total organization for total war and the success with which Germany was able to organize scarcity. The fact that the Germans successfully conscripted men. money, and materials in conditions of artificially created scarcity, rejoiced Lenin's heart for it suggested the feasibility of a socialist revolution in a land of scarcity and backwardness.

Taking issue with Mr. Carr's assertion that Lenin's idea of a conspiratorial elite was a twentieth-century concept, Mr. Wolfe expressed the view that, on the contrary, the transformation of society by large masses was a twentieth-century idea, whereas conspiracy by an elite could be traced far back in history. This type of conspiracy was not something new and thus was not a model for the twentieth century.

In closing, Mr. Wolfe noted that his picture of Lenin differed considerably from that presented by Mr. Carr, adding that he was unable to forget the Lenin who advocated shooting of "mental capitalists" and shirking workers.

To Mr. Seton-Watson, the notion that Lenin evoked support whereas Stalin imposed his will did not seem altogether fair to Stalin. Lenin had played the role of shepherd in a time of total chaos and apocalyptic hopes and fears. He had led the Russian masses out of their dreadful despair; in these circumstances the intolerant doctrinaire aspects of Lenin's personality had not been strongly felt. On the other hand, the situation facing Stalin was relatively stable. Although prevailing conditions were bearable for a majority of the population, they were intolerable from the point of view of carrying out the socialist aims of the leaders. In such a situation Lenin might not have been less doctrinaire than Stalin.

Mr. Seton-Watson next referred to some of the results of the October Revolution. Many of the changes that had come about in Russian society under the Communists would have occurred in any event. Such was the case with urbanization. The really significant difference between pre- and post-revolutionary Russian society lay in the composition of its elites. The revolution had resulted in the replacement of the very heterogeneous tsarist elite with one significantly more homogeneous, confident, and capable. This homogeneity could be attributed to three elements: residual Marxism, Great Russian or Soviet chauvinism, and a type of esthetic, literary philistinism similar to Western European bourgeois attitudes in the late nineteenth century. The tradition of the tsarist intelligentsia had not disappeared, and in the present circumstances the intelligentsia either was against or desired a reinterpretation of residual Marxism and opposed esthetic philistinism, However, there was no sign that the Soviet intelligentsia rejected Great Russian chauvinism.

Mr. Carr had no quarrel with much of what had been said. Replying to Mr. Lipson's query regarding the Bolsheviks and the obsolescence of the peasantry, he commented that he had referred only to the obsolescence of the small individual peasant unit. He agreed with Mr. Lipson that in analyzing the differences between Marxism and Leninism it was important to take account of the fact that Marx did not hold power. However, the foundation of a good deal of Lenin's thinking had been laid before he held power so that comparisons were not altogether invalid.

Addressing himself to Mr. Wolfe, Mr. Carr asserted that he did not believe in the convergence theory, but that there were common factors influencing both Soviet civilization and our own that were worth pursuing. The vital question to be asked in regard to the differences between societies was less the position of the moment than the direction in which the societies were moving. Acknowledging that he disagreed with Mr. Wolfe about Lenin, Mr. Carr observed that Mr. Wolfe had had a life-long love-hate affair with Lenin and was capable of adopting almost any attitude toward him except one of cool detachment.

Mr. Carr expressed agreement with most of the comments made by Mr. Roberts. Referring to the suggestion made by Mr. Roberts that history did not always develop in a progressive manner, Mr. Carr stated that he did not share the view held by a large number of the conference participants that the Russian Revolution was a disaster. The French Revolution had been regarded negatively for more than fifty years and assuredly in twenty or fifty years, when positive achievements were balanced against shortcomings and failures, the place of the Russian Revolution in history would be as great as that of the French.

The Relationship of Bolshevism to Marxism
— Maximilien Rubel

My subject, the relationship of Bolshevism to Marxism, can be understood in three ways: (1) as the study of the relationship of Bolshevism and its various factions to the other Russian Marxist currents, for instance, to so-called Legal Marxism and Menshevism; (2) as the confrontation of Bolshevism with Western Marxism as it evolved from the intellectual heritage of the founders of "scientific socialism"; and (3) as the examination of the relationship of Bolshevism to "original Marxism," that is, to the teachings of Marx and Engels. Although I shall concentrate on this last topic, I will have to deal, at least in passing, with the two others as well.

Let me proceed to the central topic of my paper: Did the Bolsheviks, in 1917, act in accordance with the social theory of Marx and Engels? In order to answer this question, we must define Marx's theory and compare it, not only with Bolshevik Marxism as revealed mainly in Lenin's theoretical writings, but also with the policies followed by the Bolshevik party in 1917.

In my view, the theoretical position taken by Marx and Engels with respect to the social future of tsarist Russia is a perfect illustration of their general conception of historical evolution. For this reason, it may be useful to begin by recalling their attitudes toward Russia—attitudes strongly influenced by a burning hatred for autocracy, of which tsarist Russia was then the most advanced example, as compared to Prussian monarchism and French Bonapartism. Marx was almost pathological in his distrust of Russians, a fact that did not prevent Russian liberals and revolutionaries alike—as he later complained—from singling him out for special attention. During a quarter of a century, he had never ceased to warn about Russia's messianic striving for world domination. In 1856–57, he had published in the *Free Press*, the journal of the notorious russophobe David Urquhart, a historical study written in purest Urquhartian style. To sum up the essential elements of this work (*Revela-*

tions of the Diplomatic History of the Eighteenth Century), one could not do better than cite some of Marx's own comments on Russia's early and modern history:

The bloody mire of Mongolian slavery, not the rude glory of the Norman epoch, forms the cradle of Muscovy, and modern Russia is but a metamorphosis of Muscovy . . . It was Ivan Kalita, the Mongolian slave who elaborated all the cunning of the most abject slavery into a system, and his policy remained the policy of Ivan the Great as well as of Peter the Great! Peter the Great, the creator of modern Russia, divested the old Muscovite system of encroachment of its purely local character and generalized its purpose by exalting its object, which is unlimited power. Modern Russia's drive for Constantinople is but the continuation of the policy of the Rurik dynasty which transferred its capital from Novgorod to Kiev, in order to be nearer to Byzantium. Byzantium became the model of Russian religion and civilization, as well as the aim of Russia's everlasting aspirations.[1]

In a more positive vein, Marx saw the beginning of a social revolution in Russia, in the emancipation of the peasants after the Crimean War and in tsarist policy toward the peasantry in the 1860's. But it was only when he came into contact with Russian revolutionaries that his attention turned seriously toward Russian economic and social problems. Could this nation escape the destiny of Western Europe—capitalism, private ownership, the bourgeois state? Could it perform the fundamental task of creating a new society founded on communal property and cooperative production of the peasant commune (obshchina)?

Stimulated by the economist N. F. Danielson, who translated Capital, Marx immersed himself in the study of archaic and Asiatic forms of property holding. He concluded, in agreement with the populists, that under certain conditions the Russian peasant commune offered a possible starting point for the coming social and socialist revolution in Russia, enabling the country to bypass the capitalist stage of development. At Marx's urging, in 1875 Engels published an answer to the

1. "Revelations of the Diplomatic History of the Eighteenth Century," The Free Press, February 25, 1857. The work was published in 10 issues of the Free Press (from August 23, 1856, to April 1, 1857). Marx considered it as an "Introduction" to a larger study, as he declares in Herr Vogt. It must be noted that the "Revelations" of Marx so far have not been published in the Soviet Union; they are absent from the first and the second Russian editions of Marx's and Engels' Works, and they are not included in the German edition (Werke, Berlin, Dietz) published in East Germany. There is a French edition: K. Marx: La Russie et l'Europe, translation and introduction by B. P. Hepner (Paris, 1954). For a complete and commented inventory of Marx's and Engels' writings on Russia, see H. Krause, Marx und Engels und das zeitgenössische Russland (Giessen, 1958).

criticisms of P. Tkachev, a Russian follower of Auguste Blanqui. In an open letter to Engels, Tkachev had reproached him for his ignorance of Russian social conditions and revolutionary prospects. According to Tkachev, Russia was the chosen land of socialism because it had neither a bourgeoisie nor a proletariat, but was based, instead, on communal institutions such as the *artel* and the *mir*. There remained, however, the political problem: the overthrow of tsarism and the conquest of the state by a revolutionary minority. Here, very briefly, is Engel's answer: a social revolution is certainly brewing in Russia, but it will not have a socialist character because of the absence of a strong urban proletariat and of a powerful capitalist bourgeoisie; in other words, because of the insufficient development of Russia's productive forces, which requires both capital and a bourgeoisie. According to Engels, there was no doubt that the presence in Russia of communal forms of labor and property demonstrated the deep desire of the Russian people for a cooperative mode of production, but it did not in the least prove its messianic drive for socialism, nor its independence of Western movements. Although it was menaced by the progress of capitalism, the *mir* could become the basis of Russian socialism. It could help this function only on one condition: the previous triumph of the proletarian revolution in Western Europe. Until that time, Russian (and the European) revolutionaries must mobilize all the popular forces to overthrow tsarism.[2]

Two years later, Marx himself entered the discussion. In answering the Russian publicist N. K. Mikhailovskii, who had criticized his "philosophical system" for presenting capitalism as an inevitable stage that no country could avoid, Marx objected to this improper interpretation of his thought. He asserted that his explanation of Western capitalism did not by any means claim to be a "historical and philosophical theory of the general advance necessarily imposed upon all peoples." Historical understanding could be obtained only by an empirical and comprehensive analysis of the evidence and not by a particular and philosophical theory, "the supreme virtue of which is to be supra-historical." As for Russia's social future and the hopes that the populists placed in the rural commune, Marx expressed the following opinion, based, as he wrote, on a long study of Russian and other documentary materials:

If Russia continues to pursue the path she has followed since 1861, she will lose the finest chance ever offered by history to a people and

2. F. Engels, "Soziales aus Russland," *Der Volksstaat*, April 16, 1875. (*Werke*, XVIII, Berlin, 1962, pp. 556–567.) See R. Pipes, "Russian Marxism and Its Populist Background: The Late Nineteenth Century," *The Russian Review*, October 1960, pp. 316–337.

undergo all the fatal vicissitudes of a capitalist regime . . . If Russia is tending to become a capitalist nation after the example of the West-European countries—and during the last few years she has been taking a lot of trouble in this direction—she will not succeed without having first transformed a good part of her peasants into proletarians; and after that, once taken into the bosom of the capitalist regime, she will experience its pitiless laws like other profane peoples.[3]

Marx retained his sympathy for the populists' aspirations until his death, even after serious theoretical and political disagreements had developed between them and the first Russian Marxists. He spoke sarcastically of those Russian revolutionaries

who left Russia voluntarily and . . . in order to carry on propaganda in Russia—moved to Geneva! What a quid pro quo. These gentlemen are against all political-revolutionary action. Russia is to make a somer-sault into the anarchist-communist-atheist millennium! Meanwhile, they are preparing for this leap with the most tedious doctrinairism, whose so-called principles are being hawked about the street ever since the late Bakunin.[4]

It must be noted that this criticism by Marx was directed against the Russian socialists in Geneva grouped around the journal *Chernyi Peredel* (The Black Repartition) after the split of the *Narodnaia Volia* (People's Will). G. Plekhanov, P. B. Akselrod, and Vera Zasulich, who would soon become the "Nestors" of Russian Marxism, belonged to this group. Marx considered them "anarchists" and utopians, while admiring the terrorist faction of the *Narodnaia Volia* whose members were risking their lives in Russia against tsarism. Before her flight to Geneva, Vera Zasulich had made an attempt on the life of the prefect of Petersburg and had been acquitted by a jury. She joined the *Cherny-peredeltsy* in Geneva and from there, in February 1881, she addressed a letter to Marx in the name of her group in which she asked his opinion on a major political disagreement among the Russian revolutionaries for whom it was "a matter of life and death": either the rural commune would be able to develop in a socialist direction, in which case, the revolutionaries should devote all their forces to the emancipation and development of the commune; or, it was meant to disappear, leaving the Russian socialists to speculate on the swiftness of Russia's capitalist development and restricting their activity to propaganda

3. "Marx to the editorial board of the *Otechestvennye Zapiski*," November 1877. Marx-Engels, *Selected Correspondence* (Moscow, n.d.), pp. 376–379.

4. Marx to F. A. Sorge, November 5, 1880. *Selected Correspondence*, p. 405.

among the city workers. Vera Zasulich asserted that the second thesis was that of the "Marxists." But was it that of Marx himself?[5]

Marx tried to outline his views in several drafts that contain a tentative sociological analysis of the institution of the *obshchina*. Because he confined himself to a short answer, we may assume that his illness prevented him from completing his project—he was to die two years later. Rejecting the idea of the "historical necessity" of capitalism for all the countries of the world, Marx declared in his answer to Vera Zasulich:

The analysis developed in Capital *gives reasons neither in favor of nor against the vitality of the rural commune, but a special study I made on it, searching for the materials in the original sources, convinced me that this commune is the basis of Russia's social regeneration. But so that it may act as such, the deleterious influences which assault it on all sides should first be eliminated, and then the normal conditions of a spontaneous development should be guaranteed it.*[6]

With this interpretation, Marx decided against his Russian disciples; that is, against those Marxists who no longer accepted any alternative to the development of capitalism in Russia. Capitalism in Russia was for him only one possibility: socialism could develop either through the peasant commune or through capitalism. About a year after his answer to Vera Zasulich, he signed, with Engels, the preface to a Russian edition of the *Communist Manifesto* in which the following statement appears: "If the Russian revolution becomes the signal for a workers' revolution in the West, so that both revolutions complete each other, the present Russian commune property can become the starting point of a communist revolution."[7]

After Marx's death, Engels continued the discussion with the Russian populists and Marxists, without, however, risking a definite judgment that would have decided in favor of either group.

It is no exaggeration to say that the views expressed by Engels on the early intellectual manifestations of Russian Marxism are a thorough criticism (if not a condemnation) of the political strategy advocated by the first Russian followers of Marx as well as of all political tactics

5. Vera Zasulich to Marx, February 16, 1881. *Marx-Engels Archiv*, I (Frankfurt, 1926), pp. 316–317.

6. Marx's drafts and the definite answer have been published by D. Riazanov in *ibid.*, pp. 318–342.

7. Marx-Engels, Preface to the Russian edition of the *Communist Manifesto* (1882), *Selected Works*, I (Moscow, 1950), p. 24.

adopted after his death by the new generation of Russian Marxists. Given the relevance of Engels' statements and the almost complete silence with which contemporary Marxists treat it—particularly in the "socialist" countries—it is necessary to quote some essential passages.

The following is from a letter by H. A. Lopatin, written a few months after the death of Marx, in which Lopatin reports a conversation with Engels:

We spoke a lot about Russian affairs, of the probable course of our political and social rebirth . . . Engels also thinks (as do Marx and I) that the task of a revolutionary party or party of action in Russia at present is not to propagate a new socialist ideal or even to strive to carry out that ideal, which as yet is far from being completely elaborated, with the help of a provisional government consisting of our comrades. It must be to direct all efforts either: 1) to force the tsar to convoke a Zemskii Sobor *or, 2) by intimidating the tsar, and so forth, to stir up profound disturbances which would lead in another way to the convocation of a* Sobor *or something of the kind. He thinks, as I do, that such a* Sobor *would inevitably lead to a radical, not only political, but also social reorganization. He believes in the immense significance of the electoral period, in the sense of the far greater success of propaganda than all booklets and oral information. He considers a purely liberal constitution impossible without profound economic reorganization, and therefore is not afraid of the danger of that. He believes that in the* actual *conditions of the life of the people enough material for a reorganization of society on a new basis has accumulated. He naturally does not believe in the instant implementation of communism or anything like it, but only of what has already matured in the life and the soul of the people. He believes that the people will manage to find eloquent spokesmen to voice their needs, desires, etc. He believes that once this reorganization or revolution has started no force will be capable of stopping it. Hence, one thing alone is important: to shatter the fatal forces of inertia, to get the people and society to shake off their sluggishness and inertness and to bring about disturbances which will force the government and the people to set about the interior reorganization, stir the placid ocean of the people and arouse the attention and enthusiasm of the whole nation for a complete social upheaval. The results will come of themselves, whatever results are possible, desirable and realizable for the epoch in question. All this is drastically summarized, but I cannot go into details now. And then perhaps you will not like it all. That is why I am giving you word for word other opinions of Engels' which are very flattering for the Russian revolutionary party: Here they are: "All depends now on what is done in the immediate future in Petersburg, on which are now fixed the eyes of all thinking, far-sighted and penetrating people in the whole of Europe." "Russia is the France of the present century. To her belongs rightfully and lawfully the revolutionary initiative of a new social reorganization."*[8]

In February 1885, Vera Zasulich addressed a letter to Engels asking him his opinion of Plekhanov's book *Nashi Raznoglasia* (Our Differences). In his answer Engels declared that he had read only the first sixty pages of the book, but that this was enough to acquaint him "more or less with the differences in question." Then he wrote:

First of all I repeat to you that I am proud to know that there is a party among the youth of Russia which frankly and without equivocation accepts the great economic and historical theories of Marx and has decisively broken with all the anarchist and more or less Slavophile traditions of its predecessors. And Marx himself would have been equally proud of this had he lived a little longer. It is an advance which will be of great importance for the revolutionary development of Russia. To me the historical theory of Marx is the fundamental condition of all reasoned *and* consistent *revolutionary tactics; to discover these tactics one has only to apply the theory to the economic and political conditions of the country in question . . .*

What I know or believe I know about the situation in Russia makes me think that the Russians are approaching their 1789. The revolution must break out there in a limited period of time; it may break out any day. In these circumstances the country is like a charged mine which only needs a match to be applied to it. Especially since March 13.[9] *This is one of the exceptional cases where it is possible for a handful of people to* make *a revolution, i.e., with one little push to cause a whole system, which (to use a metaphor of Plekhanov's) is in more than labile equilibrium, to come crashing down, and thus by an action in itself insignificant to release explosive forces that afterwards become uncontrollable. Well now, if ever Blanquism—the fantastic idea of overturning an entire society by the action of a small conspiracy—had a certain* raison d'être, *that is certainly so now in Petersburg. Once the spark has been put to the powder, once the forces have been released and national energy has been transformed from potential into kinetic (another favorite image of Plekhanov's and a very good one)—the people who laid the spark to the mine will be swept away by the explosion, which will be a thousand times as strong as they themselves . . . Suppose the people imagine they can seize power, what does it matter? Provided they make the whole which will shatter the dyke, the flood itself will soon rob them of their illusions. But if by chance these illusions resulted in giving*

8. H. A. Lopatin, from a letter to N. M. Oshanina, September 20, 1883. First published in *Fundamentals of Theoretical Socialism, and Their Application to Russia,* I (Geneva, March 1893). Translated from the Russian in *Reminiscences of Marx and Engels* (Moscow, n.d.), pp. 204–205.

9. On March 1 (13), 1881, occurred the assassination of Alexander II.

them a superior force of will, why complain of that? People who boast that they made a revolution always see the day after that they had no idea what they were doing, that the revolution made does not in the least resemble the one they would have liked to make . . . To me the important thing is that the impulse in Russia should be given, that the revolution should break out. Whether this faction or that faction gives the signal, whether it happens under this flag or that matters little to me. If it were a palace conspiracy it would be swept away tomorrow. There where the situation is so strained, where the revolutionary elements have accumulated to such a degree, where the economic conditions of the enormous mass of the people become daily more impossible . . . where all these contradictions are violently held in check by an unexampled despotism . . . there, when 1789 has once been launched, 1793 will not be long in following.[10]

In a conversation with Kautsky, Engels once more commented on Plekhanov's writing. We quote from a letter of Kautsky to Bernstein:

Engels is presently reading Plekhanov's latest brochure. He finds it very interesting, by and large theoretically correct, and in some passages really excellent. Coming from Engels this, certainly, is high praise. But much as he likes the pamphlet with regard to theory *he finds its* tactical *remarks—I do not wish to say false but not very well to the point. What matters today in Russia Engels says, is not a program but the* Revolution. *If it comes to that, however, the liberals, and not the socialists, will come to power. Only if under the impact of this revolution the socialist revolution will be victorious in Western Europe, this victory can have an effect on Russia and help to bring socialism to the top. Those people who will make the Revolution in Russia will not go on leading it. Their theoretical vision is not as important as their energy. Today one has to unite in Russia the energetic elements for [common] action, regardless of differences in their program, and Plekhanov is wrong in attacking the only people who right now are doing something in Russia, the Narodnaia volia, even if his position toward them is theoretically correct. What matters at this time in Russia is the fall of tsarism and the unification of all elements for this purpose, and Engels will always place himself at the side of those who act accordingly, even though their programs are incomplete.*[11]

Of particular interest are the ideas expressed by Engels on Russia's capitalistic future in his letters to Danielson who firmly retained his populist hopes in the future of the *obshchina*. Here are excerpts from Engels' letters mentioned above:

10. Engels to V. Zasulich, April 23, 1885. *Selected Correspondence*, pp. 458–461.
11. Karl Kautsky to Eduard Bernstein, June 30, 1885. E. Bernstein, *Die Briefe von F. Engels an E. Bernstein (Mit Briefen von K. Kautsky an ebendenselben)* (Berlin, 1925), pp. 172–173.

[*June 18, 1892*]: *"Could Russia, in the year 1890, have existed and held its own in the world, as a purely agricultural country, living upon the export of her corn and buying foreign industrial products with it? And there, I believe, we can safely reply no. A nation of 100 millions that play an important part in the history of the world, could not, under the present economic and industrial conditions, continue in the state in which Russia was up to the Crimean War . . . All governments, be they ever so absolute, are* en dernier lieu *but the executors of the economic necessities of the national situation. They may do this in various ways, good, bad, and indifferent; they may accelerate or retard the economic development and its political and juridical consequences but in the long run they must follow it. Whether the means by which the industrial revolution has been carried out in Russia, have been the best for the purpose, is a question by itself which it would lead too far to discuss. For my purpose it is sufficient if I can prove that this industrial revolution, in itself, was unavoidable."*

[*October 17, 1893*]: *"In the Berlin* Sozial-Politisches Centralblatt *a Mr. P. Struve has a long article on your book. I must agree with him in this one point, that for me, too, the present capitalistic phase of development in Russia appears an unavoidable consequence of the historical conditions as created by the Crimean War, the way in which the change of 1861 in agrarian conditions was accomplished, and the political stagnation in Europe generally. Where he is decidedly wrong, is in comparing the present state of Russia with that of the United States, in order to refute what he calls your pessimistic views of the future. He says the evil consequences of modern capitalism in Russia will be as easily overcome as they are in the United States. There he quite forgets that the United States are modern, bourgeois, from the very origin . . . Whereas in Russia we have a ground work of a primitive communistic character, a pre-civilization* Gentilgesellschaft, *crumbling ruins, it is true . . . the material upon which the capitalistic revolution (for it is a real social revolution) acts and operates . . . Therefore it stands to reason that the change in Russia must be far more violent, far more incisive, and accompanied by immensely greater sufferings than it can be in America. However, there is no reason to be pessimistic about such a prospect; there is no great historical evil without a compensating historical progress. Only the* modus operandi *is changed.* Que les destinées s'accomplissent![12]

Whatever ambiguity is contained in Marx's and Engels' sociological and political teachings, the intellectual legacy they transmitted to the Russian disciples—whether populist or Marxist—was quite unequivocal. They called the populists' attention to the fact that the survival and

12. Engels to N. F. Danielson, June 18, 1892; October 17, 1893. *Selected Correspondence*, pp. 527–529, 545–547.

the expansion of the rural commune depended both on the fall of tsarism and on the proletarian revolution in the West. They advised the Russian Marxists to abandon all ideological sectarianism and to concentrate their activity on a single goal: the mustering of all dynamic elements of Russian society toward the overthrow of tsarist despotism. In a conversation with a Russian visitor, A. Voden, Engels recalled Marx's answer to Mikhailovskii and expressed his hope that the achievement of power by Social Democracy in the West would coincide with the political and agrarian revolution in Russia. To the same visitor, he expressed his discontent with those Marxists, Russian and others, who were bent on selecting quotations from Marx's or from his own writings instead of thinking as Marx would have thought in their place.[13]

Paradoxical as it may seem, Marx's and Engels' political legacy to their Russian disciples was to abstain from being "Marxists" and to act within the framework of the common struggle of all the revolutionary forces aimed at the overthrow of tsarism. The whole past of the Russian people condemned the latter, even after the fall of tsarist autocracy, to undergo a long period of material transformation and political education. Marx's and Engels' own political careers were the best illustration of a social theory that defined the spontaneous activity (*Selbsttätigkeit*) of the modern working classes as the main force for bringing about a radical change in human relations and institutions. This theory declared axiomatically that the new political elites, which had had a preponderant role in revolutions occurring in the pre-capitalist class societies, would play but a secondary role in the revolutionary movements of modern times. Socialist consciousness acquired through the revolutionary struggle against the ruling class in the framework of bourgeois-liberal institutions was the absolute prerequisite of the conquest of political power in highly developed capitalist countries. "Scientific socialism" means, on the theoretical level, the use of a specific sociological method defined as "materialist." This method is characterized by two processes: (1) the choice of material standards for defining various types of society; (2) the adoption of a determinist hypothesis in the analysis of social phenomena.

A society is typologically and structurally defined by the way in which its members, strata, and classes determine their material life. In turn, the way of life and the mode of production of societies depend on the

13. A. Voden, "Talks with Engels." *Reminiscences of Marx and Engels*, pp. 325–333. From A. Voden's article: "At the dawn of 'Legal Marxism,'" in *Letopisi Marksizma*, no. 4 (1927). See also Engels to Gurvitch, May 27, 1893, quoted in G. Mayer, *Friedrich Engels*, II (The Hague, 1934), p. 426.

productive forces at their disposal. The relations between the individuals in a given society can be derived from their position in the process of production. These relations take on the hierarchical form of ruling classes and ruled classes, the former living on the fruits of the latter's labor. Class domination is embodied in an apparatus of physical, intellectual, and moral constraint destined to maintain the whole society in a dynamic equilibrium that allows and fosters the development of social wealth at the expense of the class of direct producers. This sociological notion of human life and history implies a particular approach toward the scientific explanation of collective behavior. It leaves an important place for all forms of material determinism that contribute to the molding of types of societies and at the same time recognizes men's conscious action. Far from underestimating the interference of chance in the destiny of societies, it pays sincere tribute to the collective efforts of individuals struggling to overcome the social restraints and their alienating effects.

The question whether the Bolsheviks were "properly" Marxist or whether Bolshevism is an aberration of Marxism must be approached on two levels: Did the Bolsheviks conceive of the coming Russian Revolution as a bourgeois revolution? and Did they conduct their political activities in accordance with the advice given by Marx and Engels to their Russian followers? Paradoxical as it may seem, the first question can be answered affirmatively in the sense that not only before 1917, but even after their seizure of power, the Bolsheviks thought and acted as bourgeois revolutionaries. To use a Marxist phrase, they were "objectively" bourgeois. This term applies as well to the other faction of Russian Social Democracy, the Mensheviks. Although the Russian Marxists venerated the proletariat (being at the same time distrustful of spontaneous "economic" actions by Russian factory workers), they instinctively worshipped capitalism, emphasizing dogmatically the liberating vocation of the capitalist mode of production. In this profoundly ambivalent attitude, one can find the source of Russian Marxism as the political ideology that received full expression in the Bolshevik capture of political power in October 1917.[14]

14. See the excellent remarks on the first Russian followers of Marx in Dietrich Geyer, *Lenin in der Russischen Sozialdemokratie. Die Arbeiterbewegung im Zarenreich als Organisationsproblem der revolutionären Intelligenz 1890–1903* (Köln-Graz, 1962), pp. 16–35. Although he admits that the perspective of the Russian revolution constituted the common basis between Mensheviks and Bolsheviks, M. Fainsod argues that the "kinship was more illusory than real." *How Russia Is Ruled*

At the International Socialist Congress of 1889, speaking in the name of the Russian socialists, Plekhanov emphatically pronounced the credo of Russian Marxism: "The revolutionary movement in Russia will triumph as a worker's movement or it will not triumph at all." The hegemony of the Russian proletariat was the common faith of all the Marxist groups that consequently considered with evident enthusiasm what P. Struve called the "historical mission of capitalism" in Russia. They unanimously criticized N. F. Danielson, who believed himself to be loyal to Marx's teachings in rejecting the dogma of the "historical necessity" of capitalism for his country. One might even use Marx's concept of "fetishism" to qualify this double worship of capitalism as a necessary prerequisite of socialism on the one hand, and of the working class as the guiding force of all the democratic and liberal tendencies the tsarist Russia on the other.

The outcome of the February Revolution tested the solidity of this common link between these hostile comrades. Although convinced that Russia was not ripe for a socialist economy and must, therefore, undergo the first stages of capitalist accumulation, both Marxist parties were prepared to participate in the political direction and control of the country, in spite of the fact that the peasants constituted the overwhelming majority of the population. From the beginning, both parties had a charismatic conception of the role of the intellectual elite in the europeanization of Russia. We can see this clearly in the origins of the Russian Social Democratic Party and in the hesitations of its founders to call it a "Workers' Party." They could hardly do otherwise as there were virtually no workers present.[15]

The initiative came mainly from the intellectuals who frequently expressed dissatisfaction with the purely "economic" battles of the Russian workers. In most of the political literature of the nineties, the Russian Marxists stressed the inability of the revered Russian proletariat to see further than their immediate interests, and, if Struve drew one set of conclusions from this, becoming a militant liberal, Lenin drew another. In the footsteps of Plekhanov and Akselrod (themselves disciples of Kautsky), he conceived of the party as an elite that embodied a crucial

---

(Cambridge, Mass., 1965), p. 37. The origins of Russian Marxism have been recently brought into better light owing to a number of pertinent historical studies such as: L. H. Haimson, *The Russian Marxists and the Origins of Bolshevism* (Cambridge, Mass., 1955); J. L. H. Keep, *The Rise of Social Democracy in Russia* (Oxford, 1963); and R. Pipes, *Social Democracy and the St. Petersburg Labor Movement 1885–1897* (Cambridge, Mass., 1963).

15. D. Geyer, *Lenin in der Russischen Sozialdemokratie*, pp. 105–107.

intellectual or scientific mission: to inspire the workers with a "socialist consciousness." In the last analysis, the devotion to the proletariat became for the "scientific socialists" a narcissistic adoration, and the hegemony of the proletariat became the hegemony—at first intellectual and afterwards political—of the professional revolutionaries. This explains why Akselrod was willing to offer the democrats and liberals a provisional alliance to overthrow the autocracy without disapproving of Lenin's preference for conspiratorial methods and Jacobin centralization of authority.[16]

Marx had foreseen that, once the alternative of a peasant communal regeneration was lost, Russia would have to experience a bourgeois-capitalist revolution, and that whoever was in power during the transitional period would take the required measures to achieve rapid industrial growth. By playing the role of the deposed bourgeois class, the Bolsheviks and the other Marxist and non-Marxist groups allied with them acted objectively according to the "law of the economic movement of bourgeois society." One could, therefore, say they were "Marxists" in the same way that they were "Newtonians," by moving and falling in accord with the law of gravity. Marx was prophetic when he exposed for Mikhailovskii the alternatives mentioned above. But what he could not foresee was that Russia's transformation into a state-capitalist nation would be accomplished some forty years later under the banner of "Marxism." Yet, his Russian followers had less difficulty in learning from his work the methods for building an economy based on the imminent laws of surplus value—that is to say, on capital and wage labor—than they had in learning how to build socialism. But, if they could not find in *Capital* "recipes for the kitchens of the future," they could not ignore that "capital comes to the world sweating blood and filth from all its pores."[17] It was this latter lesson that they put to work: "The political genius of Lenin consisted in giving necessity the aspect of a choice."[18] Without having the same political genius, Stalin applied the concept with the ultimate degree of thoroughness.

16. *Ibid.*, pp. 287–317.
17. *Capital*, book I, chap. XXXI.
18. R. Pipes, "Max Weber et la Russie," II, *Le Contrat social*, May 1960, p. 152. Analyzing Weber's study *Zur Lage der bürgerlichen Demokratie* (1906), Mr. Pipes comments on his pessimism with regard to the future of liberalism in Russia. Weber went so far as to doubt whether advanced capitalism in the Western countries had any genuine affinity with democracy and liberty. Likewise, he was skeptical of the efforts of "romantic populists" who glorified on the peasant commune in Russia, arguing that on the contrary, the Russian peasantry and the Russian petty bourgeoisie were leaning towards an authoritarian regime. *Ibid.*, I, March 1960, p. 76.

It is well known that from the moment he returned to Russia after the Revolution of February, Lenin bitterly fought to impose his views on his own party. "A substantial minority," writes E. H. Carr, "if not a majority, of the party seems clearly to have clung to the view, fervently held by Mensheviks and Social Revolutionaries alike, that the revolution had not yet fully completed its bourgeois stage and was consequently still unripe for its transition to socialism. On this view, the October revolution was merely a continuation and deepening of the February revolution, and did not differ from it in principle or purpose."[19] In other words, in seizing power, Lenin, his party, and allies only undertook to give body to the promises expressed by his predecessors who proved to be incapable of implementing them. The first instance was achievement of the emancipation of the peasantry: the main gainers of the revolution. It was this accomplishment that from the start impressed on the revolution its bourgeois character, as Rosa Luxemburg rightly noted. "If one employs the criteria of Western revolutions," Lenin said in May 1918, "we are now approximately at the level attained in 1793 and 1870."[20] Albert Mathiez, whose *History of the French Revolution* is tantamount to an apology of Jacobinism, draws a very impressive parallel between Bolshevism and Jacobinism and gives his argument the following conclusion.

History never repeats itself exactly. But the resemblances that our analysis has shown to exist between the two great crises of 1793 and 1917 are neither superficial nor casual. The Russian revolutionaries copy their French prototypes voluntarily and knowingly. They are animated by the same spirit . . . Times differ; civilization has marched on for a century and a quarter. But because of its backwardness, Russia resembles illiterate, agricultural eighteenth-century France more than is generally believed. It will be interesting to observe, and rich material for reflection, if the rhythm of the two revolutions follows the same beat until the end.[21]

19. E. H. Carr, *The Bolshevik Revolution*, I (Penguin Books, 1966), p. 118. In 1918, the Left Communists were to denounce Lenin's policy as petty bourgeois and capable of leading to a restoration of a capitalist economy.
20. "Immediate Tasks of the Soviet Government" article published in *Pravda*, April, 1918, V. I. Lenin, *Collected Works*, XXVII (London, 1965), p. 245. On Lenin's intellectual development after the October Revolution, see A. G. Meyer, *Leninism* (Cambridge, 1957), pp. 187–216.
21. Albert Mathiez, *Le Bolchevisme et le Jacobinisme* (Paris 1920), p. 24. English translation by T. Clement in *Dissent*, vol. II, no. 1 (1955), pp. 77–86. The Russian Revolution has often been compared with the French Revolution, particularly by Western Marxists—not to speak of Lenin himself. To mention only one authoritative voice: Karl Kautsky, who first emphasized the Jacobin and then,

Fifty years have passed since the revolution, and it does not seem presumptuous to pursue the parallel drawn by Mathiez to our present time.

At first, Lenin firmly believed that the bourgeois revolution had ended in April 1917 and that the "socialist revolution," which, in his view, had begun on October 25, 1917, was the most pressing task of the political leaders, the members of the Communist party, and of all the conscious representatives of the laboring masses. Later, he was more cautious in his diagnosis and confessed that he had "no illusions about the fact that we have only begun the transitional period of socialism."[22] He was also well aware that in Marx's social theory this "transitional period" is called *capitalism*. All the virtues of the capitalist system were proposed as models to the builders of socialism. And Lenin was forced to recall the rules of accurate bookkeeping, saving, and good discipline that "proletarian revolutionaries" had formerly scorned with justification. The realization of these administrative procedures, he declared, is "necessary and sufficient for the triumph of socialism." Since "the Russian is a poor worker," he must learn Taylorism, which has its virtue in the transition period from capitalism to socialism, its barbarous vices being those of bourgeois exploitation.[23]

As readers of *Capital*, the Russian Social Democrats were aware that the first task of the bourgeois revolution is the rapid accumulation of capital. As for the Bolsheviks, they set out to achieve this accumulation from the moment they assumed power. In addition, once the period of "War Communism" had ended, strict labor discipline, dictatorial factory management, high income differentials, and so on, were introduced into Russian society with the aim of attaining the level of development of a capitalist economy. Lenin was particularly skillful in masking the

---

the beginning of the Stalinist era, the Bonapartist features of the Bolshevik regime. See *Von der Diktatur zur Staatsklaverei* (1921); *Die Internationale und Sowjetrussland* (1926); *Der Bolschewismus in der Sackgasse* (1930). Kautsky's argumentation —particularly in his last writing—incited the criticisms of Mensheviks like R. Abramovich, who rejected the Bonapartist parallel. See "Revolution und Konterrevolution. Das neue Kautsky-Buch über Russland," *Die Gesellschaft*, no. 12 (1930), pp. 532–541. (*"Um wirklicher Bonapartismus zu werden, fehlt dem Bolschewismus der kapitalistische Klasseninhalt,"* p. 537). Among the Bolsheviks themselves the above-mentioned parallel has found a competent spokesman in the person of L. D. Trotsky, who restricted himself to denouncing the Bonapartist character of Stalin's dictatorship.

22. "Immediate Tasks.", p. 245.

23. *Ibid.*, p. 259. In a very "un-Marxist" way Lenin restricted the "socialist" character of the Soviet power in making distinctions between political criterion and the economic one, considering the first a guarantee of the socialist character of the revolution.

316 – Maximilien Rubel

economic program of his party by giving its components socialist labels. Hence, what is in fact—on its own Marxist analysis—the transition to highly developed capitalism became in his terms the transition to socialism. In defending the authority given to factory managers, Lenin said: "The irrefutable experience of history proves that . . . the dictatorship of revolutionary classes has often been expressed, supported, and carried out by the dictatorship of individual persons." Just as in capitalist economy, heavy industry demands the "subordination of thousands of people to the will of a single individual." In this way, that which Lenin believed to be true of capitalism was grafted onto the practice of Russian "communism" because the "leaps from capitalism to socialism are so long."[24]

If the historical function of Bolshevism was the accomplishment of industrialization, and, therefore, the proletarianization of Russia, then what is called "Stalinism" simply brought this work to its logical conclusion. Lenin created the necessary apparatus and gave it its goals; Stalin used this apparatus most rationally in achieving them. He became the person who embodied the "dictatorship of the revolutionary classes," but in a way and to a degree that Lenin and the older Bolsheviks were, in the last analysis, too human to foresee. The much heralded transition to socialism in Russia is, in fact, the transition to capitalism in an

24. *Ibid.*, pp. 267–268, 273. When the "Left Communist" group reproached Lenin for his "capitulation to the bourgeoisie and its servile petty-bourgeois intelligentsia" and for "making a bug-bear of state capitalism" a "most determined policy of socialization," Lenin responded that his critics "reveal their petty-bourgeois character" precisely in not understanding "the nature of the *transition* from capitalism to socialism." Then Lenin explained the word "transition": Russian economy contains elements "of both capitalism and socialism," namely a patriarchal, self-sufficing peasant economy, small commodity production, private capitalism, state capitalism, and, finally, socialist elements. The Soviet power has nothing to fear from state capitalism because in the Soviet state "the power of the workers and the poor is assured." Thus, the Bolsheviks' task is to spare no effort in copying the state capitalism of the Germans and "not to shrink from adopting *dictatorial* methods to hasten the copying of it." "Our task is to do this even more thoroughly than Peter hastened the copying of Western culture by barbarian Russia, and he did not hesitate to use barbarous methods in fighting against barbarism." Although petty-bourgeois capitalism prevails in Russia, the road to large-scale capitalism leads equally to socialism "through one and the same intermediary station called 'national accounting and control of production and distribution' " (from " 'Left-wing' childishness and petty-bourgeois mentality," article published in *Pravda*, May 9–11, 1918) *Collected Works*, XXVII, pp. 323–354. See L. Schapiro, *The Origins of the Communist Autocracy* (Cambridge, Mass., 1955), pp. 130–146. Finally, it was not the Bolshevik party but Lenin in person, or so he seemed to believe, who embodied the will of the proletariat or, as Georg Lukacs put it, he was "das zur sichtbaren Gestalt gewordene Klassenbewusstsein des Proletariats." *Lenin* (Berlin, 1962), p. 25.

agrarian, pre-industrial country. If it was carried out by party-managers, coming mainly from the milieu of the Russian bourgeois intelligentsia, who considered themselves Marxists, it was because the latter knew what was required for such a transition. This is the starting point from which any concrete analysis of the Russian Revolution and of Russian history since 1917 must proceed.[25]

If we accept Marx's approach to the process of economic development, we may say that the function of Lenin, his party, and the bureaucracy was to replace the Russian bourgeoisie, which had to assume the role of creating the material prerequisites of future socialism, that is, a capitalist economy. The Bolsheviks presented their bourgeois-Jacobin role in a socialist guise by calling the autocracy of the Bolshevik party the "dictatorship of the proletariat," because capital requires ideological means to hide its economic oppression. In Russia, Lenin, his party, and the bureaucracy played the part taken everywhere else by the middle class—and they played it very effectively, too.

In speaking of the Bolsheviks carrying through a "bourgeois" revolution, we mean to emphasize that the necessary framework in which to place their political and economic activities is not a socialist one but a capitalist one. They have only done for Russia what Marx rightly says was done, in perhaps a less organized way, by capitalists in the early years of their domination in all advanced countries. This is particularly true under Stalin's regime in its imitation of highly concentrated Western capitalism. By telescoping both stages of capitalist development as Marx had described them in the three volumes of *Capital*, they jumped quickly from the stage of so-called primitive accumulation to that of enlarged reproduction of capital. This alleged socialist economy of Soviet Russia appears, in fact, as the type of production and distribution process that Marx, particularly in the third book of *Capital*, treats as *managerial* capitalism, a form of private capitalism that arises from the expropriation of small-scale enterprises and their absorption by oligopolistic and monopolistic corporations. Managerial capitalism is characterized by Marx as the result of the divorce between the economic function of the capitalist within the production process and his social position as the owner of the means of production. In all forms of capitalism, the producer (worker) has no control over the means of production, but, on the contrary, participates in the economic process as a mere executant of incontestable orders. The essential relation is one between capital

25. For an attempt of such analysis see Maximilien Rubel, "La croissance du capital en U.R.S.S.," *Economie appliquée*, X (1957), pp. 363–408, and A. Erlich, *The Soviet Industrialization Debate, 1924–1928* (Cambridge, Mass., 1960).

and labor as economic concepts and only secondarily between individual capitalists and individual workers.

It is in this light that capitalism can be said to exist in a society without capitalists, or, in terms of a sociological analysis of power relations, in a society where the functions of capitalists in the traditional sense are fulfilled by the "agents" or "managers" of capital. The basic relation brings together capital, the exploiting capacity of the means of production, and the labor so exploited. Whether the men in control of the means of production are capitalists or managers, as in the West, or Communist state bureaucrats and managers, as in the East, is of secondary importance. On one occasion, Marx even spoke of the possibility of all the means of production in a country being owned by one capitalist or a group of capitalists who could hire managers to do the work of managing. Similarly, Lenin spoke of a "bourgeois state without a bourgeoisie."[26]

There are few statements in all Lenin's writings that are more revealing than his claim, shortly after the 1905 Revolution, that the next and successful revolution would result in "a democratic, not a socialist, dictatorship":

[Such a dictatorship] will not be able (without a series of intermediary stages of revolutionary development) to affect the foundations of capitalism. At best, it may bring about a radical redistribution of the land to the advantage of the peasantry, establish consistent and full democracy including the republic, eliminate all the oppressive features of Asiatic bondage, not only of village but also of factory life, lay the foundation for thorough improvement in the position of the workers and raise their standard of living, and, last but not least, carry the revolutionary conflagration into Europe. Such a victory will by no means transform our bourgeois revolution into a socialist revolution; the democratic revolution will not extend beyond the scope of bourgeois social and economic relationships. Nevertheless, the significance of such a victory for the future development of Russia and of the whole world will be immense.[27]

26. State and Revolution (1917), Collected Works XXV (London, 1964), p. 471.

27. The Two Tactics of Social-Democracy in the Democratic Revolution (1905), Collected Works, IX (London, 1962), pp. 56–57. Quoting this puzzling "innovation" in Marxism, J. Plamenatz writes: "If Marxism were really what Marxists think it is, this suggestion would be so fantastic that we could not believe Marx had made it. If Marxism were a coherent theory and Marxists were persons who believed in it and acted in consequence, Lenin, a real Marxist if ever there was one, could never have written this absurd and important pamphlet." German Marxism and Russian Communism (London, 1954), p. 228. There is another way of looking at these

There was no real effort on the part of Lenin to bolster his new slogan: "the revolutionary-democratic dictatorship of the proletariat and
the peasantry" in a *bourgeois* revolution and in a *capitalist* economy by
any reference or quotations from Marx's writings. In fact, Lenin's theoretical "innovation" in regard to Marx's theory can be considered a
reversal of historical materialism that is generally identified by the whole
Marxist school with Marx's main contribution to social science. There
can be no doubt that Lenin was then aware of the fact that his "slogan"
was an infringement of this theory. In 1917, however, he was apparently
happy to discover both the social force which could support his new
concept and the literal confirmation he needed, that is, the soviets and
Marx's Address on the Commune of 1871. The events of the years
following October 1917 revealed that neither the soviets nor the ideas
of Marx on the Paris Commune were suitable to give another character
to the development of Russian society and economy than that which
Lenin had defined in 1905, namely that of a bourgeois and capitalist
society.

On the basis of the above-mentioned facts, we may say that the Bolsheviks, in taking power on behalf of the proletariat in a backward
country, played the part that Marx and Engels assigned to the Blan-
quists in their own time. Bolshevism, then, must be considered as the
ideological distortion of a social theory, which gives maximum credit
to the modern class struggle as a dynamic force of social change. Not
the *parties*, but the *classes* were in Marx's conception the decisive factors
of historical change. This ideological distortion was put into effect by
the Bolshevik party by depriving the soviets of their social and political
power, and by establishing a dictatorship that, to quote Rosa Luxemburg, was "not the dictatorship of the proletariat . . . but only the
dictatorship of a handful of politicians; that is, dictatorship in the
bourgeois sense, in the sense of the rules of the Jacobins."[28]
Like almost any other revolutionary, Marx sometimes suffered from
fits of impatience that got the better of his intellectual judgment. This
is apparent in his support of the Paris Commune only a few months
after he had clearly shown why it had had to fail. In regard to the revolutionary role of organized minorities, however, he was more consistent,
and he never altered his hostile opinion. For him, "a revolution whose
soul is political, organizes, according to the limited and therefore dual

---

facts: to pretend to be a Marxist and to hold the view Lenin does is equivalent to
claiming to be a disciple of Einstein, while denying his theory of relativity.
28. Rosa Luxemburg, *The Russian Revolution* (Ann Arbor, 1961), p. 72.

nature of this soul, a dominant sphere of society at the expense of society."[29] This was his judgment in 1844, and this, we believe, applies to the events of 1917; the social soul of the revolution had been corrupted by its political leaders who acted as a class of ruling managers quite comparable, from the standpoint of the workers' interests, to the modern managerial ruling class in the Western capitalist countries. When he spoke of the methods of primitive accumulation in less developed countries, Marx wrote that "they all employ the power of the state, the concentrated and organized force of society, to hasten—hothouse fashion—the process of transformation of the feudal mode of production into the capitalist mode, and to shorten the transition. Force is the midwife of every old society pregnant of a new one. It is itself an economic power."[30] Judging from Marx's critical analysis of capitalism and bourgeois society of his time, we may safely assume that the author of *Capital* would not be misled by the features of our present-day world.

The general lesson that can be drawn from the foregoing is that the Russian Revolution of 1917 was not the work of a party guided by a theory or an ideology, but the inevitable result of the whole series of events which preceded it. In this, its history is essentially similar to that of other modern bourgeois revolutions, and its subsequent evolution has taken a course similar to that followed by other Western countries, the totalitarian phases of the latter included. With the revolution, Russia entered at last into the process of Western history, and its destiny since then has been inextricably linked with the destiny of the Occident. As Lenin formulated it in 1905, "Marxists are absolutely convinced of the bourgeois character of the Russian revolution. What does this mean? It means that the democratic changes in the political regime and the social and economic changes which have become necessary for Russia do not in themselves imply the undermining of capitalism or the undermining of bourgeois domination; on the contrary, they will, for the first time, properly clear the ground for a wide and rapid European, and not Asiatic, development of capitalism, they will, for the first time, make it possible for the bourgeoisie to rule as a class."[31] The process of transformation and assimilation that was inaugurated in 1917 by the over-

29. Karl Marx, "Kritische Randglossen zu dem Artikel eines Preussen," article written against Arnold Ruge and published in *Vorwärts*, Paris, August 7–10, 1844; *Werke*, I (Berlin, 1957) pp. 392–409. In this essay Marx demonstrated the absolute incompatibility between state and socialism: "Die Existenz des Staats und die Existenz der Sklaverei sind unzertrennlich." pp. 401–402.

30. *Capital*, book I, chap. XXXI (Moscow, 1931), p. 751.

31. Lenin, *Two Tactics*, p. 48.

throw of the bourgeoisie as a possessing class and by adopting the bourgeois and capitalist methods of economic exploitation and accumulation was long overdue, having been retarded by the heritage of centuries of tsarist absolutism. This process is still going on. In short, the Russian Revolution was before all else a necessary result of the facts of Russian history, as was its peculiar course; a course determined by the lack of the enriching Western experience of the Renaissance and the Reformation, and deprived of the development of a powerful urban bourgeoisie struggling for the emancipation of society from the state. No people can sever itself from its past, and historians have, therefore, often discovered that apparent changes in reality represent new forms of old developments.

If this thesis is correct, the problem of parties and ideologies is more approachable, for it implies that the Russian Revolution was a social as well as a political one. As in the Bonapartist Second Empire, the social basis of the new oligarchic power in Russia was represented by a new class of small landowners. To be sure, the role of the Bolshevik party and its ideology was more important than that of the other parties and ideologies, but its importance was subordinate to the process of the revolution, itself the outgrowth of numerous factors. Theoretically or ideologically, both Marxist factions favored a bourgeois revolution, and both were preparing themselves to take charge not only of the subsequent proletarian revolution—when it would take place—but also to control the forthcoming preliminary bourgeois stage as well. That fact that one faction—the one that adopted the name "Bolshevik"—was ready to precipitate a second revolution is less decisive than the common aims and attitudes that united the two. The triumph of Bolshevism was really the triumph of the Russian Social Democratic Workers' Party. This is revealed in the acts of complicity committed by the leftists among the various socialist and Marxist groups during the whole revolutionary period, particularly from the first Provisional Government to the Bolshevik seizure of power and its aftermath. When Martov, on the eve of the Bolshevik coup d'état, associated his motion condemning the Bolsheviks in the Pre-Parliament with two fundamental conditions—immediate land reforms and decisive action to bring about peace—he formulated the main points of the Bolshevik program.[32]

If the Jacobin elements in Russia finally triumphed over the spontaneously growing movement of the soviets, it was not because of the

32. For a remarkable testimony of the Mensheviks' attitude during the whole revolutionary period see Theodore Dan, *The Origins of Bolshevism* (New York and Evanston, 1964), pp. 330 ff. and, of course, the standard history of E. H. Carr.

genius of Lenin or the virtue of his party, but rather because of the political immaturity of the Russian people; their pathetic inability to take
advantage of the opportunities offered by the decay of tsarism. But there
was nothing in their history that could have given them the necessary
capability. If the word "treason" has any place in the vocabulary of historians, we should not look for guilty men or parties but to history itself.
Incapable of achieving real human emancipation, the Russian people
could only take what was offered. History does not yield Messiahs—only
managers—though the latter often try to confuse the two.

Paradoxical as it may seem, while Russian Marxist ideology has proved
a tremendous failure, Marx's social philosophy or rather, sociological
interpretation of historical development has been shown to be amazingly
correct. Marx had foreseen the Russian Revolution as a consequence of
a war that would take the aspect of "a war of races," a war in which
Germany would fight "against combined Slavic and Roman races."[33]
The strange alliance between republican France—the heir of the great
revolution—and tsarist Russia—the bastion of European reaction—was
in itself of the highest prophetic significance. Russia was thus drawn into
the historical destiny of Occidental civilization as much by her military
alliance with France as by her military defeat and the resulting inevitable revolution. Furthermore, Marx predicted the social character
of this revolution: the transformation of Russia from a rural, semi-
Asiatic society to a modern or urban, proletarian society. Can we speak
here of a *bourgeois* society? Yes and no. Yes, if we do not identify the
bourgeois regime with liberalism, because bourgeois regimes may be
totalitarian in their various forms (Bonapartism, fascism, Nazism), and
if we consider the evolution of the traditional individualistic phase of
the bourgeoisie to the bureaucratic or managerial stage. No, if we think
of the bourgeoisie in terms of individual capitalists.

What Marx could not have foreseen was that the political masters of
the Russian Revolution would claim to have acted in accordance with
his social theory, that is, with the materialist conception of history. Nor
could he have imagined that this revolutionary creation of a proletarian
society and a state-capitalist economy would be proclaimed by the ruling
class as a socialist revolution and be accepted as such by Western
scholars, oblivious of the fact that in a class society, "the ruling ideas
are the ideas of the ruling class."[34]

History sometimes makes for strange bedfellows, and such phenomena

33. Karl Marx, *Second Manifesto of the General Council of the I.W.M.A.*,
September 9, 1870.
34. *Communist Manifesto*.

have been ranged under the highly unscientific idea of "the irony of history." The year 1967 is one of such an ironic coincidence; the fiftieth anniversary of the Russian Revolution is celebrated in the same year as the one hundredth anniversary of the publication of *Capital*. It would cause no surprise if the ruling party in Russia, in celebrating these two anniversaries, should deliberately link the two together. In so doing, it would not realize how profoundly right it would be. After fifty years of managerial rule, the Bolsheviks and their allies may be aware of the fact that if *Capital* has not offered them "recipes for the kitchens of the future," it still may present an almost accurate description of their own adventures. Thus, contrary to Marx's expectations, "Oriental despotism" is undertaking the historical mission that Occidental capitalism has failed to achieve.

Comment by Shlomo Avineri on — "The Relationship of Bolshevism to Marxism" by Maximilien Rubel

Let me start by saying that I generally agree with the main thesis presented here by Mr. Rubel. I have, however, some methodological doubts, and I would like to state them at the outset of my remarks.

One of my major doubts concerns the different levels on which "Marxism" and "bolshevism" appear as historical phenomena. What exactly are we comparing? Whatever one's view of Marx's political activity may be, most of us would agree that Marx was mainly a political and social theorist, whereas Lenin was an activist who held a rather instrumentalist view of theory. If we compare what Marx said and wrote to what Lenin said and wrote, we are facing an obvious difficulty: what Marx said is crucial to the understanding of Marx as an historical phenomenon, whereas Lenin's historical impact is, of course, far more related to his political activity than to his writings. On the other hand, it would not help to obviate the difficulty by comparing what Marx *said* to what Lenin *did*.

Keeping these difficulties in mind, I would therefore like to limit myself to two aspects of the broader historical and theoretical problems implied in the issue covered by the title of Mr. Rubel's paper. These two points are: (1) Marx's statements about the chances of revolution in Russia; and (2) that small segment of Marx's writings that is directly policy-oriented and that could therefore be compared with some justi-

324 - Shlomo Avineri

fication with Lenin's political actions. I am fully aware of the limited relevance of such a comparison, yet it seems to me to cast some light on the wider issue of the place of bolshevism within the general Marxist tradition.

But let me first address myself to what I take is Mr. Rubel's central thesis, that is, that what Leninism ultimately did to Russia amounts to the introduction of capitalism and not of socialism. Provided we could agree on a semantic issue, I would wholeheartedly endorse Mr. Rubel's statement. If we mean by capitalism something totally analogous to Western capitalism, as described, for example, in Marx's *Capital*, then it does not seem plausible to argue that bolshevism introduced anything of the sort into Russia. Otherwise we shall have to argue that one can have capitalism without capitalists and without private ownership of the means of industrial production. But if what Mr. Rubel really means is not capitalism in the strict Western sense but industrialization, then there would be no difficulty in agreeing with him—and with Djilas— that this was the main historical impact of bolshevism on Russian society.

Of course, this thesis has wider ramifications, for a very plausible argument could be made that much of Marx's criticism of what capitalism is doing to the quality of human life is actually in the impact of techno-logical industrialism far more than in the impact of capitalism *per se*. And if the gist of Mr. Rubel's argument is that Marx's views about alienation and dehumanization apply today to Soviet society just as much as they apply to the capitalist West, then this is so not because the Soviet Union is capitalist in any intelligible sense of the term, but because it is an industrial society. Incidentally, Marx's critique of mod-ern society would thus have a wider scope of applicability than being just a description of nineteenth-century Western capitalism; and it seems that Engels in the essay *On Authority* had at least a vague feeling that some of the horrors of modern society are an outcome of technology and not of capitalism, that is, of the mode of production and not of property relations.

If we turn now to Marx's views about Russia, we have to face another of Marx's deep paradoxes. For though Marx's prognosis of the imminent collapse of the capitalist order has been predicated upon the structural contradictions he found in the most highly industrialized societies, he does not forecast the initial outbreak of the revolution in these countries. Throughout Marx's writings there is a strong streak which foresees the revolution as breaking out in the less developed countries, where the tension between the old socio-political order and the new economic modes of production is at its sharpest. The fact that the revolution broke out in underdeveloped Russia rather than the industrialized West does not seem to contradict Marx's writings on the subject.

In the *Communist Manifesto* Marx and Engels explicitly state that "the Communists turn their attention chiefly to Germany," which was at that time (1847) the least developed among the Western European nations. Germany, they argue, is "on the eve of a bourgeois revolution that is bound to be carried out under more advanced conditions of European civilization than that of England . . . and France." Therefore, the authors of the *Manifesto* conclude, "The bourgeois revolution in Germany will be but the prelude to an immediately following proletarian revolution."

When later Russia replaced Germany as the country "on the eve of a bourgeois revolution," Marx and Engels wrote in 1882 in their preface to the Russian edition of the *Communist Manifesto* that the social revolution might break out in Russia first and become a signal to proletarian revolution in the West.

Now I hate to add more quotations to those already cited by Mr. Rubel and he has appropriately cautioned us not to throw quotations at each other in that talmudic fashion that has sometimes become a substitute for an understanding of Marx. Yet I would like to call your attention to a letter Marx wrote to Sorge in 1877, that is extremely intriguing because it shows Marx's attempts at prediction simultaneously at their worst and best. Under the impact of the initial Russian defeats in the Russo-Turkish War, Marx writes to Sorge on September 27, 1877, as follows:

This crisis is a new turning point in European history. Russia has long been standing on the threshold of an upheaval, all the elements of it are prepared . . . The gallant Turks have hastened the explosion by years with the thrashing they have inflicted, not only upon the Russian army and Russian finances, but in a highly personal and individual manner on the dynasty commanding the army (the Tsar, the heir to the throne and six other Romanovs). The upheaval will begin according to the rules of the art with some playing at constitutionalism and then there will be a fine row. If mother Nature is not particularly unfavourable towards us we shall still live to see the fun . . .

This time the revolution will begin in the East, hitherto the unbroken bulwark and reserve army of counter-revolution.[1]

Within a few weeks Marx probably would have liked to forget that he wrote those lines because the Russian victory in the Balkans made

1. Marx to Sorge, September 27, 1877, in Marx-Engels, *Selected Correspondence*, 2nd ed. (Moscow, 1965), p. 308.

a collapse of tsarism seem even more remote than ever. Yet when a revolution did break out in Russia in 1905, and then of course in 1917, Marx's statement seemed to project quite well on the actual conditions that made the revolution possible and determined its course: military defeat, consequent loss of prestige on the part of the tsar and the dynasty, "some play at constitutionalism," and then the radical revolution. It may not be very helpful to be wrong in terms of four weeks and to be proved right in terms of forty years, but the resulting ambiguity is deeply connected with the problem that Russia and other non-Western agrarian societies, presented to Marx. In all fairness, however, one has to add that Engels was at least aware of another product of the non-Western nature of Russian society: in a letter to Marx of April 20, 1870, he warns against the social imbalance implied by the existence in Russia of tens of thousands of revolutionary students lacking a proletariat or even a revolutionary peasantry. These "officer candidates without an army" seem to Engels to be a real danger to the revolution: the Jacobinism of Tkachev, as well as the warnings of Machajski, seem already to have been prefigured here.

Let me now turn to the second issue, namely Marx's policy-oriented statements. On solid epistemological grounds Marx was always very uneasy about drawing up blueprints for future society. Yet the *Communist Manifesto* lists ten points that should serve as guidelines for the proletariat when taking power. They are all aimed at "using the political supremacy" of the proletariat in order "to wrest, by degrees, all capital from the bourgeoisie." Although these ten measures have often been mentioned in the literature, it might be helpful to compare them with the policies undertaken by Lenin on achieving power. The ten measures could be summarized as follows:

(1) Abolition of private property in land.

(2) A heavy progressive or graduated income tax.

(3) Abolition of the right of inheritance.

(4) Confiscation of the property of emigrants and rebels.

(5) Centralization of credit in the hands of a State Bank.

(6) Centralization of transport in the hands of the state.

(7) Extension of factories and instruments of production owned by the state.

(8) Equal liability of all to labor.

(9) Combination of agriculture and industry.

(10) Free education.

The unusual feature of this program is that *it does not include nationalization of industry*. It calls for the nationalization of land, the banking system, and transportation, but not of industry. Marx's plan for eliminating private control of industrial production is a far more sophisticated and shrewder one: the combined impact of (2), (3), (5), (6), and (7) will undoubtedly squeeze private industry out of business in the long run; but this would be the last and ultimate result of a long structural change in the *economy*, not the first *political* act of the revolution. Here as elsewhere Marx is thinking of the proletarian revolution in terms of economic processes rather than mere political acts.

The major difference between Marx's plan and Lenin's policies is obvious. Whereas Marx advocated (1) nationalization of land and (2) non-nationalization of industry, Lenin's policies resulted in (1) distribution of land to the peasants and (2) nationalization of industry. Of course, it could well be argued that the distribution of land was a tactical move to mobilize the support of the peasantry and detach them from the Socialist Revolutionaries, whereas the nationalization of industry was more an outcome of *stikhiinost* and pressure from below than a result of clear policies. This is, of course, true but beside the point.[2]

In nationalizing industry outright, Lenin created that economic chaos and dislocation that Marx's shrewd program had sought to avoid: Marx was well aware of the fact that outright nationalization would create immediate enemies, antagonize lukewarm adversaries, cause bottlenecks and decline in production, and even end in mass unemployment. These were the precise consequences of nationalization of industry in Russia, and the NEP was nothing else than a feeble acknowledgment of this fact; but the damage had already been done.

The land policy had similar disastrous results. Marx's call for nationalization of land was a two-pronged measure aimed both at the landholding aristocracy and the small peasantry. In his essay on *The Eighteenth Brumaire of Louis Bonaparte* Marx rightly saw the small land-owning peasantry as the major obstacle to a proletarian government. Lenin's Land Decree made Russia into the largest peasant economy the modern world has ever known. For the Russian countryside, November 1917 was really 1789. The political absurdity and unfeasibility of a peasant nation ruled by Marxists dedicated to a proletarian revolution

---

2. It is amusing that Engels did in fact envisage the dangers of such revolutionary spontaneity. In a letter to Weydemeyer of April 12, 1853, he discussed the possibility that "our party" will all of a sudden find itself in power and adds: "On such an occasion, driven by the proletarian populace, bound by our own printed declarations and plans—more or less falsely interpreted, more or less passionately thrust to the fore in the party struggle—we shall be constrained to undertake Communist experiments and perform leaps the untimeliness of which we know better than anyone else . . . I do not see how it can turn out otherwise." Marx-Engels, *Selected Correspondence*, 2nd ed. (Moscow, 1965), p. 78.

became apparent in the late 1920's and threatened the viability of the whole Soviet system. Surely few political systems in history expressed such a gap between the "economic base" and the "political superstructure." The forced collectivization of the Stalinist era was nothing else than payment of the bill for Lenin's tactical successes in 1917 in mobilizing the peasants and nationalizing, that is, destroying, industry.

That Lenin was motivated by tactical rather than theoretical reasons only accentuates the difference between the place allotted to theory in the respective world views of Marx and Lenin. Lenin's action-oriented theory usually overlooked the fact that measures dictated by tactics still can have structural effects on society. The fact that the two major structural changes in Russian society after 1917 were an outcome of tactical considerations rather than policies originating from basic principles of socialist theory again bring out the limitations of Lenin's political understanding of the revolution as compared with Marx's more comprehensive vistas.

It is to this context that I would like to address my final remark. It has to do with the international policies of the Bolsheviks in 1917. Here a similar disregard for structural consequences of merely tactical policy-decisions produced the same effect. In their 1882 preface to the Russian edition of the *Communist Manifesto*, Marx and Engels predicated the success of a social revolution in Russia on its becoming a signal for proletarian revolution in the West. This universalistic element never disappeared from Soviet ideology and propaganda, but it could hardly be discerned in their policies immediately after 1917. It certainly never was a guideline to Soviet policy when confronted with the issue of a separate peace with the Central Powers.

Again, a good argument could be made for the case that had it not been for Brest-Litovsk, the Soviet government would not have been able to hold out. Yet the readiness of the Soviet government to sign a peace treaty of that kind meant again that for tactical reasons the Bolsheviks were ready to accept a settlement that expressed the wildest expansionist dreams of the imperial German *Drang nach Osten*. Furthermore, in justifying Brest-Litovsk in terms of *Realpolitik* one may also speculate whether the Soviets could really have held out had the boundaries and the political realities in East Europe not been radically changed a few months later in the wake of the German collapse in the West.

Be that as it may (and I would not venture to speculate on those hypothetical questions), the positive effect of the treaty of Brest-Litovsk was to deal a death blow to any universalist or internationalist ideology still slumbering within the German Social Democratic Party. It was all right for Lenin to fulminate against the German "Social chauvinists," but in acceding to the German expansionists demands, the Bolsheviks paradoxically legitimized the uneasy pact the Social Democrats had with the imperial German government. Despite all their cooperation in the war effort, most of the party leaders had been uneasy about the *Burgfrieden* and wished to extricate themselves from it at the first chance. Now if the victorious Russian Revolution could accept the expansionist *Ostpolitik*, why should the German Social Democrats be debarred from backing it? And when the Social Democrats came to power in Germany, they showed as little consideration for the predicaments of the Russian Bolsheviks as Lenin had shown for their difficulties just a few months earlier.

Moral judgments are not intended, but it should be pointed out that a whole set of considerations never entered Lenin's mind. The whole course of Soviet history was determined by Lenin's policies on land tenure, nationalization of industry, and relations with Germany. On all three of those crucial issues Lenin took positions that were as diametrically opposed as possible to the directives suggested in Marx's writings. The deeper theoretical issue about the relationship between Marxism and bolshevism is not solved, of course, but on the level of policy-decisions I feel that at least one aspect of this problem has been given a fairly strong answer.

Discussion

Replying to Mr. Avineri's remarks, Mr. Rubel said that those ambiguities that existed in Marx's writings were contained in his commentaries on political events. There was nothing inconsistent in Marx's analysis of Russia's social future. Neither Marx nor Engels had entertained any illusions about the possibility of proletarian revolutions in Eastern countries; both had expected an agrarian revolution in Russia.

With regard to the question of Marx's attitudes toward the 1848 revolutions, Mr. Rubel took the position that in 1848 Marx had tried to act as a kind of mentor to the German bourgeoisie. He had even founded a democratic journal, *Neue Rheinische Zeitung*. In Marx's mind there had been no question of a Communist seizure of power in Germany. Moreover, Lenin could not have used the program from the *Communist Manifesto*, quoted by Mr. Avineri, because it had been drawn up as a transitional program for a state already possessing a well developed proletariat.

Mr. Wolfe thought that characterizing Marx as an advisor to the revolutionary bourgeoisie in 1848 was a bit too simple and that to regard the body of Marx's writing as consistent was a mistake. The *Communist Manifesto* had been addressed to the advanced sector of the proletariat; indeed, its language seemed designed to frighten the bourgeoisie. However, as soon as

Marx and Engels entered Germany they had dropped the *Manifesto* and directed their efforts toward the bourgeoisie. Then after March 1850, partly under the impact of the recession of the revolution and also under the over-powering impression of Victorian prosperity in England, they had again reversed themselves.

Mr. Wolfe went on to criticize the indiscriminate use of the terms capitalism, socialism, and class, arguing that these words had never been defined in any sort of precise, meaningful, and generally acceptable way. He also felt that Mr. Rubel had oversimplified Marx's attitude toward revolution in Russia. Whereas in some of his writings on the subject Marx appears to have had an agrarian revolution in mind, at other times his attention seems to have been focused on the possibility of a political revolution aimed at overthrowing the autocracy. It had been Marx's opinion that the collapse of the "gendarme of Europe" would greatly facilitate socialist revolutions in the more advanced European countries.

Switching from Marx to Lenin, Mr. Thompson saw a fundamental consistency in Lenin's attitude toward the possibility of socialist revolution in Russia. Lenin had always tied such a development to successful revolutions in Western Europe. Thus after seizing power he had viewed Bolshevik rule as a temporary holding action with the development of the revolution in Russia still dependent upon the victory of socialism in more advanced countries and the receipt of economic and technical aid from them. When the expected revolutions did not occur, Lenin was at a loss as to how to build socialism in Russia. He had toyed with cooperatives, electrification, and so on, but died still uncertain of a solution to the problem.

Mr. Carr disagreed with Mr. Rubel's suggestion that Lenin had pretended to establish socialism in Russia and had really introduced capitalism. He granted that in public speeches after the revolution Lenin might have been a little optimistic. However, broadly speaking, Lenin had made no pretense of introducing socialism and more than that, he had viewed NEP as a retreat from socialism. Concurring with the opinion expressed by Mr. Thompson, Mr. Carr said that down to the moment of his death Lenin was in fact still puzzling over the question of how socialism could be introduced in Russian conditions.

Mr. Carr concluded his remarks by adding the word Marxism to Mr. Wolfe's list of concepts to be used with caution. Apart from the fact that Marx was not always consistent in what he wrote and that the Russian experience had added a new dimension to Marxism, Marx was essentially a nineteenth-century thinker whose theories could not be adopted *tout court* in the twentieth century.

Referring to Mr. Avineri's remarks on the comparison of Marx's words with Lenin's deeds, Mr. Roberts said that the very difficult problem of Lenin as a writer was raised. Lenin had to be taken seriously not only as an actor, but as a writer with an ultimately consistent line of thought and despite the enormous difficulties that analysis of Lenin's often complex and seemingly contradictory writings inevitably entailed.

Taking a cue from Mr. Wolfe and Mr. Carr, Mr. Seton-Watson commented on the problems involved in using the term bourgeoisie with reference to tsarist society. He pointed out that the word bourgeoisie was sometimes used to mean simply private capitalists. More often, however, it implied a certain homogeneity among three functionally distinct middle classes: businessmen, bureaucrats, and intellectuals. These three categories had existed in medieval and modern Europe where they had tended to become homogeneous culturally and socially. But there was nothing inevitable about this development, and indeed, in tsarist Russia the ethos of businessmen, bureaucrats, and intellectuals was quite distinct. In Russia a homogeneous bourgeoisie in the Western European sense had barely existed. Moreover, neither the Russian bureaucracy nor the intelligentsia had possessed the individualist, selfish outlook of the Western European bourgeoisie. Even Russian businessmen, although individualistic in the sense of wanting private property, were not so in other respects. Thus, for example, in exchange for economic advantages they were generally willing to act as instruments of the bureaucracy.

Mr. Pipes thought that Mr. Rubel had underestimated the differences between Lenin and his fellow Social Democrats. Moreover, he did not believe it fair to say either that Social Democrats worshipped capitalism or that they looked upon democracy and collaboration with the liberal bourgeoisie merely as expedient. Most Social Democrats viewed democracy as an absolutely essential precondition to the triumph of socialism in Russia. In this respect Lenin's conception was virtually unique.

Mr. Avineri clarified his references to Marx's view of the possibilities for revolution in Russia. The point he had tried to make was that there was at least some ambiguity in Marx's allowing the possibility of a radical revolution, possibly based on the peasantry, prior to the full development of capitalism. The fact that Marx admitted an option of this kind seemed helpful in relating Lenin to Marx.

Mr. Avineri also made additional comments on the problem of the ten points in the *Communist Manifesto*. These involved more than merely liberal-democratic demands. They had been preceded by a very clear statement to the effect that the proletariat would use its political supremacy to wrest all capital from the bourgeoisie by degrees. Then too, whereas a liberal democrat might agree with a progressive income tax, he would not favor the abolition of all rights of inheritance and the centralization of credit and the means of communication and transportation in the hands of the state. These were not just peripheral stipulations, a bit left of the usual radical democratic slogans, but precisely what Marx aimed for in Germany in 1848. At least judging by the *Manifesto*, Marx appeared to have conceived this radicalization of liberal bourgeois society as something that was already part of the transition to socialism.

In reply to Mr. Roberts, Mr. Avineri commented that he had no wish to disparage Lenin as a theoretician. All he had meant to say in this regard was that there was a tendency to concentrate on Lenin as a political actor because historically Lenin's actions were more important than his theory. In Lenin there was the possibility of a gap between theory and action that did not exist in Marx because he was concerned almost exclusively with theory.

Mr. Rubel wound up the discussion by responding to the comments made by Mr. Thompson and Mr. Pipes. He agreed with Mr. Thompson that Lenin had no intention of building capitalism in Russia. Nevertheless, this, precisely, had been his function. Referring to Lenin's conception of the organization and role of the revolutionary party, Mr. Rubel also expressed agreement with Mr. Pipes's emphasis on Lenin's unique position in the Russian Social Democratic movement.

The Uses of Revolution — *Adam B. Ulam*

What was the Bolshevik Revolution for? Has it been a success? These questions might seem to provide good copy for one of those half indignant, half satirical commentaries on Western interpretations of their history with which Soviet writers like to regale their readers. But to the maker of the revolution this question would not have appeared preposterous. Practically on his deathbed Lenin pondered the meaning of the event that inscribed his name indelibly on the pages of history.

He did not express contrition or repentance. He was not the man to exclaim "Plekhanov (or Martov), thou hast conquered." But Lenin was a Marxist, brought up in the tradition that his ideology was a binding picture of social and historical reality and not merely a party program, or campaign oratory. Was the revolution according to the gospel of Marxism? And if not, what could justify this departure from the science of history? Won't the slighted Marxian gods of history take revenge for 1917?

The occasion for these reflections was Sukhanov's *Notes on the Revolution,* a garrulous, enchanting chronicle of the great events by one who, though considering himself a militant Marxist, could not accept the Great October. Here was the echo of the taunts and warnings that Plekhanov, Martov, and others had expressed before the Bolsheviks had embarked on their great adventure. Russia was not civilized enough, the level of her economy was not far enough advanced for her to embark on the path toward socialism. If the Russian proletariat tried to take power prematurely it would in the end only disgrace itself, and so on. The great strategist of the revolution had then made light of such warnings. But now it was January 1923. Lenin was lying semi-paralyzed, a virtual prisoner of the Politburo, forbidden to engage in any political activity. A few days before he had written a memorandum containing a scathing characterization of his eventual successor. His illness accentuated his fears for the future: the party he had built up was in the hands of quarrelling oligarchs; bureaucratism and Russian chauvinism were already encrusting the whole machinery of the Soviet state.

Were all those phenomena accidental, or a function of personalities, or was the explanation more fundamental? Was the decision of 1917 somehow responsible for the bureaucratic rot and oppression of 1923? Here there is a *cri de coeur* of Lenin's: What else could we have done? He writes almost incoherently, "What if the complete hopelessness of the situation, having by the same token increased the strength of the workers and peasants tenfold opened for us the possibility of laying the foundations of civilization in a different way from all other Western European countries?"[1] But the meaning is clear enough: yes, the revolution was a departure from the canons of orthodoxy. It was compounded of despair and of a unique opportunity. If spurned by the Bolsheviks, this opportunity might not have come again.

In his memorandum Lenin alternates between scornful references to Sukhanov and his Menshevik ilk: "pedant," "coward," and snatches of inner dialogue. Culture—this word in the mouths of his enemies used to infuriate him: Russia had not enough culture to build socialism: his own tactics in 1917 were uncultured; they were those of an anarchist, not of a true Marxist heir to the democratic and liberal tradition. But now intermingled with scorn is self-questioning. Yes, we did not have enough culture, we do not have it yet. But was it so wrong *first* to conquer power "and then already on the basis of the worker peasant power and the Soviet system to start catching up with other nations?" Is it not a part of the civilizing mission to begin by chasing out the landowners and capitalists "and then start the movement toward socialism? In what books have you read that such changes of the usual historical process are impermissible or impossible?"[2]

One is tempted to answer: in Karl Marx. But Lenin had other than theoretical reasons for this self-questioning. The gist of his own criticism of his party machine and its current rulers has been precisely that: lack of culture. That Ordzhonikidze could hit an opponent, that Stalin and Dzerzhinskii could whitewash such and much worse instances of grossness and oppression has been to him a source of deep humiliation and depression. They in turn could only be amazed by such squeamishness in the man who had sanctioned revolutionary terror, and who, when well, used to quote approvingly that one does not enter the realm of the revolution in white gloves and on a polished floor.

Lenin succeeds, at least on paper, in reassuring himself. Yes, the deci-

1. V. I. Lenin, *Sochineniia*, 4th ed., XXXIII (Moscow, 1954), p. 438.
2. *Ibid.*, p. 439.

sion of October 1917 was the correct one. Napoleon has rightly proclaimed: *"On s'engage et puis on voit."* And if those Menshevik pedants are shocked by the Russian Revolution, let them just wait. They will see how "new revolutions in the much more populous and socially much different countries of the East will display even more singular characteristics than the Russian Revolution." And with this defiant taunt Lenin concluded, except for his subsequent critique of Stalin's administrative methods, his literary activity.

Six years after the revolution its maker still groped for its meaning and relationship to the creed that had guided his life. If one discounts the circumstances under which the article was produced—it was written by a sick and embittered man—one is still struck by Lenin's evaluation of the great event. The revolution was not a triumphant entry into the promised land. It was the beginning of a long and tedious process of laying down the cultural foundations on which in turn could be built bases for the development of socialism. But apart from this attempt to fit the Russian Revolution into the scheme of Marxism, Lenin suggests that, Marxism or no Marxism, we are in the presence of a world revolutionary surge. Other societies, still less ripe for socialism according to the Marxist timetable than Russia had been in 1917, will go through cataclysms the likes of which orthodox Marxists cannot even imagine. That part of his prophecy has certainly been verified and is the source of Lenin's successors' most vexing dilemma on this fiftieth anniversary of the revolution.

Stalin is not usually credited with a penchant for ideological introspection. But shortly before his death he rephrased Lenin's question and reverted to the then distant events of 1917: "What should the proletariat and its party do in a country—including our country—where conditions favor seizure of power by the proletariat and the overthrow of capitalism . . . but where agriculture, despite the growth of capitalism, still remains so scattered among numerous small and medium owner-producers that there appears no possibility of raising the question of expropriating these producers?"[3] And Stalin answers, attributing his solution of the problem to Lenin: *"Favorable conditions for seizure of power by the proletariat should not be allowed to slip by;* power should be seized without waiting for the time when capitalism contrives to ruin the many millions of small and medium producers."[4] As to the original

3. J. V. Stalin, *Economic Problems of Socialism in the USSR*, quoted in *Current Soviet Policies*, ed., Leo Gruliow (New York, 1953), p. 3.
4. *Ibid.* (italics mine).

difficulty, Stalin piously rejects the forcible solution, that is, "expropriating the small and middle producers in the countryside and socializing their means of production." Yet that is precisely what he undertook and carried through in his forced collectivization. Is it credible that he could deceive himself in 1952 to the point where he came to believe that collectivization had been a voluntary process? Yet he could write about collectivization by force: "Marxists cannot agree to take this senseless and criminal course . . . since such a course would undermine every possibility of success of the proletarian revolution and would drive the peasantry for a long time into the camp of enemies of the proletariat."

Thus both the maker of the revolution and his successor have tried to soothe their ideological conscience and to fit the Bolshevik Revolution into the Marxist scheme of things. Their different emphasis is interesting. Lenin never emancipated himself *entirely* from the Social Democratic tradition. His continuous use of "culture" and "civilization" is very characteristic. Once the necessary brutal task had been accomplished, the sense of revolution had to be sought above all in changed human relations. This was to be the immediate consequence of the changed power and property structure. In the first days of the Bolshevik regime, his self-delusion on this count was so great that he would often repeat in speeches, "For the first time in Russian history the man with a rifle is not feared." This belief could not withstand his subsequent experience as the ruler of Soviet Russia. But intermittently to the very end he groped for the meaning of the revolution, not only in great historical, but also in immediate human terms. At the very end, when he saw that this element of "culture" was sadly missing in the society he had created, he still projected his dream for the future: at least the foundations for a more humane society had been laid. By curbing the party oligarchs and by introducing simple proletarians into the central party organs, one could save the Soviet system from bureaucracy and corruption. And above all, the Bolshevik Revolution had lit the beacon of hope for those eastern countries for which the orthodox Marxist would have decreed patient endurance of further decades of oppression and backwardness. The revolution had not turned out to be what it had promised in 1917, but it freed Marxism from a fatalistic bondage to the assumed laws of history and restored to the doctrine, and to the millions of people who followed it, militancy and hope.

For Stalin the retrospective justification of the revolution was much more mechanical in nature. There is no heart-searching inquiry into the "cultural" meaning of the event, into its human implications for the rulers and the ruled. One could not let a favorable opportunity of seizing power slip by. Power meant the ability to perform huge tasks of social engineering, the tasks which the orthodox Marxists would await dully for history to perform for them. An efficient organization of society and technological progress—those are the goals which have justified the revolution, just as they have justified the "criminal course" he had taken in liquidating the individual peasant holdings. Who could have asked for more at that stage of history? Lenin's musings on "culture" would undoubtedly have been dismissed by Stalin, as had his strictures on his own personality, as a sick man's lapse into sentimentality unworthy of a revolutionary, of a real Bolshevik. Had Stalin expressed himself frankly, he well might have subscribed to the philosophy enunciated by a Red Army commander to Gorky: "Civil War—it is nothing . . . I will tell you frankly, comrade, it is easy to oppress the Russian. We have so many people, everything is in a mess; you burn a village, so what? In due time it would burn by itself anyway."[5]

Both Lenin and Stalin projected in their retrospective view of the revolution their self-image: Lenin in that of a liberator who tried to lead Russia out of oppression and "uncultderedness" and save her from a pseudo-revolution; Stalin in that of a builder of a new civilization who rescued communism from theoretical and personal wranglings that threatened it with dissolution on Lenin's death and set it on a course cruel but purposeful. Both men admitted, even if in a roundabout way, that the revolutionary decision of 1917 was against the teachings of classical Marxism. But both, being Marxists, sought a vindication of this non-Marxist beginning in the subsequent Marxist content of the continuing revolution. But to some of their opponents it was this first step which prejudged decisively the future course of the revolution. Having been conceived in an un-Marxist way it would never be able to retrieve a real socialist and democratic meaning. Has the experience of fifty years helped to decide that debate?

Lenin's emancipation from the precepts of classical Marxism was, of course, rendered possible by the fact that the Great War made the whole pre-1914 world of liberal and socialist concepts appear unreal and irrelevant. It is a measure of how far we ourselves have departed from that world that the scruples and hesitations of the Bolsheviks' socialist opponents in 1917 appear to us ridiculous if not indeed as sheer imbecility. Yet being good Marxists, people like Martov and Tseretelli thought mainly in terms of historical precedents and laws. It seems incredible that a man as intelligent as Martov, who had discerned and

5. Maksim Gorky, *O Russkom krest'ianstve* (Berlin, 1922), p. 21. Gorky adds that the speaker was "in his way" a humane person who treated his soldiers well and enjoyed popularity among them.

fought Lenin's dictatorial tendencies long before 1914, would in 1917 consistently proclaim against any measure of repression against bolshevism. But this contradiction is easily explicable. Before 1914 the Russian revolutionary movement had been in the main a conspiracy and as such always in danger of being seized by a ruthless minority. But in 1917 Russia became a democracy, "the freest country in the world." To suppose that a country of 150 million free citizens could be seized and run by a minority, that the Bolshevik party, which for all the eccentricity of its leader, was a Marxist party containing many members with genuine democratic feelings would yield itself to such a design would have meant the repudiation of everything in which Martov and many others had believed and worked for, for decades. "History" taught that the main, if not only, danger to progressive revolutions lay in right-wing conspiracies and plots, in the threat of a Thermidor followed by a Napoleon. The Bolshevik Revolution prevailed largely because its opponents lived still in the nineteenth century when ideologies were held to be binding representations of social and historical reality and not merely conglomerations of slogans or quasi-religious visions.

The insistence of modern philosophy on the supreme importance of calling things by their right name finds a strong vindication in the story of the revolution. Was there anything Marxist or Social Democratic about the Bolshevik postulates and activities between April and October 1917? A large proportion if not indeed a majority of those who carried out the October coup and who stood armed guard over the infant Soviet regime during its first weeks professed themselves Left Socialist Revolutionaries and outright anarchists of various hues. Yet the allegiance or acquiescence of the working class in the large cities could not have been won by the party of only Lenin and Trotsky. It had also to be one of Marx and Engels. Most of all, the revolution could not have been preserved except in the spirit and name of Marxism. Anarchism and pacifism were sufficient to overthrow the old regime, but to retrieve Russia from anarchy and dissolution one had to have an ideology that had a concrete plan of an ordered society and of an international order. The Bolsheviks' anarchism gained them the soldiers and sailors who stormed the Winter Palace and the Moscow Kremlin, and, much more important, the passivity of the masses that simply refused to defend any vestige of the established order and its institutions. But anarchism could not have brought to the Bolshevik side the ex-tsarist officers who helped win the Civil War, the engineers and other "bourgeois specialists" who began to restore the Russian economy, and finally those members of the intelligentsia of all political persuasions who simply wanted to work for their country.

Yet as to the concrete meaning of this Marxism within the Communist setting. Lenin and his successors have always been in a quandary. A militant socialist like Rosa Luxemburg could not help wondering, for all her temperamental affinity for bolshevism, at the news of the revolution, what there was specifically Marxist about it. The very name "Soviet" chosen to baptize the society and regime they had created has epitomized the Bolsheviks' dilemma. It was a word pregnant with meaning in 1905 and 1917, symbolizing to the masses of soldiers and workers that theirs was a direct form of democracy, unlike bourgeois parliamentarism of the West. Yet, taken literally, the term was almost meaningless: Soviet society means society of councils, and very shortly it became absurd in relation to what was going on in Russia. No Western parliament was as distant from real decision making as was the whole network of soviets in Soviet Russia, say by 1925.

Having seized power and concluded peace, the Bolsheviks could have claimed that their objectives were to put Russia on her feet and to modernize their society. But again those were hardly specifically Marxist objectives, and in achieving them the Bolsheviks would have had the hearty support of most of the population and no need to set up a one-party state. Was it then the "chasing out of the landowners and capitalists" that Lenin represented at times as the *socialist*—and great—achievement of the revolution? But the fact remains that it was Lenin himself who struggled for some weeks after October against what he considered (rightly, from the Marxist point of view) as a premature nationalization of industry, who reintroduced private enterprise in the NEP, and who dreamed of interesting *foreign* capitalists to invest in Russia. Was socialism then "electrification plus Soviet power," as Lenin explained on another occasion? As with many dazzling slogans, this one will hardly withstand some reflecting as to what it actually means.

Both Lenin and his successor were much more convincing in explaining what was *not* Marxism. Workers' control of industry, he said quite rightly, was anarcho-syndicalism and had nothing to do with the precepts of Marx. And Stalin was equally correct when he characterized the plea for complete equalization of wages as "petty bourgeois" in spirit rather than socialist. This then was the negative use of the ideology: Marxism was being invoked to strip Soviet society precisely of those quasi-anarchist features that enjoyed the widest popular support, and the promise of which had contributed to the Bolshevik triumph in 1917 and in the Civil War.

In fact, much of the content of the ideology was replaced for Lenin and for his followers by the sense of commitment and struggle, accompanied by an almost Nietzschean revulsion against the pre-1914 world.

When at a meeting of the Comintern one of the foreign Communists was bold enough to suggest that a revolution after all should have the tangible results of improving the welfare of the workers, Lenin exploded: "Revolution should be undertaken only if it does not injure too much the situation of the workers. I ask, is it allowable in the Communist party to speak in such a way? That is a counterrevolutionary way of speaking . . . When we established the dictatorship of the proletariat the workers became more hungry, and their standard of living went down. The victory of the workers is impossible without sacrifices, without a temporary worsening of their situation."[6] It would be hard to imagine a statement more at variance with the spirit and message of Marxism, with its assumption that revolution itself is a rational step designed not to destroy or humiliate the rich and powerful, but to provide a concrete way of rescuing the masses from their poverty and securing the workers even during the period of transition an improvement in their material well-being. Communism tears Marxism away not only from its historico-deterministic moorings, but also from much of its materialistic setting. Marx's criticism of capitalism was not that it neglects technology and development of society's productive power, but on the contrary that its enormous stress on and effectiveness in these respects does not translate itself into a steady and concrete improvement of the people's standard of living. To assert that revolution in itself and the dictatorship of the proletariat are the supreme goals of socialism is not Marxism.

The attempt to find out what the revolution had been fought for provided the background of the political struggle of the 1920's. With the Kronstadt rebellion, the really populistic "soviet" side of the revolution went down to defeat. From then on, "Central Committee" and then "Politburo" would have been a more appropriate prefix to Russia than "Soviet." Trotsky, then Zinoviev, then Bukharin tried to reclaim Marxism-Leninism as the solid foundation in their opposition to the ascendant current of politics in the USSR, but they found out that instead of solid ground they were standing on a disintegrating ice floe. When in 1927 Trotsky attempted before the Central Committee to invoke those historico-rationalistic arguments that had been the staple of the Marxist discourse before 1917 he aroused general hilarity. As he began: "The worker in 1905 . . . ," there were shouts that Trotsky proposed to read his collected works, that instead of talking of the worker in 1905 he should tell his judges what he had said at the Iaroslav railway station a few days ago, or if indulging in historical reminiscences he should explain how he had "betrayed" Lenin between 1905 and 1914.

6. Lenin, *Sochineniia*, 4th ed., XXXI (Moscow, 1951), p. 233.

The only use of history left in Stalin's Russia was that of a police dossier. Not the Marxian categories, but first a majority of delegates, then the command of the secret police were the determining factors in political decisions.

At the Fifteenth Party Conference Stalin assured his hearers that were Engels alive he would exclaim: "May the devil take the old formulas: Long live the victorious revolution in the USSR."[7] Marxism in Russia had thus suffered a complete attrition. Its use as an official theology reminds one of the cults of those primitive tribes that have forgotten the identity and functions of their gods, but keep worshipping symbols and objects for reasons they cannot explain. Thus the worship of the revolution for what exactly the great event has brought to the lives of the millions the regime has found impossible to explain with any precision. Was socialism achieved in 1936, as Stalin declared? In 1955 his chief collaborator Molotov was publicly reproved for affirming that Russia *then* was entering the era of socialism. Nor was Khrushchev more successful in attempting to warm up the old concepts and enthusiasms. The Twenty-second Party Congress proclaimed in 1961 that in 1980 the USSR would be entering the era of communism, but beyond a set of statistics the party ideologues exhibited considerable vagueness as to how new this better world would be. And Khrushchev's successors, judging by the Twenty-third Party Congress, have already forgotten about the majestic vistas for 1980, preferring to concentrate sensibly enough on the greater abundance of consumers' goods for 1970.

On the fiftieth anniversary of the revolution, after Lenin, Stalin, and destalinization, closest to the mark seems to be the prophecy of one who had disapproved of the Bolshevik Revolution but who had acquiesced in it, though not for ideological or idealistic reasons. Gorky, in his somber assessment of the Russian peasant and of the Civil War, wrote:

. . . *and like the Jews, led by Moses out of the Egyptian bondage, so will die the half savage, dumb and heavy people of the Russian countryside . . . Their place will be taken by a new breed of people—literate, smart, energetic. I do not think that they will be the [proverbial] "pleasant and engaging Russian people" but they will be, finally, businesslike men, skeptical and indifferent to everything which does not bear directly on their needs. They will not think readily about Einstein's theories or about the significance of Shakespeare or Leonardo da Vinci, but probably they will spend money on [biological] experiments and will undoubtedly appreciate the importance of electrification, the value of an agronomist, the advantage of having tractors.*[8]

7. *15 Konferentsiia Vsesoiuznoi Kommunisticheskoi Partii (b)* (Moscow, 1927), p. 721.

8. Gorky, *O Russkom Krestianstve,* p. 43.

Subject to some corrections, not a bad picture of the mentality of the average Russian, or for that matter of the citizen of any other industrialized country. But Gorky, who thought that this emancipated Russian nation would be able to take a hard, unsentimental look at its history, would be astounded to see on this fiftieth anniversary of the revolution, Russia's past as well as her present still subject to ideological controls by a regime that claims to embody Marxism. To paraphrase what young Lenin had written about capitalism, many a Russian must feel that he suffers today both from socialism and from the insufficient development of socialism in his country.

The preceding assessment of the work of the Bolshevik Revolution can be subjected to two lines of criticism. One, that would now be classified as conservative but that really bespeaks the point of view of pre-1914 liberalism can be just stated here. The trouble, it would argue, lies with the original ideology and not with the alleged or real abandonment of it by the Bolsheviks. The rigid pseudo-scientific apparatus of Marxism made those who followed it impotent in a revolutionary situation and enabled the others who used it cynically to rationalize their lust for power and oppression. What is even worse, the distorted version of Marxism when genuinely believed in by the first generation of Bolsheviks was productive of fanaticism rather than a rational and humane approach to the problem of social transition.

What might be called the neo-Bolshevik line of criticism would still adhere to the main lines of Lenin's response to the Mensheviks: whatever pedant or bookish arguments can be adduced against the revolution or the development of communism since then, it is silly to quarrel with history or to expect progress to be achieved painlessly. The revolution was not a rape performed by a small minority upon a huge nation and eventually on the whole European civilization. It happened because the old was decayed and incapable of regeneration. Whatever the price, the revolution lit a beacon of hope for the oppressed masses everywhere, and in that sense it transformed and humanized even its enemies, for the challenge of communism was largely responsible for capitalism reforming itself and being compelled to emancipate the millions held in colonial subjugation. In the case of Russia, it is granted that the revolution brought terrible sufferings and abuses, but those have been a by-product of the country's backwardness and hence of the society's inability to perform the needed task of reconstruction under civilized conditions. Yet for all the ravages of Stalinism and the still prevailing lack of freedom, communism has imparted vitality and purpose and provided the necessary material bases for the future freer life. The work of the revolution, this argument holds, can be thus criticized in terms of nostalgia for the pre-1914 world or, an argument applicable to all great historical events, that things could have been done "differently"—that is, more humanely. But any rational activity including the writing of history and the projections for the future of politics must come to terms with reality. And if so, then the October Revolution cannot be treated as a perversion of the "good one" of February 1917, as a huge mistake, as a crime, or be subjected to historical nitpicking: this was good, that was bad, this went too far, and so on.

Many in the West would find it difficult or at least embarrassing to question the main lines of the preceding argument, a demonstration of how much of the self-appraisal of the Russian and even of the Bolshevik Revolution has entered the mainstream of Western thought.[9] But some points of this argument require a closer scrutiny.

Has Russia's advance as an industrial and over-all power been due to communism? It would be difficult to refute the thesis that, in view of the country's size, resources, and the rate of industrial growth for some decades before 1914, it would have been difficult for Russia *not* to achieve the preeminent position she holds as one of the world's two super-powers. There is something schizophrenic in the regime's boastfulness; the main element in its self-praise has always been that no other system has been able to overcome its own huge mistakes as successfully as the Soviet one, that no other nation could have endured so much in the way of mismanagement and crimes by its rulers as the Russians.[10]

As to the significance of the Bolshevik Revolution for the world at large, one is also constrained to make a few ungracious qualifications. That communism holds the unique key to a rapid modernization of a Western society is sufficiently refuted by the example of Japan. But the universality of the appeal of communism requires one comment that may serve also as the final reflection on the Bolshevik Revolution.

Communism was born out of one world war, and it experienced its greatest expansion as a consequence of another. It is strange in view of its explicit rejection of pacifism that the most potent attraction of communism was its vision of an eventual peaceful world order. In the

9. And also how unequal are the terms of the dialogue between the East and the West. Would a Soviet historian or philosopher reciprocate his liberal Western colleague's stance and grant that whatever its past crimes and present deficiencies capitalism in the last twenty years has shown an amazing power of adjustment and vitality? Or that it is likely to reform itself still further and cease entirely to be an oppressive and hostile force?

10. "We often take with one hand what we give with the other," Lenin said on one occasion. And at the Victory Banquet in the Kremlin for the Soviet commanders at the end of World War II Stalin matched this frankness: the Communist regime had made many mistakes, he said, in an obvious reference to its collaboration with Hitler in 1939–1941, and any other nation might well have chased out its rulers when the war broke out. But not the Russians!

wake of the bloodiest of wars the sacrifices and sufferings of a revolution loomed almost insignificant as against the promise of a world where the extinction of exploitation and imperialism will lead to the abolition of war and eventual universal confederation of socialist states. Capitalism had led to 1914. The Second International had proved impotent to arrest that development. Hopes for the expansion of communism after 1921 were often based on the probability of a recurrence of an imperialist war, and people as astute as Trotsky and Radek often postulated the probability and imminence of an Anglo-French or Anglo-American collision. The League of Nations was resented and abused by Soviet spokesmen not only as a possible nucleus of anti-Soviet coalitions but as a dangerous attempt to recreate a capitalist world order. Even the absolute subordination of foreign communism to the interests or, rather, commands of Stalin's Russia could be rationalized as the necessary preliminary of the establishment of a supra-national Communist world order, which, however cruel and destructive its beginnings, would eventually spare the world its greatest scourge.

Beginning with 1948 this most hopeful legacy of the Bolshevik Revolution could no longer be maintained. The Yugoslav conflict showed that communism possessed no secret formula for dissolving conflicts between states that share its basic assumptions. And with the ripening of the Sino-Soviet conflict, the tenet in which, whatever their other evasions and improvisations with the doctrine, Lenin and his companions genuinely believed—that communism provided the only true internationalism and way of abolishing war—appears as illusory as many other hopes of 1917. In the Chinese Communists' trampling upon the old formulas and cautions and extolling of action over theory, the Soviet leaders might see (though they are not likely to, historical imagination not being their strong point) parallels to the Bolsheviks' adventurous pragmatism and in their own reactions—at times pleading, at times threatening, still half-heartedly hoping for a reunion—the perplexed strivings of Plekhanov and Martov.

Comment by Hannah Arendt on — "The Uses of Revolution" by Adam Ulam

Since I belong here in the category of the layman, I feel privileged indeed to comment briefly on Mr. Ulam's fascinating reflections on the gap between ideology and practice in both Lenin and Stalin and on the way they justified it before themselves.

I have no quarrel with Mr. Ulam's evaluation of Lenin. Indeed, to look back upon the October Revolution from the viewpoint of Lenin while he lay dying seems to me singularly appropriate. Revolutions, as a rule, are not made but happen, and the Russian Revolution is no exception to this rule. But the coup of October 25, 1917, occurring within the larger context of this revolution, was entirely due to Lenin's decision and to his power of persuasion; without him, the October Revolution would never have come to pass. What happened from then on up to his death was his responsibility. Hence the questions Mr. Ulam raises—"Was the Revolution according to the gospel of Marxism? And if not, what could justify this departure?"—have the great advantage of applying a standard of judgment which was inherent in the event.

Still, there are some points in Mr. Ulam's reflections on which I would like to comment.

First, Mr. Ulam has protested elsewhere against putting Lenin alongside Stalin; from this, I suggest, it follows that the kind of justification one might put into Lenin's mind on his deathbed cannot possibly be of the same kind as for Stalin. What is at stake here is the question of the continuity of the revolution, which came up earlier in the debate following Mr. Carr's paper. While I was listening to this debate I was struck by the fact that its protagonists had one thing in common, namely, that both believed in an unbroken continuity of Soviet Russian history from October 1917 until Stalin's death. In other words, those who were more or less on the side of Lenin's revolution also justified Stalin, whereas those who were denouncing Stalin's rule were sure that Lenin was not only responsible for Stalin's totalitarianism but actually belonged in the same category, that Stalin was a necessary consequence of Lenin. This implicit consensus seems to me highly characteristic of what has been called here "the mainstream of Western thought" on the matter, and it is noteworthy that it stands in sharp contrast to recent voices in the Soviet Union. It may be interesting to mention the "first-rate row" that took place on February 16, 1966, in the Institute for Marxism-Leninism, Department for the History of the Great Patriotic War, when the book of the Soviet historian Alexander M. Nekrich, *June 22, 1941*, was discussed. Its thesis: Stalin was responsible for the Russian defeats in the early stages of the war. My source of information for the following quotations is *Der Spiegel* (no. 13, 1967, pp. 132–138). "Stalin," said Mr. Iakir (son of general Iakir, executed in 1938), "should not be called a 'comrade.' He never was a comrade, certainly not our comrade . . . Lenin had called fascism the main enemy, . . . Stalin nominated Social Democracy to be the main enemy." Moreover, as Mr. Gnedin (of the Institute for World Economy and International

Relations) explained, "We have every reason to believe that Stalin was not concerned with the defense of the country but wanted to come to an understanding with Hitler." Finally, the Russian poet Snegov denounced all attempts at justifying Stalin, enumerating Stalin's crimes— "When Hitler prepared his aggression against Poland, Stalin helped him. He liquidated all Polish Communists in the Soviet Union and outlawed the Polish Communist party . . . How can anyone be a Communist and speak calmly of Stalin, who betrayed the Communists, who liquidated almost all the delegates of the Seventh Party Congress and nearly all the members of the Central Committee duly elected by the Congress, who betrayed the Spanish Republic, Poland and all Communists in all countries?"

I have quoted these extraordinarily interesting words only in order to underline the distinction between Lenin and Stalin. Whatever Lenin had done, he could, being a Marxist, justify it by believing that he had laid the foundations for a long process, and "to project his dream into the future" was not against the letter or the spirit of Marxism. But Stalin? Even if one were to admit that he could justify his criminal methods in liquidating the peasant class on doctrinal grounds (and I would not admit it, but would agree with what Mr. Kennan had said so eloquently: this is indeed one of the great unsung tragedies of this century), on what grounds could he have justified the liquidations of the party bureaucracy, of the perfectly loyal leadership of Communist parties outside Russia, of the officer corps of the Red Army, and so on? In other words, I believe that even the cautious way in which Mr. Ulam in his paper put Stalin alongside Lenin is open to question.

Second, it sounds very plausible when Mr. Ulam says that Lenin's opponents were helpless because they still lived in the nineteenth century, which, with World War I, had just come to an end, but I wonder whether this view can actually be upheld. The point is not even that other characteristics mentioned here repeatedly—apathy, inactivity, lack of will power, but above all, fear of responsibility—were perhaps more potent factors, but that Lenin himself was still a child of the nineteenth century in so many respects although he lacked its sentimentality. Did he not seriously believe that in the society of the future one would be able to do without a penal code, since under "normal" (that is, socialist) circumstances men would know how to behave themselves and to observe "the elementary rules of social life that have been . . . repeated for thousands of years in all copy-book maxims," so that every citizen would come to the aid of his fellow citizens in case of "downright moral perverts" as "simply and readily as any crowd of civilized people, even in modern society, parts two people who are fighting, or interferes to prevent a woman from being assaulted."[1] If this is not nineteenth-century "idealism," what is?

What, then, is the explanation of Lenin's ascendancy over all his opponents inside as well as outside his party? Much has been said here to back up the theory that revolutions are not the result of conspiracies or the propaganda of revolutionary parties but the almost automatic outcome of processes of disintegration in the powers-that-be, of their loss of authority, in which case the decisive question would always be who, if anybody, steps into the power vacuum created by the disappearance of the *ancien régime*. Mr. Ulam said—in his splendid book about Lenin, *The Bolsheviks*—that the Bolsheviks did not "seize power, but picked it up." And this is entirely right—except that it was Lenin who did it rather than the party. The point is that he was the only one willing "to pick it up" *and* to keep it—which is only another way of saying that Lenin was the only man willing to assume responsibility for the revolution after it had happened without the help of anybody, least of all of the Bolshevik party. (To start a revolution in "the land of Nicholas and Rasputin" was "as easy as lifting a feather," Lenin once remarked.[2]) And since this action was clearly a departure from the Marxist time-table, the question is, why did he do it?

The main reason, I would suggest, was that Lenin, alone among the revolutionaries, understood the modern interconnection between war and revolution. He had learned the lesson of the first Russian Revolution of 1905, and perhaps of the French Commune as well, when defeat in war had touched off events in which the weakness of the regime, which otherwise might have lived on for considerable periods, suddenly stood exposed. Very soon after the outbreak of World War I, he began to think of the twentieth century as a "century of wars *and* revolutions," and he was, I believe, the only one in his own group who welcomed the war without any qualifications. He hoped for revolutions in all defeated countries in Europe; indeed, he might not have seized power without this hope. Above all, I think, he began very early to associate the notion of a "world war" with that of a world revolution. We know from Mr. Ulam's paper how accurately he predicted "revolutions of a yet unknown character in the East," and if these revolutions were unknown in character they certainly could not be found in Marx and Engels. In other words, I think that it was this insight, not to be found in Marxism, that gave him the necessary confidence for the *on s'engage et puis on voit*. He had been *prepared* where the others were not.

1. V. I. Lenin, *Collected Works*, 4th ed., XXV (London, 1964), p. 464; XXXI (London, 1966), p. 355.

2. Lenin, *Collected Works*, XXVIII (London, 1965), p. 99.

My third point concerns the soviets. Mr. Ulam is, of course, right: the term became almost meaningless in a very short time. He only forgot to add that it was far from meaningless until Lenin had done quite a bit in order to *make* it meaningless. In *The Bolsheviks*, Mr. Ulam stated: October 25, 1917, marks not only the triumph of the Bolshevik Revolution but also the beginning of the counterrevolution carried out by the same party. It was Lenin who had proclaimed, "All power to the Soviets." While the new government, the Council of the People's Commissars, was supposed to last only until the meeting of the Constituent Assembly, which—as Mr. Ferro and Mr. Anweiler advised us—was supported by soviets' resolutions from all over the country, it was the same Lenin who dissolved the Constituent Assembly, emasculated the soviets, and liquidated the Kronstadt rebellion in which the sailors had demanded no more than the fulfillment of the pledges of October. As far as Lenin's revolution was concerned, this was a point of no return. I would suggest that it was precisely the Marxist in Lenin who prevailed in these decisions. For whatever a true Soviet Republic might have been, it certainly would not have been the same as a dictatorship of the proletariat. Moreover, we know that Lenin had been greatly bothered, from the beginning, by the problem of dyarchy; in this respect he shared the conviction and prejudices not merely of the disciples of Marx, but of all political theorists and statesmen of continental Europe, who from Right to Left held that power is indivisible, that it must be centralized, and that a separation or division of powers weakens power. The only exception to this rule was Montesquieu, as we all know, and he influenced the men who made the American Revolution but neither the statesmen nor the revolutionists of Europe. Also, without denying certain anarchistic tendencies in the soviets, I would like to stress once more that the soviets had been organs of order rather than of action.

Fourth, the attrition of Marxism under Stalin is undeniable, but I am not so sure that this process began already under Lenin. The dictatorship of the proletariat—in Lenin's view a dictatorship of the Bolshevik party as the vanguard of the proletariat—was quite in accordance with Marx's views on these matters. The very word "dictatorship" was meant to indicate the provisional, transitional character of state power, since the word was still understood in its original Roman usage. I cannot agree with Mr. Ulam's view that Lenin's practical handling of the important question of state and political power was at odds with Marx's teachings or with his own theoretical convictions as stated in *State and Revolution*. For Marx as for Lenin, "The state is a special organization of force, . . . the organization of violence," whose only function is suppression—either in the hands of the bourgeoisie to suppress the working class or in the hands of the workers who "need a state only to overcome the resistance of the exploiters." Its power consists of "special bodies of armed men which have prisons, etc., at their disposal." Hence, every state is "repressive" by definition; there cannot be such a thing as a "free state." "As long as there is a state, there is no freedom; when there is freedom, there will be no state," as Lenin, paraphrasing Engels, put it, and when, after the February Revolution he called Russia "the freest country in the world," he probably meant that the country had no real government. That these notions of the nature of the state and of political power are essentially anarchistic seems to me obvious, and Lenin himself mentions as the only distinction from anarchist doctrine that, according to Marx, the state "withers away" after having been seized by the working class and transformed into the dictatorship of the proletariat, whereas anarchists believed in the immediate "abolition of the state" through the revolution. In any event, after the October Revolution, Lenin stressed that the power of the new regime was "based directly upon force and unrestricted by any law."[3] Hence, the chief distinction between a bourgeois state and Lenin's dictatorship was the absence of law, and this, according to him, meant absence of bourgeois hypocrisy. In short, it was precisely because Lenin shared Marx's fundamentally anarchistic estimate of political power and the nature of government that his own government immediately turned into an apparatus of coercion and oppression. If one needed government at all—and according to Marx it was needed for a period of transition—what else could one expect? That he then could believe that such a power apparatus could be checked and restrained by "discipline" and revolutionary morality was characteristic of his nineteenth-century mentality mentioned before.

However, confronted with the reality of Russia, Lenin added an important new thought to his essentially Marxian estimate of the role of the state. In *State and Revolution* (chapter 2, section I) he held that "The proletariat needs state power, the centralized organization of force, the organization of violence" not merely "for the purpose of crushing the resistance of the exploiters" but also (and this is entirely new) "for the purpose of building the great mass of the population— the peasantry, the petty bourgeoisie, the semiproletarians—in the task of getting the socialist economy going." This was essentially the same function the prerevolutionary party had, according to Lenin, with regard to the working class—except that now the party had acquired the power of coercion. And this, of course, changed everything; by no stretch of

3. Lenin, *Collected Works*, XXVIII (London, 1965), p. 236.

the imagination could one speak of this new "vanguard" of the proletariat as a body representing the working class. The decisive point,
however, was that coercive power had now acquired a positive function,
an eminently practical one if it should work. Seen from this viewpoint
of a strictly Leninist, non-Marxian doctrine, it looked as though Russia
was not so much skipping the capitalist stage, as Marx had hoped, as
going through that stage of enlightened despotism with its mercantile
systems (now called "state capitalism") that had preceded the capitalist
development, especially in France, had developed a huge and mostly
ineffective bureaucracy, and was brought to an end by the French
Revolution. Lenin seems to have been dimly aware of this. He praised
state capitalism as a "step forward," as "immeasurably superior to the
present system of economy" (in *"Left-Wing" Childishness*, section III),
and at the same time, in spring 1918, demanded *"unquestioning submission* to a single will, . . . that the masses *unquestioningly obey the
single will* of the leaders."[4]

The trouble with enlightened despotism has always been the scarcity
of enlightened despots. Despots are seldom enlightened because enlightened men have no appetite for this kind of power. The very fact
that Lenin on his deathbed thought of nothing but of the personalities
of his potential successors shows that he must finally have grasped this
simple matter—however vaguely and crudely—and this is all the more
impressive as his ideological convictions should hardly have permitted
him to waste the precious time left to him (he knew he was dying) on
the "subjective factor" that they all had held in such contempt. It is
indeed ironic and—if one has any sympathy with Lenin, as I have—a bit
sad to see how a movement that had staked everything on objective developments should maneuver itself so quickly into a position in which
everything depended on a "subjective factor," that is, the future ruler for
whom not even a law of succession existed. Thus we see Lenin during
the last months of his life helplessly and awkwardly (the awkwardness
of his last memoranda and letters seem to me very striking) imploring
the comrades to show more "discipline," deploring their "lack of culture" in general and Stalin's "rudeness" (what an understatement!) in
particular.

My fifth and final point concerns the question of the attraction of
communism. I agree with what Mr. Ulam said and would only like to
add two points that make the outlook perhaps a little less rosy. This
attraction is quite strong in those European countries where people are
bent on change, on a "new order of things," whereby the new order is

4. Lenin, *Collected Works*, XXVII, p. 269.

not necessarily intended to be a Communist dictatorship. (Machiavelli, no less eager for what we today call revolution and what he still called "a new order of things," knew at least "that there is nothing more difficult to carry out, nor more doubtful of success, nor more dangerous to handle, than to initiate" it.) The Communist parties, especially in France, Italy, and Greece, obviously attract the "disaffected members of society" in addition to large numbers of the working class who are convinced that they are the strongest factor in the fight for improved living conditions. Most of these people vote Communist only in order to express their opposition to the status quo, and I would not think that this state of affairs was particularly dangerous if I had more trust in the stability of the European status quo.

Potentially much more explosive is the fusion of nationalism and communism in the underdeveloped countries where the "exploitation of man by man" is still as powerful a slogan and point of crystallization as it originally was when Marx wrote *Capital.* "The beacon of hope" is there now what it once was in the West, and this hope, I think, is less the hope for peace than for a decisive shift in power. It is the same hope which St. Just voiced long before Karl Marx: "*Les malheureux sont la puissance de la terre.*" Everything we know of history refutes this statement, no revolution has ever been made by *les malheureux,* by the wretched of the earth. But who could deny the grandeur and the powerful attraction of St. Just's words?

Discussion

Opening the discussion with some general comments on the relation of Marxism to Russia's historical development, Mr. Rubel reiterated his belief that the events of 1917 demonstrated the failure of every ideology, particularly the Marxist. To be sure, Marx's sociological interpretation of historical development was perfectly correct. Thus, Marx had predicted that the result of Germany's annexation of Alsace-Lorraine in 1871 would be an alliance between republican France and the Slavic race, the ultimate consequences of which would be war with Germany and revolution in tsarist Russia. Furthermore, Marx had forecast the social character of the Russian Revolution, namely, the transformation of Russia from a rural semi-Asiatic society, to use Lenin's words, into a modern, urban, proletarian, and capitalist society. Could one properly view Soviet Russia as a bourgeois society? Mr. Rubel's answer to this question was affirmative, provided one did not identify a bourgeois regime with liberalism and allowed for the evolution of the bourgeoisie from its traditional liberal phase to a bureaucratic managerial one.

According to Mr. Rubel, what Marx could not have foreseen was, first, that the political masters of this revolution would claim to have acted in accordance with his social theory. Secondly, Marx could not have foreseen that a proletarian society with a state capitalist economy would be defined by its ruling class as a socialist society and economy, and accepted as such by Western historians and political leaders.

Referring to the remark made by Lenin on the eve of his death regarding the October Revolution, "What else could we have done?" Mr. Schapiro noted that it was a view for which he had much sympathy. In a sense, the triumph of bolshevism could be interpreted as a reaction against the futility of the whole Russian intellectual and revolutionary tradition. Speaking only of 1917, the astonishing ineffectiveness of the Mensheviks and SR's had made it inevitable that sooner or later somebody would take action; Lenin's character had led him to make the attempt. However, his sympathy for Lenin's plight in 1917 did not extend to his political policies in 1920 and 1921. There was nothing inevitable about Lenin's elimination of all dissent in the Communist party at this time or about his creation of the rudiments of the totalitarian model that Stalin was ultimately to exploit. Rejecting the notion that these policies of Lenin's were determined by Marx's doctrine of the dictatorship of the proletariat or by a danger to Lenin posed by the Mensheviks and SR's, Mr. Schapiro expressed the opinion that more than anything else they demonstrated that Lenin was not a statesman. He attributed Lenin's inability to understand the art of government to such factors as character, background, and training.

Mr. Kennan addressed himself to some of the consequences of the October Revolution on Russia's relations with the West and on development in Western Europe. Such habits of the Soviet regime as its hostile rejection of Western government and its secretiveness and suspiciousness rendered impossible the maintenance of normal relations between Russia and the Western powers. Moreover, this unfortunate effect of the revolution on international affairs was paralleled by the revolution's impact on political life throughout Western Europe. The triumph of bolshevism had split moderate socialist movements in the Western countries, thereby reducing their effectiveness, and it raised groups on the left wing of these movements that were strongly opposed to the societies in which they lived. This, in turn, weakened moderate political tendencies in a most unfortunate way and produced what today would be called a backlash on the right. Stressing that he was well aware that the leftist threat did not cause fascism, Mr. Kennan noted that it had provided the excuse for it.

Mr. Kennan added that yet another important external effect of the Russian Revolution had been to poison the relations between Europe and non-Europe, primarily Asia and Africa. There was no doubt that colonialism was bound to disappear in the modern age and that this was good. However, an unfortunate consequence of the Russian Revolution was that Europe had lost its extra-European connections in a precipitate way, in a spirit of conflict and hatred that was of little benefit either to Russia or the former colonial peoples.

Mr. Ulam prefaced his closing remarks with the comment that he did not interpret the absence of questions addressed at his paper as did Stalin at the end of the Party Congress in 1934 when he said: Nobody questioned or criticized my report, consequently I assume that everybody is in unanimous agreement with me. He had no quarrel with the remarks made by Miss Arendt. There was validity in her views regarding the fundamental nature of the criticism heaped on Stalin by Communists today. However, as far as official Soviet doctrine was concerned, although the original destalinization in 1956 tried to destroy post-1934 Stalin, it held the pre-1934 Stalin to have been a very useful gentleman. In 1961–62 Khrushchev shifted his ground and attacked Stalin from the beginning. Although he did not call collectivization a crime, he came very close to it by implying that Stalin was a murderer and criminal from the start. The current neo-Bolshevik attitude was that the process of collectivization, although influenced by criminal and destructive elements, had been in the main a good thing. In other words, a certain approval of Stalinism was still inherent in the view not only of the current leadership but of many people who had expressed the greatest reservations about Stalin's policies after 1934 and even about present conditions.

Similarly, Mr. Ulam acknowledged the validity of Miss Arendt's explanation of the reasons for the impotence of the SR's and Mensheviks in 1917. He had no doubt that ideological ties and apathy provided part of the explanation; however, he wondered whether fear was equally applicable. Many of the figures who now appeared so ridiculously indecisive had in the past been people of great courage, not above engaging in intrigues of their own.

Mr. Ulam also endorsed Miss Arendt's opinion of the importance of Lenin's understanding of the interconnection between war and revolution in the formulation of his strategy. He agreed with her remarks regarding Lenin's role in the stifling of even limited inner party democracy and Lenin's lack of understanding of power. He noted that unfortunately people who wrote about power were often people who did not have power, and that before 1917 Lenin himself had not much opportunity to exercise it.

Mr. Ulam shared Mr. Schapiro's sympathy for Lenin's deathbed query, "What else could we have done?" In October 1917 a coalition government (Martov and Chernov along with Kamenev and Zinoviev!) would have meant a continuation of the wrangling and talking that had characterized the Provisional Government period. He agreed that 1920–21 was the critical point in the destruction of the remnants of democratic feeling. At that time there was still a great deal of debate within the Communist party. Lenin might have displayed some ideological and political generosity toward dissenting views and in so doing, laid claim to being a great universal statesman. However, motivated by the belief that if one gave way a little bit, everything would fall to pieces—a notion that inspired tsarist bureaucrats before 1905 as well as today's Communist autocrats—Lenin tried to link Martov, the Kronstadt rebellion, and so forth, with fictitious White Guards, generals, and the emigration, thereby establishing himself as the dictator and originator of the Communist autocracy.

Index

Adler, Friedrich, 161
Africa, character of revolution in, 293–294; relation to Europe, 352
Agitation, as tool for recruiting labor, 43–44, 46, 47
Agriculture, subordinated to industrialization, 3–5, 16; Fedoseev on, 37–38; reform of by Provisional Government, 110; forced collectivization of, 336. *See also* Land; Peasants
Akselrod, P. B., 43, 46, 51, 304; and Marxism, 53, 312–313
Alexander II, 7, 8; murder of, 10, 14, 23, 28; Schiemann on, 67
Alexander III, 29
Algedorskii, 242
All-Army Committee, 205
All-Russian Cossack Congress, 210
All-Russian Supreme Staff, 243–244
All-Siberian Congress of Soviets, 199
Altdorffer, 69, 71–72, 82
Altfater, V. M., 242
Anarchism, 221, 278; and Russian socialism, 36; of Lenin, 60, 349; anti-intellectualism of, 61; inadequacy of, 338
Anikeev, V. V., 187
Anti-Semitism, under the tsars, 10–11, 20, 23
Antonov, V. P., 188, 189
Antonov, rising of, 271
Antonov-Ovseenko, V. N., 229, 237, 238–239, 252
Anweiler, Oskar, on Katkov, 94; on Anweiler and Wolfe, 138, 141–142; on Ferro, 163; on Geyer and Keep, 221; on Meijer, 278
April theses of Lenin, 126, 127
Arendt, Hannah, on Kennan, 24; on Pipes, 62; on Schapiro and Anweiler, 141; on Ferro, 163; on Geyer and Keep, 221; on Ulam, 344–351, 353

Armenians, and Russian nationalism, 25
Army, democratization of, 111; bolshevization of, 202. *See also* Imperial Army; Red Army; Soldiers
Artsybashev, V. P., 184
Asia, character of revolution in, 293–294; relation to Europe, 352
Aufwiegelung (subversion), agencies of, 70–71; early bungling of, 71–74; among POW, 75; attempts to foment revolution, 75–84
Austria, 21–22; Witte on, 64–65
Auswärtiges Amt (AA), assessment of possible revolution in Russia, 64, 66–67, 69; information from Schiemann, 67–69; and sedition, 70; and Stepankowski, 74; use of Russian emigrés by, 75; Russian agents of, 76; Bolshevism subsidized by, 81, 83; peace propaganda of, 82; Russian counter-measures, 84–85; effectiveness of, 86–88, 91
Autocracy, Russian, long-term weaknesses of, 1–13; effect of revolutionary movement on, 13–14; possible transformation of, 22–24; revolutionary struggle against, 39; relation of Provisional Government to, 100
Avineri, Shlomo, on Pipes, 61; on Geyer and Keep, 221; on Rubel, 323–329, 330, 331
Avksentiev, N. D., 114
Avrich, Paul, 60–61
Avtonomov, 239

Balashev, 179
Baltic Germans, and Russian nationalism, 24, 25; loyalty of to Germany, 67, 69; discriminated against, 84
Basilevskii, 240
Berlin, Sir Isaiah, on Kennan, 24; on Pipes, 52–59, 61, 62

358 – Index

Russian Research Center Studies

41. *The Soviet Industrialization Debate, 1924–1928,* by Alexander Erlich
42. *The Third Section: Police and Society in Russia under Nicholas I,* by Sidney Monas
43. *Dilemmas of Progress in Tsarist Russia: Legal Marxism and Legal Populism,* by Arthur P. Mendel
44. *Political Control of Literature in the USSR, 1946–1959,* by Harold Swayze
45. *Accounting in Soviet Planning and Management,* by Robert W. Campbell
46. *Social Democracy and the St. Petersburg Labor Movement, 1885–1897,* by Richard Pipes
47. *The New Face of Soviet Totalitarianism,* by Adam B. Ulam
48. *Stalin's Foreign Policy Reappraised,* by Marshall D. Shulman
49. *The Soviet Youth Program: Regimentation and Rebellion,* by Allen Kassof
50. *Soviet Criminal Law and Procedure: The RSFSR Codes,* translated by Harold J. Berman and James W. Spindler; introduction and analysis by Harold J. Berman
51. *Poland's Politics: Political Idealism vs. Political Realism,* by Adam Bromke
52. *Managerial Power and Soviet Politics,* by Jeremy R. Azrael
53. *Danilevsky: A Russian Totalitarian Philosopher,* by Robert E. MacMaster
54. *Russia's Protectorates in Central Asia: Bukhara and Khiva, 1865–1924,* by Seymour Becker
55. *Revolutionary Russia,* edited by Richard Pipes

* Out of print.
† Publications of the Harvard Project on the Soviet Social System.
‡ Published jointly with the Center for International Affairs, Harvard University.